THE
SCIENTIFIC AMERICAN
BOOK OF PROJECTS FOR

A FIRESIDE BOOK PUBLISHED BY

SIMON AND SCHUSTER · NEW YORK

THE
AMATEUR
SCIENTIST

Experiments and constructions, challenges and diversions in the fields of Astronomy, Archaeology, Biology, Natural Sciences, Earth Sciences, Mathematical Machines, Aerodynamics, Optics, Heat and Electronics. Selected from Mr. Stong's clearing house of amateur activities, appearing monthly in SCIENTIFIC AMERICAN, and expanded with additional information, instructions, notes, bibliographies — and postscripts, from readers.

BY C. L. STONG

INTRODUCTION BY VANNEVAR BUSH

ILLUSTRATED BY ROGER HAYWARD

TO MIL

CONTENTS

II. ARCHAEOLOGY

*facts can give pleasure to the amateur and
help his professional colleagues.*

*How a group of amateurs with professional
guidance unearthed an ancient Indian village and thereby upset some well-established
conclusions about Indian culture. Important
do's and don'ts for the beginner.*

III. BIOLOGY

*Adventures in gardening at the microscopic
level. How to experiment with weed-killers
popularly known as wonder drugs.*

*Even if you live in the city you can grow a
pioneer crop of the minute plants which may
some day become an important source of
man's food.*

*An experiment designed by a Michigan high-
school girl.*

*An Ohio high-school girl devised this appa-
ratus. She describes its assembly and operation and gives details of a typical experiment
utilizing mice as subjects.*

*An analytic technique, one of the most
powerful known to biochemists, is used to
separate chlorophyll from spinach leaves.*

V. THE EARTH SCIENCES

IX. OPTICS, HEAT AND ELECTRONICS

INTRODUCTION

A book of this sort for the amateur scientist is a decidedly interesting undertaking. It immediately raises the question of what is an amateur, and for that matter what is a scientist.

One definition of an amateur is that he is an individual who pursues a study for the fun of it. This is hardly the point. Most professional scientists get fun out of their efforts; in fact many of them get so much satisfaction and enjoyment out of their work that they devote only secondary attention to the subject of what they are paid for their efforts. Amateurs have no monopoly on enjoyment.

Another definition is that an amateur derives no income from his efforts. We hear that the great strides in science in England in the early days were made by amateurs. This is only partly true. Such scientists as Priestley, Cavendish and Boyle were men of means, who experimented and wrote on natural philosophy as a proper undertaking for a gentleman. Sterling, a Scottish clergyman, invented the first really successful engine using a fixed gas cycle, which was not improved upon much for a century, and he certainly derived no income from his efforts. Certainly one of the prime attributes of the amateur is that he does his work without thought of personal gain. For the amateur scientist, necessity is not the mother of invention.

Unfortunately, it is also customary to regard the amateur as a chap who knows only a little about a subject and who dabbles, in contrast with the professional, who knows a great deal and who creates. Of course there are many amateurs who do simple things crudely. After all, it is necessary to learn to walk before one can leap and run. I think back with much amusement to some of the things I did early in life. One evening a few years ago I spent many interesting hours with Orville Wright. We spent the whole time telling each other about things we had worked on which did not pan out, and he took me up to his attic and showed me models of all sorts of queer gadgets. I wonder how many mature scientists shudder a bit when they find students who have hunted up the old theses they presented for degrees; I know I am one of them. In fact, my old thesis has a prime fallacy in it, fortunately one that neither I nor the faculty discovered at the time. Amateurs, generally, are content to be modest, and to plug away without acclaim, recognizing that they are a long way from the top in their subjects. But every amateur has in the back of his mind, carefully concealed, the thought that some day . . . Moreover there are amateurs — I have met numbers of them — who are truly masters of their subjects, who need take a back seat at no professional gathering in their field. It was an amateur who discovered the planet Pluto, and an amateur who was primarily responsible for the development of vitamin B_1.

The motivation of the scientist, professional or amateur, is the sheer joy of knowing. In fact, that is one of the principal satisfactions of being alive. The man who learns one new thing, small though it be, that has never before been known to anyone before him in the whole history of the human race, is in the same position as the man who first climbs a difficult mountain and looks out upon a vista never before seen. Erwin Schrödinger wrote: "Art and science are the spheres of human activity where action and aim are not as a rule determined by the necessities of life; and even in the exceptional instances where this is the case, the creative artist or the investigating scientist soon forgets this fact — as indeed they must forget it if their work is to prosper." Many of the amateur scientists who contributed to this book experienced this sort of lift of spirit.

There are lots of amateur scientists, probably a million of them in this country. The Weather Bureau depends on some 3,000 well-organized amateur meteorologists. Other groups observe bird and insect migrations and populations, the behavior of variable stars, the onset of solar flares, the fiery end of satellites, earth tremors, soil erosion, meteor counts, and so on. The American Philosophical Society noted 8,000 laymen in Philadelphia alone, interested in science; and of these, 700 had made contributions to knowledge important enough to merit professional recognition. There are 200 science clubs in the city with national affiliations. Probably no other city can quite match this performance; after all Benjamin Franklin gave Philadelphia a bit of a head start, but the activity is nation-wide.

One reason, of course, is that we have more leisure today. This is due to the strides of science and its applications, which have rendered it possible to secure the necessities and some of the luxuries of life with much less labor. The days are gone when multitudes labored from dawn to dusk in order that a few might have time to think and to acquire some sort of culture. Of the dozens who have time on their hands, one or two turn to serious study, and especially to science. In the aggregate there is an army of men and women with the leisure to delve into science, and the opportunity lies before them.

This leads me to write a word about science itself. There is a prevalent opinion today that all science is carried on by great groups in expensive laboratories, using particle accelerators, X-ray spectrometers, radio telescopes and other costly paraphernalia. There is also the feeling that all true research is conducted by men who have prepared for the task by long years of patient study. Also that one has to be a genius in order to create. Now there is truth to all of this, and it is due to the national recognition and support of great scientific efforts that we are making today's rapid scientific strides forward. But this is not all the truth by any means. It took genius to discover the phenomenon of transduction of genetic characteristics, one of the greatest scientific advances of the last decade, more important than taking a shot at the moon, too complex to be explained in this short note. But it did not take great apparatus at the expense of taxpayers. All it required was glassware, chemicals, colonies of bacteria — and genius. It did not take genius in the early days for radio amateurs, supposedly crowded out of all useful radio channels, to open up a whole new part of the spectrum. Nor does it take enormous organization and support to accomplish very useful things. The great rush into atomistics and nucleonics, into space exploration, into atomic energy, has left relatively neglected great areas of what was once classical physics and chemistry. The whole vast field of biology has no such pressure of public interest behind it, and in the maze of its byways are thousands of unsolved problems. Many of them require no more than careful, patient observation and the skill to fit results into the jigsaw puzzle of advancing biological science. And who is it that has the skill? It may indeed be you.

So I introduce this book with enthusiasm. May there be many like it. And from its influence, and the influence of many good books that are appearing today, may there be satisfaction for many an amateur in science. The world is being remolded by science. It is worth while to have a part, even a small part, in its transformation.

VANNEVAR BUSH

PREFACE

Three assumptions about my readers have guided the selection of the material in this book. First, I have supposed that you revel in your simian heritage of curiosity. You take boundless delight in finding out what makes things tick, whether the object of your interest has been fashioned by nature or man. Second, you are an inveterate tinkerer. You love to take organized structures apart and put them together again in new and interesting ways — be they rocks, protozoa, alarm clocks or ideas. Third, you can usually drive a nail home on the first try, put a fairly good edge on a knife, and manipulate a Bunsen burner without broiling your thumb.

In short, I assume you are an Amateur Scientist; the projects and discussions that follow are presented accordingly.

Although every project has been tested and successfully performed by a number of amateurs you may, nevertheless, encounter difficulty in duplicating a few of the experimental results. This must be expected. Not all of the experiments are easy to do. Moreover, as mentioned here and there in the text, experimental work is beset by Murphy's Law, which holds that "if something can go wrong, it will!" Don't permit the intrusion of Murphy to discourage you. The fact that an experiment delivers an unexpected answer means simply that you have not asked the question you assume you have asked. Take comfort in the knowledge that difficulties of this kind invariably yield to the vigorous application of Goldberg's Rule: "If at first you don't succeed, try a new approach."

A final suggestion: After considerable thought the decision was made not to set up this volume like a cookbook (with lists of ingredients preceding the "recipes," etc.) or even like a lab manual. The various pieces in it give you pertinent information, as you read, in relation to the scientific points being made. Hence I urge the amateur who is about to perform an experiment to begin work only after he has (1) read through the subsection containing the experiment and (2) glanced through the entire section. That is: Don't build your telescope until you have made your-

self at least roughly familiar with all the contents of the section on Astronomy. The admonition to read through before starting work applies especially in experiments dealing with high-energy radiation, where simple but important safety measures must be taken.

I want to thank Gerard Piel, Dennis Flanagan, Donald Miller and their associates on the staff of SCIENTIFIC AMERICAN, where much of this material originally appeared, for permission to reprint it here and, most especially, for their numerous helpful suggestions and editorial assistance.

I am equally grateful to Roger Hayward, architect, optical designer and accomplished artist, whose illustrations adorn these pages. Hayward's remarkable talent for simplification is reflected both in the drawings and experimental procedures.

I wish it were possible to acknowledge properly all the contributions made by the generous readers of SCIENTIFIC AMERICAN magazine. Their keen eyes and nimble minds have spared readers the annoyance of combing out errors that might otherwise have been carried over into this volume. Without the contributions of the several experimenters named in the text there would have been no book, of course. To them goes fullest credit.

A special word of thanks is due to Dr. Vannevar Bush who, despite heavy professional responsibilities of national concern, took out time to address some words of encouragement to those who turn to science for recreation.

Finally, I cannot believe that it falls to the lot of many writers to enjoy the help of two women more wonderful than the pair behind this enterprise. Miss Nina Bourne, my editor at Simon and Schuster, has been untiring in her effort to make this the kind of book you want it to be. Her contribution has been fully matched, if not paralleled, by that of my gifted wife, who not only typed the original manuscript and read proof with painstaking care but throughout the long months of preparation displayed an understanding of (and tolerance for) the human male that professional psychologists may well envy.

C. L. STONG

I.

ASTRONOMY

1

ASTRONOMICAL DIVERSIONS

A note about the delights of stargazing and some of the fascinating instruments man has devised to overcome the limitations of his eye

How DID THE MOON acquire its mottled face? Why do some stars look red and others blue? When did the celestial fires burst into flame and what will happen when their fuel is spent? These and like questions have challenged the imagination of every age. In searching for answers man has looked up into the star-filled night and glimpsed, or thought he glimpsed, the dwelling place of his gods, the forces that shape his destiny and, more recently, the structure of his universe. No intellectual diversion has engrossed him through a longer span of history or exerted a deeper influence on his way of life.

Astronomy has always been a favored game for amateurs — since it first brought creases to the brow of Homo neanderthalensis. Merely learning to find one's way among the stars can become a rewarding experience. In the course of nightly tours the novice will encounter fascinating objects which most laymen rarely take out time to see. With the aid of a simple star chart — like the one published every month in the magazine *Sky and Telescope* — you can find the window in the Milky Way which looks out on an island universe much like our own, one shimmering with the light of 100,000 million blazing suns. Still other "suns" turn out to be great sheets of dust shining with the reflected light of stars just being born. The marching constellations soon become familiar as celestial guides, and our sun a kind of clock which appears to govern the parade. Occasional comets liven the scene as well as meteors, auroras and man-made satellites. All of these objects can be detected by the naked eye — that marvelous though unfortunately narrow portal to the stars.

Of the 100 billion stars comprising our local galaxy the eye can see a mere 2,000; and of the galaxies in uncounted billions that wheel through space beyond the Milky Way — only one. The unaided eye can distinguish color differences between the stars but it fails to analyze the spectral composition, to sense their significance. Worse, of the 22 octaves of electromagnetic radiation which stream in to us with information about events in outer space — from the long waves of radio to the ultrashort gamma rays — the eye is blind to all but the single octave called light.

To surmount the limitations of the eye astronomers have dipped heavily into scientific disciplines not directly related to the stars. The supreme advance came, of course, with the invention of the telescope. By holding up an appropriate lens in each hand and looking through the pair one can see distant objects as if they were close, a principle of optics first demonstrated by the Dutch spectacle maker, Hans Lippershey, in 1608. That the same effect could be obtained by means of a concave mirror was suggested 55 years later by the Scottish mathematician, James Gregory. Galileo Galilei based his refracting telescope, the world's first, on the lens principle in 1610. Isaac Newton made the first reflecting instrument in 1669. Between these pioneering feats and the construction of the 200-inch reflector on Palomar Mountain came all the monumental accomplishments of modern astronomy, many of them inspired by man's simple desire to extend the power of his eye. To perfect ways of collecting, bending, recording and analyzing faint rays of starlight has been the goal of some of the foremost physicists, chemists and instrument makers of the past 400 years.

In consequence, astronomy has become an experimental science as well as an observational one — a side of stargazing, incidentally, which currently attracts the majority of amateur enthusiasts.

Most amateurs agree that the questions which arise in the course of building a telescope are as fascinating as those which the instrument helps to explore. Four of the nine projects and problems which comprise this section discuss the construction and use of such instruments. For amateurs who enjoy a dash of variety in their experiments, these projects invite excursions across the boundaries of many scientific disciplines including optics, mechanics, electronics, chemistry and solid-state physics. The concluding discussions take up instruments demonstrating the value of astronomy in everyday affairs. All the projects are well within the compass of the average basement workshop and reach of the average pocketbook. Those who would hitch their hobby to the stars can make no better start than to construct the small telescope herewith described.

2

A SIMPLE TELESCOPE
FOR BEGINNERS

Although its design does not strive for optical perfection, this instrument — more powerful than Galileo's — will show you such phenomena as the rings of Saturn, the mountains on the moon, and Jupiter's satellites. Total cost: about $25

In 1926 an article appeared in SCIENTIFIC AMERICAN magazine which described how a group of amateurs in Springfield, Vt., had mastered the formidable art of constructing an astronomical telescope. The details of construction had been worked out by Russell W. Porter, engineer and explorer, and were described in collaboration with the late Albert G. Ingalls, an editor of SCIENTIFIC AMERICAN. Within a year some 500 laymen had completed similar telescopes and were well on their way to becoming amateur astronomers.

I was one of them. Like many laymen I had wanted to see astronomical objects close up, but could not afford a ready-made telescope of adequate power. Nor was I acquainted with the owner of one. The description of the Springfield telescope solved the problem. I immediately set out to make a six-inch instrument, and I had scarcely begun to use it when half a dozen of my neighbors started telescopes of their own.

It was not a very good instrument by the standards of present-day amateurs, but it showed the markings of Jupiter and the polar caps of Mars. The fact that scattered light gave the field of view a bluish cast which tended to wash out the contrast, and that the stars wore curious little tails, detracted not a bit from the satisfaction of observing. So far as I knew this was the normal appearance of the sky when it is viewed through a telescope! Over the years I made and used better instruments, and on one occasion I even enjoyed a turn at the eyepiece of the 60-inch reflector on Mount Wilson. By then, however, I had found observing almost routine. Even the Mount Wilson experience did not give me the same thrill as that first squint through my crude six-incher.

In my opinion the beginner should not attempt to make a telescope of high optical quality on the first try. Too many who do grow discouraged and abandon the project in midstream. The application of the tests and figuring techniques through which the surface of the principal mirror is brought to optical perfection is a fine art that is mastered by few. I have made more than 50 mirrors and have yet to polish a glass with a perfect figure to the very edge. For all but the most talented opticians neither the tests nor the techniques are exact. After misinterpreting test patterns and misapplying figuring techniques for some months the beginner is tempted to give up the project as impossible and discard a mirror that would operate beautifully if used. Conversely, spurious test-effects have been known to trick veteran amateurs into turning out crude mirrors by the score under the prideful illusion that each was perfect. That such mirrors work satisfactorily is a tribute to the marvelous accommodation of the eye and to lack of discrimination on the part of the observer.

Beginners may nonetheless undertake the construction of a reflecting telescope with every expectation of success. If the amateur has enough strength and mechanical ability to grind two blocks of glass together, his efforts will be rewarded by an instrument far superior to that used by Galileo. He need not concern himself either with tests or elusive figuring techniques.

The simplest reflecting telescope consists of four major subassemblies: an objective mirror which collects light and reflects it to a focus, a flat diagonal mirror which bends the focused rays at a right angle so that the image can be observed without obstructing the incoming light, a magnifying lens or eyepiece through which the image is examined, and a movable framework or mounting which supports the optical elements in alignment and trains them on the sky. About half the cost of the finished telescope, both in money and in labor, is represented by the objective mirror.

The mounting can be made from almost any combination of materials that chances to be handy: wood, pipe, sheet metal, discarded machine parts and so on, depending upon the resourcefulness and fancy of the builder. The mounting designed by Roger Hayward, illustrated in Figure 6, is representative. The dimensions may be varied according to the requirements of construction.

Materials for the objective and diagonal mirrors are available in kit form, as advertised in most popular science magazines. Amateurs with access to machine tools can also make the required eyepieces. The construction is rather tedious, however, and ready-made eyepieces are so inexpensive that few amateurs bother to make their own.

The beginner is urged to start with a six-inch mirror. Those of smaller size do not perform well unless they are skillfully made, and the difficulty of handling larger ones increases disproportionately. Kits for six-inch mirrors retail for about $10. They include two thick glass "blanks," one for the objective mirror and one (called the tool) on which the mirror is ground. The kits also supply a small rectangle of flat plate-glass that serves as the diagonal, a series of abrasive powders ranging from coarse to fine, a supply of optical rouge for polishing and a quantity of pine pitch.

As Russell Porter explained back in 1926, "In the reflecting telescope, *the mirror's the thing.* No matter how elaborate and accurate the rest of the instrument, if it has a poor mirror, it is hopeless." Fortunately it is all but impossible to make a really

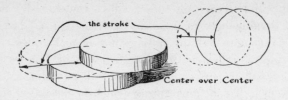

1
Details of the stroke for grinding the objective mirror of the telescope

poor mirror if one follows a few simple directions with reasonable care. The idea is to grind one face of the six-inch mirror
blank to a shallow curve about a 16th of an inch deep, polish it
to a concave spherical surface and then, by additional polishing,
deepen it increasingly toward the center so that the spherical curve
becomes a paraboloid. The spherical curve is formed by placing
the mirror blank on the tool, with wet abrasive between the two,
and simply grinding the mirror over the tool in straight back-and-
forth strokes. Nature comes to the aid of the mirror-maker in
achieving the desired sphere, because glass grinds fastest at the
points of greatest pressure between the two disks. During a portion of each stroke the mirror overhangs the tool; maximum pressure develops in the central portion of the mirror, where it is supported by the edge of the tool. Hence the center of the mirror
and edge of the tool grind fastest, the mirror becoming concave
and the tool convex. As grinding proceeds, the worker periodically turns the tool slightly in one direction and the mirror in the
other. In consequence the concavity assumes the approximate
form of a sphere because mating spherical curves tend to remain
everywhere in contact when moved over each other in every possible direction. Any departure from the spherical form tends to
be quickly and automatically ground away because abnormal
pressure develops at the high point and accelerates local abrasion.

The grinding can be performed in any convenient location that
is free of dust and close to a supply of water. The operation tends
to become somewhat messy, so a reasonably clean basement or
garage is preferable to a kitchen or other household room.

A support for the tool is made first. This may consist of a disk of wood roughly half an inch thick fastened to the center of a square of the same material about a foot on a side. The diameter of the wooden disk should be about half an inch smaller than that of the tool. All surfaces of this fixture, except the exposed face of the wooden disk, should receive two coats of shellac. The glass tool is then cemented symmetrically to the unfinished face of the wooden disk by means of pitch. Melt a small quantity of pitch in any handy vessel. Warm the tool for five minutes in reasonably hot water, then dry it and rub one face lightly with a tuft of cotton saturated with turpentine. Now pour a tablespoon of melted pitch on the unfinished face of the wooden disk and press the tool against it so that pitch squeezes out all around the joint. After the tool and supporting fixture cool, they are a unit that can be removed from the bench conveniently for cleaning, which is frequently needed. Some workers prefer to attach the wooden disk to a large circular base. The base is then secured to the bench between three wooden cleats spaced 120 degrees apart. This arrangement permits the base to be rotated conveniently.

The tool assembly is now fastened on the corner of a sturdy bench or other working support, and a teaspoon of the coarsest abrasive is sprinkled evenly over the surface of the glass. A small salt-shaker makes a convenient dispenser for abrasives. The starting abrasive is usually No. 80 Carborundum, the grains of which are about the size of those of granulated sugar. A teaspoon of water is added to the abrasive at the center of the tool and the mirror lowered gently on the tool. The mirror is grasped at the edges with both hands; pressure is applied by the palms. It is pushed away from the worker by the base of the thumbs and pulled forward by the fingertips. The length of the grinding strokes should be half the diameter of the mirror. In the case of a six-inch mirror the strokes are three inches long — a maximum excursion of an inch and a half each side of the center. The motion should be smooth and straight, center over center. Simultaneously a slight turn is imparted to the mirror during each stroke to complete a full revolution in about 30 strokes. The tool should also be turned slightly in the opposite direction every 10 or 12 strokes, or, if he prefers, the worker may shift his position around the tool. Learn to judge the length of the stroke. Do *not* limit it by means of a mechanical stop. Beginners will tend to overshoot and undershoot the prescribed distance somewhat, but these errors average out.

Fresh Carborundum cuts effectively, and the grinding is accompanied by a characteristic gritty sound. Initially the work has a smooth, well-lubricated feel. After a few minutes the gritty sound tends to soften and the work has a gummy feel. Stop at this point, add another teaspoon of water and resume grinding until the work again feels gummy. Both the mirror and tool are removed from the bench and washed free of "mud," the mixture of pulverized glass and powdered abrasive that results from grinding. This marks the end of the first "wet." Fresh Carborundum is now applied, and the procedure is continued for three additional wets. The stroke is then shortened to a third of the diameter of the mirror (two inches in the case of a six-inch mirror) for two more wets. The mirror should now show a uniformly ground surface to the edge of the disk in every direction. If not, continue grinding until this is achieved.

NOTE: Beginners occasionally report that the expected curve refuses to appear, that both glasses remain essentially flat and merely grind away. This may happen unless uniform pressure is exerted over the whole area of the mirror. Some practice may be necessary to develop the proper stroke. As a temporary expedient the mirror may be shifted gradually from side to side during the rough grinding — made to follow a zigzag path. Concavity will then develop promptly. Caution: Don't overdo it!

The ground surface now has the form of a shallow curve and must be tested for focal length. This is easily accomplished on a sunny day. The test equipment consists of a square of light-colored cardboard about a foot across which serves as a screen on which the image of the sun is projected, and a supply of water to wet the roughly ground surface of the mirror and thus improve its effectiveness as a reflector. Stand the cardboard on edge at a height of about six feet so that one side faces the sun squarely; then take a position on the shady side about 10 feet from the screen. Dip the mirror in the water and, with the ground surface facing the sun, reflect sunlight onto the screen. The image will appear as a fuzzy disk of light, doubtless somewhat smaller than the diameter of the mirror. The size of the image will change as the mirror is moved toward or away from the screen. Find the distance at which it is minimum. This is the approximate focal length of the mirror. At this stage of grinding, the focal length will doubtless be of the order of 15 feet. The object is to shorten it to six feet by additional grinding. Wash the tool, apply fresh abrasive, grind for five minutes and repeat the test. It is advisable to make a chart on which the focal length is recorded after each spell of grinding. The chart aids in judging progress toward the goal of six feet. When the desired focal length is attained, thoroughly scrub the mirror, tool, bench, utensils and all other objects likely to be contaminated with No. 80 abrasive. Grinding is then continued with successively finer grades of abrasive. The same stroke is used: two inches in length and center-over-center. Usually the second grade is No. 180, which has the texture of finely powdered sand. The grinding technique is precisely the same for all subsequent grades of abrasive; each stage of grinding is continued until all pits made in the glass by the preceding grade have been removed. Usually six wets with each grade is adequate. On the average each wet will require about 15 minutes of grinding. Examine the ground surface by means of a magnifying glass after the sixth wet. If any pits larger than average are found, continue grinding for another wet or two and examine again. Persist until all pits larger than average disappear. There is one exception to this procedure. Sometimes a stray grain of No. 80 or one of the intermediate grades will find its way into work that has reached the terminal stages of fine grinding. A scratch or groove will appear that is so deep that it cannot be removed by a reasonable amount of fine grinding. The only solution is to return to the offending grade and repeat all the intermediate work. Gloves are notorious grit-catchers. Never wear them when grinding. Try to prevent clothing from coming into contact with loose grit. Abrasives supplied with representative kits include Nos. 80, 180, 220, 280, 400, 600, FFF and rouge.

The beginner is urged to purchase an extra mirror blank. The object is to make two mirrors simultaneously, select one for immediate use and reserve the second for subsequent refinement. Those following this suggestion should grind the mirrors alternately. Complete a wet of a given grade on the first mirror and proceed with the same wet on the second. After all grinding is completed, the mirrors are polished independently.

The operations of grinding and polishing glass are similar in that both require the use of a material which is harder than glass. In grinding, the abrasive material is used between a pair of hard surfaces, either two pieces of glass or glass and cast iron. In rolling between the surfaces under pressure the hard particles erode the glass by causing tiny conchoidal fractures in its surface. Glass can be polished with the same hard particles merely by replacing the hard tool with an appropriately soft and yielding one. The theory of the polishing action is not well understood. It is clear, however, that the abrasive particles do not roll. Held firmly by a yielding medium, their protruding edges may act like the blade of a plane.

Most amateurs use a polishing tool, or "lap," of pine pitch divided into a pattern of facets and charged with rouge. To make the facets, pitch is first cast into strips about an inch wide, a quarter of an inch thick and eight or 10 inches long. An adequate mold of wood (lined with moist paper to prevent the strips of pitch from sticking) is shown in Figure 2. Melt the pitch over a hot plate, not over a direct flame. Do not overheat the pitch; it burns easily. The fumes (largely vaporized turpentine) are highly combustible, so prevent direct flame from reaching the open part of the container.

The strips of cool pitch are cut into square facets by means of a hot knife and stuck to the ground surface of the tool in a checkerboard pattern as shown. Begin by locating one facet somewhat off-center in the middle of the tool, and work outward. Adhesion is improved by first warming the tool, smearing it with a film of turpentine and warming the face of each square of pitch before placing it in contact with the glass. The pitch facets should be beveled, which can be accomplished in part by cutting the edges of the wooden divider-strips of the mold at an angle. This also

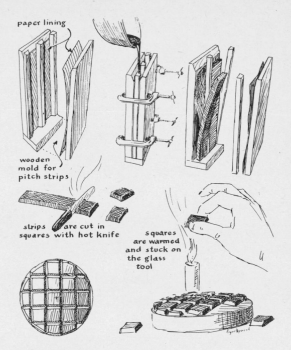

paper lining

wooden
mold for
pitch strips

strips   are cut in
squares with hot knife

squares
are warmed
and stuck on
the glass
tool

2
Preparation of pitch facets for polishing lap

facilitates the removal of the strips from the mold. Pitch yields
under pressure, so unless the facets are beveled the space between
adjacent facets soon closes during the polishing operation.

Trim all boundary facets flush with the edge of the tool by
means of the hot knife. Then invert the completed lap in a pan
of warm water for 10 minutes. While the pitch is warming, place
a heaping tablespoon of rouge in a clean wide-mouthed jar fitted
with a screw cap, and add enough water to form a creamy mixture. Remove the lap from the pan, blot it dry and, with a quarter-
inch brush of the kind used with water colors, paint the pitch
facets with rouge. Now place the mirror gently and squarely on
the lap and apply about five pounds of evenly distributed weight
to the mirror for half an hour until the pitch facets yield enough

to conform with the curve of the glass. This process is called cold-pressing. At the end of the cold-pressing interval slide the mirror from the lap and bevel the edge facets to remove any bulges that have formed.

The mirror must now be fitted with a shield to insulate it from the heat of the worker's hands. In the case of a six-inch mirror cut a disk of corrugated cardboard eight inches in diameter and notch its edge every inch or so to a depth of one inch. Center the cardboard on the unground side of the mirror, press the notched edges down along the side of the glass and secure them with several turns of adhesive tape. The cardboard form now resembles the lid of a wide-mouthed jar.

Paint the facets with fresh rouge, add half a teaspoon of water to the center of the lap and, with the heat-insulating shield in place, lower the mirror gently onto the lap. Polishing proceeds with strokes identical with those used in grinding; they are two inches long and center-over-center. When the work develops a heavy feel, stop, add half a teaspoon of water and resume. Continue polishing for 20 minutes. Then cold-press for 10 minutes. Proceed with this alternating routine until no pits can be detected when the surface is examined with a high-powered magnifying glass. If the fine grinding has been performed as directed, the mirror can be brought to full polish in three hours or less. When work must be suspended for some hours, coat the lap with rouge and cold-press without added weight. It is well to brace the mirror around the edges when it remains on the lap for some hours, because pitch flows slowly and may deposit an unbraced mirror on the floor.

The shape of the mirror is now close to a perfect sphere. The center will doubtless have a somewhat longer radius than the region near the edge. Precisely the reverse situation is desired: a curve whose radius increases from the center outward. A minute thickness of glass must therefore be removed from the center of the mirror and a somewhat lesser amount removed toward the edge. The mirror is put back on the lap and, with a fresh charge of rouge, polished by a modified stroke. The length of the stroke is not altered, but the mirror is now made to follow a zig-

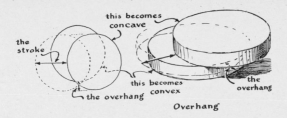

3
Details of stroke used to parabolize the objective mirror

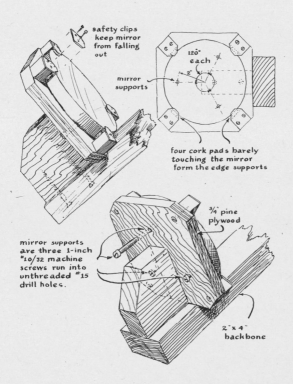

4
Details of wooden cell for the objective mirror

zag course laterally across the lap at right angles to the worker. The first stroke follows the conventional center-over-center course away from the worker but on the return stroke and subsequent strokes the mirror is zigzagged gradually toward the right until it overhangs the tool by about an inch. It is then gradually worked back across the center until it overhangs the lap on the left side by an inch. This operation is repeated over and over for 15 minutes. Simultaneously the mirror is rotated slightly in one direction during each stroke and the tool is periodically rotated in the other direction to distribute the abrasive action uniformly.

After a thorough cleaning the mirror is ready for silvering. Amateurs formerly coated their mirrors at home. But silver is difficult to apply and tarnishes quickly. Most reflecting telescopes are now

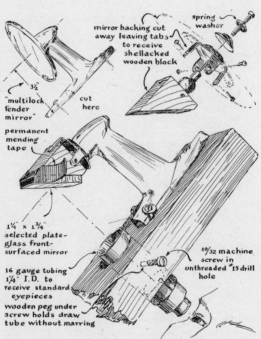

5
Modified rear-view auto mirror for supporting diagonal mirror

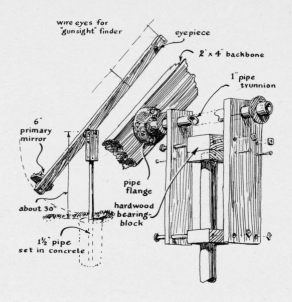

6
Simple mounting for supporting optical train of reflecting telescope

aluminized, a process too tricky to be undertaken by beginners. The mirror is placed in a highly evacuated chamber and bombarded with vaporized aluminum. On being exposed to air the metal acquires a transparent film of oxide which protects it against tarnish. Firms that specialize in this work charge about $5 to aluminize a six-inch mirror. The advertisements of many are found in the magazines of popular science. The beginner is urged to have both his objective mirror and the diagonal coated in this way.

The mounting may be constructed while the mirrors are being coated. In designing the mounting never permit appearance to compromise sturdiness. This telescope will have a maximum magnifying power of about 250 diameters and any jiggle arising in the mounting will be magnified proportionately. The objective mirror is supported in a wooden cell fitted with screw adjust-

17

ments. Fine-grinding and polishing will have reduced the focal length to about five feet. The center of the diagonal mirror is spaced approximately six inches from the focal point of the objective (about 4.5 feet from the objective), thus bending a six-inch cone of rays into the eyepiece, as shown in detail in Figure 6.

After assembly the optical elements must be aligned. Remove the eyepiece, look through the tube in which it slides and adjust the diagonal mirror until the objective mirror is centered in the field of view. Then adjust the tilt of the objective mirror until the reflected image of the diagonal mirror is centered. Replace the eyepiece in its tube and you are in business.

Those who construct this telescope will ultimately discover that it is not the best that can be built. To improve it consult the books recommended in the bibliography and tackle the fine art of figuring the second mirror by means of the fascinating tests and techniques described therein.

3

A TRANSISTORIZED DRIVE
FOR TELESCOPES

Telescopes must be turned slowly to follow the stars across the sky. A method of turning one automatically by means of a motor deriving its power from transistors is described by George W. Ginn, an engineer of Lihue, Hawaii

THE SLOW PARADE of stars across the night sky appears to be greatly accelerated when it is observed through a stationary telescope of high power, because the instrument magnifies apparent motion as well as size. In consequence objects drift across the field of view and disappear in a matter of seconds unless some arrangement is made to keep the instrument trained on them. If the telescope is mounted so that it can turn, objects can be kept in view most of the time by moving the tube manually. Hand guiding is not precise enough, however, for many types of observation. The instruments used by astronomers and a large number of the telescopes made by amateurs are therefore equipped with a mechanism to keep celestial objects automatically in view.

Most of the apparent motion of a celestial object is caused by the rotation of the earth, which amounts to one revolution in 24 hours with respect to the sun, and to one in about 23 hours, 56 minutes with respect to the stars. The fact that the hour hand of a clock turns at approximately twice this rate suggests that a clockwork could be modified to serve as an automatic drive by coupling it to the shaft of the telescope through a set of simple reduction-gears. This approach has been tried by many amateurs. Ordinary clocks, however, fall considerably short of meeting the requirements for an ideal drive. Few of them deliver enough power to overcome frictional losses in bearings of the type used by amateurs, and they do not provide enough range in speed. To track the moon accurately as it crosses the meridian a clock must run about 5 per cent slower than normal, a rate which in the latitude of New York would cause the clock to lose about an hour per day. This rate is beyond the range of the "fast-slow" adjustment of most clocks. Another serious limitation of clocks as drives for telescopes arises from the property to which they owe their usefulness as instruments for measuring time. Clocks run at constant speed, but the apparent motion of a star varies. Light from stars low in the sky passes through more of the earth's atmosphere than does light from stars higher in the sky; the light of a star near the horizon is so strongly refracted by the atmosphere that the image of the star can be seen several seconds after the star has passed below the horizon. Accordingly a drive that freezes an object in the field of a telescope pointed at the zenith permits the image to drift increasingly as the telescope is pointed at lower angles. In the most satisfactory drives provision is therefore made for continuously altering the tracking speed through a narrow range above and below its average value. Moreover, the best systems are equipped with a coarse control for changing the tracking rate by at least an order of magnitude so the tube can be quickly centered on a selected object.

Mechanical drives, such as those built around spring-driven clocks, are not satisfactory for use with portable instruments. The mainspring of most small clocks is not powerful enough to overcome frictional losses in the mounting, so an arrangement of weights must be added to supplement the energy stored in the spring. A clutch must also be inserted between the clockwork and mounting so that the tube can be disengaged for shifting the field of view from one region of the sky to another. In addition, the system must include a set of differential gears, a screw adjustment or some comparable means for making small corrections in the position of the tube without interrupting the basic motion of the clock. All this adds up to a cumbersome mechanism which is costly to make, inconvenient to use and difficult to maintain in satisfactory working order.

Much of my observing, which has included a lot of photography, has been done at elevations above 10,000 feet on Mauna Loa and neighboring volcanic peaks, where seeing is exceptionally good nearly every night of the year. Most of these locations are reached by car and on foot by roads carved from lava, which is scarcely an ideal pavement. This means that my equipment must be light and rugged enough to retain its accuracy during rough trips.

The camera and guide telescope are supported on a tripod by a mounting of German manufacture which I acquired from the University of Hawaii in exchange for adapting one of their instruments for portable use. The mounting is of the equatorial type — one shaft turns in the plane of the earth's equator and the other in elevation — and is equipped with worm gears coupled to hand wheels for following objects in right ascension and declination as well as with clamps for locking the tube in any desired position. The arrangement is adequate for casual observing and even for making photographs of short exposure. But fine visual measurements and extended exposures require more precise guiding.

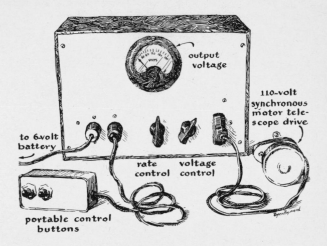

7
Exterior view of transistorized drive for small telescope

Most of these difficulties can be overcome by substituting electrical parts for the springs and gear trains — with a distinct gain in the precision of tracking. My present drive consists of a small synchronous motor of the type used in electric clocks which is energized by an oscillator-amplifier using transistors. The oscillator converts direct current into alternating current of a precisely known frequency. In effect it measures time and corresponds to the escapement of a clock. Power for the unit is taken from my automobile storage battery, which is thus analogous to the mainspring of a clock. The motor, somewhat smaller than a pack of cigarettes, is mounted on and geared directly to the mounting. A plug-in cord connects the motor to the oscillator-amplifier. The unit is about the size of a miniature radio-receiver. Another plug-in cord from the oscillator-amplifier is connected to the battery by spring clips, and a third cord runs to a control box equipped with push buttons for changing the speed of drive as desired. The control box is held in and operated by one hand during observation. The complete system, less battery, weighs five pounds. It requires no lubrication or other maintenance, is unaffected by

21

dust and retains its calibration over wide changes of temperature.

The oscillator-amplifier circuit was designed for transistors instead of vacuum tubes primarily because I wanted to learn something about transistors. Perhaps the use of vacuum tubes would have been wiser at this stage of transistor development; the choice of circuit components designed expressly for transistors is still rather narrow, particularly in the case of transformers. On the other hand, the impressive reduction in size, weight and power consumption of apparatus which is made possible by the use of transistors more than compensates the builder for time spent in modifying parts.

With the exception of the motor and the controls, the system contains no moving parts. During operation the oscillator draws direct current from the battery and converts it to alternating current at any desired frequency from 55 to 65 cycles per second. The frequency is controlled by a knob that corresponds to the fast-slow adjustment of a clock. The control covers a range of something more than 5 per cent, which is adequate for guiding telescopes and cameras less than five feet in focal length. The frequency can be doubled instantly by operating one of the two push buttons in the control box. The other button stops the oscillator. The action of the buttons corresponds to that of a set of differential gears and is used as a slow-motion traverse. By pressing the appropriate button the telescope can be moved forward or backward with respect to the stars at the rate of .25 degree per minute. The amplifier portion of the circuit steps up the output power of the oscillator to four watts at 115 volts for driving the motor, which is rated at 3.8 watts.

The oscillator circuit is of the Wein bridge type and has excellent stability. The frequency is adjusted through the 5-per-cent range by dual potentiometers and is doubled by switching out half of the .5-microfarad capacitors shown in the accompanying circuit diagram, Figure 8. Stopping the oscillator is accomplished by short-circuiting the 5,000-ohm (5K) variable resistor shown at the top of the diagram. This resistor controls the amount of energy fed back in reverse polarity from the output of the oscillator to its input and is normally set to the lowest resistance at which the os-

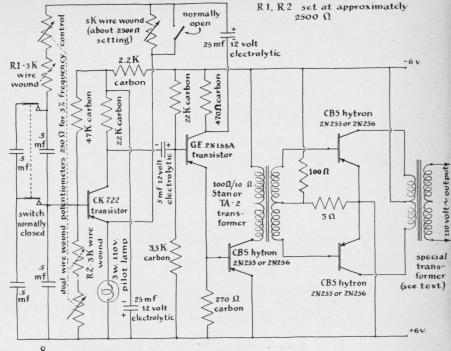

R1, R2 set at approximately 2500 Ω

5K wire wound (about 2500 Ω setting)

normally open

25 mf 12 volt electrolytic

-6 v.

R1-3K wire wound

2.2K carbon

4.7K carbon

22K carbon

dual wire wound potentiometers 250 Ω for 5% frequency control

22K carbon

470 Ω carbon

CBS hytron 2N255 or 2N256

.5 mf

.5 mf

switch normally closed

.5 mf

.5 mf

CK 722 transistor

R2-3K wire wound

3w 110v. pilot lamp

5 mf 12 volt electrolytic

GE 2N188A transistor

100 Ω/10 Ω Stan or TA-2 transformer

100 Ω

3 Ω

CBS hytron 2N255 or 2N256

CBS hytron 2N255 or 2N256

110 volt ~ output

special transformer (see text)

3.3K carbon

25 mf 12 volt electrolytic

270 Ω carbon

+6 v.

8
Circuit diagram for transistorized amplifier-oscillator

cillator will start and maintain stable operation. Switching is accomplished by relays, the coils of which are energized by the push buttons.

The circuit includes a ballast lamp for stabilizing the output voltage. The filament is connected in series with the feedback resistor so that the voltage of the circuit is divided between them. When the voltage rises, the filament warms up and the resistance increases. This has the effect of increasing the negative feedback, which in turn reduces the voltage to its normal value.

Standard construction and wiring were used. The housing of the oscillator-amplifier unit is five inches wide, six inches deep and nine inches long and is available from most radio dealers. The aluminum panel and chassis were cut to fit the case. The small transistors were mounted along with the resistors on a strip of

Formica by drilling small holes in the strip for the leads and making connections on the back. The cases of the power transistors function as "collectors," counterparts of the "plate" electrode in vacuum tubes. Voltage is applied to the cases, so they must be insulated from the chassis. Kits are available for mounting power transistors which include mica washers and silicone oil to aid in the transfer of heat to the chassis. I did not use the oil because in this circuit the units operate substantially below their rated capacity for dissipating heat. Do *not* solder connections directly to the power-transistor terminals; transistors are easily damaged by high temperature. Clips for connecting transistors into the circuit can be made from contacts salvaged from miniature vacuum-tube sockets. Connections to the emitter electrodes of the power transistors must be tight because a peak current of two amperes flows in this circuit. Two other precautions are worth mentioning. First, transistors, unlike vacuum tubes, can be damaged by applying voltage of incorrect polarity to the terminals. Second, the output stage must not be operated without a load.

The power transistors of this amplifier deliver about 4.3 volts on each side of the center tap. This must be stepped up by a transformer to 115 volts for driving the motor. Unfortunately, dealers do not stock a suitable transformer. I tried to modify a conventional filament-transformer for the job by leaving the 117-volt winding intact and rewinding the 6.3-volt secondary for the lower input voltage. Sad to relate, only 50 volts came out of the high side. After stewing over this development for a day or so, and consulting *Radio Engineers' Handbook* for data on transformer design, it became apparent that heat losses in the iron core caused by the high density of the magnetic field were eating up the profits. Apparently 6.3-volt filament-transformers are designed with a minimum of iron and copper, adequate performance being achieved by operating the iron core at a high magnetic-flux density. If 25 per cent of the energy is wasted in heating the core, nobody cares because the energy is being taken from the 110-volt power line and amounts to only a few watts. After calculating the losses for several values of flux density and wire size, I picked the best combination and rewound both coils of the transformer. The primary was replaced with 48 turns of No. 18 enameled magnet-wire on each side of the center tap; the secondary, with 1,560 turns of No. 32 wire. This reduced the flux density from 98,000 lines per square inch to 41,000 lines and reduced the and has a cross-sectional area of 7/8 square inch. Any core of about this size and weight should work satisfactorily. Smaller cores would require more turns. The losses are proportional to the weight of the core and the square of the flux density. The core of an audio-frequency transformer would doubtless perform better because the laminations are thinner and are made of the highest quality magnetic iron.

The power transistors operate alternately, so only half of the primary coil carries current at one time. If the transformer were operating from a conventional alternating-current source of four volts, the primary coil could be a single winding of 48 turns. If 12-volt operation is desired, the number of primary turns must be doubled. The output in this case would be about nine watts, so the wire size of the secondary winding would have to be increased to No. 30, and a larger core would be required to provide additional space for the larger wire size.

The new set of coils delivered an output of 90 volts, as measured by a meter of the rectifier type. Further investigation disclosed that the low indication was caused by the irregular shape of the voltage wave, a response induced by the motor. A .5-microfarad capacitor connected across the output coil of the transformer corrected the wave form and raised the indication to 110 volts. The voltage rises somewhat when the frequency is doubled, but this is not a disadvantage because the torque of the motor would normally drop at the higher frequency. The higher voltage tends to maintain constant torque.

A few bugs remain in this pilot model. The oscilloscope shows some highly unconventional and mysterious wave forms here and there. Other builders will doubtless find ways to improve the circuit, and I will welcome a report of their results. But the bugs have no discernable effect on the operation of the unit. When I compare its output with that of the 60-cycle power line, the power frequency varies most. Operation in the field is simplicity itself. Set up the telescope, plug in the cords, adjust the speed and you are ready to observe.

It is assumed that amateurs who undertake the construction of this device will have some experience with electronic circuits. Others are urged to solicit the cooperation of a neighboring radio "ham." Some reading is indicated for those inexperienced with transistors; I can recommend the booklet on 2N255 and 2N256 transistors published by CBS Hytron of Lowell, Mass. Similar booklets covering equivalent transistors made by other manufacturers are available through most radio dealers.

4

AN ELECTRONIC STAR-TWINKLE SUPPRESSOR

Twinkling starlight, a source of delight to the casual stargazer, presents the astronomer with a major problem by blurring his photographs of celestial objects. Robert Leighton, a nuclear physicist at the California Institute of Technology and an ardent amateur astronomer, explains how he minimized the blur by means of an apparatus with which he made photographs of the planets considered to be the clearest ever exhibited

IT IS A COMMON BELIEF that very large telescopes, such as the 100-inch and 200-inch reflectors of the Mount Wilson and Palomar Observatories, should show fine detail of the moon and planets because the resolving power of a perfectly figured telescope lens, for objects situated at a great distance, is supposed to improve as the diameter of the objective lens is increased.

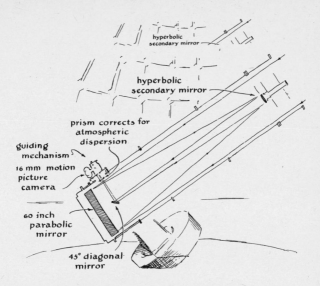

9
Leighton's guiding device applied to optical system of the 60-inch telescope at Mt. Wilson Observatory

According to the so-called Rayleigh criterion, the resolving
power of a telescope is expressed numerically by dividing 4.5 by
the diameter of the objective in inches. The quotient gives the
smallest angular separation, in seconds of arc, at which two equally bright point sources of light can be distinguished. Any pair separated by a smaller angle will merge because of the wave nature
of light and be seen as a single point. Hence if the performance of
the huge telescopes were limited only by their optical quality,
they would indeed give breathtaking views of the planets.

Although the big instruments are virtually perfect in their optical and mechanical construction, and have surpassed their expected performance in the applications for which they were designed, there is very little likelihood that they will ever show
planetary detail to the limit of their theoretical capabilities. In
fact, there is good reason to believe that the best planetary and
lunar photographs will be made with telescopes of but 30 to 40
inches aperture.

An observer at the eyepiece of a relatively small telescope can see millions of tiny craterlets and other structures less than a thousand feet wide on the moon, but no lunar photograph has yet pictured detail less than about a mile in extent. Again, the ring system of Saturn has never been adequately photographed. Most photographs show only the two main rings and the largest division, whereas the faint crape ring is very clear visually in small telescopes, and at least two other divisions are recognized. The canals of Mars may be a third example. Their failure to appear on any of the many thousands of photographs that have been made of this planet is the cause of a long-standing controversy regarding their existence. Many qualified observers have reported seeing them. Others, apparently equally qualified, see not a trace of them. Even a single convincing photograph could settle the question of their existence.

These examples, particularly that of the lunar craters, clearly establish that a wide gap exists between well-substantiated visual observation and the corresponding photographic results. The fundamental cause of this discrepancy is to be found not in any lack of optical perfection of the telescope itself, but rather in the optical unsteadiness of the earth's atmosphere, which is brought about by thermal nonuniformities always present throughout it. This, coupled with the need for several seconds' exposure, leads to relatively poor photographic resolution, no matter how large or how small a telescope is used.

The degree of optical steadiness of the atmosphere is called the "seeing." One effect of the turbulence is visible to the naked eye as the scintillation or "twinkling" of the stars. As the thermally inhomogeneous regions move past the observer's line of sight, they act upon the light rays passing through them, thereby producing a constantly changing deviation and phase shift. Neighboring rays interfere with one another and cause the observed color and brightness changes. In times of good seeing the atmosphere is relatively calm and thermally uniform and there is little or no naked-eye stellar scintillation. During bad seeing, on the contrary, the atmosphere is quite nonuniform thermally and a large degree of scintillation is visible.

The atmospheric turbulence that leads to poor seeing arises from many causes. It may be created by local warm objects (such as motors, vacuum tubes or observers near the telescope itself), by a difference in temperature between the telescope tube and the surrounding air, or by nearby chimneys or factories which emit heat. More basically, the inhomogeneities are caused by large-scale convection currents which accompany cloud formation and thunderstorms, or by turbulence between atmospheric layers having different temperatures and wind velocities.

The character of the seeing can be viewed telescopically in considerable detail by observing an out-of-focus image of a bright star. The pattern you see resembles the bands and spots of sunlight on the bottom of a slightly agitated pool of water. They are in constant motion. Slow-moving patterns with sharp boundaries generally signify nearby heat sources, and these can often be tracked down by careful observation. Fast-moving patterns can usually be seen sweeping across the objective in one or more directions; these are caused by winds somewhere in the atmosphere.

The effect of the seeing upon the quality of an image formed by a telescope depends upon the "cell size" of the seeing. This refers to the size of the region over which the air temperature is sufficiently uniform so that a parallel light beam passing through such a region to the telescope is negligibly distorted. The part of the objective that receives such a beam forms a perfect image. If the cell size is substantially smaller than the telescope aperture, the objective will encompass several such cells, with the result that a number of separate images are formed by the telescope. These then combine to form a blurred image on which fine detail cannot be resolved. If only a few such cells cover the aperture, the separate images may be individually visible. Each star or other object is split into a small cluster. This is often the case with fine detail such as the craters of the moon or the Jovian satellites.

At the other extreme the seeing cell size may be much larger than the telescope aperture, so that the entire objective acts as a unit and the resultant image is clear and sharp. But the image will move irregularly about some average position. These irregular excursions are often as large as one or two seconds of arc, which is several per cent of the angular diameter of Mars or Jupiter. Under given conditions of seeing it is clearly disadvantageous to use an aperture larger than the seeing cell-size. This aperture will yield a brighter image, though it will show less detail.

What is the best size of telescope, then, for visual observation? It ought to be large enough to take advantage of the best seeing (*i.e.*, largest cell size) that is reasonably likely to occur. The maximum size thus depends upon the geographical location, for at each location there is a certain distribution of seeing conditions throughout the year, and on each night there is a corresponding maximum useful aperture for visual observation. On most nights, even at a favorable location, this will be less than three or four inches. On many it may be as large as 10 or 12 inches. But apertures as large as 50 or 60 inches very seldom can be used with maximum effect. The greatest telescopes, such as the 100-inch and 200-inch reflectors, will encounter seeing conditions fully matching their apertures only once in many years. Indeed, no astronomer who has used the 200-inch Hale telescope has yet reported star images less than about three tenths of a second of arc in diameter. This size corresponds to the theoretical resolving power of a 15-inch telescope! Obviously a visual observer gains no advantage at the eyepiece of the huge telescopes.

If we now consider the photographic situation, a new element enters the problem. This is the requirement that a sufficient exposure time be provided to yield a satisfactory photographic image. Because of this the advantage of a smaller aperture disappears, since the fainter image corresponding to the smaller aperture requires a longer exposure and will therefore move about more on the film, yielding a blurred image. Thus for photographic purposes it is almost immaterial whether a large or small aperture is used, so long as it is at least as large as the seeing conditions will permit for visual observation.

It should now be clear why direct vision has proved superior to photography for the observation of lunar and planetary detail. For visual observation of a sufficiently bright object, it is of no great importance that the image be steady, so long as it is sharply defined, because the eye is able to follow the irregular excursions of the image that are brought about by the atmospheric instability. For photographic observation, on the contrary, it is quite necessary that the image be both sharply defined and steady for the duration of an exposure. Furthermore, a visual observer has a great advantage in being able to ignore the times when the image is distorted and to remember the moments when it is excellent, while the photographic plate indiscriminately records all the accumulated fluctuations.

Yet in spite of the marvelous ability of the eye to catch, and the brain to retain, fleeting glimpses of extraordinarily fine detail, we cannot regard the situation as anything but unsatisfactory. The eye is not a quantitative measuring instrument, and the brain is not always objective in what it records. The accuracy, objectivity and permanence of the photographic record are as much to be desired here as in other fields of science.

A number of possibilities exist for removing or relaxing the limitations that the turbulent atmosphere imposes on stellar photography. The most obvious of these is to try to exploit those very rare nights when a large telescope actually will perform better than a small one. Unfortunately this requires more than a steady atmosphere; it also requires that a suitable object be available in a favorable location to photograph. In the case of the moon, this immediately reduces the likelihood of such a coincidence by at least a factor of four, and in the case of Mars, by a factor of at least 40, not allowing for the fact that the most favorable oppositions of Mars occur when it is low in the sky for the majority of the large telescopes in the world. It would be the sheerest accident if any ordinary photograph of Mars taken with the 200-inch telescope within the next century were to show detail worthy of its tremendous resolving power!

In contrast with the performance of the 200-inch, the chances of good seeing improve so rapidly with diminishing aperture that a telescope of 40 or 50 inches might be used effectively for planetary photography, provided photographs were taken almost continuously during every reasonably steady night. But this would require reserving a large portion of the observing time for such use. Such a program probably could not be justified except possibly for a limited time, such as during a very favorable opposition of Mars.

Clearly the economic justification of the big telescope does not lie in its ability to resolve minute details of bright, relatively close objects. Rather, its immense light-gathering power is largely exploited for photographing objects too faint or remote in space for smaller instruments.

We cannot hope to take the much-desired photograph of Mars by the mere expedient of building ever more powerful telescopes. How, then, may we approach the job?

Although no ideal solution is known at present, several possibilities have been suggested and some have been tried with promising results. One is to remove directly the main cause of the problem: the atmosphere. This could be done by taking the telescope away from its traditional bedrock foundation and lifting it above most of the atmosphere in a rocket, a balloon or a high-altitude jet aircraft.

A different line of attack, which shows considerable promise, involves the use of electronic image intensification. The aim here is to reduce the required exposure time so drastically that the image from a relatively small telescope could be utilized. A system based on this principle has been tested at the Lowell Observatory at Flagstaff, Ariz. It yields enough intensification to permit a 30-fold reduction in exposure time. The image thus has less time for wandering about on the film, and smearing is reduced accordingly. This is essentially a closed-circuit television system utilizing an image-orthicon pickup tube connected through an amplifier to a picture tube. The picture tube is then photographed with a camera whose shutter is suitably synchronized with the picture. With this method the possibility also exists of detecting electronically the moments when the image is sharpest and building up a complete exposure out of many selected shorter intervals. It is too early to evaluate the capabilities of the new electronic methods, but doubtless much will be heard of them in the future.

During the past few years I have experimented with a third approach in which an electronic guiding system is used to cancel out most of the motion of the image on the film. I observed that during good seeing the image of a planet tends to move as a whole, rather than to change in size or shape. This motion is erratic, but the image remains within one or two seconds of arc of some average position. Most important, the image moves slowly enough so that the design of an electromechanical servo system capable of following it appeared practicable.

After the usual number of false starts, I assembled a guiding device and tested it on an artificial planet in the form of an illuminated hole two millimeters in diameter in a metal sheet. This spot of light could be moved in a pattern that simulated the image movement of a planet under average seeing conditions. The assembly was then coupled to a modified 16-millimeter motion picture camera and mounted on the tube of the 60-inch reflector on Mount Wilson [*see Fig. 10*]. The resulting pictures show at least as much detail as was visible to the eye at about 750 power.

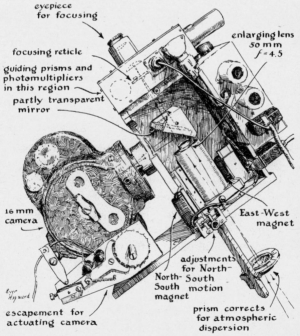

eyepiece for focusing

focusing reticle

guiding prisms and photomultipliers in this region

partly transparent mirror

enlarging lens 50 mm f = 4.5

16 mm camera

East-West magnet

adjustments for North-South motion

North-South magnet

escapement for actuating camera

prism corrects for atmospheric dispersion

10
Close-up view of the optical system and camera of Leighton's drive

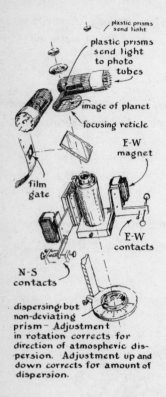

plastic prisms
send light

plastic prisms
send light
to photo
tubes

image of planet

focusing reticle

E-W
magnet

film
gate

E-W
contacts

N-S
contacts

dispersing: but
non-deviating
prism - Adjustment
in rotation corrects for
direction of atmospheric dispersion. Adjustment up and
down corrects for amount of
dispersion.

11
Optical train, including photo cells
and guide-magnets, of Leighton's
electronic drive

The device operates in this way. A small enlarging lens of about
$f/4.5$ focal ratio is mounted on a doubly pivoted carriage, as shown
in Figure 11. The carriage permits the lens about half a millimeter
of transverse motion in any direction. The two components of this
motion are governed by two small electromagnets whose pulls are
balanced against springs. The light from the telescope forms an
image in the normal focal plane of the telescope, proceeds past this
plane through the enlarging lens, reflects from a partly reflecting
diagonal mirror, and comes to a new focus at the film plane of the
motion picture camera. Part of the light proceeds through the
partly reflecting diagonal mirror and comes to a focus on a reticle,
where it can be viewed by an eyepiece. Two small reflecting
prisms with sharp edges project slightly into this latter beam

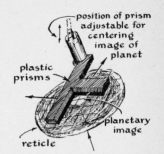

12
Deflecting prisms made from
single sheet of Lucite

from two directions at the focal plane and throw a small amount
of the light into each one of two photomultipliers [*Fig. 12*]. The
signals from these tubes are amplified in separate direct-current
channels and are fed into the electromagnet coils that determine
the position of the magnifying lens. The system seeks a stable
condition wherein a certain amount of light is entering each photo
tube. If the telescope image moves by a small amount, the amount
of light entering the photocells changes, and the system responds
in such a way as to cancel out this motion. This negative feedback
is, of course, not capable of completely canceling the erratic motion,
but it reduces it by a factor of about 10. In this way seeing fluc-

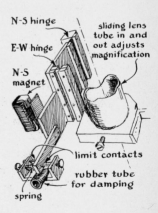

13
Details of slow traverse contacts,
hinges and lens adjustment

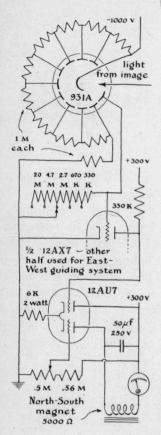

14

Circuit diagram of system for shifting star image in North-South direction. Identical circuit handles East-West shift

tuations, mechanical vibration and driving errors are essentially canceled out through a frequency range extending from zero vibrations per second up to approximately two vibrations per second.

An additional feature that is a great convenience, but not a necessity, is that there are relay contacts on the lens carriage which act as limit switches to prevent the electromagnets from having to work outside their designed range. If this pre-set range is exceeded, the corresponding slow-motion drive of the telescope is automatically applied so as to bring the electromagnet back into the center of its operating range. Thus, once adjusted, the guider

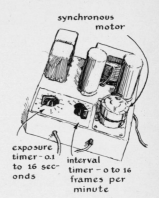

15
Electronic control for timing exposure
and shifting film

will track and center a planet image for the duration of an entire observing night. Indeed, except for focusing the image on the reticle and rotating the telescope dome now and then, the entire operation is automatic, including the timing of each exposure and the advancing of the film. The timing system is shown in Figure 15.

Through the use of this device one of the two serious disadvantages of a long exposure is essentially removed: the relative motion of the image as a whole with respect to the film is neutralized. But it is still necessary to match the diameter of the telescope objective to the seeing cell size, so that the image will be sharply defined over the greater part of the exposure time.

I used 16-mm. Kodachrome film with exposure times that varied from two seconds for Jupiter to 16 seconds for Saturn. Exposures were usually made at the rate of two frames per minute over a period of a few hours, and the best of the resulting images were later selected for enlargement.

5

AN ASTROPHYSICAL
LABORATORY IN YOUR
BACK YARD

*With adequate accessories the telescope becomes a
tool of immense power for probing the mysteries of
the universe. One of these, the spectrograph, literally
converts the instrument into a laboratory*

STRIP THE TELESCOPE of its setting circles, clock drive,
plate holder and related accessories and you put it in a class with
a blind man's cane. Like the cane, it informs you that something is
out in front. Shorn of appendages, the telescope tells you next to
nothing about the size, temperature, density, composition or other
physical facts of the stars. Not more than 20 celestial objects, counting such classes of objects as comets, star clusters and nebulæ,
appear through the eyepiece as interesting patterns of light and
shade. Only one, the moon, displays any richness of surface detail.
All other bodies look much as they do to the naked eye. There is a
greater profusion of stars, of course. But the telescope adds little to
the splendor of the firmament.

That is why the experience of building a telescope leaves some
amateurs with the feeling of having been cheated. A few turns
at the eyepiece apparently exhaust the novelty of the show, and
they turn to other avocations. Other amateurs, like Walter J. Semerau of Kenmore, New York, are not so easily discouraged. They
pursue their hobby until they arrive at the boundless realm of astrophysics. Here they may observe the explosion of a star, the slow
rotation of a galaxy, the flaming prominences of the sun and many
other events in the drama of the heavens.

Semerau invested more than 700 hours of labor in the construction of his first telescope, and confesses that what he saw with it

seemed like poor compensation for the time and effort. He hastens to point out, however, that there were other satisfactions, the solution of fascinating mechanical and optical problems. To anyone with a fondness for craftsmanship these are no mean compensations and, considered in these terms, Semerau feels his first telescope was the buy of a lifetime.

Accordingly he went to work on a 12½-inch Newtonian reflector, complete with film magazine and four-inch astrographic camera. Both were assembled on a heavy mounting with an electric drive, calibrated setting-circles and slow-motion adjustments. He could now not only probe more deeply into space but also do such things as determine the distance of a nearby star by measuring its change in position as the earth moves around the sun. To put it another way, he had made his "cane" longer and increased his control of it. When the sensitivity of modern photographic emulsions is taken into account, Semerau's new instruments were almost on a par with those in the world's best observatories 50 years ago.

During these 50 years, as Cecilia Payne-Gaposchkin of the Harvard College Observatory has pointed out, we have gained most of our knowledge of the physics of the universe. Most of this knowledge has come through the development of ingenious accessories for the telescope which sort out the complex waves radiated by celestial objects.

Semerau now decided that he had to tackle the construction of some of these accessories and to try his hand at the more sophisticated techniques of observing that went with them. He went to work on a monochromator, a device which artificially eclipses the sun and enables the observer to study the solar atmosphere.

Having built the monochromator, Semerau felt he was ready to attempt one of the most demanding jobs in optics: the making of a spectrograph. Directly or indirectly the spectrograph can function as a yardstick, speedometer, tachometer, balance, thermometer and chemical laboratory all in one. In addition, it enables the observer to study some remarkable magnetic and electrical effects.

In principle the instrument is relatively simple. Light falls on an optical element which separates its constituent wavelengths or colors in a fan-shaped array, the longest waves occupying one edge of the fan and the shortest the other. The element responsible for the separation may be either a prism or a diffraction grating: a surface ruled with many straight and evenly spaced lines. The spectrograph is improved by equipping it with a system of lenses (or a concave mirror) to concentrate the light, and with an aperture in the form of a thin slit. When the dispersed rays of white light are brought to focus on a screen, such as a piece of white cardboard, the slit appears as a series of multiple images so closely spaced that a continuous ribbon of color is formed which runs the gamut of the rainbow.

The explanation of why this should be so stems from the fact that when atoms and molecules are, in effect, struck a sharp blow by a hammer of atomic dimensions they ring like bells. The ear is not sensitive to the electromagnetic waves they emit, but the eye is. All light originates this way. Just as every bell makes a characteristic sound, depending upon its size and shape, so each of the hundred-odd kinds of atoms and their myriad molecular combinations radiate (or absorb) light of distinctive colors. The instrument physicists use to sort out the colors, and thus identify substances, is the spectroscope.

The colors appear as bright lines across the rainbowlike ribbon seen (or photographed) in the instrument when the source is viewed directly. If the light must traverse a gas at lower temperature than the source, however, some of the energy will be absorbed. Atoms of the low-temperature gas will be set in vibration by the traversing waves, just as a tuning fork responds when the appropriate piano key is struck. Evidence of such absorption appears in the form of dark lines which cross the spectrographic pattern. Hence, if one knows the composition of the emitting source, the spectrograph can identify the nature of the intervening gas. Moreover, as the temperature of the source increases, waves of shorter and shorter length join the emission, and the spectrum becomes more intense toward the blue end. Thus the spectral pattern can serve as an index of temperature.

The characteristic lines of a substance need not always appear at the same position in the spectrum. When a source of light is moving toward the observer, for example, its waves are apparently shortened — the phenomena known as the Doppler effect. In consequence the spectral lines of atoms moving toward the observer are shifted toward the blue end of the spectrum. The lines of atoms moving away are shifted toward the red. Velocity can thus be measured by observing the spectral shift.

When an atom is ionized, *i.e.*, electrically charged, it can be influenced by a magnetic field. Its spectral lines may then be split: the phenomenon known as the Zeeman effect. Intense electrical fields similarly leave their mark on the spectrum.

These and other variations in normal spectra provide the astrophysicist with most of his clues to the nature of stars, nebulæ, galaxies and the large-scale features of the universe. The amateur can hardly hope to compete with these observations, particularly those of faint objects. However, with well-built equipment he can come to grips with a rich variety of effects in the nearer and brighter ones.

As Semerau points out, the beginner in spectroscopy is perhaps well advised to tackle the analysis of the nearest star, our sun, and then consider moving into the deeper reaches of space.

Walter J. Semerau explains how he built a spectrograph for exploring the dramatic processes at work on the surface of the sun

IF YOU ARE CONSIDERING the construction of a spectrograph and are willing to settle for the sun you can shuck off a lot of labor. Because it is so bright, a three-inch objective lens, or a mirror of similar size, will give you all the light you need. The rest is easy. Many amateurs have stayed away from spectroscopes because most conventional designs call for lathes and other facilities beyond reach of the basement workshop, and many are too heavy or unwieldy for backyard use.

About four years ago I chanced on a design that seemed to fill the bill. My employer, the Linde Air Products Company, a division of the Union Carbide and Carbon Corporation, needed a special spectroscope for industrial research and could not find a commercial instrument that met their specifications. The Bausch & Lomb Optical Company finally located a design that looked promising. As things worked out, it was adopted and is now on the market. My instrument, shown in Figure 16, is a copy of that design.

The concept was proposed by H, Ebert just before the turn of the century. The instrument is of the high-dispersion, stigmatic type and employs a plane diffraction grating. As conceived by Ebert, the design was at least 50 years ahead of its time. In his day plane gratings were ruled on speculum metal, an alloy of 68 per cent copper and 32 per cent tin which is subject to tarnishing. This fact alone made the idea impractical. Ebert also specified a spherical mirror for collimating and imaging the light. Prior to 1900 mirrors were also made of speculum metal. It was possible but not practical to repolish the mirror but neither possible nor practical to refinish the finely ruled grating. Consequently a brilliant idea lay fallow, waiting for someone to develop a method of depositing a thin film of metal onto glass that would reflect light effectively and resist tarnishing. Then John Strong, now director of the Laboratory of Astrophysics and Physical Meteorology at the Johns Hopkins University, perfected a method of depositing a thin film of aluminum on glass.

The process opened the way for many new developments in the field of optics. One of these is the production of high-precision reflectance gratings ruled on aluminized glass. Prior to being coated the glass is ground and polished to a plane that does not depart from flatness by more than a 100,000th of an inch. The metallic film is then ruled with a series of straight, parallel saw-tooth grooves — as many as 30,000 per inch. The spacing between the rulings is uniform to within a few millionths of an inch; the angle of the saw-tooth walls, the so-called "blaze angle," is held similarly constant. The ruling operation is without question one of the most exacting mechanical processes known, and accounts for the high cost and limited production of gratings.

In consequence few spectrographs were designed around grat-

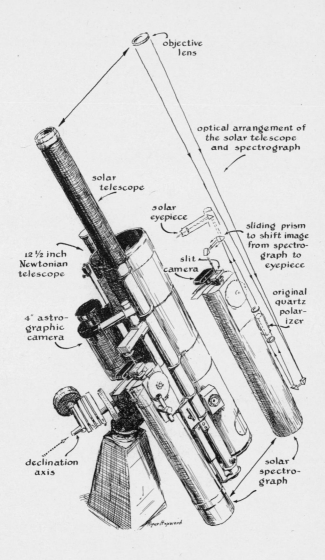

objective
lens

optical arrangement of
the solar telescope
and spectrograph

solar
telescope

solar
eyepiece

sliding prism
to shift image
from spectro-
graph to
eyepiece

12 ½ inch
Newtonian
telescope

slit
camera

original
quartz
polar-
izer

4" astro-
graphic
camera

declination
axis

solar
spectro-
graph

16
Semerau's telescope, astrographic camera, monochromator and spectrograph mounted on common equatorial drive

43

ings until recently. About five years ago, however, Bausch and Lomb introduced the "certified precision grating." These are casts taken from an original grating. It is misleading to describe them as replicas, because the term suggests the numerous unsatisfactory reproductions which have appeared in the past. The Bausch and Lomb casts perform astonishingly well at moderate temperatures and will not tarnish in a normal laboratory atmosphere. The grooves are as straight and evenly spaced as those of the original. The blaze angle can be readily controlled to concentrate the spectral energy into any desired region of the spectrum, making the gratings nearly as efficient for spectroscopic work as the glass prisms more commonly used in commercial instruments. Certified precision gratings sell at about a tenth the price of originals; they cost from $100 to $1,800, depending upon the size of the ruled area and the density of the rulings. Replicas of lesser quality, but entirely adequate for amateur use, can be purchased from laboratory supply houses for approximately $5 to $25.

The remaining parts of the Ebert spectrograph — mirror, cell, tube, slit and plate holder — should cost no more than an eight-inch Newtonian reflector. Depending on where you buy the materials, the entire rig should come to less than $100. By begging materials from all my friends, and keeping an eye on the Linde scrap pile, mine cost far less.

There is nothing sacred about the design of the main tube and related mechanical parts. You can make the tube of plywood or go in for fancy aluminum castings, depending upon your pleasure and your fiscal policy. If the instrument is to be mounted alongside the telescope, however, weight becomes an important factor. The prime requirement is sufficient rigidity and strength to hold the optical elements in precise alignment. If the spectrograph is to be used for laboratory work such as the analysis of minerals, sheet steel may be used to good advantage. For astronomical work you are faced with the problem of balancing rigidity and lightness. Duralumin is a good compromise in many respects. Iron has long been a favored material for the structural parts of laboratory spectrographs because its coefficient of expansion closely approaches that of glass. When mirrors are made of Pyrex, an especially tough cast iron known as meehanite has been used to counteract the effects of temperature variation.

The optical elements of my instrument are supported by a tube with a length of 45 inches and an inside diameter of 8¼ inches [see Fig. 17]. The walls of the tube are a sixteenth of an inch thick. The eight-inch spherical mirror has a focal length of 45⅝ inches. The grating is two inches square; it is ruled with 15,000 lines per inch. The long face of the saw-tooth groove is slanted about 20 degrees to the plane of the grating. The width of each groove is 5,000 Angstrom units, or about 20 millionths of an inch. Such a grating will strongly reflect waves with a length of 10,000 A., which are in the infrared region. The grating is said to be "blazed" for 10,000 A. A grating of this blazing will also reflect waves of 5,000 A., though less strongly. These waves give rise to "second-order" spectra which lie in the center of the visible region: the green. In addition, some third-order spectra occur; their wavelength is about 3,300 A. Waves of this length lie in the ultraviolet region.

The angle at which light is reflected from the grating depends upon the length of its waves. The long waves are bent more than the short ones; hence the long and short waves are dispersed. A grating blazed for 10,000 A. will disperse a 14.5-A. segment of the first-order spectrum over a millimeter. My instrument thus spreads a 2,200-A. band of the spectrum on a six-inch strip of film.

The film holder of my spectroscope is designed for rolls of 35-millimeter film. Light is admitted to the holder through a rectangular port six inches long and four tenths of an inch wide. By moving the holder across the port, it is possible to make three narrow exposures on one strip. This is a convenience in arriving at the proper exposure. The exposure time is estimated on the basis of past experience for one portion of the film; the interval is then bracketed by doubling the exposure for the second portion and halving it for the third.

The most difficult part of the spectrograph to make is the yoke which supports the grating. Much depends on how well this part functions. It must permit the grating to be rotated through 45 degrees to each side, and provide adjustments for aligning the

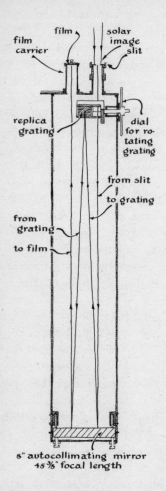

film carrier

film

solar image slit

replica grating

dial for ro- tating grating

from slit

to grating

from grating

to film

8" autocollimating mirror
45⅜" focal length

17
Optical train of diffraction
type astrospectrograph

grating with respect to the mirror. The ruled surface must be located precisely on the center line of the yoke axis, preferably
with provision for tilting within the yoke so that the rulings can
be made to parallel the axis. In my arrangement this adjustment
is provided by two screws which act against opposing springs, as
shown in Figure 18. The pressure necessary to keep the grating
in the parallel position is provided by four springs located behind
it. Two leaf springs, one above the other, hold the grating in

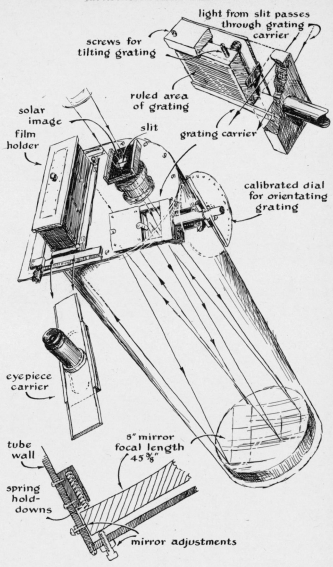

light from slit passes through grating carrier

screws for tilting grating

ruled area of grating

grating carrier

solar image film holder

slit

calibrated dial for orientating grating

eyepiece carrier

tube wall

spring hold-downs

5" mirror focal length 45 ⅝"

mirror adjustments

18
Spectrograph assembly showing details of diffraction grating mount *(upper right)* and mirror cell *(lower left)*

place. The assembly is supported by an end plate from which a shaft extends. The shaft turns in a pair of tapered roller-bearings which, together with their housing, were formerly part of an automobile water-pump. A flange at the outer end of the housing serves as the fixture for attaching the yoke assembly to the main tube. It is fastened in place by two sets of three screws each, the members of each set spaced over 120 degrees around the flange. One set passes through oversized holes in the flange and engages threads in the tube. These act as pull-downs. The other set engages threads in the flange and presses against the tube, providing push-up. Adjusting the two sets makes it possible to align the yoke axis with respect to the tube.

The shaft of the yoke is driven by a single-thread, 36-tooth worm gear that carries a dial graduated in one-degree steps. The worm engaging the gear also bears a dial, graduated in 100 parts, each representing a tenth of a degree. The arrangement is satisfactory for positioning spectra on the ground glass or film but is inadequate for determining wavelengths.

All plane gratings should be illuminated with parallel rays. Hence the entrance slit and photographic plate must both lie in the focal plane of the mirror. Small departures from this ideal may be compensated by moving the mirror slightly up or down the tube.

The spectral lines of the Ebert spectrograph are vertical only near the zero order and tilt increasingly as the grating is rotated to bring the higher orders under observation. The tilting may be compensated by rotating the entrance slit in the opposite direction while viewing the lines on a ground glass or through the eyepiece. The effect is aggravated in instruments of short focal length.

The cell supporting the mirror, and its essential adjustments, are identical with those of conventional reflecting telescopes. If no cell is provided and the adjustment screws bear directly on the mirror — which invites a chipped back — then no more than three screws, spaced 120 degrees apart, should be used. This is particularly important if the screws are opposed by compression springs; more than three will almost certainly result in a twisted mirror.

The plate holder is equipped with a 48-pitch rack and pinion, purposely adjusted to a tight mesh so each tooth can be felt as it comes into engagement. It is this arrangement that makes it possible to move the film along the exposure port and make three exposures on each strip of film. Lateral spacing during the racking operation is determined by counting the meshes. Although the magazine accommodates standard casettes for 35-mm. film, it is not equipped with a device for counting exposures. I merely count the number of turns of the film spool and record them in a notebook.

The back of the plate holder is provided with a removable cover so that a ground glass may be inserted as desired. It also takes a 35-mm. camera, a convenience when interest is confined to a narrow region of the spectrum such as the H and K lines of calcium or the alpha line of hydrogen. The back may be changed over to an eyepiece fixture which may be slid along the full six inches of spectrum. This arrangement provides for a visual check prior to making an exposure; it is especially helpful to the beginner.

Care must be taken in illuminating the slit. If the spectrograph has a focal ratio of $f/20$ (the focal length of mirror divided by the effective diameter of grating), the cone of incoming rays should also approximate $f/20$ and the axis of the cone should parallel the axis of the mirror. The slit acts much like the aperture of a pinhole camera. Consequently, if the rays of the illuminating cone converge at a greater angle than the focal ratio of the system, say $f/10$, they will fill an area in the plane of the grating considerably larger than the area of the rulings. Light thus scattered will result in fogged film and reduced contrast. Misalignment of the incoming rays will have the same effect, though perhaps it is less pronounced. Baffles or diaphragms spaced every three or four inches through the full length of the tube will greatly reduce the effects of stray light, such as that which enters the slit at a skew angle and bounces off the back of the grating onto the film. The diaphragms must be carefully designed, however, or they may vignette the film.

The components are assembled as shown in Figure 18. The

initial adjustments and alignment of the optical elements can be made on a workbench. An electric arc using carbons enriched with iron, or a strong spark discharge between iron electrodes, makes a convenient source of light for testing. The emission spectra of iron have been determined with great precision, and the wavelengths of hundreds of lines extending far into the ultraviolet and infrared (from 294 to 26,000 A.) are tabulated in standard reference texts. Beginners may prefer a mercury arc or glow lamp because these sources demand less attention during operation and emit fewer spectral lines which are, in consequence, easier to identify. The tabulations, whether of iron or mercury, are useful for assessing the initial performance of the instrument and invaluable for calibrating comparison spectra during its subsequent use.

Recently I have been concentrating on the spectroscopic study of sunspots. To make a spectrogram of a sunspot you align the telescope so that the image of the sun falls on the entrance slit. The objective lens of my telescope yields an image considerably larger than the slit. The image is maneuvered, by means of the telescope's slow-motion controls, until a selected sunspot is centered on the slit, a trick easily mastered with a little practice. The spectrum is then examined by means of either the eyepiece or the ground glass. The spot is seen as a narrow streak which extends from one end of the spectrum to the other. The adjustments, including the width of the entrance slit, are then touched up so the lines appear with maximum sharpness.

Successive spectral orders are brought into view by rotating the grating through higher angles. The upper spectrum of Figure 19 shows the first order. The one beneath is made in the second order. Note that although fewer lines per inch appear in the second order, there is no gain in resolution. Shifting the grating for the detection of a higher order is analogous to substituting eyepieces of higher power in a telescope. You get a bigger but proportionately fuzzier picture. The film magazine is substituted for the eyepiece and three exposures made in both the first and second orders. In many cases the range of intensity between the faintest and brightest lines exceeds the capacity of the film to register contrast. Three exposures, one estimated for the mid-range intensity and the other two timed respectively at half and twice this value, will usually span the full range.

Gases in the vicinity of a sunspot often appear to be in a state of violent turbulence. At any instant some atoms are rushing toward the observer and others away. The spectral lines show proportionate displacement from their normal positions in the spectrum — the Doppler effect — and register as a bulge in the central part of the line occupied by the sunspot. This explains the

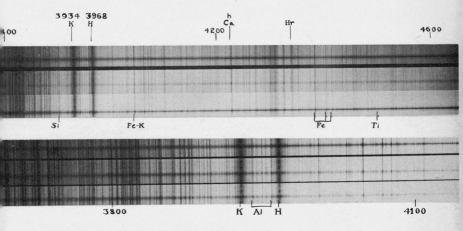

19
Sunspot spectrograms made by Walter J. Semerau. The first-order spectrum is at the top; the second-order, at the bottom

dark streak extending through the center of the spectra reproduced in Figure 19.

A portion of this same spectrum, photographed in the fourth order and enlarged photographically, appears in Figure 20. It includes the H and K lines of calcium, at wavelengths of 2,933 and 3,960 A. respectively. Observe that a segment in the center of each of these two lines — the segment representing the sunspot — is split. The light streak occupying the area within the split section is referred to as "emission over absorption" and, in this

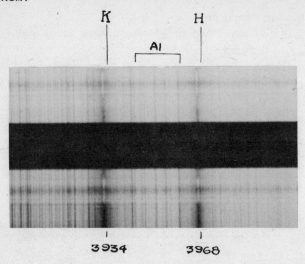

20
Sunspot in the fourth spectral order with splits in K and H lines indicating presence of calcium gas 100,000 miles above sun's surface

instance, indicates the presence of incandescent calcium at an altitude of about 100,000 miles above a region of cooler matter in the spot. Had the glowing calcium been lower, its emission would have been absorbed by the intervening solar atmosphere and it would have photographed as a dark absorption line. My interpretation of this spectrogram is that a solar prominence, carrying incandescent calcium from the sun's interior, arched up and over the sunspot. We are looking down on top of it. Reconstructing such events from evidence buried in the myriad lines of spectra is an endless challenge and one of the hobby's many fascinations.

6

USING SHADOWED STARLIGHT
AS A YARDSTICK

As the moon crosses the night sky it eclipses all stars in its path, just as it occasionally eclipses the sun. When detected and timed electronically, the fleeting star shadows thus cast by the moon can be used for locating geographical points on earth with great precision. The construction of an instrument for observing such lunar occultations is described

WHERE, PRECISELY, AM I? This is one of those easy-to-ask, impossible-to-answer questions. You must settle for an approximation. If you ask it while touring U. S. 80 from Plaster City, Calif., to Los Angeles, you may be content with the knowledge that you are less than a mile from Coyote Wells. But if you are an amateur astronomer setting up a telescope at the same site, you would prefer map information to the effect that you are at Latitude 32° 44′ 01″. 29 North; Longitude 116° 45′ 24″ .00 West.

Not even this seemingly precise pinpointing, however, would satisfy Colonel J. D. Abell and his associates in the Army Map Service. New methods of navigation, such as Loran, have disclosed gross errors in cartographic data. Particularly inaccurate are the positions of the oceanic islands; some important atolls in the Pacific appear to be as much as half a mile or more off their true positions on the map.

The personnel of Colonel Abell's bureau, in conjunction with the 30th Engineer Group under Colonel William C. Holley, has developed an ingenious method of surveying by astronomical occultations. By timing the shadow cast on earth when the moon intercepts the light of a star they have learned to measure points thousands of miles apart to an accuracy of 40 feet or better.

Our trouble, according to John A. O'Keefe, chief of the Research and Analysis Branch of the Army Map Service, stems from the basic fact that we don't know which way is straight up! If we had some way of pinpointing our zenith we could draw maps to any desired accuracy. In other words, if accurately known positions on the earth were correlated with one another by locating them with reference to the known positions of stars when they are at the zenith, the correlations would enable the cartographers to draw a good map of the world.

In principle the job is simple. You wait until a selected star of known position is directly overhead and clock it. Accurate timing is necessary because the relationship of the earth's surface to the sky changes continually as the earth rotates. Time signals broadcast from the U. S. Bureau of Standards' station WWV make precise clocking easy.

The usual instrument used for locating the zenith is a transit, which relies on a plumb bob or its counterpart, the bubble level. The source of error resides right here in these two gadgets, according to O'Keefe. Both the plumb bob and the bubble are thrown out of true by local irregularities in the density of the earth's crust which distort the gravitational field. Attempts have been made to correct for local deviations, but "this sort of guesswork gets you nowhere," says Floyd W. Hough, chief of the Service's Geodetic Division. "Even if you could estimate the effect of surface features accurately, you still would need information about conditions underground. Density varies there, too, and generally in the opposite direction."

The Army men decided to fix positions on the earth by timing occultations of stars by the moon as it moves across their positions in the heavens. One method of using the moon as a geodetic instrument is to photograph its position in relation to stars in the background at a given instant; it has been possible in this way to get fixes accurate to a tenth of a second of arc, which means locating positions on the earth with an accuracy within 600 feet. However, considering that this distance is more than twice the width of an aircraft runway, the desirability of still greater accuracy is obvious. The Army Map Service set out to improve on the accuracy of fixes by the moon's occultations.

The best telescopes, such as the 200-inch reflector on Palomar Mountain and the largest refractors, have a theoretical resolving power considerably better than .1 second of arc. But you cannot carry them from place to place on the earth, and furthermore their resolving power has practical limits, imposed by poor seeing conditions, distortion of the optical train by variations of temperature and so on. Above all there is diffraction, the master image-fuzzer, which arises from the wave character of light itself. Because adjacent waves interfere with one another, the light from a distant star does not cast a knife-sharp shadow when it passes the edge of the moon. Waves of starlight grazing the moon's edge interact, diverge and arrive at the earth's surface as a series of dark and light bands bordering the moon's shadow. The first band, the most pronounced, is about 40 feet wide.

The solution hit upon by O'Keefe and his associates was a new way to use a telescope which makes it capable of incredible resolution. They developed a portable rig (which amateurs can build) that plots lunar positions to within .005 second of arc as a matter of everyday field routine — resolution equivalent to that of an 800-inch telescope working under ideal conditions! It can also do a lot of other interesting things, such as measuring directly the diameters of many stars. It can split into double stars images which the big refractors show as single points of light. Some observers believe that it could even explore the atmosphere of a star layer by layer, as though it were dissecting a gaseous onion. Of greatest interest to the Army, the method measures earth distances of thousands of miles with a margin of uncertainty of no more than 150 feet!

The telescope that yields these impressive results has a physical aperture of only 12 inches. The design — a Cassegrain supported in a Springfield mounting — follows plans laid down by the late Russell W. Porter, for many years one of the world's leading amateur telescope makers.

The secret of the instrument's high resolving power is in the way it is used rather than in uniqueness of optical design. The telescope is trained on a selected star lying in the moon's orbit and is guided carefully until the advancing edge of the moon overtakes and begins to cover the star. Depending on the diameter and distance of the star, it may take up to .125 of a second for the moon to cover (occult) it completely. During this interval the edge of the moon becomes, in effect, part of the telescope — like a pinhole objective with an equivalent focal length of 240,000 miles. As the edge of the moon passes across the star, the intensity of the starlight diminishes, and the differences in intensity at successive instants are measured. It is as if a 240,000-mile-long tube were equipped at the distant end with a series of slit objectives — with the moon covering one slit at a time. The resolving power depends upon the great focal length.

The tiny successive steps in the starlight's decay are detected by a photomultiplier tube and a high-speed recorder. In principle the measurement of terrestrial distances by lunar occultation resembles measuring by the solar eclipse technique. The moon's shadow races over the earth's surface at about 1,800 feet per second. Except for differences in instrumentation and the mathematical reduction of results, the eclipse of the star is essentially the same kind of event as the eclipse of the sun. The insensitivity of the eye prevents star eclipses from making newspaper headlines, but photomultiplier tubes respond to such an eclipse strongly. They also detect the fuzziness caused by diffraction at the edge of the moon's shadow. The most prominent diffraction band, as previously mentioned, is some 40 feet across — the limit to which measurements by occultation are carried. The sharpest drop in starlight registered on typical recordings spans .015 second of time. Since the moon near the meridian has an average apparent speed of about .33 of a second of angular arc per second of time, the recorded interval of .015 of a second corresponds to .005 of a second of arc. This is the instrument's effective resolving power.

Any amateur who owns a Springfield mounting equipped with a high-quality mirror of eight inches aperture or larger can convert for high resolution work at a cost which is modest in proportion to the gain in performance. What he needs is a photomultiplier tube, a power supply, an amplifier and a high-speed recorder.

The photocell costs about $150. The amplifier must be of the

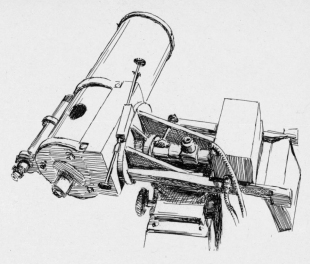

21
Springfield mounting equipped for photoelectric occultation work

direct-current type with a linear response good to at least 200 pulses per second. The recorder should be a double-channel job — one pen for registering time signals and the other for starlight. The Brush Development Company of Cleveland markets a recorder of the recommended type along with a companion amplifier for about $1,000. With a little ingenuity the amateur can contrive adequate counterparts for substantially less. He also needs a filter to cut out the 400- and 600-cycle tone of WWV, so beloved of musicians. These units are available through dealers in radio equipment for about $15.

The eyepiece must be equipped with a cell for the photomultiplier tube and with a pinhole aperture for screening out unwanted moonlight. The pinhole (about .010 of an inch in diameter) is made in a metal mirror assembled in the eyepiece tube at an angle of 45 degrees, as shown in the drawing [*see Fig. 22*]. A Ramsden eyepiece focuses on the pinhole. In operation the mirror is seen as a bright field with a small black speck, the pinhole, in the center. The star's image appears against the mirror as a brighter speck on

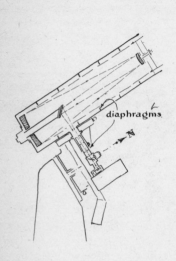

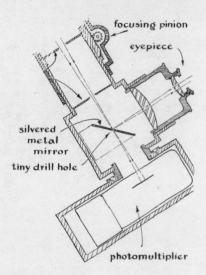

22
Schematic diagram of optical train *(left)* and details of ocular equipped with silvered stop and photomultiplier *(right)*

the bright field. Thus it is easy to guide the image into position over the pinhole. When properly centered, some starlight strikes the edge of the pinhole, forming a small brilliant ring surrounding a jet-black speck. The ring aids in subsequent guiding.

Occultation observing has attracted a substantial following among amateurs in recent years. In the U. S. their interest in the work has been stimulated by the Occultation Section of the American Association of Variable Star Observers, whose offices are at 4 Brattle Street, Cambridge 38, Mass. Their world-wide observations, made by eye and timed by chronograph, are forwarded to Flora M. McBain at Greenwich, England. She supervises the mathematical reductions. The results of occultation observations have been used to establish irregularities in the rotation of the earth and to improve the tabulations of the moon's orbit.

Dirk Brouwer of the Yale University Observatory, who has made an exhaustive interpretation of the observations collected during the past century, sees an opportunity in the new photoelectric technique for the group to make an impressive addition to its already substantial scientific contribution. The photoelectric cell betters the response time of the eye (estimated at about .1 second of arc) by 100-fold or more and eliminates human variables. Thus it makes possible far higher accuracy in timing occultations. Moreover, the high-resolution aspect of the technique opens a whole new and relatively unexplored field for original work by amateurs. As Professor Brouwer points out, star occultations, like solar eclipses, can be observed only in certain regions at particular times. A world-wide network of amateur observatories equipped for high resolution work could cover many more star occultations in any year than are accessible to the great telescopes of Southern California.

One serious drawback that prevents utilizing the full potential of the increased accuracy at present is the irregularity of the moon's surface. If these irregularities are not allowed for in the calculations, the resulting position of the moon will frequently be off by several tenths of a second of arc. And if the star happens to be occulted at a point on the moon's limb where a high peak or low valley is located, the result may be off in extreme cases by two seconds of arc. A new study of the irregularities of the moon's surface by C. B. Watts at the United States Naval Observatory in Washington, expected to be completed soon, should make it possible to correct for the deviations with an accuracy matching the sensitivity of the photoelectric technique.

Figure 23 shows a pair of typical curves, recording the occultations of a sixth magnitude star and an eighth magnitude one. Note the jaggedness of the fainter star's curve. This is due to "noise," a term borrowed from radio and telephone engineering to describe random fluctuations in the output current of an amplifying device. The output of noise increases when the volume or "gain" control of the amplifier is turned up to compensate for a weak input signal. Noise originating in the photomultiplier (the principal source) can be reduced by chilling the tube with dry

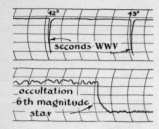 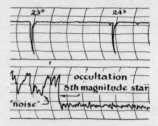

23
Occultation graphs automatically recorded by system showing comparative noise background of 6th magnitude star vs. 8th magnitude

ice. The sharp drop in each curve marks the interval of occultation. Its steepness is determined principally by the diffraction pattern. In the case of some big stars, such as Antares, the effect of size can be seen in a flattening of the curve.

When a double-star system is occulted, the curve drops steeply for a time, indicating occultation of the first star, then levels off, and falls steeply again when the companion is occulted. The duration of the flat portion of the curve is the measure of the pair's separation. Some curves of Antares and other large stars show bends and twists which seem to come from bright and dark parts of the star's disk as well as from the stellar atmosphere. The proper interpretation of these records, however, is still considered an open question by some astronomers — another indication of the opportunity the technique presents to an amateur who enjoys original work.

"There is far better than an even chance that we shall stumble onto much that we didn't expect," O'Keefe says. "We are examining stellar disks with greater resolving power than ever before. We shall certainly find a lot of close, fast binary stars. Perhaps we shall also find stars with extended atmospheres and all that. In occultations of very bright stars we are in a position to detect very faint, close companions. I really do not see how anyone getting into this sport can miss hooking some information of value, and he might catch a really big fish."

24
Relative position of moon with respect to stars and zenith

Incidentally, if a college man with a background in astronomy faces induction into the armed forces and the idea of occultation work appeals to him, he would be well advised to communicate with the Army Map Service in advance. The bureau is on the lookout for likely candidates.

In many respects photoelectric occultation seems almost too good to be true. Neither poor seeing nor diffraction within the instrument has the slightest effect on the high resolving power of the method, and it is as precise when the moon occults a star low in the sky as overhead.

"The whole thing no doubt, gives the impression that a rabbit is being produced from a hat," says O'Keefe. "It appears most surprising that such a powerful method for detailed examination of the sky should have gone unexplored for so long. This, of course, we enjoy. Our group did not invent the technique: it was suggested by K. Schwarzschild in Germany and A. E. Whitford in the U. S. It has not been exploited before because people simply could not believe that it works. But if I can get people to disbelieve thoroughly in something which is done before their eyes, then I have at least entertained them — and myself."

7

A UNIVERSAL SUNDIAL

Turn a globe of the earth so that your location is on top, then align its axis with the North Star, and you have a sundial that shows the season of the year, the regions of dawn and dusk, and the hour of the day wherever the sun is shining. Richard M. Sutton, professor of physics at the California Institute of Technology, gives detailed instructions for mounting the globe and using it to clarify the apparent motions of the sun

IF YOU LEAVE A TENNIS BALL undisturbed in the closet for a week it turns completely around in space seven times! This simple fact, which ordinarily escapes notice, can be put to good use. Most people would say that the ball has not moved at all, yet they would admit the intellectual fact that the earth turns on its axis. The ball is turned by the earth around an axis parallel to that of the earth, and at just the rate at which the earth turns: 15 degrees per hour.

If we combine the fact that the ball turns completely around once a day with an equally simple fact, we can convert any globe of the earth into a remarkable universal sundial that tells more about sunlight, the earth's motions in space and the conditions of sunlight in distant lands than might be supposed. The second fact is that the light falling on the earth from the sun comes in a flood of substantially parallel rays. Because of the great distance of the sun (some 93 million miles), even the extremes of a diameter of the earth are struck by rays that diverge by only .005 degree. This means that the angle subtended by a line 8,000 miles long seen at a distance of 93 million miles is about 1/200 of a degree. The significance of this fact will be apparent below.

The rules for setting up the globe are simple and easily followed. It is rigidly oriented as an exact copy of the earth in space, with its polar axis parallel to the earth's axis, and with your own home town (or state) right "on top of the world" (where most of us like to think we belong anyway!). First turn the globe until its axis lies in your local meridian, in the true north and south plane that may be found by observing the shadow of a vertical object at local noon, by observing the pole star on a clear night, or by consulting a magnetic compass (if you know the local variation of the compass). Next turn the globe on its axis until the circle of longitude through your home locality lies in the meridian just found. Finally tilt the axis around an east-west horizontal line until your home town stands at the very top of the world. If you have followed these three steps, then your meridian circle (connecting the poles of your globe) will lie vertically in the north-south plane, and a line drawn from the center of the globe to your local zenith will pass directly through your home spot on the map.

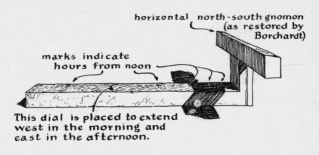

horizontal north-south gnomon
(as restored by Borchardt)

marks indicate
hours from noon

This dial is placed to extend
west in the morning and
east in the afternoon.

25
Egyptian sundial from the period of Thothmes III, 1500 B.C.

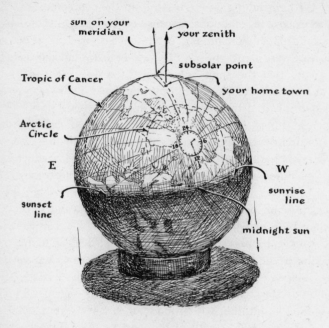

26
The global sundial, showing the North Pole on June 21

Now lock the globe in this position and let the rotation of the earth do the rest. This takes patience, for in your eagerness to see all that the globe can tell you, you may be tempted to turn it at a rate greater than that of the turning of the earth. But it will take a year for the sun to tell you all it can before it begins to repeat its story.

When you look at the globe sitting in this proper orientation — "rectified" and immobile — you will of course see half of it lighted by the sun and half of it in shadow. These are the very halves of the earth in light or darkness at that moment. An hour later the circle separating light from shadow has turned westward, its intersections with the Equator having moved 15 degrees to the west. On the side of the circle west of you, the sun is rising; on the side east of you, the sun is setting. You can "count up the hours" along the Equator between your home meridian and the sunset line and estimate closely how many hours of sunlight still remain for you that day; or you can look to the west of you and see how soon the sun will rise, say, in Japan. As you watch the globe day after day, you will become aware of the slow turning of the circle northward or southward, depending upon the time of year.

Let us take an imaginative look at the globe as it sits in the sun. Suppose it is during those days in June when the sun stands near the zenith in our new state of Hawaii. The globe dial shows that it is still sunlight at 9:30 p.m. in Iceland, that the midnight sun is shining on the North Cape of Norway. It is between late and early afternoon on the U. S. mainland, being about 6 p.m. in New York and 3 p.m. in San Francisco. The eastern half of South America is already in the darkness of its longer winter nights. The sun has recently risen *next day* in New Zealand and the eastern half of Australia, and most of China and Siberia are in early-morning light, whereas in Japan the sun is already four hours high in the sky. Alaska is enjoying the middle of a long summer day with the sun as high in the sky as it ever gets. Seattle is in early afternoon about two sun-hours ahead of Honolulu in the midst of a 16-hour day, while Sydney, Australia, is just starting a day with only 10 hours of sunlight.

Now you don't have to be in Honolulu to see all this happening. Your own globe tells it to you. The same is true for persons who set up their globes in Fairbanks, Honolulu, Tokyo, Caracas, Havana or anywhere else. They will all see exactly the same story at the same time if in each place they have taken the small trouble to set up their globes for their own home towns as directed. If we choose, we can follow the progress of the circle of light and dark through the year. Three months later, for example, when the sun has returned close to the celestial equator, and when it passes day by day close to the zenith along our own Equator, we will see the circle between light and dark apparently hinged on the polar axis of our globe. This is the time of the equinoxes, when every spot on earth has 12 hours of light and 12 hours of darkness. On December 21 the sun will have gone to its position farthest south, now failing to light any spot within the Arctic

Circle but lighting the region within the Antarctic Circle completely (as you may see by stooping and looking at the lower part of your globe).

From its position farthest south, the sun starts its way north again at a rate that may seem painfully slow for those in northern latitudes who wait for spring. By March 21 it has again reached the Equator, and we find it at the vernal equinox, the astronomers' principal landmark. Through the centuries this was the time for the beginning of the year. Only as recently as 1752 did December cease to be the 10th month of the year, as its name implies. January 1, 1752, was the first time that the calendar year began in January in England and the American colonies! At the vernal equinox in March there is a sunrise lasting 24 hours at the North Pole, and a sunset lasting 24 hours at the South Pole. Now, as the months advance, we will find that on June 21 this circle of light has advanced to its position farthest north. Sunlight does not enter the Antarctic Circle on the bottom side of your globe at all, but it extends clear over the North Polar region to the Arctic Circle beyond. At noon in your garden on this day you will see how people living on the meridian 180 degrees from your home are enjoying the midnight sun, provided they live within the Arctic Circle. Thus in imagination we have made a complete trip around the earth's orbit and have watched the progress of sunlight during the 365 or 366 intervening days — all right in the garden.

It is not easy to appreciate the fact that the sun's rays are parallel as they fall on the earth. Let me suggest a simple experiment. On a bright morning take a piece of pipe or a cardboard tube and point it at the sun so that it casts a small, ring-shaped shadow. Now if at the very same moment someone 120 degrees east of you — one third the way around the world — were to perform the same experiment, he would point his tube westward at the afternoon sun. Yet his tube and yours would necessarily be parallel to within a very small fraction of a degree. If you point the tube at the sun in the afternoon, and someone far to the west simultaneously does the same in his morning, his tube will again be automatically parallel to yours. This experiment will help explain how it is that, when our globes are properly set up, people all over

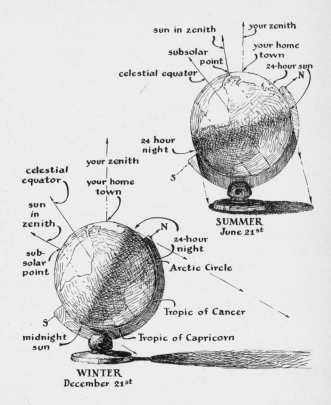

sun in zenith
your zenith
subsolar point
your home town
celestial equator
24-hour sun
N

24 hour night
your zenith
your home town
celestial equator
S
sun in zenith
SUMMER
June 21st
sub- solar point
N
24-hour night
Arctic Circle
S
Tropic of Cancer
midnight sun
Tropic of Capricorn
WINTER
December 21st

27
The illumination of a global sundial during winter and summer

the world who are in sunlight will see them illuminated in just the same way.

How easy it is, with this global dial, to imagine oneself in a distant land, seeing the sun in that sky at that time of day. A pin held at any point on the globe immediately shows the direction of the shadow of a man standing at that spot. Your globe has become a "terrella," a little earth that shows what the big earth is doing in space.

It was from long experimenting with a precision sundial drawn on the floor of my office at Haverford College that I slowly came to the idea of this dial. I had developed that dial to the point where I could tell the time within five seconds. But the global dial is more exciting. When it came to me, I was enthralled by its simplicity and profundity: to be able to see at a glance everything about sunlight all over the world without budging from my own garden or office. However, I had a strong feeling that an idea so simple and universal could not have escaped intelligent people at other times and other places. I have now learned that it was recognized some 300 years ago, when globes were playthings of the wealthy. People were then regarding their world with new understanding, made much richer by the great sailing explorations and the increasing recognition of the earth's sphericity. To be sure, the early Greeks had seen that the earth must be a sphere. For example, Archimedes based his great works on floating bodies on a proposition that reads: "The free surface of any body of liquid at rest is part of a sphere whose center is the center of the earth." Imagine that for 200 B.C.! There is much evidence in the writings of the Greek mathematicians that they appreciated this fact. Their estimates of the earth's size were correct in principle and not bad in actual result, but men seem to have ignored their observations and the reasoning behind them until the great age of exploration which we date from Columbus and the discovery of the New World.

In a book on sundials by Joseph Moxon, first published in 1668, there is a description of "the English globe, being a stabil and immobil one, performing what ordinary globes do, and much more." Moxon, who was hydrographer to Charles II (and whose book was dedicated to Samuel Pepys, Principal Officer of the Navy), ascribes this globe to the Earl of Castlemaine. It seems certain that the globe existed in London by 1665. In 1756 another global sundial was described by Charles Leadbetter. Consider the delightful title of Leadbetter's book: "MECHANICK DIALLING, or the New Art of Shadows, freed from the Obscurities, Superfluities, and Errors of former writers upon the Subject — the whole laid down after so plain a method that any person (tho' a Stranger to the Art) with a Pair of Compasses and Common Ruller only, may make a Dial upon any Plane for any place in the World, as well as those who have attained to the greatest Knowledge and Perfection in the Mathematics. A work not only usefull for Artificers but very entertaining for Gentlemen, and those Student at the Universities that would understand Dialling without the Fatigue of going through a Course of Mathematics." They knew how to make full use of a title page in those days!

Leadbetter tells how to erect an immobile stone sphere and inscribe a map on it. He says: "According to their true latitudes and longitudes (for various spots on earth) you may discover any moment when the Sun shines upon the same, by the illuminated parts thereof, what Places on Earth are enlightened, and what Places are in darkness. . . . The Extremity of the Shadow shows likewise what Places the Sun is Rising or Setting at; and what Places have long Days; these with many more curious Problems are seen at one View, too many to be enumerated in this place. The dial is the most natural of all others because it resembles the Earth itself, and the exact manner of the Sun's shining thereon." Leadbetter suggests that a pin be placed at each pole in order to use the global sundial to tell time. Around each pin are 24 marks — one every 15 degrees — corresponding to the hours; the time is read by noting the position of the pin's shadow with respect to the marks. I, too, have used this system. Leadbetter adds: "As you see, that [pin] at the North Pole will give the hour in summer, that at the South Pole the hour in Winter."

There is *no* spot on earth with which we do not at some time during the year share the light from the sun. One might object that surely the nadir, that spot directly beneath our feet on the other side of the earth, has no sunlight while we ourselves have it; but atmospheric refraction keeps the sun in the sky longer than geometry alone predicts, making every sunrise about two minutes early and every sunset about two minutes late.

It is easy to tell from the global sundial just how many hours of sunlight any latitude (including your own) will enjoy on any particular day. All you need to do is to count the number of 15-degree longitudinal divisions that lie within the lighted circle at the desired latitude. Thus at 40 degrees north latitude in summer the circle may cover 225 degrees of longitude along the 40th

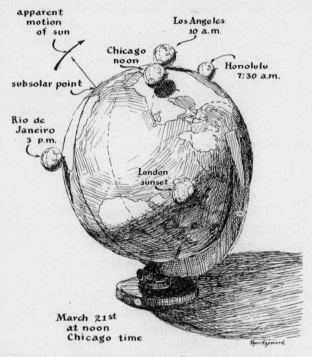

apparent
motion
of sun

Los Angeles
10 a.m.

Chicago
noon

Honolulu
7:30 a.m.

subsolar point

Rio de
Janeiro
3 p.m.

London
sunset

March 21st
at noon
Chicago time

28
Rectified globes anywhere on earth show the same lighting

parallel, representing 15 divisions or 15 hours of sunlight. But in
winter the circle may cover only 135 degrees, representing nine
divisions or nine hours. As soon as the lighted circle passes beyond
either pole, that pole has 24 hours of sunlight a day, and the
opposite pole is in darkness.

One or two other concepts may make the dial even more useful. First, we can answer the question: Where is the sun in the
zenith right now? Can we find the spot on earth where men find
their shadows right at their feet? Easily. Hold the end of a pencil at the surface of the globe and move it until its shadow is
reduced to its own cross section. When the pencil points from
the center of the sun to the center of the globe, the spot on the

map where its end rests corresponds to the point immediately beneath the sun. Better still, if you use a small tube instead of a pencil, you can let the sunlight pass down the tube to cast a ring-shaped shadow at the point beneath the sun. This point is important, because it gives the latitude and longitude of the sun at that moment and locates the center of the great circle of daylight. Ninety degrees around the globe in any direction from that point is a point where the sun appears on the horizon, either rising or setting. At the north and south extremes of the circle between light and darkness are "the points where sunrise and sunset meet." In June, for example, the southern point shows where the sun barely rises and then promptly sets in Antarctica, and the northern point (beyond the North Pole) shows where the midnight sun dips to the horizon and immediately rises again.

To find the point directly beneath the sun still more accurately, you can construct a simple cardboard tripod. Just cut three identical pieces of cardboard and fasten them together with gummed paper as shown in the accompanying illustration [see Fig. 29]. When the tripod stands on a level table, the line joining the three vanes is vertical. When the tripod rests on the surface of your globe, the line extends outward along a radius of the globe. If you move the tripod about until the shadow of its three vanes disappears into three lines, you find the subsolar point at the junction of these lines. Once you have found the subsolar point, and hence the exact location of the sun in our system of coordinates, it is a simple matter to count off the hours since or until your local noon, to tell your local sun-time, to forecast the time until sunset and to tell how long it is since sunrise. You can also determine these things for locations other than your own.

Perhaps this little sundial, so simply set up, will clarify the apparent motions of the sun, caused of course by the earth's daily rotation on its axis and its annual revolution around the sun. Surely it is fun to bring so much of the system of the world into your garden. The global dial can give one a fuller appreciation of the sunlight on which all men depend. If it thereby strengthens your feeling of kinship for people far away, the instrument will have served you well.

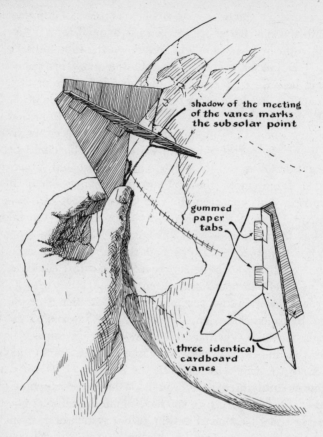

shadow of the meeting
of the vanes marks
the subsolar point

gummed
paper
tabs

three identical
cardboard
vanes

29
Triangular fixture for locating the subsolar point

8

A SUNDIAL THAT KEEPS
CLOCK TIME

Richard L. Schmoyer, an engineer of Landisville, Pa., discusses aspects of the sundial frequently overlooked by laymen. The accuracy and utility of dials are considered, and instructions given for constructing an instrument which can be adjusted to keep clock time, including daylight-saving, anywhere in the Northern Hemisphere

WHY IS IT that a man who owns a perfectly good watch and several clocks will buy or build a sundial? It is not enough to say that a sundial makes a pleasant ornament in the garden. A deeper answer is that there is considerable intellectual charm in a device which, though it is motionless, converts the constantly changing motion of the sun into accurate time.

A sundial that tells the time with any real accuracy is exceedingly rare, of course, and those that tell clock time are all but unknown. The problem is that the earth moves faster along its orbit in January than it does in July, and the height of the sun's path across the sky changes every day. But sundial-making holds other attractions for its enthusiasts than the utility of the finished instrument.

In the course of developing a sundial, one is exposed to a fascinating and well-defined mixture of mathematics, geometry, geography and astronomy. The design of a sundial challenges our creative talents, and its construction puts our craftsmanship to an exacting test. Finally, the designer who permits the primary time-telling function of the sundial to control its form adds spice to the project. Hardware in pleasing though strange and unexpected shapes often emerges from the equations which describe the ever-changing slant of the sun's rays.

These inducements led me to design a sundial last year which has become a continuing source of pleasure both to me and to my neighbors. With only a few simple settings during two seasons of the year the sundial can be made to indicate accurate clock time. It can be adjusted to the latitude and longitude of any point in the Northern Hemisphere, including those areas where clocks are changed for daylight-saving time. Clock time can be read from it to an accuracy of about one minute, even when the sky is covered by a light overcast.

Most people find sundials attractive, so one must not altogether dismiss their ornamental properties. The structure of my dial was derived from the armillary, a traditional form which continues to enjoy wide popularity. Those primarily concerned with the appearance of a sundial admire the geometric perfection of the armillary's nested rings, representing latitude, longitude, tropics, celestial equator and the ecliptic. Much the same pleasing quality is found, however, in the unsymmetrical crescent of the early and late moon. The armillary can be converted to this form by eliminating all except the rings representing latitude and longitude and opening these at one of the sides where they join at right angles. When tapered and strengthened, these rings become nested crescents, as shown [see Fig. 30].

The transformation from armillary to nested crescents demonstrates how a pleasing shape can emerge from a functional necessity. A good time-telling device should always fulfill its mission. The armillary falls short of this ideal. During part of each day its pattern of ornamental rings casts shadows on the time-scale, which is carried on the inner face of the equatorial ring. Worse, in the seasons of the equinoxes (March 21 and September 23) the scale lies in continuous shadow because the plane of the ring then parallels the sun's rays. By eliminating the useless rings and opening the functional pair into crescents the time-scale is exposed to the sun without obstruction.

The structure of a sundial which indicates clock time is simple in concept if not in the making. The crescents are supported at their edges by an arrangement of bolts, slots and clamps so they can be rotated in their respective planes. The latitude crescent is made in two parts with a flange at the inner end of each. Bolts pass through the flanges and through a slot in the longitude crescent. When the nuts are tightened, the assembly becomes a rigid unit. Similarly, the edge of one member of the latitude crescent is clamped between the jaws of a split pedestal which extends up from the base. By loosening a single wing-nut the whole assembly can be rotated in the plane of the latitude crescent and in azimuth.

A pair of holes are drilled in the latitude crescent on the diameter which coincides with the axis of the equatorial crescent. These holes serve as bearings to support the gnomon. It is to the unique shape of the gnomon, which compensates for the effect of the eccentricity of the earth's elliptical orbit and the tilt of its axis, that this sundial owes its property of keeping clock time. If the earth followed a circular orbit around the sun, and if its axis were perpendicular to the plane of the ecliptic, the straight gnomon of the conventional sundial would indicate clock time. The time shown by clocks is that of a fictional sun which leads the real sun by as much as 16 minutes or lags behind it up to 14 minutes, depending upon the observer's location and the season. This difference is known as the equation of time and is shown graphically as the analemma on globes, a closed curve in the form of a figure eight.

The gnomon of my dial is related to the analemma but differs from it in that the halves of the figure are seperated and the ends are stretched somewhat. Structurally the gnomon consists of a strip of cast metal bent at a right angle along its length. The apex of the angle is opened to form a thin slot. It is supported at the ends by shafts which turn in the bearings of the latitude crescent. The halves of the gnomon are bent into almost symmetrical compound curves with respect to the long axis and are therefore complementary. When either half is turned to face the sun, the curved ribbon of light which passes through the slot corresponds with the equation of time for half of the year, the remaining six months being represented by the other half. Time is indicated by the thin line of light from the slot which falls on the time-scale between shadows cast by the halves of the gnomon.

The portion of the curved slot through which the rays pass to the time-scale depends on the declination of the sun. In summer, sunlight falls on the dial at a high angle and reaches the time-scale through the upper part of the slot, where the curvature just compensates for a "slow" sun. The reverse is true in the fall, when the sun is low. The winter sun is also mostly slow, and in the spring the sun goes from slow to fast to slow to fast again. Whatever the season, the sun's declination selects an appropriate portion of the curve to offset the equation of time.

Some difficulty is encountered during the period from about December 1 through January 15, when the sun lingers close to its lowest path across the sky. During this same period, however, it speeds up with respect to the fictional sun. A lag of some 11 minutes becomes a lead of about nine minutes. The simultaneous change in declination is very small. A similar event takes place in reverse during the weeks preceding and following the summer solstice on June 21, when the real sun falls behind the fictional one, again accompanied by little change in declination. To accentuate the sundial's response during these periods, the curvature of the slot is stretched out. The gnomon must also be moved axially in its bearings, the amount of shift being determined by a stop on the shaft. The adjustment is made by hand according to a scale of dates engraved on the gnomon, as shown in Figure 30.

The designing of the gnomon, though tedious, is not difficult. One first determines the rate at which a ray of sunlight moves across the time-scale. This depends on the diameter of the crescent on which the scale is engraved and on the related distance between the scale and the gnomon. Multiply 3.1416 by the diameter of the equatorial crescent and divide the product by the number of seconds in a day. In the case of a 13-inch crescent the result is .000473. This number is used for computing the distance and direction by which the curved slot must depart from a straight line for successive weeks of the year. This procedure can be illustrated by constructing a graph of the curve for one face of the gnomon. First draw a straight line equal to the radius of the proposed

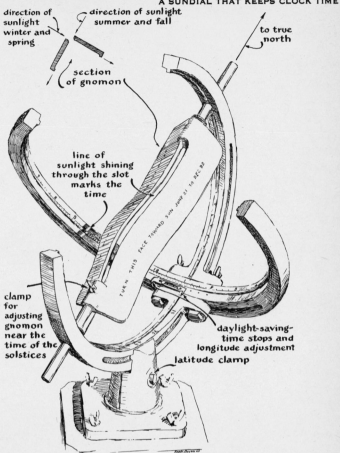

direction of
sunlight
winter and
spring

direction of sunlight
summer and fall

to true
north

section
of gnomon

line of
sunlight shining
through the slot
marks the
time

TURN THIS FACE TOWARD SUN JUNE 21 TO DEC. 22

clamp
for
adjusting
gnomon
near the
time of the
solstices

daylight-saving-
time stops and
longitude adjustment

latitude clamp

30
The Schmoyer sundial for telling clock time by the sun

crescent and erect a perpendicular of about the same length above
and below one end of the line. The base line represents the sun's
mean elevation (0 degrees) on September 23. Next, with the end
of the base line as the point of origin, extend a line to the perpendicular at an angle of 21 degrees, 34 seconds *above* the base
line. This represents the sun's elevation on July 15. Now make a
similar angle of 21 degrees, 47 seconds *below* the base line. This
corresponds to the sun's elevation on December 1. Angles above

the base line are regarded as positive and are designated "plus"; those below are considered negative. Next, draw in angles at weekly intervals for all intermediate dates. A table showing the sun's angular elevation throughout the year can be found in any ephemeris and in many almanacs. These references also carry a table for the equation of time and list the difference between solar time and clock time in minutes and seconds. The curve for one face of the gnomon is plotted from these values. (If the thickness of the material from which the gnomon is constructed exceeds .01 inch, the curvature of the trailing edges must depart from that of the faces to avoid shadow. The same basic procedure is used in computing all curves, however.) For September 23 the equation of time has a value of -7 minutes, 35 seconds, which is equal to -455 seconds. Multiply this interval by the rate at which the ray of sunlight moves across the time-scale of the dial. In the case of my dial the computation is: $.000473 \times -455 = -.215$. This product represents the distance in inches by which the curve of one edge of the slot in my gnomon departs from the perpendicular. (In plotting the curves all negative values are directed to the left of the perpendicular and positive values to the right.) The remaining points of the curve are similarly plotted for all intermediate dates at weekly intervals.

The ends of the curve must be stretched out, as mentioned earlier. To accomplish this a perpendicular line is drawn through the point of origin and divided by a series of four points spaced a quarter of an inch apart both above and below the base line. With these points as successive origins draw in the sun's declination *above* the base line for the dates July 8, July 1, June 26 and June 21 and *below* the base line for the dates December 7, 12, 17 and 22. Similarly draw in the sun's declination on the other half-face for June 1 to 21 and December 22 to January 15. The ends of the curves are then plotted from the equation of time by the method described. The full-scale drawing is then ready for translation into hardware. All major parts of my sundial were cast in aluminum. The layout was drawn directly on the wood from which the patterns were made. The time-scale is divided into

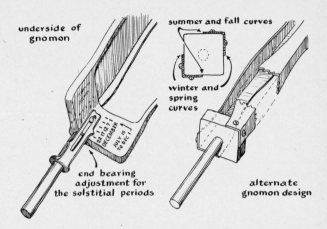

underside of gnomon

summer and fall curves

winter and spring curves

end bearing adjustment for the solstitial periods

alternate gnomon design

31
Detail of gnomons. Adjustment for solstitial periods *(left)* and alternate method of constructing gnomon *(right)*

hourly intervals of 15 degrees each and subdivided into minutes as desired. The graduation representing noon lies in the plane of the meridan.

NOTE: A copy, in reduced scale, of the layout of Schmoyer's gnomon may be procured without charge by forwarding a request, *along with a stamped, self-addressed envelope,* to the Amateur Scientist Department, SCIENTIFIC AMERICAN, 415 Madison Avenue, New York 17, N. Y. Schmoyer has volunteered to have duplicate castings of the sundial made by his local foundry upon request by those who wish to purchase a ready-made set. His address is: Landisville, Pa.

9

THE MOON IN "3-D"

With the aid of a mirror, and your own nose as a measuring rod, the photographs in Figure 32 will give you a "3-D" view of the moon. How the pictures were taken

GEORGE W. GINN of Hilo, Hawaii, submits the stereo photographs of the moon shown in Figure 32. The upper pair of views gives the illusion of three dimensions when viewed with the aid of a thin mirror. Stand the mirror vertically with respect to the plane of the page and align the edge with the boundary separating the right and left views. If the glass is a foot high, let the tip of your nose touch the upper edge and look toward the view behind the mirror.

The lower pair is printed for viewing either "cross-eyed" or, in case you are not blessed with this talent, by means of a conventional stereoscope. With a bit of practice, most persons can perfect the art of cross-eyed viewing. Hold the page in your left hand about a foot from your eyes. Now place the tip of your right index finger between the views, focus both eyes on the fingertip and slowly move the finger toward you. When your finger reaches a certain distance, you will become conscious of four indistinct moon images in the background. Move your finger until the inner images merge. Then shift your focus to this center picture. The moon will appear clear, sharp and in three dimensions.

In commenting on his lunar stereos, Ginn writes: "The views were taken with a three-and-a-half-inch objective of 42 inches focal length. My telescope has provision for placing an Exakta camera at the prime focus in place of the eyepiece. The penta-prism finder of the camera makes a fair eyepiece. The image of the moon on the film is three eighths of an inch in diameter and has been enlarged about six diameters.

32
Stereoscopic photographs of the moon to be viewed by the "cross-eyed" method *(below)* and by a mirror *(above)*

"The two halves were taken seven hours apart, allowing the earth's rotation to provide the base line. For true perspective they would have to be viewed at a distance of about 20 feet."

II.

ARCHAEOLOGY

1

SHOULD THE AMATEUR DIG?

When you discover a promising site (mound, outcropping of artifacts, etc.), run, or write, to the nearest natural history museum. You will get a warm welcome and guidance. Frank H. H. Roberts, Associate Director of the Smithsonian Institution's Bureau of Ethnology, explains how the amateur can collect artifacts under professional guidance and contribute to archaeology

ARCHAEOLOGY FASCINATES MOST PEOPLE. It is the means by which the past is made to live again, and it opens up new and exciting perspectives of time. The study of man's early history, growing out of the pleasant pastime of gathering antiquities for curio cabinets, long ago passed the stage where stone axes were thought to be thunderbolts and arrowheads were looked upon as "fairy stones," when the man who found a pot was called an archaeologist and he who found two became a great archaeologist. It has become a very complicated subject with numerous ramifications.

The material remains which an archaeologist is lucky enough to find are only the starting point. They must be studied in relation to the environment in which they are found. The place where the people who made the objects lived will tell far more of the story than the objects themselves, because its climate and natural resources at the time were determining factors in the growth and development of the cultures which produced the artifacts. Detailed studies of the soil in which the objects lie, and a complete record of what is found there, are absolutely essential, for the process of excavating destroys the source of information. For that reason professional archaeologists have been loath to encourage laymen to make a hobby of archaeology and have insisted that excavations should never be undertaken except by an experienced person. This

33
Excavated Indian skeleton

attitude on the whole is not snobbishness, as many amateurs believe, but is the outgrowth of a real concern for irreplaceable information.

What constitutes the difference between a professional and an amateur is not easy to define. Is the mark of a professional full-time employment at the job, or is it organized training and skill? Some men who make their living as archaeologists are purely amateur in that they have had virtually no training in the techniques of the science, while on the other hand some of those who are concerned with archaeology only as a pastime would qualify as professionals in skill and experience.

To most people the word archaeology is synonymous with digging. Its glamour as an avocation certainly comes in no small part from the fact that in many of us there still lingers the small boy's delight in hunting for buried treasure. But an amateur can also profitably engage in other phases of archaeology which will not only give him satisfaction but contribute to knowledge. One can carry out many interesting archaeological projects without touching a shovel.

A person interested in the traces of aboriginal occupation of the area in which he lives can obtain considerable pleasure from preparing a map showing their location and character. Getting the necessary information for such a map entails walks about the countryside and enjoyable chats with the local residents. Many farmers keep the "curios" turned up by their plows and generally are delighted to show and talk about them. The research may even require a bit of reading in a library to determine what Indian tribes lived there in former days or to find out if there are references to the archaeology of the area. In the course of tramping about the fields the investigator may find an occasional arrowhead, other stone implement or potsherds. A record giving information as to how and where they were found will make a useful supplement to the map and may prove helpful to some professional when a comprehensive study is made of the region. If you find a number of artifacts, it is useful to sort them according to types and show their distribution.

A map of this kind becomes still more valuable if it indicates the types of vegetation and the general character of the topography. By comparing it with old maps, often available in local historical society libraries, you may be able to find changes that have occurred in the terrain since the earlier maps were made. The earlier character of the ground may have had a definite bearing on the location of an Indian village, and often it explains conditions which might otherwise be puzzling. Old maps also occasionally lead to the discovery of archaeological features which were destroyed by cultivation and are no longer apparent on the ground.

Collecting arrowheads of course is one of the most popular hobbies. Some people collect them mainly by purchase or trade. Those who buy their artifacts run considerable risk of having fraudulent objects palmed off on them, as there are a number of men in the U. S. who are experts at making "Indian" things. In any case, a collection by purchase has little actual value, because there is no record of where the artifacts were found. Occasionally a large collection containing very fine specimens is offered for sale after the death of its owner and, much to the disappointment of the heirs, brings far less than expected, even less than the original cost of the

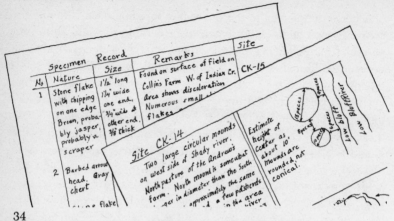

34
Typical archaeological records and map of site

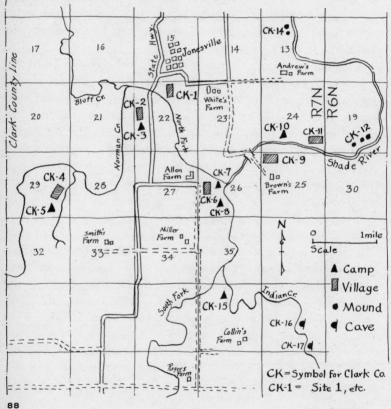

items, solely because no information accompanies them. Every person who makes a hobby of collecting arrowheads or other aboriginal objects should keep a careful record of where and how each was obtained, asking the seller for this information when a piece is purchased. Each specimen should be numbered and listed in a notebook, so clearly that anyone can readily identify it.

In recent years there has been an encouraging trend toward the organization of societies by laymen interested in archaeological subjects. Many of these groups seek the help and advice of professionals and are making a serious effort to follow accepted archaeological procedures. Some of the local groups have formed state-wide societies, and in the eastern U. S. several state societies have combined in a regional association.

State organizations and local societies have developed programs of investigation and contributed considerably to the archaeological knowledge of their own regions. In Connecticut and Massachusetts, for example, some excellent excavation projects have been carried out by amateurs under the general supervision of a few professionals. In Missouri amateur societies have cooperated with the University of Missouri in making surveys to locate and record all archaeological manifestations throughout the state. Their work has been particularly helpful because it has been done in areas which will be flooded before long by the construction of large dams. In Texas local societies have salvaged materials which were being destroyed by construction operations and have kept a valuable record of their activities.

Contrary to a rather widespread impression, the professional archaeologist is not opposed to the amateur and is not continually seeking to keep him from what can be a worthy avocation. What the professional is anxious about is that the amateur should learn the best procedures and do his work properly. The sincere amateur will find that most professionals are more than willing to advise and assist him with his problems and to suggest ways in which his efforts can be of service.

2

THE EXCAVATION OF
WAPANUCKET NO. 6

Maurice Robbins, director of the Massachusetts Archaeological Society at Attleboro, Mass., tells how a group of amateurs with professional guidance unearthed an ancient Indian village on the shore of Assawompsett Pond in Plymouth County and thereby upset some well-established conclusions about the culture of the first Americans. Important "do's" and "don'ts" are included for the beginner in archaeology

WHEN THE AMATEUR sees ancient relics being destroyed by earth-moving machinery, when he realizes that there are not enough professionals to excavate even a small percentage of the available sites, mere talk or even the enactment of laws will not dissuade him from taking a hand in "dirt archaeology." The only alternative, in my opinion, is to educate and cooperate. As the old adage puts it: "If you can't lick 'em, join 'em!" The soundness of this approach to the "amateur problem" was demonstrated by our Society during the recent excavation near Middleboro, Mass., of an Indian village dating back to 2300 B.C.

Most of the work at this site, which was designated Wapanucket No. 6, was performed by members of the Cohannet Chapter of the Massachusetts Archaeological Society. The group is composed of shoe craftsmen, electricians, a florist, a clergyman, a newspaper reporter, a professor of history, several engineers, and other laymen, ranging in age from about 20 to over 60. During the five years prior to their work at Wapanucket No. 6 these amateurs had taken courses in cultural anthropology and archaeological techniques that were offered free by the Society's Bronson Museum at Attleboro. During the summers the group had also excavated a number of

35
Stakes mark the position of post molds at entrance to lodge. Chalk line
marks contour of walls

minor sites in the immediate vicinity, where the usual archaeological pattern of the northeastern states was found.

In the course of this preliminary work the amateurs learned a lot
about the dusty volume in which the story of man's rise is recorded,
and about the characters in which the volume is written: those of
stone, baked clay, bone and stained soil. They encountered at first
hand the ancient authors who wrote without effort to conceal their
faults or enhance their virtues. Such errors as may creep into the
story, the amateurs learned, are those of translation and are charge-
able to the reader.

Most important, the group came to have deep respect for a
unique weakness of the book: the fact that the very act of reading
destroys it! No sentence, much less a paragraph, can be scanned in
the original but once. They learned that those who would enjoy the
thrill of being the first — and the last — to turn the ancient pages
assume a heavy responsibility. They must pay for the privilege by
reading carefully and recording all data in detail so precise that

others in this or future generations may correct errors in the original translation.

By the time work began at Wapanucket No. 6, much was known about the Indians who for some thousands of years had inhabited the region. But following the excavation it became apparent that a number of prior conclusions, particularly those concerning certain people who lived here some 3,000 years ago, would have to be altered considerably. In general, three cultural levels are encountered in the northeastern states. As one sinks his shovel into the earth at favored sites, arrowheads and related artifacts of the most recent Indians are turned up near the surface; at lower levels the remains of older cultures are found. The deepest layer is associated with a people who appear to have come into the area between 6000 and 5000 B.C., and it records what is called the Paleo-Indian occupation. Little is known about these ancient wanderers beyond the fact that they made fluted spear points of the Folsom type, also found in the U. S. Southwest. What may have happened to these early tribes is anybody's guess. They simply disappeared. If any clue to their fate remains, it has yet to be discovered.

The intermediate layer, the one next above the Paleo-Indian, records the period of Archaic occupation. This culture persisted for some 4,000 years: from about 5000 B.C. to 1000 B.C. The remains of these people trace a gradual but pronounced cultural evolution. Implements made in 5000 B.C. exhibit less finish and variety than those of 1000 B.C.

Distinctions between the two types of artifact have enabled archaeologists to divide the Archaic period into early and late components. Wapanucket No. 6 was the site of late Archaic occupation. Although the nature of the period is the subject of considerable discussion among archaeologists, it is agreed in general that the economy of these Indians was based on hunting, fishing and food-gathering. Agriculture and clay pottery were unknown. The bow and arrow did not come into use until late Archaic times. Prior to this the Archaic people hunted and fought with lances and spears.

Finally, at about 1000 B.C., the "Woodland" cultures arose. These peoples were primitive farmers who raised corn, beans, pumpkins and squash. They were also excellent potters and pro-

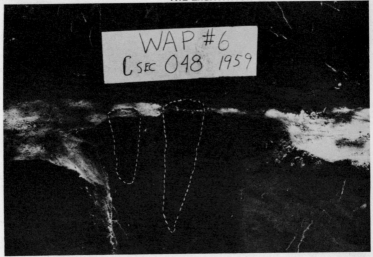

36
Molds of posts that supported walls of a lodge appear as soil discoloration. (Dotted outline added for clarity)

duced handsome clay vessels. Because of a plentiful and secure supply of food the Woodland people could live together in fairly large communities and build permanent villages.

The agricultural traits of the Woodland people had a far-reaching effect on their culture. Freedom from the necessity of roaming the countryside in search of food left them time to think of non-material things. After a few centuries they accordingly developed fairly complex social, religious and political systems. Their culture began to take on the aspect of what one might call a proto-civilization.

Early explorers from Europe arrived in Massachusetts during the final stages of the Woodland period. Thus we have excellent descriptions of the lodges in which the Woodland people lived, and we know the meaning of at least part of their expressive language. Unfortunately, from the point of view of the archaeologist, the camp and village sites that appealed to the Woodland people were precisely those selected by their predecessors.

Accordingly it is quite the usual thing to find a Woodland site superimposed upon one of the Archaic period. The tools left by both groups are often mixed, particularly at sites that show the mark of the Colonial plow. However, by the methods of typology — by analyzing artifacts according to types known to be the product of each culture — the archaeologist can recognize the presence of more than one assemblage of tools and can for the most part separate them into groups according to their time of origin. For example, the preference of Archaic Indians for projectile points with stems is well known; grooved axes and certain types of gouges are also characteristic of the period. Moreover, the Archaic Indians developed a special technique for sawing, grinding and polishing stone, by which they fashioned knives of a characteristic crescent shape and vessels of soapstone. These are positive clues to Archaic occupation.

Until recently the nonmaterial aspects of the Archaic culture were practically unknown and the subject of much speculation. Because agriculture was not practiced during this period, the Archaic Indians were entirely dependent upon wild plants and animals. Any appreciable concentration of people living in such an economy would have resulted in a rapid depletion of the necessities of life, or so it was thought.

In consequence the discovery of an Archaic village was considered most unlikely. Stone tools from this early period had been found in rock shelters and at open sites; it was assumed that the shelters built by the Archaic people must have been flimsy affairs of which no vestige could possibly remain. This conclusion seemed reasonable because the Archaic people were so preoccupied with the eternal quest for food and so dispersed by the environment in which they lived that they would have neither the time nor the opportunity for any but the most rudimentary social, political or religious concepts. How wrong the work of the amateurs at Wapanucket No. 6 has shown these conclusions to be!

The site lies on the northern shore of Assawompsett Pond. Originally this area was a part of the old mother colony of Plymouth. Assawompsett is the largest natural body of fresh water in Massachusetts, covering some 2,200 acres. It forms a part of the drainage system of the Taunton River, which together with its many tributaries provided the aboriginal inhabitants with an easy means of travel. A few hours in their dugout canoes would take them to the seacoast or to interior forests.

The northern shore of the lake is formed by a sand dune flanked by swamps and small streams. Its wave-cut front rises steeply out of the water to a height of 24 feet, and its top offers several acres of level, well-drained land. This area has been the site of aboriginal occupation since the advent of man into New England.

In the spring of 1956 a reconnaissance party from the Cohannet Chapter excavated several random test-squares in the wooded area just back from the lake front. The appearance of Indian refuse pits, fire-cracked stone, and chips remaining from the manufacture of stone implements quickly confirmed our hope that the area had once served as an aboriginal campsite.

The prerequisites of a controlled archaeological "dig" are a careful survey of the area to be examined, the determination of levels in relation to some permanent object (such as a large rock or a survey marker) and the establishment of an excavation grid or checkerboard pattern of carefully measured lines for subsequent use in charting the precise location of all objects discovered. These were

37
Age of charcoal in this hearth was determined by the radio-carbon dating method to be 4,250 years, ± 300 years

the first order of business. Numbered stakes were set at two-meter intervals to outline an area 52 meters long and roughly parallel to the shore.

Next the group removed a thin layer of topsoil along the first line — the so-called base line. Then it began the heavy work of scraping away larger areas of topsoil an inch at a time and examining each freshly exposed surface for evidence of human occupation. Fragments of worked stone, artifacts, hearths, pits or any other indication of aboriginal habitation were located both horizontally and vertically with reference to the numbered stakes and were entered upon printed record cards prepared for the purpose.

The data from these cards were entered upon a chart or progress plan of the area; notes were kept of the type of soil encountered, the content of hearths or pits and the position of post molds: discolorations in soil marking the location of posts which had decayed to dust centuries ago. (Post molds are easy to recognize. Upon removal of the topsoil, the tops of the molds appear as dark circular stains in the surrounding yellow soil. A vertical cut then reveals the cross section of that portion of the original post which was embedded in the earth. The majority of the molds found at Wapanucket No. 6 had smooth sides which curved to a sharp point at various depths.) Information of this sort, together with numerous photographs, constituted the field notes upon which the group based its final conclusions.

As digging progressed and artifacts began to accumulate, the group became aware that none of the material was characteristic of the Woodland period; it was wholly Archaic in appearance. The trend could not be taken seriously at this early stage of excavation, but it was sufficiently pronounced to stimulate interest. The molds of posts began to form new and unfamiliar patterns in the records.

As the weeks passed and the artifacts maintained their Archaic character, the group began almost unconsciously to speak of this as an Archaic site. In our more conservative moments, however, we still doubted our diagnosis. The majority of the artifacts — the tops of the post molds and of pits and hearths — were appearing at about the same depth as that at which objects typical of the Woodland period had been found at other sites in the area.

Several perplexing questions arose. How was it possible for these evidences of occupation to have been preserved with so little disturbance since Archaic times? Why was so favorable a location free from all indication of a Woodland occupation? Were we to abandon the concepts concerning the limitations of a hunting, fishing and food-gathering economy, so firmly established by many authorities? Could we justify the existence not only of a permanent abode but also of a whole Archaic village?

On the basis of our findings the answers to all of these questions had to be yes. Our charts showed undeniable evidence of at least three lodges — structures larger than any known from the Woodland period — and a floor plan that had never, so far as we could determine, been uncovered before. The implements were without exception those of a late Archaic culture. Although a respectably large area had been excavated at this stage of the work, not a single incongruous artifact had appeared.

During the following two seasons four additional lodge floors of the same unique pattern were found. By this time a total of 556 post molds had been charted, and the excavations had been extended a

38
Portion of site demonstrating method of excavation

reasonable distance in all directions without uncovering another floor. We agreed that the complete village had been exposed.

The pattern of the mold array established the existence of an entirely new type of floor plan that was repeated in seven instances. In the construction of these seven houses, pairs of posts had been driven into the earth in two concentric circles. The pairs of posts were placed on radial lines from the center of the structure and driven vertically into the earth. The pointed vertical section of the molds indicated that the posts were driven rather than set in a previously prepared hole. This suggested in turn that the height of the wall was no greater than that of a post which could have been driven by a man standing on the ground. At one point in each structure the walls bypassed each other to form a short protected entranceway. Six of the structures, apparently dwellings, averaged about 31 feet in diameter. The seventh, believed to have a ceremonial function, was 66 feet in diameter and possessed internal posts not found in the smaller lodges. The Note accompanying plan [*Fig. 39*] shows the arrangement of this unique Archaic village, the first to be located in the Northeast.

During the excavation of an Indian site certain features are encountered that in the final report are called pits or hearths, depending upon their appearance, content and vertical position in the ground. Basin-like depressions at or near the surface that contain charcoal, particularly those surrounded by hard, reddened soil, are usually called hearths. Thirty-nine such hearths are recorded at Wapanucket No. 6. Comparable but somewhat larger basins are commonly called pits. Many of these pits contain carbonized material and burned stone and are assumed to have served the final purpose of a receptacle for camp refuse. A pit numbered 29 is of particular importance at this site. The age of a sample of carbon taken from it was established by the geochronometric laboratory at the University of Michigan at $4,250 \pm 300$ years (approximately 2300 B.C.).

The burials at Wapanucket No. 6 were found a few yards south and west of Lodge Floor No. 1. These consisted of four deposits in large oval pits. The cremated remains of human skeletons had been placed in the southwestern quadrant of each pit. In two instances

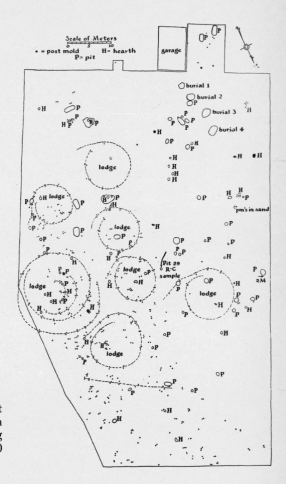

39
Map of Wapanucket
No. 6, the site of an
Indian village dating
back to about 2300
B.C.

grave goods had also been included, and in one instance a considerable quantity of red paint in the form of iron oxide was also present. Burial No. 2 contained a deposit of four stone gouges, a stone
plummet (thought to be a fishing weight) and two sharpening
stones, surrounded by a mass of red paint. In Burial No. 3 a large
crescent-shaped knife of ground slate (called a semilunar knife)
and a sharpening stone were found. Sharpening stones of this type
were made only by late Archaic Indians.

Prior to the discovery of the burials two large features had been found nearby to which our group was unable to assign a satisfactory function. They consisted of carefully laid stone platforms some 10 feet in diameter. The flat stone slabs were reddened and cracked by the intense heat, and a large amount of charcoal had accumulated about and upon the platforms. The platforms are too large to be classed as hearths, and we were at a loss to account for them. With the discovery of the cremation burials their purpose became clear. These were the crematory pits where the initial phase of the funeral rite was conducted.

The group recovered a total of 1,167 stone artifacts from the village area, including one or more implements of each type in the basic tool kit of the inhabitants. The chipped tools included projectile points, lance or spear points, knives, drills, scrapers and assorted woodworking tools. These accounted for more than 80 per cent of the stone objects recovered. The balance of the implements were those made by the sawing, grinding and polishing techniques typical of the late Archaic period.

Much of the information represented by the material dug up at Wapanucket No. 6 is in direct conflict with earlier ideas concerning the culture and manner of life in Archaic times. It is evident that the occupants of Wapanucket No. 6 led a semi-sedentary existence. That they chose this location for convenience rather than defense seems obvious. Living atop the highest ground on the shore of the lake, they would have been a conspicuous part of the landscape. The very size of these lodges creates an impression of permanence and security. They could easily have accommodated at least 100 individuals.

The explanation doubtless lies in the size of the lake. Here at Assawompsett, with its tidal streams, was an abundant supply of food that we, in our ignorance of wilderness life, had failed to take into account. In spring the annual run of shad, and probably salmon and trout, would have provided an abundant food supply. Here migratory birds might be expected to congregate, and in the swamps surrounding the site there must have been considerable game. After a winter spent in ranging the forests to the north and west in small family groups, an ancient people would turn quite

PIT 27

40
Grave goods in precise position occupied at Wapanucket No. 6

naturally to this favored site by the lake. Here could be found a welcome change from the red-meat diet of the winter. A plentiful store of smoked fish could also be prepared against a time when game was scarce. In their great ceremonial lodge the villagers could celebrate the rites required by their religious beliefs, and here those who had departed during the winter could be laid to rest.

Thanks to the initiative and dedicated efforts of a small group of amateurs, a chapter from the ancient book has been carefully preserved and, with the help of specialists, translated. Much new knowledge has been added to our meager understanding of the northeastern Archaic occupation, and more may result from detailed study of the group's records. The group is now constructing a complete reproduction of the village in miniature at the Bronson Museum, so that all may see how the citizens of Wapanucket village lived centuries before Tutankhamen was laid to rest in his tomb at Thebes.

III.

BIOLOGY

1

HOW TO CULTIVATE
HARMLESS BACTERIA

*The growth of the minute plants called bacteria can
be selectively encouraged or retarded by the use of
techniques familiar, on the large scale, to farmers.
Two New York City medical students, Henry Soloway
and Robert Lawrence, explain how to garden at the
microscopic level and, in particular, how to experiment with the weed-killers popularly known as wonder
drugs*

THE SERIES OF EXPERIMENTS which follow are designed
to demonstrate how certain bacteria are affected by bacteriostatic
agents, drugs which retard the growth of selected bacteria. In testing such substances you first cultivate a selected bacterium in an
environment which encourages its growth, subject it to the bacteriostatic agent and then measure the result. Bacteria, like other
forms of life, have preferences in foods, temperature, moisture and
so on. Hence no universal culture medium, in which all organisms
thrive equally, has been developed. Media must be compounded
according to the preferences of the bacteria under study. However,
one medium in which some thousands of organisms thrive consists
of beef broth, the familiar consommé of the dinner table, which
has been refined and specially treated. It is used both in liquid
form and, when thickened by the addition of agar, as a stiff jelly.

As in ordinary farming, "weeds" must be kept down. One is often
interested in the characteristics of a single species of bacterium,
and since the size of the organism makes "weeding" impractical,
intruders must be prevented from gaining a foothold in the first
place. This is accomplished by killing all microscopic life in the
environment of the experiment except the desired organism. The

culture medium and all equipment is sterilized, exposed only to sterilized air and otherwise kept scrupulously aseptic during the experiment.

Preparing for the experiments

THESE CONDITIONS CAN BE MAINTAINED if the amateur provides himself with an aseptic transfer chamber in which all critical operations are performed. This can be a simple wooden box two feet high, two feet wide and three feet long. It is fitted with a glass top, a small door and a pair of holes in one side large enough to admit the hands and forearms comfortably as shown in Figure 41. The cracks should be calked with cotton or sealing compound. A short pair of muslin sleeves may be tacked around the holes to serve as barriers against the outside air. Inside the box one should place, among other things, an alcohol lamp or Bunsen burner, and a small atomizer of the nosespray type containing Lysol or Clorox.

Glassware should include two dozen Petri dishes, which have flat bottoms about four inches in diameter, sides about half an inch high, and are fitted with covers. The experimenter will also need three Erlenmeyer flasks of one-liter capacity and half a dozen of the quarter-liter size, a half-dozen test tubes of 20-milliliter capacity and a rack for supporting them, a dozen one-milliliter pipettes and a special rubber bulb or syringe for filling them, a 50-milliliter graduated cylinder, a wax pencil for marking the glassware, a dissecting needle fitted to a pencil-sized wooden holder, a small loop of thin wire fitted to a similar handle, a glass stirring rod about eight inches long, and a pair of tweezers. All these things should be assembled, together with the special wooden box or transfer chamber, on a substantial bench located where the materials will not be disturbed.

All the materials are then sterilized. Petri dishes and pipettes are tightly wrapped in lots of six in brown paper. Larger items are wrapped individually. Test tubes and Erlenmeyer flasks may be plugged with wads of absorbent cotton instead of being wrapped in brown paper. The glassware is then placed in an oven and heated to 325 degrees Fahrenheit for at least two hours. None of

glass set in mastic
calking compound

muslin sleeves tacked
to armholes

door

seal all joints with cotton
or calking compound

41
A sterile transfer chamber designed for amateur construction

the packages should be opened nor the cotton removed until the glassware is used.

Dehydrated culture medium, both plain and in the form of an agar infusion, may be ordered through your local druggist from the Difco Laboratories, Detroit, Mich., or from the Baltimore Biological Laboratory, Baltimore, Md. A principal object of the experiment, however, is to provide the amateur with experience in the basic techniques of culturing bacteria. The beginner is therefore urged to prepare his own culture medium.

Here is the recipe. Stir a pound of freshly ground hamburger

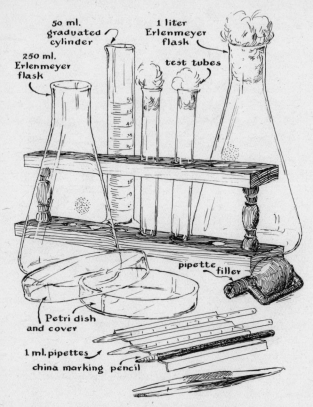

50 ml. graduated cylinder

1 liter Erlenmeyer flask

250 ml. Erlenmeyer flask

test tubes

pipette filler

Petri dish and cover

1 ml. pipettes

china marking pencil

42
Essential equipment for experimenting with bacteria

into a liter of distilled water and put it in the icebox (at about 40 degrees F.) for 10 hours. Then skim off the fat which rises to the top and filter the remaining liquor through a single thickness of clean muslin. Add distilled water to bring the liquor back to a full liter, then add five grams of peptone and five grams of ordinary table salt and stir until the salt is dissolved. Pour 50 milliliters into a second flask and set it aside. Then add 15 grams of agar to the 950-milliliter portion.

Bacteria, like other organisms, are sensitive to the acid-base balance of the medium in which they grow. Those grown in this experiment prefer a neutral medium. The two solutions just prepared will be slightly acid; they must accordingly be adjusted to neutrality (pH 7) by adding precisely enough sodium hydroxide to counteract the acid. Mix 10 grams of sodium hydroxide in a liter of distilled water. Test the beef broth with a piece of blue litmus paper. An acid broth will turn the blue paper red. The sodium-hydroxide solution will turn red litmus blue. Add a drop or two of sodium hydroxide to the liquor, stir, and with the glass rod put a drop of the solution on a piece of blue litmus. The paper in contact with the drop will probably turn pink. Add more sodium hydroxide to the liquor and test again. Continue this until the test drop causes no change in the color of either red or blue litmus.

Each container of liquor is then heated almost to 212 degrees F. for half an hour. This will precipitate the proteins in the liquor. The proteins are removed by passing the hot liquor through coarse filter paper. Each filtrate is again brought up to volume by adding distilled water.

One hundred milliliters of the hot agar medium are poured into each of six Erlenmeyer flasks, which are then stoppered with wads of absorbent cotton. Five milliliters of the liquor containing no agar are poured into each of 10 test tubes, which are similarly stoppered.

The media are now sterilized. The containers may be placed in boiling water for half an hour on each of three successive days. They may alternately be sterilized in a pressure cooker. Put the containers inside the cooker, add two inches of water and pressure-cook for 20 minutes. Be sure to cool the cooker slowly. Rushing the job by quenching the cooker with cold water will cause the internal pressure to drop suddenly and the vessels of hot medium to boil over. Stoppered tubes of tap water and other solutions may be sterilized by either of these methods.

Any nonpathogenic strain of bacteria may be employed for the demonstration of bacteriostasis. *Micrococcus pyogenes* var. *albus*, *Proteus vulgaris* or *Alcaligenes faecalis* can be used in the experiment and may be purchased at low cost from the American Type Culture Collection, 2112 M Street, N.W., Washington 6, D.C. Amateurs may wonder why one should go to the expense of buying bacteria if they are plentiful in the air. You can, of course, grow your own simply by exposing a quantity of the culture medium to the air and incubating it for 24 hours. Let us emphasize that this is pointless and can be dangerous. It is pointless because the average amateur has no means of identifying the microbes he has caught. It is dangerous because there is some possibility of capturing and cultivating disease organisms. Incidentally, media that have been used should be sterilized and discarded immediately. The strains recommended are inoffensive and have the further advantage of being accessible to all workers. Results of experiments may accordingly be compared. Purchased cultures can be perpetuated indefinitely by keeping them in beef broth at room temperature and inoculating a fresh tube of medium (by putting a drop of the old culture into it) every other day. If the culture can be stored at 40 degrees F., the growth of the bacteria is slowed and new media need be inoculated only once every six days.

The bacteriostasis experiment

To PERFORM THE BACTERIOSTASIS EXPERIMENT, first place a test tube of sterile beef broth, the tube containing the flourishing culture, and the wire loop inside the transfer chamber. The chamber is sprayed thoroughly with germicide and the droplets are allowed to settle for five minutes. The alcohol lamp or Bunsen burner is lit and the wire loop heated to redness as far as the handle. Hold both test tubes obliquely in the left hand and the sterile wire loop in the right, as illustrated by Figure 43. Remove both cotton plugs from the tubes with the last two fingers of the right hand. The mouths of both tubes are passed slowly through the flame. The wire loop is then dipped into the flourishing culture for about a second, withdrawn and inserted into the tube containing the sterile broth. Both cotton plugs are replaced and the wire loop is again sterilized by heating to redness. To avoid contaminating the pure culture the beginner should run through these operations with empty tubes a few times for practice.

The freshly inoculated tube is permitted to incubate for two hours at room temperature and is then stored at 40 degrees F. At the end of 24 hours the tube is swirled in front of a light. The pres-

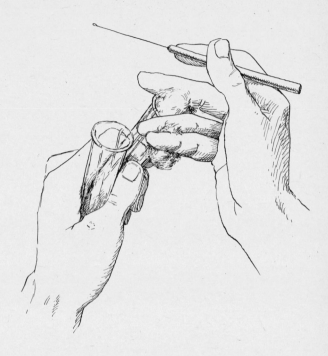

43
How to hold test tubes while transferring bacterial cultures with a loop

ence of sediment indicates that the inoculation has "taken." The purchased culture may then be sterilized and discarded. If at the end of 24 hours there is no sediment, the procedure should be repeated. It is useless to wait another 24 hours.

Antibiotics for diagnostic purposes may be procured through your local druggist under the trade name Bacto-Sensitivity Disks. If they are not available in stock the druggist may order them from Difco Laboratories, Detroit 1, Mich. Each drug is shipped in a sterile vial, 50 disks to the container, and in three concentrations — low, medium and high. The following antibiotics are available in this form: aureomycin, bacitracin, chloromycetin, dihydrostreptomycin, erythromycin, magnamycin, neomycin, penicillin, polymyxin B, streptomycin, terramycin, tetracyline and viomycin.

The bacteriostasis test consists in exposing a series of increasingly concentrated cultures of bacteria growing on plates of agar medium to the action of the drugs. A zone of inhibition around the Bacto-Sensitivity Disks indicates that the organism is sensitive to the antibiotic. The sensitivity of an organism may be evaluated by tabulating zones of inhibition according to the table shown in Figure 44.

SENSITIVITY	CONCENTRATION		
	LOW	MEDIUM	HIGH
very sensitive	zone	zone	zone
sensitive	no zone	zone	zone
slightly sensitive	no zone	no zone	zone
resistant	no zone	no zone	no zone

44
A simple table showing the sensitivity of an organism to an antibiotic of varying concentration

A duplicate set of plates is used as a control for detecting contamination. Begin the experiment by placing the following materials in the sterile transfer chamber: (1) a liter of sterilized tap water, (2) two packages of sterile Petri dishes, (3) a dozen sterilized one-milliliter pipettes and the sterilized rubber squeeze bulb, (4) a water bath heated to 112 degrees F. in which have been placed six Erlenmeyer flasks of agar medium, (5) a test-tube rack containing six test tubes, (6) the was pencil, and (7) an open bowl of germicide.

The packaged glassware is opened and the cotton stoppers removed from the culture and test tubes. A small tuft of sterilized cotton is placed in the neck of each pipette. Nine milliliters of sterile tap water are poured into each of the six test tubes. The following operations are then carefully performed, each piece of glassware being labeled or coded as it is used. Fit the squeeze bulb to a pipette and with it transfer one milliliter of the culture to a test tube of tap water. This tube is labeled 1:10, indicating that it contains one part of culture in 10 by volume. The tube is swirled for 30 seconds to assure thorough mixing. Remove the squeeze bulb from the pipette and drop the used pipette in the bowl of germicide. Select another sterile pipette and transfer one milliliter of the 1:10 mixture to a tube of tap water. Mark this tube 1:100. Again swirl the 1:100 mixture for 30 seconds, drop the used pipette into the germicide and with another sterile pipette transfer one milliliter of the 1:100 mixture to the third tube of tap water. Mark this tube 1:1,000 and proceed in the same way with the remaining tubes, labeling them 1:10,000, 1:100,000 and 1:1,000,000.

A specimen of melted agar medium is now poured from each of the six Erlenmeyer flasks into six Petri dishes, each dish being labeled to correspond with the flask from which it is poured. The dishes are then covered with their glass tops and set aside to harden. After these control plates have been poured, each batch of melted medium remaining in the flasks is inoculated with one of the dilutions in the test tubes. Pipette one milliliter of the dilution into the appropriately labeled flask. Drop the used pipette into the bowl of germicide. The flasks are stoppered with cotton and swirled gently for 30 seconds to mix their contents. The water dilutions are sterilized and discarded.

The control plates are incubated two days at 80 degrees F. The transfer box can be made to double as an incubator by fitting it with a 100-watt bulb controlled by a thermostat of the type used in tropical-fish aquariums.

Twelve Petri dishes, the Bacto-Sensitivity Disks and a pair of forceps are next introduced into the transfer chamber. The chamber is sterilized as before. Two Petri dishes are then filled from each of the six inoculated flasks, each pair being labeled to show the culture dilution. The dishes are permitted to stand for about 20 minutes until the agar solidifies. The forceps are then passed through the flame, the Bacto-Sensitivity Disks opened and the disks placed carefully on the agar medium by means of the forceps. The weaker disks are placed on one plate of the pair and the stronger on the other. (If three drug concentrations are being tested the number of cultures must be increased accordingly, of course.) One way to keep track of the disks is to draw a radius on the back of each Petri dish with the wax pencil. The disk of aureomycin is then placed on this line. All other disks are placed alphabetically, according to the name of the drug, in a clockwise circle. Crowding should be avoided; if space is limited, the last disk can be placed in the center of the plate. Covers are then placed on the dishes, and the culture is left to incubate for two days at 80 degrees F.

The effects of the several drugs and their concentrations on the various concentrations of bacteria are then evaluated by observing the growth on the plates and the rings around each drug where growth has been inhibited. The results may be tabulated by using a minus sign to indicate no growth and a plus sign for inhibition. The presence or absence of a zone of inhibition — *and not the diameter or area of the zone* — indicates the sensitivity to the antibiotics. Any growth on the control plates indicates contamination and invalidates the experiment. The test plates should be reread after four days of incubation, then sterilized and discarded.

Charting the effect of the drugs

AN INTERESTING MODIFICATION of the test permits the experimenter to chart the effect of the drugs with respect to time. Thus he can study the interval following inoculation at which each antibiotic exerts its action, and the rate, if any, at which it loses its effect. This requires the construction of a relatively simple light-meter capable of reading the relative transmission of light through a test tube. Bacterial growth in beef broth increases the turbidity of the broth and reduces its transparency. When the broth is placed in a test tube its turbidity — and hence its population of bacteria — can be measured by the light-meter. The device consists of a lamp and lens for focusing a beam on the side of a test tube, a photocell on the other side of the tube for receiving the transmitted light, and a microammeter for reading the output of the cell. The light source, lens assembly, test tube and photocell are mounted in an appropriately compartmented and light-tight box [*see Fig. 45*].

Here the operations are conducted in test tubes rather than agar. A tablet of antibiotic is dissolved in 10 milliliters of sterile tap water (in the aseptic transfer chamber). Dilutions of this solution are prepared as before, so that six dilutions span the range from 1:10 to 1:1,000,000. Observe that in this case it is the drugs, not the cultures, which are diluted. One milliliter of each of the dilutions

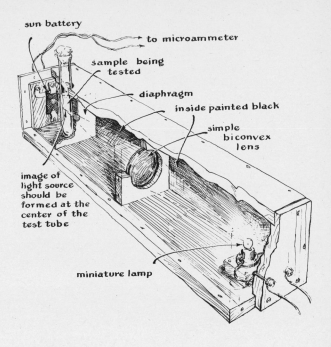

sun battery

to microammeter

sample being tested

diaphragm

inside painted black

simple biconvex lens

image of light source should be formed at the center of the test tube

miniature lamp

45
A homemade light meter for measuring the density of a bacterial culture

is added to a sterile test tube which contains four milliliters of beef broth.

The tubes are then inoculated with one loop of bacteria from a two-day-old beef-broth culture and left to incubate at 80 degrees F. At equal intervals during the incubation, say every three hours, the tubes are gently swirled and their turbidity is measured by means of the light-meter. Turbidity is then plotted against time. The result is a set of graphs showing bacteriostatic activity. The test tubes should be inspected for optical uniformity by means of the light-meter before they are used. Professional light-measuring instruments used for this test are usually calibrated in accordance with Beer's law, which states that, for solutions of a given substance in a given solvent, light will be absorbed in proportion to the thickness of the solutions.

Graphs made with instruments calibrated arbitrarily will show accurate rates of bacteriostatic effect, although the curves will not necessarily conform to those drawn with the aid of professional instruments. Tests which employ light-measuring devices can have great practical value because they show which antibiotic can be employed most effectively against a bacterium about which no data have been collected. They also disclose whether a known bacterial strain has mutated to become more resistant to a given drug.

Isolating unusual colonies and developing new strains

IN THE COURSE OF EXPERIMENTS employing plates of agar medium one may occasionally observe a small colony flourishing within the circle of inhibition. The chances are that this is a contaminant. There is always the possibility, however, that the organism is a mutant, a new strain which has been naturally selected over the original strain susceptible to the drug. All such unusual colonies should be isolated and cultured. (A portion of the colony is lifted from the plate with the tip of the dissection needle and transferred to fresh medium for incubation.) Tests can then be performed to learn if it is in fact a mutant or merely a contaminant.

Radiation is known to increase the mutation rate of all living organisms; thus it is possible to develop new strains by exposing cultures to X-rays. The homemade X-ray machine described in Section IX by Harry Simons is capable of inducing such mutations. The experimenter is cautioned, however, to avoid exposure to the X-rays. The culture should be placed in front of the tube and the machine operated by remote control from behind a shield, as suggested by Simons.

2

GROWING ALGAE ON A
WINDOW SHELF

*A casual stroll in the woods led the late I. C. G.
Cooper, a naval architect of New York City, into the
fascinating realm of algae culture. Here are his directions for isolating, identifying and growing the minute
plants which may some day become an important
source of man's food*

ONE AFTERNOON, many years ago, I started out for a
pleasant walk in our neighboring woods with William T. Davis, an
amateur naturalist and one of the founders of the Staten Island
Institute of Arts and Sciences. He had volunteered to teach me how
to identify some of our local wildflowers. His enthusiasm was con-
tagious, and before the afternoon was over the bug had bitten me.

During the next few months I gathered and mounted a lot of
flowers and weeds. Before long it became evident that I was a little
late with my discoveries; the specimens I collected were already
represented in the Institute's display cases. It seemed pointless to
go on duplicating work already well done. Then one evening at the
end of a field trip I took a short-cut home by way of the beach and
noticed a strange clump of seaweed waving back and forth in the
low tide. I took off my shoes and waded in. After I had pulled up
a specimen of the plant, I had an idea: Why not make a study of
Staten Island's marine flora?

Although that first specimen turned out to be only a common
variety of rockweed, it occupies a special place in my collection
because it introduced me to the thallophytes, the grand division of
the plant kingdom occupied by the algae.

You don't need a scientist's background to get fun out of collecting algae, especially the big ones. You simply float them in

whole or in part onto a sheet of paper and let them dry. The leaf-like parts of many consist of only two layers of cells coated with a clear pectinous substance. They dry on the paper without apparent thickness, like ink, and few artists paint more colorful or exotic abstractions.

Things went along nicely for a couple of years, and my original rockweed grew into quite a substantial collection. Then the job became rough. As I worked my way down the scale of algal sizes, the number of species increased all out of proportion. Identification became difficult. The reference texts, which fully describe the giant kelps and often carry colored illustrations of them, become sketchy when you get down to the species that make a pocket magnifier handy.

Without knowing it would make matters worse, I bought a microscope. The first look through it almost ended my new hobby. Here was no man's land. I could not even distinguish between plants and animals, much less identify the plants. A single drop of fluid scraped from a stalk of marsh grass would hold scores of organisms, including animals that grow in branching patterns like plants and plants that swim by means of whiplike tails and eat like animals! At this point I want to put in a good word for the patience of our museum's curators and that of my fellow members in the New York Microscopical Society. They finally succeeded in teaching me how to recognize a chloroplast when I saw one, and also to identify the cellulose walls which aid in distinguishing one biological kingdom from the other.

But learning how to tell plants from animals was only a beginning. Each drop of liquid that appears under the microscope's objective contains a unique population. Before I could complete a census, the drop would evaporate and destroy the individuals. How do you introduce order into a scramble like this, and where do you begin?

It is a good idea, the curators advised, to commence by narrowing your field. Staten Island is not large as islands go, but in terms of its algal population it is vast. In naively undertaking the collection of all our local "seaweed" I had staked out too much territory. After years of sampling the immensely various populations of algae in the island's waters, I decided I would have to limit myself to the less abundant algae of the soil.

As a rule, algae are not too difficult to find in the soil once you have picked up a bit of experience in handling cultures and the microscope. But separating them into individual species and exploring their structure and behavior can get you embroiled in all sorts of puzzles and complications. Fortunately the phycologists and bacteriologists have solved the hard problems of method, and it is not difficult to adapt their techniques to an amateur's studies.

I use the so-called "soil-water" culture method advocated by E. G. Pringsheim of Cambridge University. In effect the algae grow in a miniature artificial pond — a glass jar of nutrient solution covering a bottom of mud [see Fig. 46]. The pond is prepared by partly filling a wide-mouthed glass container — such as a peanut-butter jar — with nutrient solution, adding a tablespoonful of soil and then sterilizing the whole in an autoclave. The pond is then inoculated with the specimen of soil to be investigated. A pinch does the job. The pond is kept at room temperature and exposed to light during incubation; a window having a northern exposure is a good light source.

After incubation is completed — when the characteristic green "scum" appears in quantity — a smear of the culture is transferred to an agar plate where it continues to grow. If the smear has been made carefully, distinct colonies of the various organisms will appear here and there on the plate. You then pick out one of these with a glass needle or a micropipette and inoculate a second sterile pond with it. What you thought was a colony of identical organisms will likely prove to be a mixture — but the second pond will be less motley than the first. You continue this cycle of operations until your species appear in splendid isolation — or your patience gives out. Sometimes I wonder if it is possible to develop a perfectly pure culture of anything.

Single-celled algae are enveloped by the same pectinous substance that causes the giant kelps to dry on paper so beautifully. This sheath is usually alive with bacteria. Just try to kill them without killing the algae! Irradiation by X-ray or ultraviolet light in measured doses tends to kill the bacteria without destroying all the

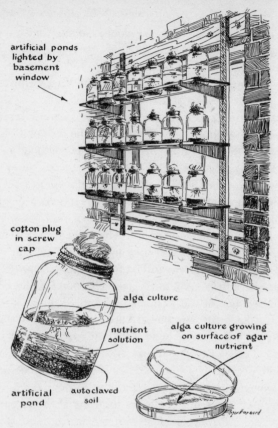

artificial ponds
lighted by
basement
window

cotton plug
in screw
cap

alga culture

nutrient
solution

alga culture growing
on surface of agar
nutrient

artificial
pond

autoclaved
soil

46
Cooper's setup for the cultivation of algae from the soil

algae. But even if you succeed in knocking out the bacteria without damaging the plant, you still face the job of separating the alga from the culture without contaminating it and of inducing it to grow in a fresh pond.

The artificial-pond technique always leaves you with a number of chemical unknowns. I hope the spectroscope will eliminate some of them. The growing culture takes part of its nourishment from elements added to the solution and part from sterilized soil. The first are under your control. If we could grow cultures by pure hydroponic methods, a lot of question marks that come with the soil would vanish. But that would necessitate a comprehensive knowledge of the organism's nutrient requirements in advance of growing a culture of it.

Hence we combine the major elements — nitrogen, potassium, magnesium and others common to all plants — in the nutrient solution and rely on the "mud phase" to supply the minor ones plus other unknown factors such as vitamins. The mud also serves as a reservoir and a place of reduction and synthesis for keeping the heavy metals in solution. Incidentally, the proper soil for the pond's bottom must be found by trial. After a lot of sampling, I located one that works unusually well. A large quantity of it was sterilized at one time by autoclaving and stored in sealed containers for future use.

Friends sometimes ask what I do with an alga when it has been isolated and added to the collection of cultures. In a way that is like asking a philatelist what he does with his stamps. If he is a good philatelist, he preserves them carefully and tries to learn something from them. Preserving live algae is no less satisfying nor more difficult than caring for any other plant.

If you give them light, water and food, and maintain the temperature they prefer, they glow with health. In turn they challenge you to discover how they react to such things as subtle changes in diet; how, when and by means of what mechanism they reproduce; what products their metabolism yields — and the countless related secrets of their life processes. In accepting this challenge you can,

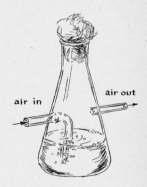

47
Aeration flask for algal culture

as they say, dive in as deeply and stay down as long as you wish. I have been at it now for some years without getting more than my feet wet.

Those who enjoy hydroponics like to develop nutrients, and I have had some success in this work. One series of experiments ended in a solution which seems to work better for me than those listed in the reference texts. You lay out a set of slightly differing ponds in a rectangular grid, with a single element in the nutrient progressively diluted more and more in each vertical row. The entire grid is inoculated and kept under observation.

A detailed record of the culture's reaction in each pond is made. The experiment can be continued by simultaneously altering the strength of two elements in each vertical row, then three elements and so on. An analysis of the accumulated record discloses the ideal concentration of each element in the nutrient for the species under study. Incidentally, a culture subjected to this study becomes a tool of great power and subtlety for investigating unknown nutrients. The alga's reactions when transferred to the unknown nutrient provide an indication of the ingredients present and, in some cases, a quantitative measure of their concentrations.

Once a culture has been standardized, that is to say, brought to a reasonable state of purity and provided with the preferred nutrient, it suggests endless other experiments. If the alga employs sexual reproduction, for example, you can attempt to mate it with a near relative and create a hybrid. It is interesting to modify a plant's diet and observe the result.

A heavy concentration of nitrogen can cause *Chlorella*, an alga which may become commercially important, to increase its production of protein from about half its weight to almost 90 per cent. In contrast, putting Chlorella on a starvation diet of nitrogen boosts fat production from something under 10 per cent to more than 70 per cent. The commercial implications are obvious.

It is easy to see how such metabolic gymnastics can fascinate the amateur. Learning to observe such changes, to take the plants apart and measure the substances of their bodies, or those that appear as by-products, will bring you into contact with as many fields of science as you have time and talent to enjoy.

3

HOW TO TRANQUILIZE A RAT

The power of certain new drugs to calm disturbed animals is demonstrated by the use of rats in an ingenious experiment designed by Sara E. Southwick, a high-school girl of Midland, Mich. She tells how to build and use the apparatus and gives the procedure for establishing experimental controls. A method for assessing the damaging effects of the drugs is described

FOR MY SCIENCE FAIR PROJECT during my senior year in high school, I set up a controlled experiment to test the effect on rats of chlorpromazine, one of the new tranquilizing drugs. Tranquilizers were making news at the time, particularly in the treatment of mental disease, and this caught my interest. According to medical reports, the side effects of the tranquilizers had not been fully catalogued, and it seemed likely that a science fair project based on one of them would have a good chance of scoring high on originality.

Chlorpromazine has the property of quieting mental patients who are restless, overactive and abnormally elated. Would the drug have a similarly depressing effect on normal animals? If so, how would it affect other aspects of their functioning?

As subjects for the experiment I obtained six white rats, all males from the same litter. During the first phase of the experiment three rats were selected at random for treatment and the remaining three were reserved as controls. Each animal was tagged for identification. Midway through the experiment the treatment was switched; the controls were put on the drug, and the group previously treated became the controls. I called this the "crossover" phase. It served as a check against previous results. Otherwise all animals were maintained under identical conditions as closely as possible, and each was given a standard ration of food and water on a fixed schedule. The experiment continued for five months as a spare-time activity.

A thorough physical examination was made of each animal at the beginning of the experiment, both to assure that the animals were in good health and to provide comparison data for subsequent use. The effects of the drug were then observed by measuring changes in activity, intelligence, blood composition, pulse rate, body temperature, weight, respiratory rate, external features, sexual behavior, internal organs and metabolism. The animals were treated by administering chlorpromazine along with their food, initially at the rate of five milligrams of the drug per kilogram of body weight.

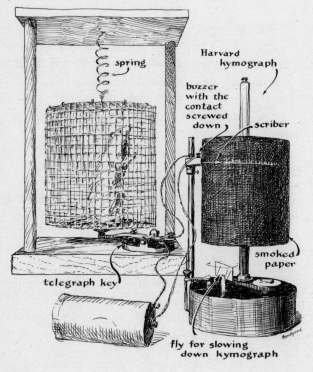

48
Cage, telegraph key and kymograph to measure the activity of a rat

After one week the dose was increased to 15 milligrams; somewhat later, to 20 milligrams.

Reaction to the drug was immediate. The treated rats became quieter than the control group. Their movements were slower and more deliberate. To measure the difference I designed a "jiggle cage" consisting of a box of quarter-inch wire mesh covered at the bottom with a sheet of heavy aluminum foil of the kind used by bakers.

The cage was suspended by a weak spring from the bottom of a small table consisting of a seven-inch square of half-inch plywood fitted with legs of wooden dowel stock. The movements of the caged rat caused the cage to jiggle up and down and actuate the handle of a telegraph key in contact with the bottom of the cage. The key closed an electrical circuit between a battery and the coils of a modified buzzer. The buzzer contacts were closed; a wire stylus was attached to the armature. The stylus pressed against the smoked drum of a kymograph on which the movements of the rat registered as sharp vertical pips in an otherwise smooth trace. I borrowed the kymograph from the biology department of the Midland High School. It is not too difficult, however, to make such a drum recording-device. [One is described in Section V.] A recording speed of some three inches per second, equivalent to the speed of a six-inch drum turning at about one revolution per minute, is adequate for this experiment.

The activity of each rat was measured daily for one hour in darkness (when rats are commonly most active). Copies of two recordings are shown in the accompanying illustration [Fig. 49]. These show the activity of the same rat before and after the drug had been administered.

The effect of chlorpromazine on intelligence was tested by means of a changeable maze in which both the pattern of the paths and the obstacles (rectangular partitions) could be altered. The animal was required to crawl under a partition or jump over it, depending on whether the partition was turned so that its opening was at the top or at the bottom. The maze was covered so the animals would not be distracted during the run.

To test the adjustment of the rats to change, the maze was altered

49
Top record reflects activity of untreated rat; bottom, treated rat

four times for each group of animals during the course of the experiment. In the beginning the control rats required about seven
runs to learn the maze, during which the time of the run dropped
from eight minutes to 30 seconds. The treated group required substantially more practice to achieve comparable performance; at
first these rats actually lost ground. The reaction of the rats was
even more significant during the crossover phase of the experiment.

During the crossover phase the rats in the control group learned
to run the maze, with practice, in five seconds. When they were
under the influence of chlorpromazine, however, none of these rats
could do better than one minute. In contrast, the previously treated
rats, after recovering from the drug, learned to run a new pattern
in five seconds. Furthermore, when the crossover phase was started,

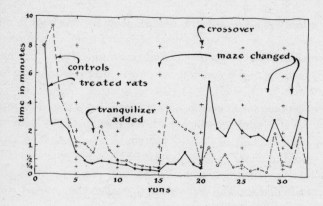

50
Graph compares the performance of treated and untreated rats in a maze

the drug caused the controls to forget a maze pattern they had mastered. From this it would appear that the drug has a depressing effect on memory as well as on intelligence.

Does the drug similarly depress organic functions? This was investigated in part by examining changes in the blood of the rats. The blood was taken by clipping the tip of the rat's tail. Incidentally, I quickly learned that rats are not as cooperative in all parts of the experiment as one could wish; blood sampling is a case in point. I first tried to hold the animals in one hand while taking the specimen with the other, but soon adopted the technique of wrapping them in a towel. Later I borrowed a glass vessel especially designed for the purpose.

Standard clinical pipettes were used for withdrawing two specimens of blood from each rat: one specimen to ascertain the number of red blood cells; the other to test for the number of white blood cells. The pipettes are fitted with a short length of suction tubing; one simply places the glass tip in the fluid and withdraws enough to reach the .5 mark etched in the glass. Sufficient diluting fluid is then drawn into the pipette to reach the top mark.

When one is sampling white cells, the top mark is 11; in the case of red cells the mark is 101. The diluting fluid for white cells (which causes the red cells to disintegrate) consists of one part by volume of hydrochloric acid to 100 parts of distilled water. The red-cell specimen is diluted by a fluid consisting of .5 gram of mercuric chloride, five grams of sodium sulfate and one gram of table salt dissolved in 200 cubic centimeters of distilled water. This solution causes the white cells to disintegrate.

Blood cells are counted with the aid of a special chamber that divides the field of view into a pattern of uniform squares, somewhat like a sheet of graph paper. If one encounters difficulty in procuring a counting chamber, a rough estimate of change in the relative number of white cells and red cells can be made by comparing stained specimens. I borrowed a chamber.

The red-cell count remained constant throughout the experiment for both treated and untreated rats. But the white-cell count increased substantially during the time the animals were on the drug, averaging 22,000 cells per cubic millimeter during treatment as

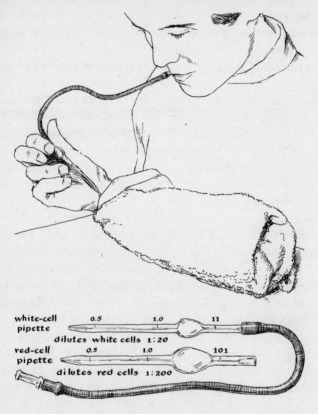

white-cell
pipette

0.5   1.0   11

dilutes white cells 1:20

red-cell
pipette

0.5   1.0   101

dilutes red cells 1:200

51
Pipetting a specimen of rat blood

against a normal count of 14,000. Counts were taken of all rats once each week for the first three weeks after the beginning of treatment.

Measurements made during the crossover phase were identical with those recorded at the beginning of the experiment. In one exceptional case, however, both groups yielded identical counts. This occurred after the experiment had been running two months and suggests that the rats may have developed some tolerance for the drug.

Stained blood-specimens were examined with the aid of a microscope equipped with a 10-power eyepiece, an oil-immersion objective of 97 power, and dry objectives of 43 power and 10 power. The combinations of eyepiece and objectives gave magnifying powers of 970, 430 and 100 diameters. The instrument was borrowed from the Midland Hospital.

The technique of making differential smears is not difficult if one carefully follows a standard procedure. The microscope slides must be cleaned thoroughly. Ordinary household detergents, particularly those containing a soft abrasive powder, make a satisfactory cleaning agent. A drop of blood is first placed near the end of a freshly cleaned slide. The end of a second slide is then held at an angle of about 45 degrees at a point between the drop and the center of the second slide, so that the drop wets the lower surface of the upper slide. The fluid will immediately spread by capillary attraction across the line of contact between the two slides. The second slide is then quickly pushed forward toward the far end of the first. This distributes the specimen *behind* the top slide in a film which adheres to the lower slide. Do not place the drop in front of the top slide and push it with the end of the glass; the cells will be forced to flow between the two slides and may be broken.

The smear is allowed to dry until it becomes tacky, and then is stained. I used Wright's stain, which can be procured through most drugstores. It is made into a solution consisting of .3 gram of powdered stain mixed with three grams of glycerin and 97 cubic centimeters of methyl alcohol. A drop of the solution is applied to the

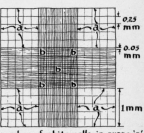

52
Pattern of chamber for counting
blood cells

number of white cells in areas 'a'
times 50 = cells per cubic mm
number of red cells in areas 'b'
times 10,000 = cells per cubic mm

slide and allowed to stand for three minutes. A drop of buffer solution is then added. This consists of 1.63 grames of potassium phosphate and 3.2 grams of sodium phosphate dissolved in a liter of distilled water.

The ingredients of both formulas, incidentally, may be cut in proportion if smaller quantities are desired. After the buffer has worked five minutes the slide is washed gently with distilled water, permitted to dry in open air and then placed under the microscope for examination.

The differential smears from rats under treatment showed a 20-per-cent increase in the white cells known as lymphocytes, and an equal decrease in neutrophil white cells. Again, however, one measurement made two months after the beginning of the experiment proved exceptional and suggested the development of tolerance to the drug.

As another index of reaction to the drug the pulse rate of all animals was taken twice during each phase of the experiment. This proved somewhat difficult because the pulse rate of a healthy rat is about 375 beats per minute, and, as I discovered, this rate is almost doubled by the administration of chlorpromazine. Accordingly, accurate counts could not be made by listening to the rats' heartbeats with a stethoscope.

I solved the problem with the aid of an ordinary magnetic-tape recorder. The rat was held against the microphone and a recording of the heart sounds made at a tape speed of 7.5 inches per second. The record was next played back at 3.25 inches per second and the beats counted by ear against a stop watch. The count was then multiplied by two. (The absolute tape speed, which varies with the make of the machine, is not important. One is only concerned with the ratio of speeds.)

Rats tend to become excited when placed against the microphone, so they should be permitted to settle down for a few minutes before the recording is made. The pulse rate of tranquilized rats averaged 639.6 beats per minute, as against 389 beats per minute for the controls. The slightly higher than normal rate of the controls is explained by the excitement of the rats at being handled.

The body temperature of tranquilized rats was also found to be abnormally high, averaging 100.1 degrees Fahrenheit as against an average of 99.7 degrees for the controls. The average difference is not great. But in every instance the lowest temperature observed in a treated animal was above the highest temperature among the controls. This fact, when considered together with the elevated lymphocyte and decreased neutrophil counts, suggests that the tranquilized rats had contracted an infection of some sort. This was further indicated by their behavior. Some appeared to be sick part of the time. The temperatures were taken with a conventional rectal thermometer.

A careful record of body weight was made daily, along with the weight of food and water consumed. Early in the experiment the ratio of water to total body weight changed in a direction that suggested that the drug was causing dehydration, but this was not supported by the crossover observations. Both groups made comparable gains in weight throughout the experiment [*see* Fig. 53].

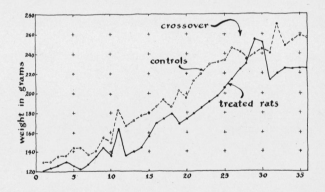

53
Graph compares the weight of treated and untreated rats

Chlorpromazine lowers the respiratory rate of rats substantially. Tranquilized rats average 72 inhalations per minute as against 95 for the controls. The rates coordinate well with the relative activity of the two groups. Counts were taken three times during each phase of the experiment.

A close check was made throughout the experiment of the external appearance of the rats in both groups. I observed a number of obvious differences. Minor skin eruptions developed within a few days after each animal was put on the drug. In addition, the hair of the treated rats became rough and shed readily. In the case of the first group to receive the drug, violent muscle tremors occurred when the animals awakened from sleep. This, however, was not observed in the group treated during the crossover phase. The behavior of the groups also suggested that, at least in rats, chlorpromazine acts as a sexual stimulant.

Tendencies to jaundice sometimes follow the administration of chlorpromazine, according to reports in the professional journals. This reaction appeared in both groups of rats approximately two weeks after treatment was started. Their eyes became pale and their feces lost color. To check possible damage to the liver an autopsy was performed on one control and one treated rat 17 days after the beginning of the crossover phase. Sections of liver tissue were taken from both rats and preserved in xylol. Both specimens showed abnormality. The damage appeared more extensive in the animal that was undergoing treatment at the time the autopsy was performed. This part of the experiment was interesting, but because the observations were limited to two animals the result could not be considered conclusive.

No diabetic effect was observed. The qualitative test for this reaction was made by a procedure which I learned at the Midland Hospital that requires the use of chemically treated test-strips that one must either purchase or borrow. The strip is dipped in the urine of the animal; if sugar is present, the tip of the stick turns blue within a minute.

Metabolism was measured by a variation of the method devised in 1890 by the noted British physiologist J. S. Haldane [see *How to Measure the Metabolism of Animals*, page 135]. Essentially the test consists in supplying the animal for a known interval with air containing a minimum of water vapor and carbon dioxide and then subtracting the weight lost by the animal from the weight of the water vapor and carbon dioxide exhaled during the test interval.

This gives the weight of oxygen absorbed by the animal, and

when this figure is divided into the weight of exhaled carbon dioxide (adjusted for the molecular weights of oxygen and carbon dioxide), the result is equal to the respiratory quotient of the animal. My apparatus consisted of an air pump (a water-powered aspirator) and five flasks of one liter each connected in series. The initial flask in the series contained approximately 600 cubic centimeters of Ascarite, a commercial preparation that has the property of absorbing carbon dioxide. The second flask held a comparable amount of anhydrous calcium chloride, which absorbs water vapor. The intake of the second flask was coupled to the exhaust of the third, a

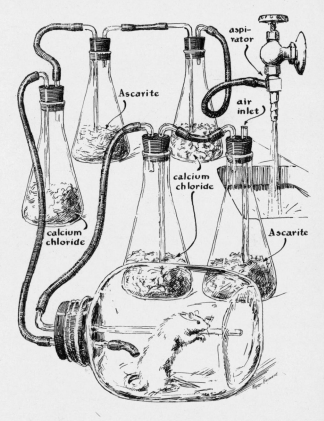

aspirator

Ascarite

air inlet

calcium chloride

calcium chloride

Ascarite

54
A homemade apparatus for measuring the metabolism of small animals

wide-mouthed jar capped with a close-fitting stopper, which served as the animal chamber. The intake of the animal chamber led respectively to flasks of calcium chloride, Ascarite and calcium chloride.

All containers and the animal were weighed individually before and after a test interval of one hour. The weight (in grams) lost by the rat was then divided into the product of the weight gained by the fourth and sixth flasks multiplied by .7282 (the ratio of the molecular weights of oxygen and carbon dioxide).

Only two animals remained in each group at the time the respiratory quotient was measured, the other pair having been used for the autopsy. The respiratory quotients of the rats then under treatment were .56 and .58, whereas those of the control rats were .82 and .65. Here again the sample was too small to yield reliable figures. Differences in the individual determinations show a spread, however, which suggests that the lower activity of the tranquilized rats is accompanied by a correspondingly low respiratory rate.

From this experiment it would seem that a rat is tranquilized by the steady administration of chlorpromazine, but with at least temporary cost to its health. The drug depresses the animal's memory and intelligence, alters the composition of its blood, invites infection, increases its pulse and body temperature, lowers its metabolism, induces abnormal sexual stimulation and damages its skin, hair and liver.

4
HOW TO MEASURE
THE METABOLISM OF ANIMALS

While casting about for a project to enter in a science fair, Nancy Rentschler, a high school student in Mayfield, Ohio, hit on an interesting apparatus for measuring the rate at which animals utilize food. She describes its assembly and operation, and gives the details of a typical experiment with mice as subjects

DURING MY HIGH-SCHOOL DAYS I once came across a textbook diagram of an apparatus to measure animal metabolism. It had been designed for dog-sized animals and therefore presented a space requirement considerably beyond my available facilities. The process sounded so fascinating, however, that I could not put it out of my mind. I didn't know very much about metabolism. But it seemed to me that I could learn if the apparatus could be scaled down to the size required for a mouse. I was further stimulated by the fact that the apparatus, if it could be designed, should stand up well against the 220 exhibits scheduled for entry in our science fair. I began to work on the project late in January and performed my first experiments about a month later.

The mice and the apparatus

THE MICE I USED were purchased through a pet shop. They had been inbred for three generations. At first I found it a bit difficult to handle them, but soon I learned to pick them up by the tail. After a week or so the mice became quite tame, although occasionally one would lose its temper during an experiment and try to bite the experimenter.

For the purpose of my experiments I divided 15 mice into four groups, three in one group and four in each of the others. By placing each group on a diet or medication which differed from that of the others, I could study the effects of these differences on the metabolism of the animals. I followed the experimental method devised by the noted British physiologist J. S. Haldane in 1890. The apparatus consists mainly of an animal chamber and five flasks of chemicals interconnected by tubing so that a controlled stream of air can flow through the system [see Fig. 51, How to Tranquilize a Rat].

The purpose of the apparatus is to measure the amount of oxygen taken up by the animal, and the amount of carbon dioxide expelled. The ratio of oxygen inhaled to carbon dioxide exhaled by the animal during a given period indicates the rate of its metabolism, and is called the "respiratory quotient." This quotient varies with the diet of the animal. When the animal is fed a carbohydrate such as sugar, the ratio is 1. When it is fed fats, the ratio varies slightly with the composition of the fat but averages .7. The ratio for proteins also varies, but averages .8. The ratio of alcohol is .667. The respiratory quotients of normal animals under average conditions usually lie between .72 and .97.

Each flask of the apparatus is fitted with a rubber stopper and two glass tubes about half an inch in diameter. One tube reaches to within an inch of the bottom of the flask and the other just passes through the stopper. Air entering the flasks through the longer tubes is exhausted through the shorter ones. The first and fourth flasks in the series (not counting the animal chamber) are filled to a depth of about three inches with soda lime, which absorbs carbon dioxide. The second and third flasks contain the same amount of calcium chloride. The fifth flask is charged with pumice stone and sulfuric acid. These last three flasks absorb water vapor. Ideally all three should contain pumice and sulfuric acid.

I found the pumice difficult to prepare, so I made enough for one flask (to satisfy myself that I could prepare it) and "made do" with calcium chloride in the other two. The pumice is used in lumps about half an inch in diameter. Mine came from cosmetic counters, which proved to be a costly source. I learned later that chemical supply dealers list pumice at 50 cents a pound.

The stone is activated by heating it to redness with an acetylene torch and dropping it, while it is still hot, into concentrated sulfuric acid. The excess acid is then allowed to drain off. The soda lime is prepared by mixing lime with a solution of sodium hydroxide in the proportion of one ounce of sodium hydroxide (by weight) to two and a half ounces of water (by volume). Lime is added until the mixture becomes dry. The powder is then separated from the coarse particles by means of a fine sieve and discarded. Large lumps are broken down. It is the intermediate fragments — those which pass through a sieve of five meshes per inch — that are used for charging the flasks. The absorbing power of soda lime does not last long, and I had to make additional batches as the experiments progressed.

My animal chamber was a two-quart canning jar. I found it necessary to shield the exhaust tube of the chamber to keep it from pinning the mice. Before I added the shield, this happened several times, spoiling the experiment and injuring the mouse. The shield is merely a short length of rubber tubing with a slit or a few holes cut in it. It is slipped over the shorter glass tube inside the chamber. No damage is done when a mouse brushes against the end of the tube because the slit provides a second exhaust port.

The entire system must be airtight. Close-fitting stoppers should be used and all joints coated with either wax or plastic cement. The rubber tubing should be as short and straight as possible, and should be tightly fitted to the glass tubes. Air was pulled through the apparatus by means of an aspirator attached to a water faucet.

Air normally contains about 3 per cent carbon dioxide and a varying amount of water vapor. Both are removed by the first and second flasks. Thus air free of water vapor and carbon dioxide flows into the animal chamber. The animal inhales oxygen and exhales carbon dioxide and water vapor. The latter are absorbed by the remaining flasks.

The increase in weight of the third flask indicates the amount of water vapor given off by the animal. The fourth and fifth flasks measure the amount of carbon dioxide (which reacts with the soda lime in the fourth flask to form carbonic acid). The fourth and fifth flasks must be weighed together because the soda lime may give up moisture to the dry air and thus lose weight.

In setting up the apparatus for a test run, the last three flasks are weighed, the fourth and fifth together. The animal is then placed in the chamber, which is stoppered and weighed. The test run is timed from this moment. The chamber is now connected to the apparatus and the air pump started. I ran the mice in each group for a total time of one hour. At the end of this period the pump is stopped and the chamber removed from the apparatus, stoppered and weighed again. The third, fourth and fifth flasks are also weighed.

The respiratory quotient may now be calculated. The combined weight of the mouse and chamber at the beginning of the run minus their weight at the end of the run equals how much weight the mouse has lost. The weight of the third flask at the end of the run minus its weight at the beginning equals the amount of water absorbed by the calcium chloride and lost by the mouse. The weight of the fourth and fifth flasks at the end of the run minus their weight at the beginning equals the amount of carbonic acid formed.

The total weight of water and carbon dioxide absorbed minus the loss in weight of the mouse equals the weight of oxygen absorbed. The respiratory quotient is determined by multiplying the weight of the carbonic acid by the fraction 32/44 and dividing the result by the weight of oxygen absorbed. The quantity 32/44 is the ratio of the molecular weight of oxygen to that of carbon dioxide. Its use in the equation indicates the amount of carbon dioxide represented by the carbonic acid.

The metabolism experiment

I USED TWO of my four groups of mice to study the effects of diet on metabolism. With the other two groups I investigated the metabolic effect of the activity of the thyroid gland. The first group of four mice was given only water. Although mice normally live about nine days without food, these died after four days. It is likely that they contracted pneumonia because their resistance was low. Their respiratory quotient dropped slightly from the beginning of the experiment but stayed within the normal limit of .7 to 1 for the first three days. It plunged sharply just before the animals died. Oxygen consumption, however, decreased at a constant

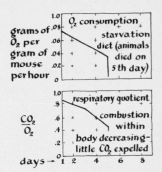

55

Metabolic graphs of starved mice

rate throughout the period of observation. At the conclusion of the experiment I plotted graphs of both oxygen consumption and respiratory quotient [*see Fig. 55*].

In the second group of mice a 17 per cent solution of ethyl alcohol was substituted for water. Each mouse also received one gram of rabbit pellets per day beginning on February 26. On March 4 I found the mice shivering and huddled together in their cage. Fearing that they might die if a test were attempted, I fed them immediately and wrapped them in warm rags. Their ration was doubled for two days and then lowered to a gram and a half on the third day. One mouse died on March 9 and another the following day. I attempted to study the remaining two in the metabolism cage but their rate of respiration was so low that no results were detectable at the end of a two-hour run.

According to a doctor friend whom I consulted during the experiments, the mice in this group died of semi-starvation and extreme intoxication ending in pneumonia and shock. The oxygen consumption of the group increased sharply during the first three days of the test, dropped for two days and then climbed gradually to a peak just before the animals died. The respiratory quotient, although low, remained within normal limits almost to the end. A restricted diet with an excess of alcohol causes fat to accumulate in the liver and retard some of its functions. The results of this experiment were also plotted in graphs [*Fig. 56*].

On February 27 a group of four mice was started on a mixture of

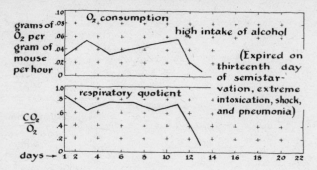

56
Graphs showing metabolic reaction of mice to alcohol

powdered rabbit pellets into which .1 per cent of desiccated thyroid gland had been mixed. Because this medication stimulates the thyroid the mice, which were permitted to eat as much as they would consume, gained weight steadily during the experiment. At one point the apparatus developed a defect and two mice suffocated. I continued with the remaining pair. Oxygen consumption appeared to drop during the final days of the experiment, but this too may have been due to a defect in the apparatus. The respiratory quotient remained below normal almost from the beginning and indicated no trend [*Fig. 57*].

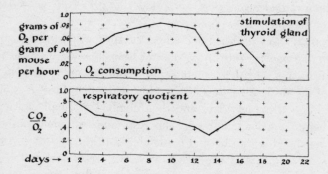

57
Plot of metabolic reaction to stimulated thyroid glands in mice

140

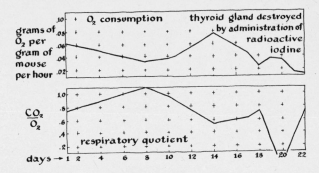

58

Graph of metabolic reaction of mice to the gradual suppression of thyroid gland activity

The final group of three mice was injected with 100 microcuries of radioactive iodine (I-131) on February 26. This proved to be an overdose which destroyed the thyroid gland in about four weeks. The injections were administered in a medical laboratory, where the mice were kept for three days. Upon their return they were supplied with as much water and rabbit pellets as they would consume.

The outward appearance of the group did not change during the period of the test. Oxygen consumption fell gradually during the first eight days and then increased to about double the minimum value on the 14th day. Thereafter it dropped more or less gradually to 10 per cent of its initial value on the 22nd day. The respiratory quotient also varied widely during the experiment but showed a gradual decrease until the final day of the run, when it shot up from a near zero value to normal [*Fig. 58*]. These changes were expected because the thyroid was slowly deteriorating and its production dropped in proportion.

5

CHROMATOGRAPHY

By washing a mixture of complex substances through a glass tube packed with a powdered absorbent such as calcium carbonate, you can separate and recover the constituents. In the following experiment this analytical technique — one of the most powerful known to biochemists — is used to separate chlorophyll from spinach leaves

WITHIN THE PAST 10 YEARS thousands of amateurs have discovered the fascination of chromatography, or "adsorption analysis," as the process is sometimes called. Despite the fact that the Russian botanist Michael Tswett described the chromatographic method in 1906, it did not come into general use even among professionals until 1930. In less than two decades chromatography has opened new avenues to knowledge, created new industries, expanded old ones and made substantial contributions to the health and well-being of millions.

No description of the chromatographic method has surpassed in clarity or conciseness that originally set down by Tswett: "If a petroleum ether solution of chlorophyll is filtered through a column of an adsorbent (I use mainly calcium carbonate which is stamped firmly into a narrow glass tube), then the pigments, according to the adsorption sequence, are resolved from top to bottom into various colored zones like light rays in the spectrum, so the different components of a pigment mixture are resolved on the calcium carbonate column according to a law and can be estimated on it qualitatively and quantitatively. Such a preparation I term a chromatogram, and the corresponding method, the chromatographic method. It is self-evident that the adsorption phenomena described are not restricted to chlorophyll pigments, and one must assume that all kinds of colored and colorless chemical compounds are subject to the same laws."

In essence chromatography requires only three pieces of apparatus: a container for holding the sample, the chromatic column and a second container for catching the spent liquid as it drips from the bottom of the tube. After the column has been packed with adsorbing material, a portion of the sample solution is poured in at the top of the tube. This is allowed to percolate down the column for perhaps a tenth to a quarter of its length. In doing so it usually forms a solid band of color characteristic of the solution under investigation. Clear solvent is then washed down the column, and the process of separation begins. Each substance has a characteristic affinity for the solvent and for the adsorbent. Chromatographers commonly refer to this property as the adsorbent's or solvent's "activity." The activity ratio determines the position a particular substance will occupy on the column relative to others in the mixture from which it is being separated. Substances most weakly held in solution and most strongly attracted to the adsorbent will adhere to the uppermost particles of the column. Those less strongly attracted to the adsorbent will be washed down farther, the distance depending upon each substance's relative adsorption ratio, and the separated substances will form a characteristic pattern of bands in the column. Extracts prepared from some green leaves, for example, show more than 20 distinct bands, ranging from dark green through various shades of orange, pink, yellow and delicate violet to white, the colors identifying the various xanthophylls, flavoxanthins, luteins, carotenes and related pigments.

The operation of washing the column with clear solvent is known as "development." As fresh solvent flows down the column, some molecules detach themselves from the adsorbent, join the solution and move down to regions of less concentration. Here they are readsorbed. The activity of both the solvent and adsorbent appears to vary with the concentration of the substance under analysis; hence a given substance may pass out of and into solution many times in the course of its journey down the column. At first the bands are narrow and bunched near the top of the column. As development continues, all the bands progress toward the bottom and grow wider and more distinctly separated. A fully developed chromatogram displays a series of distinct, cleanly separated bands, varying in width in proportion to the amount of each substance in the mixture.

The separated, purified substances can then be extracted in one of two ways: either by washing the successive bands out of the bottom of the column with solvent, or by pushing the cylinder of adsorbent out of the tube, separating the bands with a knife and removing the substance with a solvent. If the chromatogram is sucked to dryness, it slips readily from the tube. Some workers scoop the adsorbent out of the tube one band at a time with a slender spatula.

Thousands of different adsorbents and solvents have been tried. The selection of the most effective combination for each purpose remains largely a matter of cut and try. The following lists of adsorbents and solvents, which will resolve most of the mixtures the amateur is likely to prepare, were drawn up by William T. Beaver, a student at Princeton University and winner of a Westinghouse Science Talent Search award. The adsorbents are listed in approximate order of decreasing activity; the solvents, in the reverse order:

ADSORBENTS

1. Activated alumina
2. Charcoal
3. Magnesia
4. Silica gel
5. Lime
6. Magnesium carbonate
7. Calcium carbonate
8. Sodium carbonate
9. Talc
10. Powdered sugar

SOLVENTS

1. Petroleum ether
2. Carbon tetrachloride
3. Carbon disulfide
4. Ether
5. Acetone
6. Benzene
7. Methyl or ethyl alcohol
8. Water
9. Organic acids
10. Aqueous solutions of acids or bases

Sometimes more than one solvent may be used, either in combination or successively. For example, a small amount of benzene may be mixed with the weakly active solvent petroleum ether to speed up the development of bands. Care must be exercised, however, not to make the solvent so active that it washes the bands from the column immediately. After the bands of a cylinder of adsorbent have been cut into blocks, they may be treated with a strongly active solvent for the swift and complete extraction of the principal substances. This is called elution, and the solvent or combination of solvents used for this purpose is the "eluent." Most of the common adsorbents and solvents are inexpensive; some are found in nearly every home. Beaver advises the beginner to purchase chromatographic supplies from a chemical supply house. Those found in the home are likely to be contaminated, and a minute amount of foreign matter can confuse the result. Chromatography is an extremely sensitive technique, comparable in its field with the classic knife-edge test used by amateur telescope makers.

"The very fact," says Beaver, "that there are few fixed ground rules recommends chromatography as an avocation. Not even the most advanced professional can prescribe a hard and fast procedure for setting up and operating a chromatic column. The field is so new that it is open to all comers. The amateur has a good chance of making a worthwhile contribution to the technique."

The glass column may range from a fraction of an inch to several inches in diameter, depending upon the coarseness of the adsorbent, the nature of the substance to be adsorbed, the quantity of material available and like considerations. Most workers prefer to use tubes somewhat less than an inch in diameter. Usually the column is 10 times as high as it is wide. For the separation of some isotopes, however, slender tubes 100 feet or more in length have been used. The bottom of the tube is pinched in and stoppered with a tuft of cotton or glass wool to provide support for the adsorbent. Such tubes are available through most chemical supply houses, but they may be made readily at home from glass tubing.

Most of the difficulty experienced by beginners arises from failure to pack the column uniformly. Unless the adsorbent is evenly distributed, the bands are likely to be ragged and overlap. Tswett put in dry, powdered adsorbent a little at a time, and tamped each bit firmly into place until the column reached the desired length. Subsequent experience has modified his procedure in numerous ways. After a layer is packed into place, the surface may be loosened somewhat with a spatula so the succeeding one will join it more uniformly. Ordinary wooden dowel stock, squared at the end and slightly smaller than the inside diameter of the tubing, makes a good tamping tool. Some adsorbents settle into place satisfactorily if the tube is merely jarred while being slowly filled. Other adsorbents can be introduced in the form of a mud or paste, suction being applied simultaneously. Chromatographers agree that packing the column is an art. Like all arts, its mastery comes largely through practice.

Most workers use the standard tests that have been devised to choose appropriate solvents and adsorbents for specific jobs. One of the most popular consists in placing about a teaspoonful of adsorbent in a shallow dish, shaking it into a wedge-shaped layer on the bottom, dissolving the mixture to be tested in a weak solvent, putting a few drops of this on the thin edge of the adsorbent with a micropipette, and then trying various solvents and combinations of solvents in order of increasing activity [*see Fig. 59*].

Amateurs who get into this field will undoubtedly come sooner or later to paper chromatography, which makes the whole thing easier. The "column" in this case is a strip or sheet of paper, enclosed in a saturated atmosphere to prevent evaporation. The paper is moistened with solvent, and then a drop of the solution to be analyzed is applied to the upper edge or an upper corner of the sheet. The

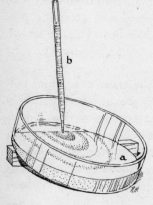

59
Convenient method of testing solvents and adsorbents

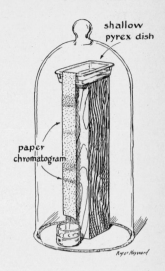

shallow
pyrex dish

paper
chromatogram

60
Chromatography with paper strip
(enclosed to retard evaporation)

sheet is then bent over and dipped into a shallow dish of the solvent
to be used for development. The solvent flows down the hanging
sheet by capillary action, carrying the substances to be resolved
with it. These adsorb as spots along the paper — the counterparts
of bands in the conventional column. When development has carried the lowest spot close to the bottom, the sheet may be removed
from the solvent, rotated 90 degrees and reinserted. Each spot then
becomes the point of origin for a new chromatogram. If the resolved fractions are comprised of subtle mixtures, the components
of each fraction will array themselves across the sheet. What you
have then is a "two-dimensional" chromatogram as shown in Figure 60.

Tswett likened the bands on his column to the rays of colored
light emerging from a prism in a series of colors. The two-dimensional chromatogram carries the analogy further by subjecting each
"ray" to a second analysis, with increased resolution comparable
with that achieved optically when physicists pass a colored light
from one prism through a second. Many amateurs use the paper
technique as a test method for identifying the fractions of a mixture
qualitatively and follow it with a conventional column for quantitative determination.

As Tswett predicted, the chromatographic method resolves color-less fractions just as readily as colored ones. During recent years much work has been done in colorless chromatography. Many tech-niques have been developed to make these substances visible. The presence of amino acids, for example, is detected by spraying the extruded adsorbent, or the paper chromatogram, with ninhydrin, which turns these normally colorless substances a light purple. Other substances fluoresce under ultraviolet light. If a drop of or-dinary blue-black ink is placed on a strip of chromatographic paper and developed with alcohol, several bluish bands, representing the ink's content of iron compounds and dyestuffs, form along the length of the strip. Under an ultraviolet lamp the dried paper shows many other bands, ranging in color through the reds, oranges and greens. With a second chromatogram using a known substance as a control, one may identify an unknown (but suspected) substance by comparing the positions of the respective bands on the chromato-grams. In a chromatographic column colorless fractions may also be detected by their differential blending of light transmitted through the column or by polarization of the light. Recently some substances have been tagged by radioactive isotopes and detected by photo-graphic processes, but these techniques generally lie beyond reach of the facilities commanded by the average amateur.

The extraction of the chlorophylls, carotenes and xanthophylls from spinach leaves can serve as a highly colorful introduction to the chromatographic technique. The following experiment, sug-gested by Beaver, should be made in a well ventilated room be-cause the solvents are highly volatile and inflammable. Moreover, fumes from one, wood alcohol, are poisonous.

Into columns made of 10-millimeter glass tubing about a foot long, fire-polished at one end and flared at the other to facilitate filling, is packed the adsorbent (Merck's alumina standardized according to Brockmann, of 80 to 200 mesh). It is packed in suc-cessive small portions while jarring the tube. Suction materially re-duces the development time; Roger Hayward's drawing [*Fig. 61*] shows how to set up the column for use with a vacuum flask. An alternative, omitting the vacuum provision, is shown in Figure 62.

Ten grams of dried spinach leaves are steeped in 100 milliliters

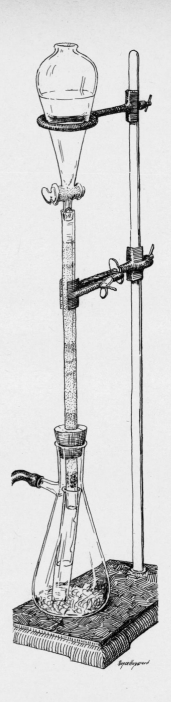

62
A chromatograph column
arranged for gravity feed

61
A vacuum chromatograph column

of wood alcohol for 24 hours. The material is then filtered and the residue is washed with an additional 50 milliliters of wood alcohol. This extract is shaken with 50 milliliters of petroleum ether; 100 milliliters of water are added, and the solution is placed in a separatory funnel. After a distinct separation has taken place, the lower alcohol-water layer is discarded, and the upper petroleum ether layer, containing the extract, is filtered.

You run about half of this extract into the column of alumina and then develop the column with benzene. The first fraction to pass down the column is a fairly narrow yellow-orange band of carotene. It is followed by much wider pink and yellow bands of xanthophylls. These are familiar pigments that cause wooded countrysides to take on the colors of fall after frost has killed the chlorophyll. Fractions of these pigments may be collected as they emerge from the bottom of the column and evaporated to dryness. The two groups (carotenes and xanthophylls) may then be further resolved into their components by dissolving them in a few milliliters of petroleum ether, passing them through fresh columns and developing with benzene-petroleum ether or, for greater eluent activity, with pure benzene.

In the column the chlorophylls form a dark green band. The band is scooped from the column; the pigments are washed out with five milliliters of wood alcohol, and the solution is filtered. The filtrate is put in a separatory funnel with five cubic centimeters of petroleum ether, and five milliliters of water is added. The petroleum ether extracts the chlorophylls, and the water and alcohol form a separate layer which can be poured off. Then the petroleum ether extract is washed several times with water and run through a column packed with powdered sugar (sucrose) in the form of a slurry with petroleum ether. Now you develop the column with petroleum ether. The chlorophylls separate into two components — a yellow-dark-green band of beta-chlorophyll near the top of the column and a bluish-green band of alpha-chlorophyll farther down.

Because of its vital role in photosynthesis, chlorophyll has become the glamor plant-pigment in popular imagination. But many amateur chromatographers find the carotenes just as interesting. Unlike the chlorophylls, which act as catalysts, the carotenes play a direct chemical role, both in animals and plants. They appear to be essential to the body's manufacture of vitamin A, and they play a part in the mechanisms of vision and sex. As the name implies they may be extracted from carrots.

To extract carotene you grind five grams of dried carrot root to dust in a mortar and then add 50 milliliters of a mixture of equal parts of wood alcohol and petroleum ether. Shake the mixture thoroughly, add five milliliters of water and pour into a separatory funnel. The carotenes, plus xanthophyll esters, are concentrated in the petroleum ether layer that forms at the top. Separate this layer and concentrate it by evaporating some of the fluid, leaving 20 milliliters. Then add three milliliters of a solution of 5 per cent sodium hydroxide in wood alcohol, which saponifies the xanthophyll esters so they can be removed by washing. Wash the mixture several times with 85 per cent wood alcohol in water; then wash several times with pure water to remove traces of wood alcohol.

Now let the petroleum ether separate from the water and then filter it. The yellow-orange solution that remains bears the complex of carotenes. To separate them, pass about half of the solution into a column of alumina and develop the column with a mixture of benzene and petroleum ether in the ratio of 1 to 3. You will get three well-defined bands, containing, from the top down, gamma carotene, beta carotene and alpha carotene. You can recover the pigments either by washing them successively out of the column or by extracting them from the separate bands of adsorbent with wood alcohol.

Chromatography is a far more subtle method of separation than the traditional chemical techniques of distillation, precipitation with reagents, and crystallization. Fortunately for amateurs, it is also a method of beautiful simplicity.

6

ZONE ELECTROPHORESIS

When a solution of chemical compounds is applied to an electrified sheet of porous paper, each compound migrates in the electrical field at a rate and in a direction determined by its own characteristic charge. Amateurs can use this phenomenon for analyzing chemical mixtures of extreme subtlety. The construction of a simple apparatus and its use are described

WITHIN RECENT YEARS biochemists and others have acquired a powerful new tool for separating intimately related compounds: the electrophoresis apparatus. The word *electrophoresis* means "borne by electricity." In a broad sense the movement of charged pith balls in an electrostatic field is an electrophoretic effect. So is the Cottrell process for eliminating smoke particles from flue gases by passing them between electrodes of high potential difference. After picking up a charge from one electrode, the particles are attracted to the other, where they clump and fall into a collecting bin. The electrodeposition of colloidal rubber suspensions on electrodes of special shape — a process widely used in the manufacture of rubber gloves and other common articles — is another example.

But electrophoresis is the special name given to the technique of separating molecular mixtures into fractions. Most suspensions of molecules in water are charged and hence can conduct an electric current. Even molecules which normally do not carry a charge tend to adsorb ions from the water. Some molecules pick up more charge than others, depending upon their chemical nature and the concentration of ions in the solution.

If the ionic concentration (pH) is properly adjusted, all closely related molecules, such as those of the proteins, appear to adsorb charges of the same sign. Consequently when they are subjected to an electric field they migrate in the same direction, although at rates which vary with the amount of charge on each member of the family. Many amateur microscopists have observed such migration on a gross scale with objects such as blood cells or protozoa. If a voltage is applied across a drop containing cells in suspension, the cells will migrate. Alexander Reuss first described the experiment 148 years ago, and it was a favorite of Michael Faraday.

To analyze molecular mixtures, the Swedish chemist Arne Tiselius hit upon a radically different scheme. He poured the material to be studied into the bottom of a U-shaped tube and carefully laid a buffered solution on top in each arm of the U so that sharp boundaries formed between the mixture and buffer. When a current was passed through the three-part solution, the material under analysis migrated down one arm of the U and up the other. Each of its fractions moved at a characteristic rate. The boundaries of each fraction were made visible by an elaboration of the schlieren optical technique devised by Léon Foucault for testing the figure of parabolic mirrors and lenses. Like the ruling engine for making diffraction gratings, the Tiselius technique of "free" electrophoresis is simple in principle. Like the ruling engine, too, the method appears easy until you set up the apparatus and try to make it work! In this domain the gifted professional appears safe from amateur challenge.

A less precise yet powerful method of zone electrophoresis has found wide application during the past ten years and the following description of it has been made possible through the cooperation of H. G. Kunkle of the Rockefeller Institute. In the zone method, particles move in liquid that fills the spaces of a finely divided solid instead of a U-tube. Molecules of like kind migrate as distinct zones which can easily be identified and recovered as purified products. Porous solids of many kinds can serve as the medium. One medium frequently used is filter paper. Zone electrophoresis thus bears a superficial resemblance to partition chromatography. The electrophoretic separation, however, depends not upon the properties of solubility and adsorption, as in the case of chromatography, but upon the electrical charge carried by the molecules of the substance that is being analyzed.

The amount and sign of the charge picked up by compounds in

solution depend both upon the chemical nature of the compound and upon the pH, or acid-alkaline balance, of the solvent. Molecules which normally carry a weak charge, such as the slightly alkaline proteins, are highly sensitive to changes in pH. A small shift in acidity or alkalinity can cause a substantial change in the rate at which such particles migrate and may even reverse the direction of their movement. One therefore selects for the solution electrolytes (sources of charge) which have a "buffering" action: that is, which tend to supply positive and negative ions to the solution at a rate precisely offsetting that at which ions are removed or dissipated. Many common salts have a strong buffering action, although table salt (sodium chloride) is not one of them.

If you take up electrophoresis you will have to find your own way through woods where few trees are blazed. Except for protein chemistry, you must develop your own electrolytes, buffers and solid media, and must find out by experiment just what voltages and current densities work best for the substance under analysis. The field of electrophoresis has barely been scratched. If you enjoy original work, you can dig in almost anywhere, certain that you are breaking fresh ground.

To give you a start, the essentials of an apparatus which uses filter paper as the solid medium are illustrated in Figure 63. You can set it up and put it into operation in a single evening.

The ends of the paper dip into two vessels containing an electrolytic solution connected through carbon electrodes to a source of direct current. To retard evaporation of the solution the paper is sandwiched between a pair of glass plates. The plates, about two inches wide and eight inches long, are cut from quarter-inch plate glass. As a safety precaution it is a good idea to round the edges and corners of the glass on either a whetstone (using water as a lubricant) or on a sheet of glass smeared with a slurry of carborundum.

It is desirable to maintain an even pressure of the glass on the filter paper, so that migration proceeds in a symmetrical and reproducible pattern. Pressure improves the sharpness of the zones, because it reduces the amount of fluid in the paper. However, if the pressure is too high, it will bend the glass and distort the zones. Some workers have attempted to solve the problem by using plates

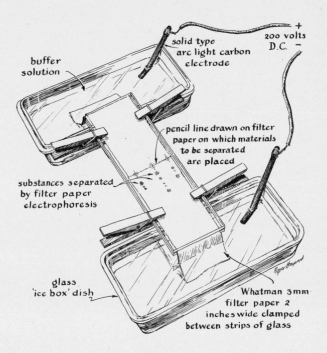

buffer solution

solid type arc light carbon electrode

+ 200 volts D.C. –

pencil line drawn on filter paper on which materials to be separated are placed

substances separated by filter paper electrophoresis

glass 'ice box' dish

Whatman 3mm filter paper 2 inches wide clamped between strips of glass

63
A simple setup for experimenting with zone electrophoresis

an inch or more thick. The bottom plate is supported by a flat base and the top one rests on the paper as a weight. Others suspend the paper from glass rods laid across the buffer vessels. The apparatus is then covered by a bell jar and operated in a buffer-saturated atmosphere. The latter method has the disadvantage that the buffer tends to gravitate toward the low point of the strip with consequent distortion of the pattern of separation.

Capillary effects between the glass plates and the paper also introduce some distortion. This is minimized by coating the plates with a thin film of grease. Vaseline will work, but not so well as silicone grease of the type used for lubricating the stopcocks of chemical glassware.

Glass containers of any convenient shape can be used as buffer

vessels. Heavy Pyrex icebox dishes, available from hardware dealers, work as well as specially made glassware. The principal considerations in the selection of containers are chemical inertness and
enough weight so the empty vessels will support the plates, paper
strip and clamps without upsetting.

Chemical inertness is a major consideration in the choice of electrodes. Most professionals use platinum, but carbon rods will work.
Avoid the cored carbons used in sun lamps. These cores are charged
with finely divided metal (to enrich the emission of ultraviolet rays)
and will contaminate the solution. Carbon electrodes from dry cell
batteries are ruled out for the same reason. Solid carbons designed
for low-intensity motion-picture projectors are good and can be procured from theater-supply dealers.

The amount of electric current needed varies with the substance
under analysis. A rectifier capable of operating between 50 and 300
volts at an output of 20 milliamperes will be ample for most work.
You may get a good rectifier from a junked radio receiver. Just connect a 40,000-ohm wire-wound resistor (of the type fitted with an
adjustable tap) across the filter condenser. The resistor should be of
at least the 10-watt size. Take the output from across the ground
side of the resistor and the tap. If no old radio set is at hand, you
can get the parts specified in the drawing [*Fig. 64*] from radio-sup-
ply dealers.

It is frequently desirable, particularly during the experimental
phase of analyzing unknown substances, to maintain either a constant voltage across the paper strip or a constant current through it.
Power supplies with automatic regulating features can be constructed, but they are costly and complex. Good results can be
achieved with a manual control. Substituting a continuously variable potentiometer for the tapped resistor makes adjustment easy,
and the knob will protect your fingers from the hot resistance
element. If the current is limited to 15 milliamperes or less the
rating of the potentiometer need not exceed 10 watts.

Almost any soft paper will demonstrate zone electrophoresis. You
can use strips cut from white blotters, paper towels, cleansing tissues,
even the unprinted parts of old newspapers. Clear, reproducible
patterns, however, require a specially made paper of uniform

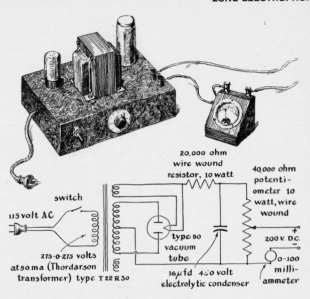

20,000 ohm
wire wound
resistor, 10 watt

40,000 ohm
potenti-
ometer 10
watt, wire
wound

switch

115 volt AC

type 80
vacuum
tube

200 V. D.C.

275-0-275 volts
at 50 ma (Thordarson
transformer) type T 22 R 30

16 μfd 450 volt
electrolytic condenser

0-100
milli-
ammeter

64
Power supply for zone electrophoresis apparatus

texture and free of contamination. A good paper is Whatman
3MM, supplied in 600-foot rolls by the Fisher Scientific Company
of New York City, which also has most of the chemicals used in
electrophoresis experiments. You can order the Fisher materials at
drug stores.

The separation of the artificial coloring used in a cheap wine is a
nice electrophoretic project for a beginner. You can make your own
mixture for analysis by adding a few drops of food coloring to grape
juice. For an electrolyte you can use a weak solution of common
salt buffered with a small amount of baking soda (sodium bicarbonate). Later you can investigate electrolytes made with other
salts, many of which provide their own buffering action.

Food coloring migrates nicely in an electric field of 25 volts per
inch at a current of 10 milliamperes. This means that the buffer-
moistened filter paper should have a resistance of about 2,500 ohms
per inch. To obtain this value of resistance you will have to experi-

ment with various dilutions of the electrolyte. Begin by drawing enough tap water to fill the icebox dishes to within half an inch of the top. Put all this water in one container and add a level teaspoon of salt. After it dissolves, immerse the paper strip in the solution. Remove the strip, blot it thoroughly and clamp it between the glass plates. Then pour the solution into the icebox dishes, suspend the ends of the paper in it, connect the power supply to the solution through the carbon electrodes and adjust the potentiometer or tapped resistor to the prescribed potential of 200 volts.

If the resulting current is less than 10 milliamperes, turn off the power, remove the strip, return the solution to the common container, add more salt and try again. Usually a level teaspoon of salt for each 12 ounces of water produces the desired conductivity, but the amount needed varies with the purity of the tap water. Finally add a quarter teaspoon of baking soda for each 12 ounces of solution. (It will affect the resistance only slightly.)

After you have an electrolyte with the proper resistance, draw a light pencil line across the middle of a fresh strip of filter paper, dip the strip into the buffered electrolyte, blot it and then apply a very small drop of wine to the pencil line with the blunt end of a tooth-pick. The wine should first be concentrated by letting it evaporate at room temperature to half or less of its normal volume. Now spread a film of grease on the inner faces of the glass plates. Clamp the paper between them, seal the edges of the plates with grease, immerse the protruding ends of the paper into the buffer and switch on the power.

If the wine sample contains artificial coloring, in about five minutes the edge of the wine spot nearest the anode should become sharper and the edge toward the cathode should grow fuzzier. Within an hour a blotch of dye, probably comet-shaped, will have migrated a substantial distance from the point of origin. As the process continues, comets of other colors, each a constituent of the dye, will trail the first one down the length of the paper as shown in Figures 65 and 66. The dye fractions in the wine should be fully resolved in about six hours. (The blotch made by the wine itself will move little, if at all.) By spacing drops along the pencil line you

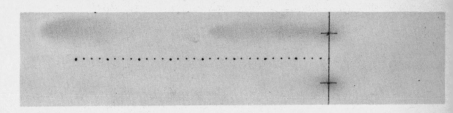

65
Electrophoresis separations of imported Chianti wine *(top)* and an inexpensive domestic Chianti to which coloring has been added *(bottom)*

can analyze several samples of fluid simultaneously on the same strip of paper.

The tendency of zones to smear, trail, assume comet shapes and otherwise depart from sharpness is one of the undesirable features of zone electrophoresis on filter paper. It represents a challenge to the experimenter. In general the drier you can run the filter paper (or other solid medium), the sharper the zones will be. Within limits dryness can be achieved by applying heavy pressure on the glass plates: in effect you try to squeeze out the buffer. The spots should be dry enough so that you can rub your hand across the

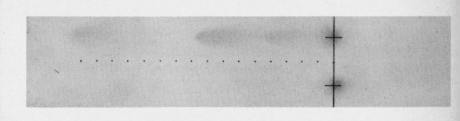

66
Electrophoretic analysis of pure grape juice *(top)* and grape juice colored with vegetable dyes *(bottom)*. Note migration of dyes

paper as it comes from the apparatus at the end of a run without smearing the pattern. The amateur who resolves the dilemma of applying enough pressure without bending the glass will make a contribution to science.

Substances which migrate more rapidly than others along the electrophoretic paper are said to have "high mobility." Mobility is determined in large part by the strength of ionization of the particles. Measuring the mobility of substances is an interesting project for beginners. You simply time the rate of migration of each substance along a scale ruled on the strip of paper, using a control buffer of a certain pH and concentration. Stains used for coloring organisms to show them under the microscope make nice test specimens. A particularly good series is eosin Y, methylene blue, basic fuchsin, malachite green, Bismarck brown, safranine and gentian violet. The chemical properties of these stains are listed in reference texts. Each migrates in a saline solution at a characteristic rate. Figure 67 shows the relative migration rates of positively ionized methylene blue (*top*) and basic fuchsin (*bottom*), and negatively ionized eosin Y (*middle*). These were resolved on filter paper with

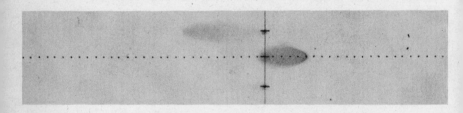

67
The migration of methylene blue *(top)* and basic fuchsin *(bottom)*

a saline solution buffered with sodium bicarbonate. The same test showed that the malachite green stain migrates an inch per hour at 70 degrees Fahrenheit under 200 volts and 10 milliamperes.

Amateurs who wish to have a go at something more sophisticated may enjoy trying to separate blood proteins. This entails the sacrifice of a few drops of blood. You will also need access to a centrifuge (to extract the serum from the blood), a few grams of the barbiturate veronal and a liter of 95 per cent ethyl alcohol.

Dampen the filter paper with barbital buffer adjusted to pH 8.6. After blotting the paper, deposit five thousandths of a milliliter of serum on the ruled strip with a calibrated micropipette. Then clamp the paper between the plates and seal it with silicone grease.

A potential of 15 volts per centimeter and a current of 15 milliamperes will resolve a specimen in five or six hours; however, the pattern may show traces of smearing. Four volts per centimeter and four milliamperes increases the time to 12 hours but yields sharper patterns. Blood-serum fractions are difficult to see. The albumin can be made more strikingly visible by labeling it with a few crystals of bromphenol blue. After the albumin has migrated an arbitrary distance, say seven centimeters, the paper is removed and dipped for two minutes into a solution of 95 per cent ethyl alcohol saturated with mercuric chloride, to which 1 per cent bromphenol blue is added. The strip will emerge from the stain a deep yellow. It is then washed repeatedly in water containing a thousandth part of acetic acid. On contact with water, the yellow changes to a deep blue. The color gradually disappears from the paper during washing but is retained by the protein fractions. Figures 68 and 69 show typical sepa-

68
The pattern of blood proteins from a normal individual

rations of blood proteins taken from two individuals, one in normal health and the other diseased. The density of the spots in each pattern indicates the amount of protein in each fraction. From right to left Figure 68 (normal serum) shows albumin, alpha-one globulin, alpha-two globulin, beta globulin and gamma globulin. The dense spot at the left in Figure 69 is characteristic of the bone disease

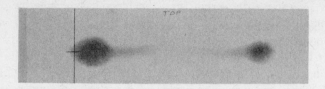

69
The pattern of blood proteins from an individual suffering from myeloma

myeloma. Other diseases produce characteristic patterns which serve as valuable aids in diagnosis.

The result of an amateur's first attempt to fractionate albumin (the white of chicken egg) is shown in Figure 70. The smeared pattern explains this experimenter's passion for anonymity. Here the buffer was salt, baking soda and water.

A number of techniques have been devised for making quantitative measurements of protein patterns. In one the strip is sectioned into eighth-inch segments. The dye in each is then quantitatively eluted in a two milliliter solution of 1 per cent N-sodium hydroxide and read, after an hour or so, on a colorimeter. The resulting values are plotted as points. The smooth curve drawn through them is equivalent to the curve derived by free electrophoresis.

As mentioned earlier, zone electrophoresis is not limited to filter paper. It is interesting to compare the behavior of a given test substance and buffer in media compounded of starch grains, silica gel,

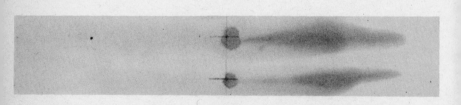

70
An amateur's first attempt to fractionate the white of an egg

activated alumina and similar materials, as well as the reaction of various buffers with respect to a given medium. A slab of starch, for example, is easy to prepare. Put a pound of potato starch into a sieve lined with filter paper. Wash the starch for 30 minutes and pour it as a batter into a rectangular mold. The slab (about ⅜ inch thick) is then thoroughly blotted, and with suitable carbon electrodes it can be used in principle just like filter paper. The only limit to variations in the physical arrangement of the apparatus is set by the ingenuity of the worker. It is possible, for example, to adapt electrophoresis for the continuous separation of material in gross amounts. At least one amateur telescope maker prepares colloidal rouge by means of continuous electrophoretic separation. Buffer is allowed to flow down a wide strip of filter paper by capillary attraction. It drips from the bottom edge of the paper into a container below. The rouge mixture is fed onto the paper from a continuously flowing micropipette near the top. Electrical contact is made with the edges of the strip through wicks saturated by buffer. Fractions not ionized flow down the strip vertically. Ionized fractions take a diagonal course, the steepness of which depends upon the strength of the ionization. A scallop is cut into the bottom of the strip in line with each fraction, and collecting vessels are placed beneath the points.

IV.
THE NATURAL SCIENCES

1

"NATURE'S UNIMPORTANT PUZZLES"

About a great amateur naturalist, Walker Van Riper

IN APPRAISING THE CONTRIBUTIONS to science of the late Walker Van Riper, a retired investment banker of Denver, Colorado, who devoted his final years to nature study, A. M. Bailey, director of the Denver Museum of Natural History, has said, "Van Riper was the perfect answer to the small museum director's prayer. You couldn't possibly pay him what his extraordinary skills were worth, yet he did the job simply for the joy of doing it — and did it better than anyone else could have done it."

Van Riper made a hobby "of investigating nature's unimportant puzzles," as he liked to say — of pecking away at question marks among animals which make no difference to man one way or the other. With his high-speed camera, for example, he proved that rattlesnakes do not bite. They stab. He also exploded the popular belief that the deer fly can break the sonic barrier. His precisely timed photographs of the creature in flight show that many common insects can easily outstrip it. At the time of Van Riper's death in 1960 he was deeply involved in the question: When a housefly lands on the ceiling does it execute a wing-over, a slow roll or a half loop? Of all his many projects, however, perhaps none was more fascinating than his continuing investigation of hummingbirds.

2

THE DELIGHTS OF
HUMMINGBIRD STUDY

No bird is more amenable to intimate observation and few pose more unanswered questions. The late Walker Van Riper devised brilliant techniques for attracting hummingbirds and studying their habits. Here are some of his methods, described in his words

PROBABLY NO OTHER BIRD is so amenable to intimate observation as the hummingbird. Fairly accurate answers can be obtained to such questions as: What does it eat and how much? How fast and in what manner does it fly? What is its size and weight? How are the young cared for? Besides its convenience as a subject, the hummingbird is the most beautiful, vivacious, bold and, in my opinion, by far the most interesting of birds.

These words may sound a bit extravagant, but they are well backed by authority. John Gould, the great British ornithologist of the 19th century, loved the hummers beyond all other birds. His five-volume *A Monograph of the Trochilidæ, or Humming-Birds* testifies to this. Eugène Simon, head of the Entomological Society of France, produced a highly valuable work on the classification of hummingbirds which took 30 years in the making. Simon had dedicated his life to the study of spiders, but during an expedition to Venezuela to collect spiders he was "seduced" by the hummingbirds and decided thereafter to divide his labors between his first love and his second. Considering that there are some 600 species of the Trochilidæ, more than in any other bird family, their taxonomy is no mean task. In fact there is a word for a specialist on hummingbirds: "trochilidist."

Hummingbirds belong exclusively to the New World. Most

of the species are tropical. Only 14 breed regularly in the U. S. On the eastern slope of the Rockies in Colorado we have three species — the broadtailed, the rufous and the calliope. The first is *the* hummer of this area, nesting in the mountains, the foothills and in city gardens. It is very similar to the ruby-throated hummingbird, the only species seen in the eastern half of the country.

The rufous and calliope hummingbirds show up here only during their return migration to Mexico from the north, where they breed in the summer. The rufous probably has the longest migratory movement of any hummingbird: it nests as far north as southern Alaska. It also has another distinction: it was first described by none other than Captain Cook. On his third and last voyage he was given some rufous hummers by the natives of Vancouver Island.

Usually by mid-July a fair number of the migrants from the north arrive here. The mature males come first and stay only two weeks or so. They are followed by females and the young. The young males often stay into September, sometimes outstaying the resident broadtails. The calliope is the smallest of our hummers, weighing about 2.5 grams — the weight of a dime. You could send about a dozen of them by first-class mail for a four-cent stamp!

The amenability of hummingbirds to close-up observation and experiment is due primarily to the fact that they are extraordinarily fearless, probably because they have no natural enemies of importance. Coupled with their eagerness for food and readiness to accept artificial food, this makes them excellent laboratory residents.

The artificial food for hummers is a syrup comparable to the flower nectar on which they usually feed. Hummingbird fanciers have a great variety of notions about the best kind of syrup. I once made a preference test with a mature female broadtail. I set up a series of bottles side by side with different mixtures: sugar solutions in water at various concentrations; sugar, orange juice and water; honey and water; honey, orange juice and water. The bird showed a clear preference for the syrup made of one part sugar to one part water (*i.e.*, equal proportions by weight). Incidentally, the feeding bottles were in my garden: to keep out

71
Apparatus setup used in weighing a hummingbird

bees and wasps the aluminum cap had only a tiny hole (an eighth of an inch) which was big enough for the hummingbird's bill; to keep out ants I smeared a band of sticky material around each bottle.

I next set up an experiment to determine the amount of syrup consumed daily by my bird, together with its relationship to her weight. The hummer fed from a single botttle while resting on a wire perch hanging from a postal scale [see Fig. 71]. By remote control I tripped a camera to photograph the scale reading and record the weight of the bird. It averaged 4.3 grams (less than one sixth of an ounce), and the bird consumed each day an average of 1.8 grams of sugar — 42 per cent of her weight.

Intake of fuel at this rate is astonishing. Oliver Pearson has shown that the hummingbird has the highest metabolic rate of any warm-blooded animal so far measured. In calories my bird ate 1.7 calories of sugar per gram of its body weight per day — more than 30 times the daily rate of food intake needed by a man doing moderately hard physical labor. And this bird by no means limited her feeding to my bottle: she also ate insects and flower nectar each day!

For several years I maintained a hummingbird feeding station in a bit of rough yellow-pine and scrub-oak country on a ranch 25 miles south of Denver, where it is possible to assemble many more birds than can be attracted to a single city garden. I was able one summer to take a cenus of the hummingbird population on the ranch.

Early in May I put out some feeders of a new type designed by Erwin Brown [see Fig. 72]. It was made of a five-ounce jelly

72
Broadtail hummingbirds surround the feeder used in a population experiment. A male is at the right; a female, at the left

container with a red lock-top. A hole in the center of the lid admits the neck of a pop bottle, and four eighth-inch holes are spaced around the perimeter. These holes admit the hummingbird bill, but not bees or wasps. The lid is fastened to the bottle with a couple of three-quarter-inch hose washers, one above and one below. The bottle is filled, the cup fastened to the lid, then the whole is inverted and hung. There is little evaporation, and it may be assumed that the entire output of this feeder goes to hummingbirds alone.

On June 20 I had half a dozen of these feeders distributed in an area about a mile square. I estimated that the number of hummers, all broadtails, then feeding at my station was 66. A few nests had been found and, judging from these, most of the hens in the area were sitting on eggs at the time. By July 11, as these hatched, the population rose to 118.

At this point the first migrating rufous appeared. The coming of the first male rufous is always an exciting event, for he is spectacularly beautiful. The rufous is sometimes called the golden hummingbird. His back is the color of burnished copper, and he has a gorget (throat patch) which is described as "of a surpassingly vivid fiery red or metallic scarlet changing to crimson, golden and even brassy green." The metallic shine and changing hues of the gorget are due to refraction and reflection of the light by minute elements in the structure of the scale feathers.

The rufous is the most pugnacious and aggressive of our hummers. A bit smaller than the broadtail, but meaner, he takes little time to demonstrate who is boss. Within 24 hours after arrival the rufous males have taken over command of every feeding bottle. In flight they make a distinct buzz, like that of a bumblebee, in contrast to the whistle of the male broadtail. The young male broadtail at first flies with a hum, like his mother, but he acquires whistling wing slots when his second set of feathers develops.

With the coming of the migrants my hummingbird population jumped to 132. As more broadtail young joined the feeders, it increased gradually to a high of 166 on July 24. The population then declined steadily and was down to 70 by the end of the month. It stayed at that level for most of August, dropped to 39 by September 4 and to zero by the 11th.

During July, when the population was at its peak, I occasionally supplied only a single feeder, generally a red bowl, in order to concentrate the birds for observation and pictures. This often brought together a flock of 25 or 30 hummers — fighting, chasing, diving and investigating around the bowl. When I sat in my car, some would fly in the window and hover a foot from my nose to look me over. When I put up my photographic apparatus, the birds investigated the camera, lights, lens — everything shiny, and especially everything red. If I held the red bowl in my hands, half a dozen birds would alight on my hands or the rim of the bowl to feed at once [*see Figures 73 and 74*].

73
Hummingbirds show no fear. Male broadtail on right; female, left

74
The hummingbird makes an ideal subject for amateur study

It was an easy matter to get pictures of my subjects in all positions — flying, feeding, sitting. Exact positioning is important,
especially for color shots of the brilliant male gorgets, which flash
in full glory only when the bird is turned toward the light and
head-on to the camera. The photography of hummingbirds is a
highly interesting art. A few of my friends and I have formed the
most exclusive of all scientific societies — the Society of Trochilidographers (photographers of hummingbirds). The art requires
the special high-speed electronic flash invented by H. E. Edger-
ton of the Massachusetts Institute of Technology. An exposure
of one 5,000th of a second will stop a hummingbird's wings fairly
well; a 20,000th of a second stops them cold. We usually use three
lights — two at the camera and one on the background, which
would be black without it. Color, as well as black and white, is
practical and successful with this setup.

The pictures on these pages showing hummingbirds in flight

were made at a 20,000th of a second. One of them is a rare photograph of a male calliope [*see Fig. 75*]. This little rascal is rather uncommon in our parts, only a few coming through in migration. I had not had more than a bare glimpse of two or three and had never got a chance at a picture until R. J. Niedrach, curator of birds at the Denver Museum, discovered one feeding on a patch of matrimony vine last summer.

75
Male calliope hummingbird, showing the gorget streaked with white

We tried every trick in our repertoire to introduce the calliope to a feeding bottle, but he was single-mindedly intent on the matrimony vine and would not be enticed. So I finally had to set up my camera and lights near a prominent plant and wait him out. I made myself as comfortable as possible with a camp chair and umbrella (it was hot) and sat 25 or 30 feet away with a remote-control button in my hand. In a week's waiting I managed to get three or four good shots. I had to take him on a dark background, because a background light spooked him just enough to keep him away from the target spot.

There is an old argument about whether a hummingbird can fly backward. The Duke of Argyll, in a Victorian work of some merit, held that it was physically impossible for any bird to do this and that observations to the effect that the hummingbird did were purely illusory. The dispute is comparable to the modern one about whether a baseball curves. In both cases the high-speed flash has given a clear answer: a curve can be thrown; the hummingbird can fly backward.

One of our pictures shows the hummingbird in the act [*Fig. 76*]. Three flashes were set off in rapid succession. We used a black velvet background — an essential in multiple-exposure photography. The camera shutter was open for a few seconds. The first flash shows its bill dipped in the feeding bottle and starting to withdraw backward; the next two catch it backing up.

A pair of successive flashes can determine the speed of a flying bird, and three or more will give both speed and acceleration. C. H. Greenewalt, a member of our society, has published some interesting results for nuthatches and chickadees flying to and away from a feeding table. These measurements are of some importance, for ornithological literature is loaded with inaccurate and contradictory figures. I recently looked up the speed of the duck hawk in three natural history books which happened to be lying on my reading table. One gave the speed as 80 miles per hour, another 180 and the third 270! My own incomplete experiments have so far failed to show the duck hawk diving at more than 57 miles per hour.

Various speeds have been reported for the flight of the hum-

76
Repetitive flash shows hummingbird flying backward from left to right

mingbird. My guess is that most of these are greatly exaggerated. In this field it is fairly safe to assume that the better the observation, the slower the speed. Ordinary experience shows that we are very likely to overestimate the velocity of small objects nearby. A bee seems to zip past your nose at bullet-like speed, but it actually does not exceed 10 miles per hour.

The dive-bombing flight of the male broadtail hummer probably shows him at his greatest speed. A well-known ornithologist once told me that he thought this was the highest velocity attained by any bird. A male broadtail in courtship display before a female flies past her, generally near the ground, soars straight up 40 to 50 feet, poises there for a moment, and then swoops down past her and soars again, tracing a deep U-shaped arc. He repeats this performance several times. His fast power dive produces a loud tinkling whistle, which rises in pitch with increasing wingbeat until he reaches his greatest velocity at the bottom of the dive.

I set up my camera with the electronic flash timed to go off twice, the interval being a hundredth of a second. This system works satisfactorily to time the diving speed of a barn swallow, but in many trials I was unable to get an accurate measure of the hummer's dive. You have to be a super wing-shot to hit a diving hummer on the nose.

I was, however, able to get a good measure of the hummer's speed in straightaway flight as one chased another away from his feeding bottle. This maneuver looks faster than it really is; actually it does not exceed the hummer's speed in ordinary level flight. In 14 measurements the chasing speed ranged from around 18 to 29.2 miles per hour [*Fig. 77*]. I think the reason it does not go higher may be that the bird is slowing up as it approaches the intruder, the objective being not to hit him but to make him fly away.

I attacked the problem of the diving speed in another way, without the camera. I noticed that a female would often perch on a bush near a feeding cup, and this pause would stimulate a male to do his stuff. The male generally soared to the height of the highest tree at the place before diving. After measuring the height of the tree, I timed a considerable number of dives by different birds with a stop watch. Assuming that the velocity reached at the bottom of the dive is twice the average for the whole dive, I calculated the hummer's top speed to be 61.2 miles per hour.

The hummingbird has been called the most aerial of all birds. It never walks or hops. To turn around on a perch, it takes wing for the turn. If it wishes to move half an inch to one side, it flies there. Sometimes a mother bird will even feed its nestlings on the wing, hovering above the baby instead of alighting on the nest. In order to photograph this I had to lower a nest from a tree to a convenient position near the ground. I sawed off a limb containing a nest of fledglings 25 feet up on a yellow pine, and with ropes I lowered the limb by four stages on successive days

77
Broadtail male hummingbird photographed at speed of 29.2 miles per hour while chasing an interloper from a feeding cup

[*Fig. 78*]. The little hen was a bit disturbed by all this, but not too much.

I have tried this nest-lowering stunt several times. It can be done with other birds, but I know of none that will sit as tight as the hummer sometimes does. After I got the limb down to a convenient level, I found that to train my camera on the nest I had to move a branch on the upper side of the nest out of the way. I sawed it through and attached a hinge, so that it could be kept in the accustomed position but could be swung out of the way when I wanted to take pictures of the nest. It turned out that this fold-back of the branch excited the hen just enough so that she fed her babies on the wing more often than not. All of which was just what I wanted [*Fig. 79*].

78
Lowering a hummingbird nest. (*Note: The nest is at right inside the fork of two limbs*)

79
A female hummingbird feeds her young while hovering

The broadtail hen builds the nest, incubates the eggs and raises the babies with no assistance of any kind from the male. In fact, there is some evidence that she selects the nest site and starts building before she picks out a mate, and after the briefest possible association with him, returns to the nest and resumes her domestic duties. The mating is so brief that in many years of hummingbird watching I have never seen it, and it has been seen only a few times by others. These little birds are independent individuals: save for the mother's care of the young, they show little tolerance for one another's company.

The male is never allowed to perch near the nest. Nor is any other bird, for that matter. The female's attack is a kind of dive-bombing: she zips down on an intruder from a couple of feet above, just brushing its back. No harm is done, but the repeti-

80
Two female broadtails threaten each other in flight

tion of the act — zip, zip, zip, back and forth — soon drives the objectionable one away. I have seen female broadtails chase many kinds of birds in this way.

For aggressiveness, though, the males take the prize. Chasing and fighting are the order of the day around the feeding bottles. Occasionally the sound of contact between two birds can be heard, and two or three times I have known of birds being knocked out. The male will peck at its mirror image, at a stuffed hummer and even at just the stuffed head and gorget of a male hummer. Females also fight sometimes with other females [see Fig. 80]. But in both sexes the belligerency usually goes no further than threatening behavior. Its purpose seems to be to chase away an intruder or rival, rather than direct combat.

Some years ago a party of us trochilidographers, camping in

the Huachuca Mountains in southern Arizona, found a young male blue-throated hummingbird which we named "Junior." One evening an approaching hawk caused a clatter in a chicken yard about 50 yards away. Tiny Junior, seeing the hawk from his lookout atop a nearby apple tree, went for the hawk and actually put it to flight!

The life span of the hummingbird is still unsettled. I have known of one which lived five and a half years in captivity and have an unconfirmed report of another that lived to 11. One of my friends had a hummer nest in his garden seven years in succession.

The act of mating, as I mentioned, has rarely been observed, and the few accounts of it differ greatly. It has been reported to take place both on the wing and on the ground. One report of the calliope says: "As he passed the female, she fluttered and hung head downward on her perch. The male alighted above her, with vibrating wings, and coition took place in that position."

There are still many questions to be investigated. Doubtless the day is far distant when it can be said that all answers are known about the life history of this most fascinating of birds.

3

RAISING MOTHS
AND BUTTERFLIES
AS EXPERIMENTAL ANIMALS

Some Lepidoptera can be of great value as experimental animals. How the late Colonel Otto H. Schroeter, a leading amateur lepidopterist, cultivated unusual species and prepared them for study

AT THE AGE OF 73 the late Colonel Otto H. Schroeter of Quaker Hill, Conn., was still chasing butterflies. Except for time out while he studied engineering as a young man in his native Germany, he was at it for more than six decades, including the years when he was employed as construction superintendent in the Panama Canal Zone by the Isthmian Canal Commission.

What fascination kept a busy construction engineer at the hobby of butterfly-collecting for a lifetime? One explanation is a service that Colonel Schroeter was able to perform several years ago for Carroll M. Williams, the eminent Harvard University zoologist who uses insects to study basic processes. Williams needed a large insect for investigation of metamorphosis and was stymied for lack of supply until he heard about Schroeter and his collection of giant silkworms.

"Our relationship with Colonel Schroeter," wrote Williams, "is certainly an excellent illustration of how the amateur can make a distinct contribution to science and share the satisfactions of scientific investigation. The amateur occupies a very special place in entomology because a high proportion of the so-called 'professionals' begin as amateurs. (Later on, incidentally, the complexities of work in a laboratory and an institution may cause them to wish they had remained amateurs!)

"As far as I can judge, Colonel Schroeter was the first to introduce to this country for scientific study and experimentation a wonderful array of 'wild silkworms.' These creatures live in distant parts of the world such as India, Malaya and the slopes of the Himalayas. Colonel Schroeter developed contacts in all these places and has made available to a number of universities and governmental laboratories, including our own, a rich variety of material.

"Certain species of the silkworms have proved strategic for particular types of scientific studies. For example, we have repeatedly called on Colonel Schroeter for specimens of *Antheraea mylitta*, the so-called giant tussah silkworm of India. This exotic creature is one of the world's largest insects, the full-grown caterpillar weighing about 45 grams (almost an eighth of a pound!). It is easy to see how scientists can use beasts of these proportions to answer chemical and physiological questions which would be quite inaccessible in ordinary insects.

"The Colonel has also made available to us considerable information, derived from his own breeding experiments, concerning the care and feeding of these strange species."

Several years ago a number of newspapers featured a picture of Schroeter with an 11-inch moth which he had reared from an egg the size of a matchhead. This big fellow is an *Attacus edwardsi*. Its wings are various shades of brown and yellow and contain transparent windows. Specimens caught in the Philippine Islands have a wing span of 14 inches. Larvæ of the Atlas species of this moth feed on ailanthus leaves — "the tree that grows in Brooklyn." Scientists have not shown much interest in the Atlas caterpillar even though he is far from being a pigmy. He is green, finger-sized and has blue horns on his head. His body looks as if he's frosted with a sugar coating. The natives informed Colonel Schroeter that he was delicious!

Another species that fascinated Colonel Schroeter is the *Thysonia aprippina*. It is a native of Brazil. Those bred at Quaker Hill have even larger wing spans than the *Attacus atlas*, which is usually listed as the largest moth in the world. Colonel Schroeter enjoyed startling visitors by handing them its cocoon — an object the size

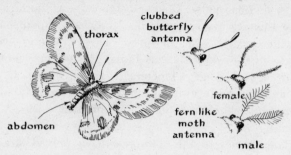

81
Antennae readily distinguish moths from butterflies

of a small sweet potato. The proportions of the moth which comes out of it are easy to imagine.

"Newspaper reporters make so much fuss over the big fellows," Colonel Schroeter once explained, "that they overlook the really interesting specimens. Take the hybrid luna, for example. Seven years ago an amateur friend of mine in India airmailed to me a dozen cocoons of the Indian moon moth. When the adults emerged some months later, it was evident that they were closely related to the American luna. The two species have about the same shape and size and their wings bear a similar general coloration — a light bluish-green. The wings of the Indian species are distinguished by two patches of red. I decided to try crossing them and finally succeeded."

Colonel Schroeter began this experiment by acclimatizing the foreign species, which meant breeding several generations of the foreigners at Quaker Hill, letting them adapt to local forms of their favorite food plants and to the new environment generally. Then he selected a likely female of the foreign species and mated her with a local male.

He invented a simple gadget to help assure a successful mating. Most amateurs tack a female to a tree by one of her wings and wait for her to attract a mate. "The chief drawback of this technique," Schroeter explained, "is that the female's attraction is not limited to mates of her species. When you pin your specimen to a tree you invite predators — other insects, birds and tree toads

— to a free dinner. Too often when you come back you find nothing but a pair of wings. Moreover, when you immobilize a single wing the female is apt to thrash around and injure herself.

"To overcome this difficulty I made what I call a 'mating panel' — a rectangle of Celotex 18 inches long and a foot wide. A screw eye in the center holds a leash of thread, the other end of which is fastened around the female's thorax. With freedom to crawl around on the surface of the panel, she usually quiets down after a few seconds of fluttering. The panel is then suspended by picture wire from the tip of a branch where it is out of reach of tree toads and free to swing in the breeze. The movement frightens most birds away.

"Moon moths mate at sundown. The next morning the female is transferred to a large paper bag in which she deposits her eggs in two parallel rows. After the eggs have been laid, the bag is cut into little squares, each holding eggs. These are fastened with bits of Scotch tape to the leaves of food plants and surrounded with a bag to prevent the larvæ from escaping when the eggs hatch. If you are lucky, the larvæ thrive and metamorphosis gets under way.

"Sometimes the experiment works, but more often it fails. The eggs may be sterile, disease may strike, the food may not be correct. Murphy's law, which states, 'if something can go wrong, it will,' makes no exception of entomology. The failures, however, can be as interesting as the successes, because they pose problems of finding out what went wrong, where and when. In the case of the moon-luna experiment, nature threw the book at me. But in the end I was rewarded with a beautiful hybrid which bore the characteristics of both parents. Its wing markings fade from bright green into greenish-blue and trail through orange to pink at the wing tips. It is probably the only offspring of this combination in the world."

Colonel Schroeter explained that most Lepidoptera mate readily in captivity. In a single season he bred more than 5,000 individuals. Eggs came to him from all parts of the world — sometimes in goose quills and other strange containers. Cocoons arrived in balsa boxes from South America and in bamboo cylinders from the

Orient. While there is a law against indiscriminate importation of insects into the U. S., the Government issued to Schroeter a special importing license, subject to strict controls.

"Don't let the import restriction on foreign material keep you out of amateur entomology," he urged. "You can collect domestic species to your heart's content without fear of ever exhausting our known varieties. Reference texts and catalogues list them by the thousands, and scores of new descriptions are added each year.

"You will find caterpillars wherever plants grow. The next time you go for a walk, whether in the park, a meadow or merely in your back yard, take along a paper bag, a piece of string, some note paper and a pencil. When you find a caterpillar, jot down a short description of it — the color, size, markings and such other information as you think will help you recognize the creature when you meet another like it. Make a similar record of the plant on which it was feeding. If you already know the name and nature of the plant, so much the better. Be sure to include the date, approximate time of day and notes on the weather. Then put the bag over the twig or weed on which your specimen is feeding and tie the end closed so it cannot escape. Check up on it a day or so later. You will likely discover that the leaves have been eaten. If so, shift everything to a fresh batch of leaves. You may have to repeat this several times.

"Eventually you will find that your specimen has vanished and a cocoon has taken its place. With luck you may catch the caterpillar in the act of spinning its cocoon. Make full notes of its methods and how long a time it spends in the process. When the cocoon is complete, break off the twig to which it is attached and transfer operations to a small cage, which you can make of window screening. Place the cage outdoors in a location matching as closely as possible that where you found the insect. Some species prefer sunny locations; others do best in shade. After days or weeks — depending upon the species and the season of the year — the adult will emerge, and you will have the thrill of discovering the exotic creature your caterpillar was destined to become."

By starting with the caterpillar instead of with the butterfly, according to Colonel Schroeter, you learn to recognize at first hand three of the four stages in the life cycle of your insect — larva, pupa and adult. Your notes now give purpose to your future field trips. You hunt for another caterpillar and cocoon of the same species. With luck you may even come across an adult female in the act of laying her eggs. When they have been mounted and labeled, you have the complete life cycle of the insect and the beginning of a collection of scientific value. Although thousands of adult moths and butterflies have been catalogued, the life cycle of a majority of those in nature still awaits description — an ideal project for the amateur who enjoys original work.

One attractive feature of amateur entomology, Schroeter pointed out, is the fact that you never run out of interesting projects for your spare hours. Collecting and breeding are merely two facets of the hobby's many sides. For convenience in study, collections must be mounted and labeled. This can be an absorbing pastime the year around. Only the most perfect specimens are selected for mounting. They are killed and stored against the day when bad weather forces you to remain indoors.

You first stun the insect by pinching the lower side of the thorax lightly between your thumb and index fingers. The thorax is the part of the body directly back of the head, to which the wings are attached. Stunning is necessary to prevent the insect from fluttering and damaging itself when you drop it into the killing jar. The jar can be any wide-mouthed container with a tight-fitting cover. A layer of absorbent material, such as plaster of Paris, is placed in the bottom and saturated with a tablespoon of Carbona. Some amateurs prefer poisons such as potassium cyanide, but they are dangerous and unnecessary. The dead specimen is stored in a triangular envelope folded from a rectangular sheet of paper as illustrated in Figure 82. The envelopes are numbered to correspond with the entries in your notebook.

In about a week the dead insects become hard and brittle. They must be "relaxed" or softened before mounting. You put the dried insects into a jar containing a rubber sponge or other absorbent moistened with water to which a few drops of carbolic

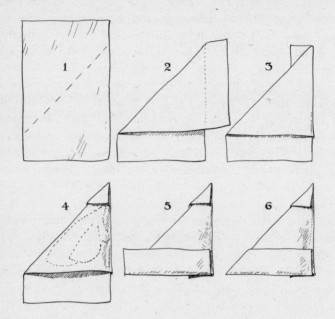

82
Method of folding paper envelopes for storing specimens

acid have been added. The acid prevents the formation of mold or other micro-organisms. A couple of blotters placed between the insects and the sponge will prevent them from getting too wet. After two or three days they are ready for mounting.

Details of the procedure are illustrated in Figure 83. A convenient outfit for mounting specimens consists of a spreading board, two slender strips of glass, tweezers, scissors, pins and a supply of thin cardboard. A spreading board is easily made from balsa or Celotex, with a groove in the center for the body of the insect. The slight upward slant of the board on each side of the groove makes allowance for the tendency of the wings to droop as they age. Mounting outfits can be bought from a supply house; the Butterfly Art Jewelry, Inc., of 289 East 98th St., Brooklyn, N. Y., for example, lists a kit including spreading board, forceps,

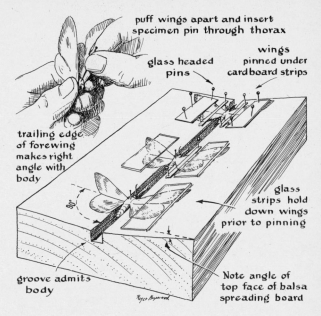

puff wings apart and insert
specimen pin through thorax

glass headed
pins

wings
pinned under
cardboard strips

trailing edge
of forewing
makes right
angle with
body

90°

glass
strips hold
down wings
prior to pinning

groove admits
body

Note angle of
top face of balsa
spreading board

Roger Hayward

83
Equipment and steps used in mounting specimens for display

pins, a display case and other essentials plus 10 tropical butterflies for practice mounting. Similar materials are available from
the Standard Scientific Supply Corp., 36 West 4th Street, New
York, N. Y.

To mount the specimen you grasp it by the lower side of the
thorax, part the wings by blowing lightly, and thrust a pin through
the thorax from the top. The pin should be inserted into the
insect just far enough to bring the point of wing attachment
level with the surface of the spreading board when the pin has
been forced into the bottom of the groove. Then blow the wings
apart again and place the specimen on the board, weighting down
the wings with strips of glass. Each glass is lifted in turn just
enough to permit pulling the forewings forward by means of a
pin inserted behind one of the heavy veins. When the trailing

edge of the forewing makes a right angle with the axis of the body, it is pinned down with strips of cardboard as shown. Wider strips of cardboard are then pinned in place of the glass weights. The specimens will be dry enough in about a week for transfer to the display case.

Eggs and pupæ are mounted without special preparation. Cement the eggs to paper strips of contrasting color. Pin the pupa as though it were a dried adult. A larva must be degutted and inflated before mounting. After killing, place the larva on a square of blotting paper and, with a fine scalpel, enlarge the anal orifice slightly. Then, beginning at the head, squeeze the viscera out by rolling a pencil down the body. The carcass is restored to normal shape by inflating it with a syringe, which you can make yourself. Heat a section of quarter-inch glass tubing to a dull red and quickly draw one end into a fine nozzle, somewhat thinner than the small end of a medicine dropper. Fit the large end with a rubber bulb. You then inflate the larva by inserting the nozzle into its anal opening and squeezing the bulb sharply. The anal opening is closed with a bit of Scotch tape until the tissues harden.

For convenience in subsequent study, specimens are generally pinned to the bottom of a glass-topped display tray. Many arrange the eggs, larva, pupa and adult of each species as a group. Among the catalogues compiled to aid the beginner in identifying his specimens are *The Butterfly Book* and *The Moth Book*, by W. J. Holland.

Colonel Schroeter gave his entire collection of thousands of specimens to the University of Connecticut. J. A. Manter, the University's zoologist, writes: "The Schroeter collection is the most colorful that I have ever seen. Every division of world macrolepidoptera is represented by rare specimens, and it is especially remarkable because of their excellent condition. Such a collection is often spoken of as an 'Oh, my!' one—the reaction it evokes from visitors as the trays are successively pulled into view. Colonel Schroeter's devotion to amateur entomology has resulted in a lasting contribution to science from which future generations of students will derive both knowledge and enjoyment."

The late William Morton Wheeler, the great Harvard ento-
mologist, once summed up the joys of the amateur in these words:
"We should realize, like the amateur, that the organic world is
also an inexhaustible source of spiritual and aesthetic delight. Especially in college we are unfaithful to our trust if we allow biology to become a colorless, aridly scientific discipline devoid of
living contact with the humanities. We should all be happier if
we were less completely obsessed by problems and somewhat more
accessible to the aesthetic and emotional appeal of our materials.
It is doubtful whether, in the end, the growth of biological science
would be appreciably retarded. It quite saddens me to think
that when I cross the Styx, I may find myself among so many professional biologists, condemned to keep on trying to solve problems, and that Pluto, or whoever is in charge down there now,
may condemn me to sit forever trying to identify specimens from
my own diagnoses while amateur entomologists, who have not
been damned professors, are permitted to roam at will among
the fragrant Elysian meadows netting gorgeous, ghostly butterflies until the end of time."

4

BIRD-BANDING FOR
THE AMATEUR

*By mastering the techniques of attaching numbered
bands to the legs of birds, and becoming a licensed
bird-bander, you can make a valuable contribution
to science in your own back yard. Various aspects of
the hobby are discussed. Then Mrs. John Gillespie of
Philadelphia explains how you can get started*

SAMUEL JOHNSON, an opinionated man on any sub-
ject, had a theory that swallows, like frogs, spent the winter
hibernating in the mud at the bottom of rivers and lakes. Unlike
many of his pronouncements, this one was not delivered purely
off the cuff; the irascible doctor actually conducted experiments.
He captured a number of swallows and cemented bits of colored
cloth to their tail feathers. He later recovered some of the marked
feathers at the water's edge and triumphantly produced them
as proof of his theory.

The good doctor overlooked the fact that birds molt their
feathers, but his approach to the scientific problem was not entirely without merit. Bird-marking is today a large and fruitful
enterprise. At the turn of the present century Danish ornithologists hit upon the scheme of tracing the travels of wild birds by
banding them with a ring of light metal fastened loosely around
a leg. A serial number and other information is marked on the
band, and whenever a bird is recovered, the information is reported to a central clearing house. The system was soon adopted
throughout the world.

In the U. S. the sponsorship of bird-banding, started by the
American Bird Banding Association, was taken over in 1920 by

the Federal Government. The project is now a branch of the Fish and Wildlife Service, with headquarters at Patuxent Research Refuge, Laurel, Md.

Almost nine million birds have been banded since the U. S. program started; some 300,000 to 400,000 are tagged each year. A total of more than three quarters of a million marked birds have been recovered. There are about 2,000 cooperating bird-banders, professional and amateur.

The object of bird-banding is to collect scientific data on the migration, dispersal and age of wild birds. It helps in the study of such characteristics as homing instinct, mating habits, navigation ability, flyways, and related patterns of behavior.

Since only a small fraction of marked birds are recovered, it is desirable to band large numbers of them and to station banders and observers over the widest possible area. Hence you are strongly encouraged to take up this avocation.

It is an activity that you can pursue in your own back yard, or that can take you afield on rugged adventure. It costs very little in cash and pays richly in diversion and discovery. All bird-banders must be licensed, because the trapping of wild birds without a license is prohibited in the U. S. Any citizen 18 years of age or over may apply to the Fish and Wildlife Service for a license. The applicant must prove that he can identify the various species and subspecies of birds and must give as references the names of three people with recognized ornithological qualifications.

Upon meeting these requirements the bander is issued a Federal permit and a supply of numbered aluminum bands of assorted sizes — free of charge — together with record forms and instruction pamphlets. He must then apply for a local permit in any state where he expects to do banding. He supplies his own traps and incidental equipment. At least once a year he must report to the Bird Banding Office, giving prescribed data on each bird he has banded or retaken.

Trapping and banding a bird without injuring it is an art, and no novice should undertake it without expert guidance. The Gillespies were two of the foremost bird-banding experts in the

84
One of the four flyways of the Canada goose

U. S., according to Lorene McLellan of Philadelphia's Academy of Natural Sciences. Mrs. Gillespie says that the precise number of years she has been a bander is outside the scope of this discussion, but in evidence of her experience she proudly exhibits a photograph of a common tern which she and her husband banded in New Jersey on August 5, 1923.

Mrs. Gillespie advises that one convenient way to band birds is to do it while they are still in the nest and unable to fly, but they must be sufficiently developed to hold a band that will be large enough when they are fully grown. This method is particularly suited for banding birds that nest in colonies and for eagles, ospreys and other birds of prey. For songbirds, ground-feeders and some wildfowl, bird-banders use a different technique, resorting to guile and temptation. They bait traps of various designs with tempting food. A bird that feeds on the ground, such as the native sparrow, readily follows a trail of food into a trap. Some banding traps are constructed on the principle of the maze; some are like funnel fish-traps; some have a trigger arrangement which closes the entrance automatically when a bird enters. There are also types of traps for catching birds that do not usually run on the ground. Properly conducted, trapping does birds no harm. Traps are never left "set" when the bander is absent, so that much of the time birds run in and out, feeding freely.

Birds live in a world full of constant danger and surprise, Mrs. Gillespie reminds you. The experience of being trapped, if they are deftly handled and quickly released, is less disturbing to them psychically than an encounter with a cat. Within a few minutes the experience is all but forgotten. The birds usually remember the food, however, and this memory often brings them back. Sometimes a bird walks into a trap again within five minutes after it has been released. Now and then one retraps itself so persistently that it becomes a nuisance.

Banding a bird after it has been caught may be a painful experience — to the bander, not the bird. Some tough-looking specimens, such as the blue jay, usually submit with little struggle. On the other hand, cardinals and the seemingly meek purple finches may attack with a ferocity that sends the bander away

85
Banded grackle showing proper method
of grasping bird

nursing a blood blister. Eagles, according to Mrs. Gillespie, belie their fearsome reputation; the parents will flutter timidly at a distance of 50 feet or more, uttering feeble, unconvincing cries, as a bander climbs to their nest and casually places numbered bands on the legs of their young. But watch out for their cousins, the ospreys! A collaborator of the Gillespies, Frederick C. Schmid, once was nearly knocked out of a tree by an osprey which left the deep trail of its talons across his face.

As each bird is tagged, the bander records the serial number, the date, the kind of bird and if possible its sex and weight, and the location where it is banded. When a banded bird is recaptured, alive or dead, its recovery is reported through the Fish and Wildlife Service to the original bander. Thus a bander gradually accumulates case histories on individuals of many species. The record files of the Gillespies contain many hundreds of cards, some of which trace migratory cycles extending over periods as long as 15 years.

Few small birds survive longer than two years in the wild state, although their maximum expectancy is believed to be 9 to 12 years in nature and 18 to 20 years when protected in captivity. Mortality is appallingly high among young birds: generally 60 to 80 per cent in the first six months. Consequently most banders prefer to invest the extra time and effort required to band adults; the chances of recovering grown birds are much better.

More than 600 species of birds have been banded in the U. S. Mallard ducks lead all the others: banders have marked about half a million of them. After the mallard duck in order come the chimney swift, common tern, pintail, herring gull, song sparrow, robin, starling and purple grackle. Amateur banders account for about two thirds of the banding activity, the remainder being done largely by government technicians and professional ornithologists.

Even a relatively low percentage of recovery can yield significant and sometimes dramatic information about bird migrations. From recoveries of just half a dozen birds it has been learned that the arctic tern nests in the Arctic Circle and winters in the Antarctic, an annual round trip of at least 25,000 miles!

Migration takes many forms. Some species follow relatively narrow routes; others range half a continent or more. There are birds that never travel farther than between a valley and its neighboring hill. The cardinal does not migrate at all; it makes every effort to acquire a small, exclusive territory for itself, and if the climate permits, it stays there as long as the place suits it.

The Gillespies have given much study to the mating and nesting habits of back-yard birds. One of their case histories concerns a pair of house wrens they banded one spring. After the wrens had raised a brood and the fledglings had left the nest, the female became interested in a second mate which had been hopefully building a nest nearby, and she mated with him to produce a second family that summer. The next spring the female returned to the Gillespies' birdhouse and again started the season with a banded male they suspected to be her first mate of the preceding season, though they could not catch him. The male soon abandoned her, leaving her to raise the brood alone. Again she found a second mate and raised a second family. Late in July the Gillespies caught her first mate nesting two blocks away. He returned to one of their birdhouses the next summer, but the female did not appear again. Two or three years seems to be the average life span for a house wren.

"One year," said Mrs. Gillespie, "we tested the homing instinct of a female cowbird. A cowbird, like the European cuckoo, builds no nest and lays her eggs in the nests of other birds. She is not lacking, however, in a homing or maternal instinct. We carried our cowbird to various places some distance away from the nest several times and each time she returned promptly after we released her. Once she was released in the center of Wilmington, Del., 20 miles from home, and she was back in our trap within three hours. The late William I. Lyon of Waukegan, Ill., sent a banded cowbird to be released in Denver, Col. Twenty-five days later it was back in Waukegan. Many believe that performances of this kind are confined to homing pigeons. Actually many wild birds demonstrate a much stronger homing instinct than do the highly trained pigeons."

A by-product of bird-banding is the opportunity to collect and study parasites. Mites, flies, ticks and lice can easily be removed from the birds while they are being handled. One bander whose brother specialized in research on malaria was able to help by taking blood smears of migratory birds, thus providing information on how malaria may be spread by bird carriers.

The Gillespies found especially thrilling the banding of ospreys, or fish hawks, which have the fierce nature usually attributed to the American eagle. They banded 457 ospreys and had reports on 70, an unusually high percentage. Forty were reported dead within a few months of the time when they were banded as nestlings. Some were found near their birth sites several seasons later. Osprey nestlings banded in July are usually well on their way south by fall. But one osprey was found in Florida less than seven weeks after it was banded, whereas his brother was still in Pennsylvania at Thanksgiving time.

"While we welcome reports of the travels of ospreys," said Mrs. Gillespie, "we regret that information generally comes only through their untimely deaths. They feed exclusively on fish and are no menace to the farmer but are often killed because they are mistaken for eagles. One of our ospreys, shot by a farmer in West Virginia, made local newspaper headlines: 'Eagle Killed By Local Hunter.'"

86
A banded eaglet in nest

"Our most unusual recovery was that of an osprey banded in Cape May County, N. J., on July 16, 1939. It covered 6,837 airline miles between that time and December 16, 1939, when it finally encountered a bullet in Rio de Janeiro. We feel sure that it did not fly in a beeline but probably followed coastlines and explored riverways, so its total distance must have been much greater than the airline routes.

"Our bird-banding work has been rich in unusual and varied experiences. There is nothing like the excitement of a nesting colony, where the air is full of flashing wings and wild screams, and young birds are everywhere about. Our activities have taken us to unfrequented beaches, deep woodlands and vast marshlands. We have enjoyed contacts with all sorts of people, not only in this country, but throughout the Americas and West Indies."

Anyone who finds a banded bird, dead or alive, will greatly assist the work of ornithologists by sending the band or its number to the Fish and Wildlife Service, along with a statement of the circumstances of the finding. The report should be made to the Bird Banding Office, Patuxent Research Refuge, U. S. Fish and Wildlife Service, Laurel, Md. Give your name and address, the date and the location where the bird was found. If you caught the bird alive, release it with its band; if the bird is dead, remove and flatten the band and send it in with your report. The Service will inform you of the known history of the bird, and notify the bander of the recovery. Many bird-banders make it a custom, when they get a notification from the Service, to write the finder.

5

HOW TO LIVE WITH REPTILES
AND AMPHIBIANS

One way to find respite from the rush of twentieth-century life is by observing the leisurely ways of the reptiles. But how does one keep snakes, lizards or turtles happy and healthy at home? Here are suggestions from Robert H. Wilson, Assistant Professor of Industrial Hygiene at the University of Rochester School of Medicine and Dentistry

MOST PEOPLE are somewhat afraid of snakes and other reptiles, and not without reason. After all, a few reptiles *are* poisonous, and not everyone can immediately tell which are dangerous and which are not. But reptiles are interesting animals, and the amateur who chooses to learn something about them can gain much pleasure from observing them. Consider, for example, the well-known fact that, because reptiles have no internal mechanism to regulate their temperature, they must warm or cool themselves by means of their behavior. The pattern of this behavior is fascinating to observe, as are many other aspects of reptilian life. The trick is how to observe them.

It is not easy to study reptiles in nature. Most of them are shy animals that rapidly disappear at the approach of *Homo sapiens.* Even in the Southwest, a veritable reptile sanctuary because of its desolation and sunny weather, one must have infinite patience to observe these animals going about the absorbing business of staying alive.

A much more satisfactory approach is to keep them in the home. They are not good pets in the ordinary sense. You cannot teach a snake or a lizard to do much more than respond when you approach with food. The rewards come in observing at first hand the ordinary life functions of these unusual creatures. Watching a healthy snake shed its skin still fascinates me, even though enough cast skins now hang in one of my windows to obscure the view. The courting activities of some of the small desert lizards are at once comical and enthralling. And a particular satisfaction comes in raising a juvenile reptile to impressive size and health.

If one recognizes the fact that reptiles have specialized dietary requirements, the rest of reptile-keeping is relatively simple. It is even inexpensive, provided one controls one's enthusiasm for collecting specimens. Of the 40-odd reptiles of various species in our house, we bought only four, all pet turtles, from a store.

The rest were acquired by gifts, trades, hatching and capture. The most important route of acquisition is the first. Once it becomes known in the neighborhood that you like snakes, your collection will grow as small and large boys appear at your door with boxes and paper bags. Trading specimens with reptile fanciers, especially those in parts of the country remote from yours, can bring in a wealth of species that you are not likely to see any other way. Capturing your own specimens has all the thrills of the hunt, and can enrich the dullest countryside.

The art of capturing snakes is greatly simplified by the cut-down golf putter shown in Figure 87. With this tool it is easy to pin down the snake so that it may be taken by hand as illustrated. Another useful accessory is a net made by stitching one end of a tube of muslin to a heavy wire ring and tying the other end with a string. A fairly long handle should be attached to the wire ring. Tying the end of the net shut simplifies the problem of transferring a netted snake, particularly a biter, into a bag. The net should be deep enough so that a half-turn of the handle closes the net on itself but leaves room for the snake at the bottom.

Snakes are caught where you find them. A slow drive down a deserted road at night will frequently turn up an amazing number of snakes, particularly in the Southwest. Turning over stones and rotted logs is also productive, but in rattler country this should not be done with bare hands; use your snake putter or a stick. Most of my snake-catching is done by the putter-and-net technique.

87
A recommended method of catching and holding a snake

Traps are not satisfactory for capturing snakes, but they are quite successful with lizards. Two kinds of trap are illustrated here [*Fig. 89*]. Spoiled meat inside such traps will attract those lizard species that have a well-developed sense of smell. A simple box trap is preferable for desert regions where shade is scarce, because lizards seek the shade when the sun becomes too hot for their comfort. The box may be two feet square and six inches deep. It is closed at the top with a wooden door and at the bottom with a wirescreen. Two or three two-inch holes are drilled in one side about half an inch from the bottom.

The trap is placed with the holes on the shady side, and jiggled down into the sand until the bottom of the holes are flush with the surface. The box is then covered with sand (except, of course, for the side with the holes). This keeps the temperature inside the box from rising too high in the hot sun. Lizards approaching from the shady side will find the holes and enter the box. Once inside, they will stay for several hours during the heat of the day. The specimens should be harvested two or three times before the heat subsides.

Netting lizards is usually unsatisfactory because they are far quicker than the netter. The lizard is much less likely to scamper off if it is approached with a noose at the end of a trout-fishing rod. The noose can then be maneuvered over the lizard's head and pulled tight simply by raising the rod. The noose should be made of silk thread rather than nylon, because nylon tends to curl.

88
How to grasp a frog without injuring it

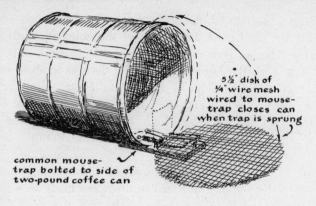

5½" disk of ¼" wire mesh wired to mouse-trap closes can when trap is sprung

common mouse-trap bolted to side of two-pound coffee can

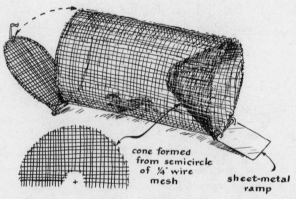

cone formed from semicircle of ¼" wire mesh

sheet-metal ramp

89
Two designs of traps for catching lizards and other small animals

Turtles that are accustomed to sunning themselves on half-submerged logs can be trapped by assembling four logs in a rectangle and suspending a net in the water beneath it. The turtles come out of the water from the outside of the rectangle, but they may depart to the inside, particularly if the turtle-trapper appears suddenly from the right direction.

They can be kept from climbing out of the trap by studding the inside of the enclosure with nails that point downward at an angle. Turtle collecting should be done with the knowledge that a number of species are protected by law. The desert tortoise, for example, is protected throughout its range, and the penalty for possessing one can be as much as $500. Eastern turtles that are protected include the box turtle and the wood turtle.

All reptile specimens are best transported in muslin bags 18 inches wide and a yard long. The bags should have double seams so that the specimens will not become entangled in loose threads. When poisonous snakes are transported, an external tab should be attached to the bottom of the bag so that one can empty the bag without exposing oneself to a bite.

Once you get the captive home, you must think of where to put it. A good container for small reptiles that cannot climb is an aquarium. Of course a wooden box will do as well, though it is desirable to fit the box with a glass front so that you can easily observe what is going on inside. With nonaquatic reptiles it is necessary to cover the box with a snug (but not airtight) cover. Snakes especially have a rare talent for finding a small opening.

I use several different kinds of cover: wire screen, perforated masonite and occasionally glass, raised slightly from the top of the container to provide adequate ventilation. The design of the cover is governed largely by the animal inside. Wire screen is generally unsatisfactory for snakes. They have a tendency to rub their noses on the screen and injure themselves. For some of the stronger species of snake a sturdy top is needed, and Masonite fills the bill. A glass cover is used when it is desirable to keep the temperature and the humidity high.

Most discussions of reptile-keeping emphasize the importance of avoiding decorative effects in the cages, pointing out that sanitation is a problem and that the humidity resulting from the presence of plants is detrimental. I do not agree with this. Animal cages in the home should be attractive. Moreover, the animals themselves appear to feel more at home in cages that roughly approximate their natural habitat.

One can divide cage climate into broad categories — for example, desert, temperate-zone region or bog — and select plants and other surroundings that are compatible. Properly managed, a reptile cage can be as decorative as the handsomest aquarium.

One warning; reptiles to be placed in a decorated cage should be carefully inspected for mites. Once introduced into such a cage, mites hide themselves in crevices and are almost impossible to eliminate.

The sanitation problem is most easily met by placing a deep layer (one to two inches) of aquarium gravel in the bottom of the cage. It is a simple matter to pick up excreta and contaminated gravel with a scoop and to replace the gravel from time to time. Many terrestrial reptiles are fond of burrowing on occasion, and aquarium gravel is a good medium in this regard because it does not pack or cake.

The illumination of the cage is important, both for the welfare of the animals and for satisfactory viewing. Most reptiles do best at temperatures slightly above 70 degrees Fahrenheit, the desert species preferring temperatures as high as 100 degrees. I achieve good temperature-control by balancing the radiant heat of incandescent lamps against the heat loss through the sides of the cage and by whatever air circulation there may be.

Reptiles govern their body temperature by absorbing heat in varying amounts from their surroundings. Incandescent lamps at the top of the cage, together with the judicious location of furniture such as rocks or sticks at various distances from the light source, permit the animals to select their own temperature conditions. It is astonishing to observe how quickly these not especially bright creatures learn that they can warm up most quickly by climbing to the highest point in the cage. When several lizards are in a cage and the light comes on after a cool night, an amusing scramble for top position usually ensues.

An effective source of light and heat is the 75-watt spotlight lamp available in most hardware stores [see Fig. 90]. The reflector of the lamp is highly efficient for both visible and infrared radiation, and incidentally lends itself to dramatic lighting effects. The radiation is concentrated, however. It is therefore important to direct it so that the animal can get out of the beam and avoid overheating. I usually mount the lamp so that the front of the glass envelope is about 10 inches from the highest piece of furniture in the cage.

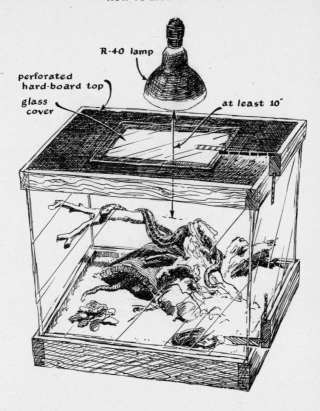

R-40 lamp

perforated
hard-board top
glass
cover

at least 10"

90
A terrarium made of wood, glass and perforated Masonite

The main problem in keeping reptiles is to provide them with
the proper diet. Few reptiles are vegetarians, though some turtle
and lizard species will eat lettuce. The rest demand meat in various forms. Most turtles will eat any kind of meat proffered (including a bit of finger if you are not quick). Cod or ocean perch
seems particularly tasty to aquatic turtles. Several of the more
terrestrial species thrive on dog food, particularly Pard.

It is important to remember that the aquatic turtles (all those
sold in variety stores) are unable to eat when they are out of
water. The turtle bowls sold with them are almost always inade-

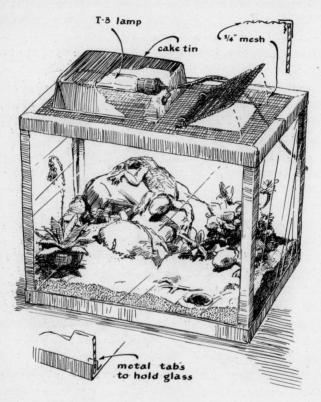

91
An aquarium modified to hold small reptiles

quate. Such a turtle is properly kept in an aquarium measuring at least 10 inches wide and 12 inches long. The aquarium should contain six to eight inches of water, a sunning platform and an ample heat source such as the 75-watt spotlight lamp. One should be forewarned that these turtles will grow, some of them to as much as eight or 10 inches long if they are properly nurtured.

Most of the lizards are insectivores, eating moths, flies, beetles, grubs, grasshoppers and so on. Such prey are not easy to come by in the winter, and it is almost impossible to convert a lizard to foods such as beef or fish. However, there are solutions to the problem.

Meal worms can be bought in pet stores. These worms, the larval form of the darkling beetle that commonly occurs around granaries, are a splendid food for insectivores, apparently supplying all the important trace nutrients.

Recently I have found that Russell Vance of Lincoln, N. Y., maintains a year-round supply of crickets that bids fair to revolutionize the keeping of reptiles. It is not difficult to raise meal worms in amounts sufficient for one or two small lizards, but a larger lizard can put away 75 to 100 worms a week. This calls for a rate of production that is difficult to maintain in the home. Moreover, some lizards ignore meal worms. The crickets, however, are a different story. In the first place, they are larger, so that even our fairly sizable African agamid is satisfied with three or four. Second, they do not contain so much chitin, the horny substance of the insect skeleton.

If a small lizard is fed a steady diet of meal worms, the indigestible chitin of the worms may actually block its gastrointestinal tract. Crickets also seem to provide more dietary essentials than do meal worms. My lizards are all in much better health as a consequence of the shift to crickets. My one insectivorous snake, a member of the smooth green species, eats crickets to the exclusion of all other food.

The snakes are probably the most fascinating of all the reptiles. All snakes are carnivorous. In most cases this means one must supply them with mice or rats for food, although water and ribbon snakes will eat fish (minnows or thawed pieces of frozen fish). Garter snakes can be induced to eat chopped earthworms mixed with hamburger; later they can be graduated to hamburger alone.

Working as I do in a biomedical laboratory, procurement of mammalian food for my specimens is no problem. I simply set up a breeding colony of mice in an out-of-the-way corner and harvest as needed. Our rat colony generally produces an adequate surplus to supply my modest needs. The less fortunate reptile-keeper, however, can doubtless make arrangements with a biological or medical laboratory for a supply of surplus rodents, usually at a reasonable cost.

Breeding in the home is not recommended. It is accompanied

by an odor problem that even the most tolerant wife can seldom ignore.

Of the readily available snake species, some are more adaptable to the home terrarium than others. The list is headed by bull snakes, which are unusually docile. I have picked up wild bull snakes in the deserts of Nevada and Idaho that struggled no more than those in my cages. Corn, fox and rat snakes are somewhat more excitable, but still adapt nicely to confinement.

An unusually charming little specimen is the red-bellied snake, which grows to a maximum length of 10 inches. These require a steady diet of small angleworms or garden slugs (the brown ones, not the gray), which are easily raised in leafy litter, with lettuce and chicken mash as food.

Most of the racers and coachwhips are best left *in situ*. They are nervous and irritable, and they bite severely. The poisonous varieties should be left strictly alone. (I must confess that I have a couple of juvenile Great Basin rattlers that I caught in Idaho last summer; I keep telling myself that as soon as they are big enough I shall give them to the zoo.) Although many of the pit vipers (which group includes the rattlesnakes) are attractive and interesting, the risk is severe. Moreover, not all neighbors are as tolerant and understanding as mine.

Perhaps the most important item in reptilian diet is an adequate supplement of vitamins. Virtually all reptiles are sun worshipers, and in captivity they must have vitamin D to compensate for the lack of sunshine. My procedure, which seems to work extraordinarily well, is to include one or two drops of Abdec per ounce of drinking water. The water-soluble polyvitamin preparation appears to suit reptiles ideally.

The effect of vitamins can be most dramatic. A reptile specimen that is lethargic and off its feed can become a ravening brute ready to eat almost anything one or two days after the direct administration of one or two drops of Abdec. Once the reptile is in condition, the maintenance dose in drinking water seems to be sufficient. Turtles are particularly sensitive to the lack of vitamins and should be given a direct dose every month or so.

Reptiles can be watered in several ways, depending on the

species. A snake will drink from any dish large enough to admit its head and an equal length of neck. Some lizards will drink from a dish; others, from a watering bottle. Some, such as the anoles, or "circus chameleons," must be watered with a dropper or by sprinkling the plants in their quarters.

When one keeps reptiles in the home, it is difficult not to be anthropomorphic about them. Lowly though they are, reptiles are individualistic, and one cannot avoid assigning them personalities. In the final analysis, why not? Each animal has a behavior pattern that is partly instinctive but partly the result of experiences during its lifetime. To me it seems only reasonable that individuality should develop.

My three bull snakes are an excellent example. All were taken at the Nevada Test Site of the Atomic Energy Commission, and they look pretty much the same. Yet there are marked behavioral differences among them. One of them, which was caught as a very young specimen, has been in captivity most of its life, and probably as a consequence has come to enjoy being handled. It rests quietly for long periods in the hands of anyone who will hold it. Another of the snakes, almost identical in appearance, was mature when taken, and although evidently satisfied with the food supply and creature comforts, has never really resigned itself to handling, preferring to wander about unconstrained when released from the cage. The third snake is intermediate between the first two; it enjoys a trip but is willing to settle down after it has investigated its surroundings.

The challenge of keeping these animals, coupled with the opportunity to observe at first hand their functions and behavior and, above all, their remarkable adaptations to their environment, make reptile study in the home a particularly rewarding avocation. The formal background requirements are certainly minimal. I am an engineer and my biological training consists of only one year of high-school biology. I find, however, that I have absorbed an astonishing amount of biology and zoology without half trying.

V.

THE EARTH SCIENCES

1

HOW TO KNOW THE ROCKS

To the amateur who learns to "read," in rocks, the history of the earth's ever-changing surface, mineral collecting can become doubly rewarding. On the following pages methods are suggested for classifying minerals by crystalline structure, chemical composition, and physical characteristics

AT ONE TIME or another nearly everyone starts a rock collection. It may begin with a curiously shaped stone picked up at the beach, a glittering fragment found along a mountain trail — any eye-catching bit from anywhere. Perhaps the specimen is clear, glass-like and flecked with yellow. Could it be gold? Stone after stone is lugged home and the collection grows, sometimes into a dust-catcher of considerable size. Then interest wanes and one fine day, about the time of spring housecleaning, the whole assortment is dumped on the trash pile, or, at best, becomes an ornamental border for the flowerbed.

How different the history of such collections might be if those who do the collecting would spend a few hours learning how to read the stories written in the rocks. Thousands of amateur mineralogists have mastered this easy language, many with little more equipment than a keen pair of eyes, normal curiosity and any of a dozen or more excellent reference books. Collecting, studying and experimenting with minerals can be enjoyed throughout the year, and few avocations offer as much variety, activity and interest.

It has been said that a stone, when examined closely, will be found to be a mountain in miniature. Of many stones this is indeed true. If a fragment of common granite, for example, is viewed under a magnifying glass of reasonable power, its uniform gray or pink surface breaks up into innumerable discrete features.

92
Typical crystalline forms of minerals.
Galena *(top)*, quartz *(middle)* and
snow *(bottom)*

Some take the form of exquisitely shaped crystals, almost as hard as gem stones. Others are soft and can be split into thin sheets. Still others present a milky appearance and break into fragments that assume the spiral shape of a sea shell. In some specimens the minute mountain of granite appears to have been folded, cracked and cemented together again — features reproduced on a giant scale by real mountains.

Once in a great while you may have the good luck to find a mineral ore and thus, in miniature, strike it rich. Incidentally, by the time the beginner has analyzed a half dozen stones he will develop much respect for the equipment that the lowly "desert rat" carries beneath his hat.

Among the other normally unseen constituents, granite contains enough atomic energy in the form of uranium not only to melt the whole rock but to refine the chemical elements of which it is composed and to reassemble them into any compounds desired. Technology is not yet equal to this task, of course. But with the development of the breeder reactor we know how to "burn the rocks," and, eventually, we may learn how to prepare them for our backs and stomachs. As Miss Elizabeth Morley, an avid amateur mineralogist and former school teacher of Philadelphia, Pa., says, "There's a lot more to rocks, even to the meanest pebble on the beach, than meets the casual eye and immensely more to prospecting than a geologist's pick and grub stake!"

Miss Morley's mineral collection, which includes specimens ranging from talc to diamond, got its start one day in 1922 when one of her eighth-grade pupils asked for permission to demonstrate a crystal radio set before his class. Its galena crystal captured Miss Morley's imagination. When the wire "cat's whisker" was adjusted, music came out of the rock! Miss Morley never quite recovered from the astonishment of that moment, and she decided then and there to learn the how and why of the silvery bit of stone which at that time she could not even name.

In the course of learning that galena shares with a number of other minerals the curious property of conducting electrical currents more readily in one direction than the other, she also learned that it breaks into cube-shaped fragments when struck a sharp blow, that chemically it is a compound of sulfur and lead, that it has a hardness of 2.5 (it can be marked by the fingernail) and a specific gravity of 7.6. But the discovery that converted her to amateur mineralogy was the fact that the mineral kingdom, like the animal and vegetable kingdoms, has a taxonomy of its own which draws a distinction between individuals quite as sharp as that which locates man in one biological category and his pet fish in another.

Minerals today are classified according to their chemical composition, and beginners in mineralogy are urged to learn the classification system. Under this system most minerals can be labeled as a member of one of the following species: sulfide, oxide, halide, carbonate, borate, phosphate, sulfate, tungstate, molybdate, uranate or silicate. In each species there are thousands of individual minerals — metallic or non-metallic.

All minerals are chemical compounds made up of two or more of the 92 naturally occurring elements. Nine elements account for the great bulk of minerals, and indeed for 95 per cent of the earth's crust. They are oxygen, silicon, aluminum, iron, calcium, sodium, potassium, magnesium and hydrogen. In addition three others, though quantitatively small, are important components of minerals. These three are carbon, chlorine and sulfur.

Because most minerals are composed of a very few elements, many specimens can be identified at a glance. More than 99 per cent of the specimens collected by the average amateur can be analyzed without elaborate equipment or methods. Others require detailed examination. This usually begins with a test for hardness. The standard scale of hardness, ranging from 1 to 10, is based on the relative hardness of a selected group of minerals. From the softest to the hardest it runs:

1. Talc
2. Gypsum
3. Calcite
4. Fluorite
5. Apatite
6. Orthoclase
7. Quartz
8. Topaz
9. Sapphire (Corundum)
10. Diamond

Kits containing the first nine of these minerals in sizes handy for use in the field can be procured for a dollar or so from firms specializing in mineralogical equipment, such as Ward's Natural Science Establishment of Rochester, N. Y., and Eckert Mineral Research Co. of Florence, Col. With a little experience the amateur can make a good estimate of hardness with the aid of quite ordinary materials.

Minerals of hardness 1, for example, crush easily between the fingers and usually have the greasy feel of talcum powder. Those of hardness 2 can be scratched by the fingernail. A common pin will scratch the hardness 3 group and those of hardness 4 yield readily to the blade of a penknife. Members of group 5 are difficult to scratch with a knife. Those in group 6 will scratch a knife. The hardest particles in granite (quartz) are of hardness 7. Thus a specimen of granite is useful in estimating the hardness of materials lying beyond the range of 7. The hardness test should be made on a fresh surface exposed by chipping a small corner off the specimen, as weathering processes soften the surfaces of exposed rocks.

Having noted the specimen's hardness, the mineralogist next tests for streak. The specimen is rubbed against a small plate of unglazed porcelain or an equivalent material. Usually it makes a streak on the white porcelain surface. This enables the mineralogist to see the true color of the specimen: thus a rock that appears brown to the eye may make a distinctly red mark on the white porcelain. This color, together with the specimen's hardness and other tests, will guide the collector to the identity of the specimen as tabulated in a reference text.

Next an estimate should be made of the specimen's general physical character. Some minerals can be flattened by a hammer, and thus are said to be malleable. Others, such as copper, can be stretched and therefore are ductile. If the specimen can be cut by a knife, like a piece of hard tar, and yet shatters under a sharp blow, it is sectile. Those that bend easily and remain bent are called flexible. Some forms of sandstone exhibit this characteristic. Others are brittle and shatter like glass when struck with a hammer or when bent beyond their yield point. Finally, many minerals, such as mica, are elastic.

The next clue to identification is the mineral's density, which can often be estimated simply by hefting it; no one needs a sensitive balance to tell a block of lead ore from one of gypsum. An advanced amateur can easily construct his own balance for determining specific gravity with reasonable accuracy. Suspend a pan from a hook by a spring or rubber band. From the bottom of this pan at the center suspend a second one a few inches below it. Hang the apparatus from a bracket so the lower pan comes to rest a few inches above a flat surface, such as the top of a table.

Next, set a pan of water beneath the balance so that the bottom pan is immersed to a depth greater than the height of the mineral sample.

Measure the distance, as accurately as possible, between the edge of the upper pan and the top of the table or other supporting surface. Identify this distance, N_1. Now place the specimen in the *upper* pan, the dry one, and again measure the distance between the pan and the supporting surface. Identify this distance, N_2. Finally, transfer the specimen to the submerged pan. (The vessel must contain enough water to fully submerge the specimen.) Measure the distance between the edge of the *upper* pan and the supporting surface while the specimen is fully submerged. Identify this distance as N_3. The specific gravity is then computed by the formula:

$$\text{Specific gravity} = \frac{N_1 - N_2}{N_3 - N_2}$$

Specific gravities of minerals range from 1.7 (borax) to 8.1 (cinnabar) or more. The specific gravity of sulfur is 2.05; gypsum, 2.3; quartz, 2.66; feldspar, 2.6 to 2.75; talc, 2.8; diamond, 3.5. The densities of metals extend over a much wider range. Some of the common ones: magnesium, 1.8; aluminum, 2.5; zinc, 7.1; silver, 10.6; gold, 19.3; platinum, 21.5. Comparing the specific gravity of gold with that of quartz, the major constituent of sand, it is easy to see why the grains of precious metal settle so readily in the bottom of the prospector's pan and why the Jolly balance for determining specific gravity became almost the symbol of the assayer's office during the days of the great gold rush.

Other readily ascertained clues to a mineral's identity are its appearance under light (daylight and ultraviolet), its electrical and magnetic properties, its crystal structure, its taste and its odor.

Minerals reflect, absorb and transmit wavelengths of light according to their chemical structure. Hence each presents a characteristic surface texture and color. Some, like the silvery mineral galena, show a pronounced metallic luster; the color may range

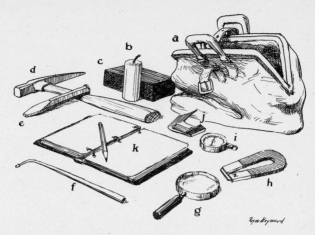

93
The tool kit of the amateur mineralogist

from light gray through silver, yellow and dark brown to purple. Others, chiefly the non-metallic minerals, show a glass-like luster that ranges through pearly and silky to glistening. Some are as transparent as clear glass; others appear milky or translucent, opalescent or iridescent.

One of the most striking optical properties of many minerals is that of fluorescence: they glow in vivid, characteristic colors when exposed to ultraviolet light. The phenomenon was first observed as a property of fluorite many years ago. Unfortunately fluorescence is not very useful analytically. Some specimens of a given mineral fluoresce readily while others show little if any activity. Some respond to a limited range of wavelengths in the ultraviolet spectrum and others to the whole spectrum. Save for rare examples such as willemite from the vicinity of Franklin, N. J., which emits a bright green glow, fluorescence cannot be depended upon as an analytical test. Nevertheless, most amateur mineralogists own inexpensive ultraviolet lamps for use in displaying their collection.

A number of minerals exhibit electrical qualities. Galena, as mentioned previously, presents greater resistance to the flow of current in one direction than in the other. Thus it is a rectifier and can be used for the detection of radio waves and related electrical applications.

This same property is characteristic of certain compounds of copper, silicon, germanium, uranium and others. Quartz and tourmaline in their crystalline forms show what is called piezoelectricity — an electrical effect produced by squeezing the specimen. This property, plus the fact that quartz is one of the most elastic materials found in nature, accounts for the extensive use of this mineral for generating small alternating electrical currents of constant frequency. Thin wafers of quartz, properly mounted in electrical circuits, can be made to vibrate at rates of 50 million pulses per second, and electrical clocks driven from quartz crystal oscillators keep time accurately to less than a second's deviation per year!

Lodestone is the classic example of a magnetic mineral. This naturally occurring magnet will pick up bits of iron or steel and in other ways behave like a horseshoe magnet. When powdered, its particles cling together, and iron filings sprinkled on paper covering a lodestone arrange themselves in the form of the specimen's magnetic pattern. Other minerals containing iron, nickel

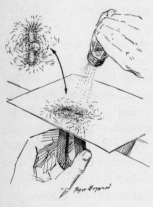

94
Test for the mineral magnetite

or cobalt also show magnetic properties — some being attracted to a magnet and others, like lodestone, behaving as a magnet.

As for taste and odor, halite (the prospector's name for ordinary salt) of course tastes salty; many potassium compounds taste bitter; those of aluminum cause the mouth to pucker; many iron compounds have a sour taste; a few varieties of limestone and other compounds of sulfur give off the odor of rotten eggs when crushed; some shales have a distinctive earthy odor; some minerals of arsenic smell like garlic.

A pencil, notepaper and a reference book are all the equipment a beginner needs to start in mineralogy, but as he goes on he will add certain other simple articles and tools. One is a light, strong collecting bag, either of the knapsack type or with hand grips. Then he will want a trimming hammer, with a flat head for cold-chisel work and a sharp edge for trimming specimens; a cold chisel of tempered steel, about six inches long with a ⅝-inch cutting edge; a magnifying glass with a power of 7 to 14 diameters; a pocketknife; a streak plate of unglazed porcelain; chemical reagents, including dilute hydrochloric acid and cobalt nitrate or chloride, and a record book.

This last is perhaps the most important item in the mineralogist's entire kit. An exceptionally good record book is available from the Eckert Co.; it provides for entering the complete history of each specimen, including the location where it was found, the date, its characteristics, a description of any experimental work made on the specimen and the results.

Unless one has access to a museum or other institution owning comprehensive collections, a good reference book listing the characteristics of the principal minerals is indispensable.

Many amateurs add a camera to their field kit. Often the geological character of the locale from which a specimen is taken helps in its identification. Moreover, photographs taken in the field and associated with the written history of specimens add greatly to the interest of collections.

As the collection grows it invites more elaborate experimental analysis, ranging from the detailed study of each specimen's crystallography to chemical and physical tests with the advanced techniques of the modern laboratory. Some of these may be undertaken successfully by the beginner who has a bit of spare room on his workbench.

The simple blowpipe test, for example, yields powerful results. It requires a flame (candle, alcohol lamp or Bunsen burner), a small block of charcoal, a little powdered borax, a short length of nichrome wire and a tapered blowpipe. Blowing into the tube, the worker directs the flame onto a small fragment of the specimen lying on the charcoal block. The fusability of the mineral is a clue to its identification; some minerals are readily fusible and others resist the hottest flame.

The flame of the blowpipe is made up of two concentric cones, the outer one pale violet and the inner a bright blue. The inner cone is deficient in oxygen. When subjected to the heat of this cone, many metallic oxides give up their oxygen to the burning gas and are thereby reduced, or refined. Conversely the outer

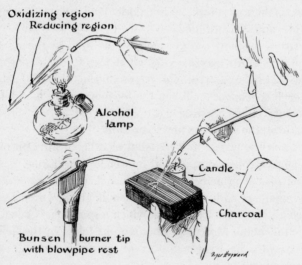

95
Sources of flame for the blowpipe test

cone is rich in oxygen and will, therefore, oxidize many minerals. Such oxides differ in color from the original mineral, and reference books list these changes along with the other clues to the specimen's identity.

Similarly many specimens react characteristically when immersed in a solution of hot borax. To make this test a small loop is formed at the end of the nichrome wire. The loop is brought to a yellow heat with the blowpipe, dipped into the powdered borax and returned to the flame, where the powder adhering to the loop is melted. The red-hot globule of melted borax is then dipped into a crushed sample of the specimen and returned to the flame. As the sample enters into solution with the borax it reacts chemically and a characteristic color appears which changes, often radically, as the globule cools.

Within a surprisingly short time the beginner will learn to identify a large number of rocks in his locality. He will meet or communicate with other collectors and exchange specimens not available in his immediate vicinity. And if he has a flair for experimental chemistry, he will discover that nature has stocked almost every hillside with an assortment of raw materials rivaling those carried by many supply houses — all free for the taking.

Where did these compounds originate? Under what conditions? How much time did nature lavish on their formation? In seeking answers to these questions the amateur may be lured into the broader field of geology — in which he will come to observe at first hand the frozen remains of creatures that disappeared from the earth long before the advent of man, to explore the ooze of ancient seas, to examine the explosive forces that have shaped our planet.

2

THE ATTRACTIONS OF AMATEUR SEISMOLOGY

The hobby of an amateur seismologist is described and directions given for locating the source of distant earthquakes by the vibrations that shake your own back yard. Some typical seismographs. An eminent seismologist invites the amateur to give the professionals a helping hand

To FIND A HAPPY AMATEUR, as good a place as any to start is in the basement of a cottage at Elma, N. Y. There, in a tiny corner cubicle that looks like a photographer's darkroom, is one of the most interesting seismological stations in the U. S. It is owned and operated by Harry H. Larkin, Jr., who during business hours is vice president of Larkin Warehouse, Inc., in nearby Buffalo. An amateur meteorologist and seismologist, Mr. Larkin is a cooperative observer for two branches of the U. S. Government. He makes regular weather reports to the U. S. Weather Bureau, and whenever his instruments record an earthquake, he dispatches his readings by teletype to the U. S. Coast and Geodetic Survey. Mr. Larkin's special interest in seismology is the study of microseisms, the constant tiny tremors of the earth that seem to link the planet's structure with its weather but are still an unsolved puzzle.

The earth sciences have fascinated Mr. Larkin for as long as he can remember. As a boy he used to visit every weather station within range of the family car with his father. Later, after taking up flying, he began his career as a meteorologist by installing a barograph in the Larkin den. Today his back yard bristles with rain gauges, thermometer shelters, towers supporting anemometers, wind vanes, sunshine recorders, time-lapse sky cameras —

a full complement of professional instruments. Some years ago Mr. Larkin's growing reputation as a cooperative weather observer prompted a professional seismologist to invite him to help in the investigation of microseisms. Mr. Larkin added two sheets of recording paper to the daily dozen already coming off his instruments and embarked hesitantly on what has since become an absorbing and often thrilling experience. As he puts it, "I entered seismology through the back door and can perhaps be described best as an amateur meteorologist with seismology as a hobby, or *vice versa*."

Practically everything a seismologist knows comes from the interpretation of wavy lines traced on a sheet of paper, and to understand seismology one must first understand the instrument that makes this record. The heart of the seismometer is a pendulum, which serves as the sensing element. Its movement records the strength and character of each tremor of the earth. The standard Weichert seismometer of the professionals is a complicated affair with a 175-pound pendulum and a stone foundation extending down to bedrock. But the instrument in Mr. Larkin's basement is astonishingly simple [*Fig. 96*].

On a slab of concrete embedded two feet deep in clay beneath the basement floor stand two slender, upright cylinders: one to measure earth movements in the east-west direction, the other, north-south. Inside each cylinder is a taut vertical wire with a small copper vane attached to it. The vane is the "pendulum," though it extends out horizontally from the wire, instead of hanging. When the earth trembles, the vane swings slightly. A beam of light, reflected from a mirror on the vane, makes a tracing of this movement on a roll of photographic paper wrapped around a slowly rotating drum. In essence, that's all there is to it.

This instrument is known as a torsional seismometer. It is comparatively inexpensive and can be bought in kit form and assembled in a few hours by any amateur. The apparatus was made available commercially by the late William F. Sprengnether, Jr., president of the Sprengnether Instrument Company of St. Louis.

The sensing element consists of a copper vane about a quarter-

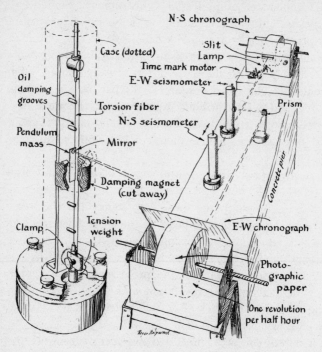

96
Wood-Anderson torsion seismograph used by Harry H. Larkin, Jr.

inch wide and an inch and a half high, attached along one edge
to a hairlike wire held taut by a vertical framework. When earthquake waves or other tremors move the assembly back and forth,
the vane rotates in precise response. The swinging of the vane
twists the wire slightly, which accounts for the name "torsional"
seismometer.

A small mirror with a focal length of one meter is cemented
to the vane. A light beam reflected from it, acting as an optical
lever, amplifies the vane's movements and registers them on
photographic paper carried by the recorder.

The recorder is simply a metal box containing a drum to carry
the photographic paper. Driven by a small synchronous motor,

the drum revolves at the rate of one revolution in 30 minutes and also moves along its axis. Thus the light beam makes a helical trace on the record sheet. The beam comes from a small lamp in a tubular housing attached to the front of the recorder. At regular intervals the time is marked automatically on the record sheet. These marks were made by means of an electric clock.

"The cost of a single instrument," says Larkin, "including material for a room and pier but not providing for an accurate clock, should not be much over $200. This figure will yield, more or less, to the amateur's ingenuity and patience. The cost of photographic paper will run around $25 per year.

"Because newspapers rarely feature accounts of earthquakes you may entertain the notion that amateur seismologists, like soldiers, spend most of their time waiting for something to happen. It is true that many days may intervene between major quakes. But microseisms, tracing their patterns on the sheet hour after hour and day after day, are an endlessly diverting show. The study of these tremors alone is an undertaking that well justifies building a station. Some microseisms record the tiny shakings of the earth by storms at sea. Some appear to be associated with low pressure systems in the atmosphere. Some come in harmonious groups from no-one-knows-where. Some appear fixed, as standing waves. Others crisscross in random array. The pattern is ever-changing: waves that herald tomorrow's weather, waves that record the onward travel of yesterday's cold front, perhaps even waves that still reflect the earth's dying response to an ice age long past.

"But the greatest thrill is to catch the dramatic reverberations of an earthquake, sometimes from far across the globe. Three kinds of waves record this happening. The first is the P or pressure wave, a compressional wave like that of sound, in which the wave motion is in the direction of the waves' travel. The next is the S or shake wave, which vibrates at right angles to the waves' path. Finally there is a long L wave, undulating like a water wave, which journeys around the surface of the earth.

"The three waves travel at different speeds. An earthquake is

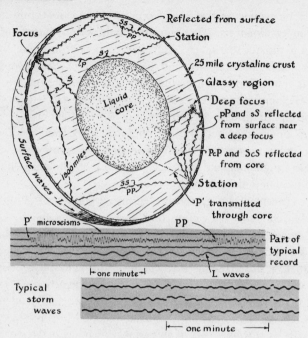

Reflected from surface
Station
Focus
25 mile crystaline crust
Glassy region
Deep focus
pP and sS reflected from surface near a deep focus
PcP and ScS reflected from core
Liquid core
Station
P' transmitted through core
Surface waves L
1800 miles
P' microseisms
PP
Part of typical record
one minute
L waves
Typical storm waves
one minute

97
Origin and types of earthquake waves

heralded by the sudden appearance on the seismometer scroll of the harsh jagged pattern of P waves, which speed through the earth at five miles per second. After a minute or so, depending on how far the quake is from the station, the P waves begin to die. But the show is far from over. Soon the slower S waves (three miles per second) arrive, as abruptly and violently as the first. They mark a very different pattern, easily distinguishable from the P. Some time later, again depending on the distance of the quake from the station, come the lazy, snake-like L waves (two and a half miles per second) that close the show. The difference in speed between P and S waves makes it a simple matter to determine from a travel-time chart the distance they have traveled and the time when the quake occurred.

"Time and distance data provide clues in the structure of the earth. The waves are reflected by its layers of differing material; some of them literally bounce around inside the earth. The reflected waves, differing slightly from those that travel directly to the station, tell something about the depth of these layers. Furthermore, S waves are not detectable at a distance of more than 7,000 miles, indicating that they are blocked somewhere in the depths of the earth. Since S waves can travel only through a solid, this suggests that the earth has a liquid core. The core also slows the passage of P waves; those that have passed through the core are designated P'."

Most earthquakes originate in the outer crust of the earth, but shocks from levels all the way down to about 400 miles have been recorded. Deep-focus earthquakes are recognized by the absence of L waves and the presence of wave trains which have been reflected from the surface above.

Paradoxically, the catastrophic events that accompany major earthquakes, as well as some minor ones, stem from terrestrial processes so gentle that they escape the eye of most persons. This year, for example, erosion will plane away at the uplands; volcanoes will erupt fresh lava; creeping masses of molten rock far beneath the surface will lift some mountains a little higher; rivers will distribute sediment over the floor of the oceans. All these shifting loads will exert new forces on rocks buried as deep as 400 miles. As the rocks crack and slide during the next 18 months the earth will liberate some 200 trillion trillion ergs of energy, which will touch off at least 1,500,000 earthquakes. Of these, some 15,000 will cause minor damage. Another 1,500 will locally shatter chimneys. Between 50 and 100 will be strong enough to register on every seismograph in the world. Some 15 or 20 will pack enough power to trigger local landslides, wreck bridges and level the most durable stone buildings. One of these quakes may be catastrophic.

The magnitude of earthquakes is measured by a scale based on the height to which the pen or light beam of a standard instrument will swing when a quake occurs at a specified distance from the station. On this scale a great shock such as the Japanese quake in December, 1946, has a magnitude of about 8.6; an atomic explosion may produce a quake rated at 5.5, and a mild quake that causes dishes to rattle in the vicinity of the quake center has a magnitude of 2.5.

Earthquakes of course are sporadic and unpredictable. Mr. Larkin's seismometer has recorded two or three major shocks in a single day, while at times several weeks or more pass without a large one. On the average his station registers about one major quake every five days.

The U. S. Coast and Geodetic Survey, with the cooperation of Science Service and the Jesuit Seismological Association, mails out cards after each major earthquake giving the "epicenter" (source) and time of origin of the quake. Any amateur who operates a seismological station as a cooperative observer may get on the mailing list to receive the cards by writing to the Survey. With this information and travel-time charts, it is an easy matter to review seismograph records and become proficient in interpreting them.

By analyzing the wave motion of light, man has solved riddles of celestial mechanics lying billions of miles beyond the trembling surface on which he dwells. But the earth waves, which might tell us a great deal about our own planet, have been comparatively neglected. Do mountain-building convection currents flow within the earth's plastic core? Is that core plastic, liquid — or neither? Although the seismograph was invented 110 years ago, science has yet to resolve these and related questions.

Thousands of telescopes have been built by laymen, but the number of amateur seismographs in existence is very small. Professional seismologists have appealed repeatedly for amateur cooperation. To make a really detailed plot of the earth's interior, something still to be achieved, science must assemble observations from a closely spaced network of seismological stations.

Our present knowledge of what lies beneath the earth's surface is vague and indistinct. In general, it is believed that the granite crust extends down about 30 miles. Then, like the progressively thicker rings of an onion, comes a layer of basalt and glassy rock to a depth of about 420 miles, and below that to some 1,800 miles a layer or "mantle," probably composed of metallic oxides. The core, roughly 4,100 miles in diameter, is believed to be liquid, but its exact consistency is unknown. Some theories call for convection currents in this plastic mass, supplying the forces that build mountains. But these are only informed guesses and must remain so until seismology assembles enough facts to bring into clear focus the picture of what lies such a relatively short distance beneath our feet.

Seismologists would like to have many additional workers and a closely spaced network of observing points to supplement the stations now thinly distributed over the North American continent.

Here is a frontier awaiting exploration, one in which the professional geophysicist eagerly invites the amateur's help. Father Joseph Lynch, S.J., head of Fordham University's seismological observatory, has said: "There is a seismological job to suit everyone's purse and everyone's ability — there is seismic work for all — but no financial remuneration." That, indeed, would seem to qualify seismology as an amateur pursuit.

3

AN ELECTRONIC SEISMOGRAPH

From a war-surplus magnet, some scrap metal and a few electronic parts you can build an instrument of great sensitivity for detecting earthquakes and recording the ever-present "microseisms" that herald the approach of violent storms. The apparatus was designed specifically for amateur construction by E. W. Kammer, an instrumentation specialist for the U. S. Navy. Its total cost, excluding a graphic recorder, should not exceed $75

THE GRAPHS in Figures 98 and 99 show how the earth jiggled a seven-room house in Alexandria, Va., on November 29, 1952, at 12:55 p. m. The onset of a quake was announced by the arrival of a pressure (P) wave at 12:55:35 [*Fig. 98*] and was followed several minutes later by the secondary or "S" wave [*Fig. 99*]. The record was made on a novel seismograph designed especially for amateurs by E. W. Kammer, an instrumentation specialist for the U. S. Navy. As may be seen, quite a lot was happening during those minutes. The thickness of the trace line, prior to the quake, was caused by traffic streaming into and out of Washington, D. C., a few miles away. Similar nearby traffic disturbances account for some of the small, sharp peaks. The gentler over-all modulation represents an approaching area of low atmospheric pressure. The longest rises and falls reflect a violent storm building up at sea off the Carolinas. Some 12 hours later its full fury struck and drove the recording pen off the sheet.

These waves are called microseisms. They are minute vibrations endlessly rippling through the earth's crust in response to the interplay of myriad forces, both natural and man-made. They are so faint that it is unlikely anyone in Alexandria other than Kammer was conscious that the earth was shaking.

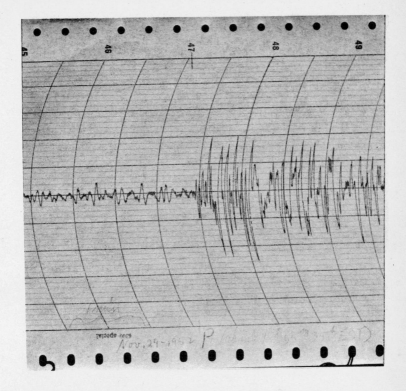

98
Seismogram showing microseisms *(left)* and onset of P wave heralding an earthquake

Earth waves are to the seismograph what light waves are to the telescope. Just as the telescope reveals cosmic details too dim or far away for the eye to see, the seismograph enables scientists to catch glimpses of the earth's internal structure. And as the telescope reports new comets and exploding stars, so, too, the seismograph provides a running account of unusual activities: sudden spurts in the growth of new mountains, readjustments of internal forces in response to surface erosion, the collapse of subterranean caverns, the interplay of stresses set up by tides and

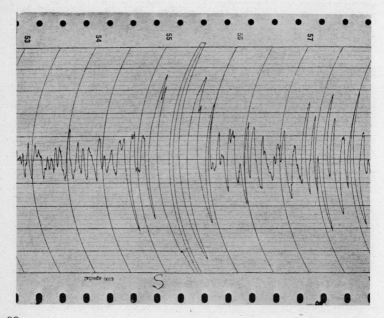

99
Arrival of S wave marking second phase of earthquake phenomena

shifting air masses. Thus the seismograph is an instrument for investigating from a safe distance some of the most awesome spectacles staged on earth, as well as the only known tool for studying the planet's interior beyond a depth of six or seven miles.

It is regrettable that amateurs thus far have not been much attracted by seismology. Kammer believes that three mistaken impressions have discouraged amateurs from taking up seismology. First, most laymen think that nothing much happens to a seismograph until an earthquake comes along; and judging by accounts published in newspapers, quakes seem to be few and far between. Second, laymen look upon seismograph records as a rather dull succession of squiggles which earthquakes convert into a hopeless scramble. Finally, the instrument strikes most laymen as a formidable piece of machinery. The few on public display feature massive frameworks anchored to concrete piers set in bedrock. The amplifying levers pivot on sapphire jewels. Finely wrought clocks drive precision drums carrying cylinders of smoked paper that look messy to handle. Certainly such an instrument lies beyond the pocketbooks and home-workshop capabilities of most amateurs.

Kammer admits that seismology owes much of its interest to earthquakes. Their waves do a lot of bouncing around on the layers inside the planet before registering on the instrument. That is why earthquake waves carry so much information about the places they have been. "If you are looking for action," says Kammer, "then don't bother with TV. Get a seismograph. With a little experience the records become not only easy to read but exciting. You can tell at a glance whether a quake originated on the other side of the globe or only a few thousand miles away, whether it was a disturbance at the surface or a readjustment of deep forces. What seem meaningless wiggles become to the experienced observer images of a coastal region sinking beneath the sea, a distant storm center, the birth of a volcano — or merely a tell-tale trace that follows your wife as she walks from the kitchen to the living room."

Kammer says that if he had to use one of the old museum-type seismographs his enthusiasm for seismology would probably dwindle. "I don't think I could work up much zest for a steam-driven bench saw today, either." Fortunately, in our electronic age all engines have shrunk in size and cost, including the seismograph. The instrument Kammer has designed for amateurs sits on a plate only 20 inches long by 10 inches wide [see Roger Hayward's drawing, Fig. 100]. It consists of three units: a seismometer, an amplifier and a recorder. A horizontal beam, pivoted at one end, carries a coil of insulated copper wire at the opposite end which swings between the poles of a permanent magnet. This pickup coil serves as the bob of the seismometer's pendulum. Flexible leads connect the coil with a line leading to the amplifier, which, if desired, may be located a mile or more away from the seismometer. The amplifier drives an electrical registering pen. Kammer uses a standard 5-0-5 milliampere Esterline-Angus re-

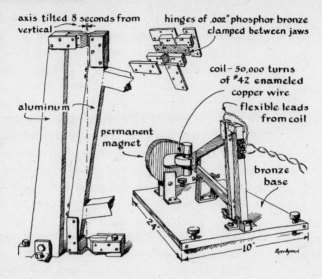

axis tilted 8 seconds from
vertical

hinges of .002" phosphor bronze
clamped between jaws

coil - 50,000 turns
of #42 enameled
copper wire

flexible leads
from coil

aluminum

permanent
magnet

bronze
base

24

10"

100
Details of Galitzin-type electronic seismograph adapted for amateur
construction by E. W. Kammer

corder which he purchased on the war-surplus market.

In addition to permitting the seismometer to be located at a
remote point favorable to it, the design has other advantages over
old-type seismographs. Because it contains no delicate parts, the
unit may be moved without the risk of disturbing its adjustment.
The equilibrium position of the seismic coil is not critical, nor,
for that matter, is the position of any of the parts with the exception of the Cardan-type hinges. These must be in good alignment
or unpredictable forces will be set up when the pendulum is near
its zero position.

Kammer's pickup coil is scramble-wound with 50,000 turns of
number 42 B-S gauge enameled copper wire, but both the number
of turns and wire size may be varied. The coil swings between the
poles of a war-surplus magnetron magnet. An electromagnet
would serve as well. The size of the air gap between the poles

and the thickness of the coil is unimportant as long as adequate clearance is maintained.

Kammer says that it is desirable to increase the voltage output from the seismometer by increasing the number of turns in the seismic coil until critical damping can be obtained by connecting a resistance of several megohms across it. The increased signal level permits the use of fewer stages in the amplifier. The unit is fitted with a cover to shield it from stray electrical and magnetic effects.

The circuit is so arranged that a small battery can be switched momentarily across the seismic coil, thereby driving it as a motor and deflecting it from its normal position of equilibrium. Upon disconnecting the battery, the coil is again connected across the input to the amplifier. In this way the free period of the un-damped seismometer oscillation as well as the proper value of damping resistance can be determined without disturbing the cover.

Perhaps the chief advantage of Kammer's instrument is the control it gives the observer over the character of the record. Unlike instruments that employ optical levers and record on photo-sensitive papers, the electronic seismograph's records can be observed continuously as they are being written. Faint, closely spaced microseisms can be enlarged at a twist of a knob to show as much detail as desired, while large-scale disturbances can be reduced, thus preventing the pen from swinging off the record sheet.

As presently designed, the instrument has only one questionable feature. It is a "velocity" type seismograph; the electrical output of the seismic coil varies in proportion to the *velocity* of the pendulum rather than its *displacement*. Professional seismologists are interested in the shape of the displacement wave — the amount of the earth's excursion on either side of the point of equilibrium — rather than in the velocity of the excursion.

Velocity graphs can be converted to displacement by performing a single integration, easily accomplished with one of the commercially available integrating devices or by feeding the output of the amplifier into an electronic integrating circuit of the type recently developed for electronic analog computers. These circuits are simple to build and the parts do not cost much. But Kammer says it is surprising how much you can learn from a straight velocity graph. He does not use an integrator.

The most remarkable of the three units is the amplifier, which responds to frequencies extending from three cycles per second down to one cycle in twenty seconds. Kammer deliberately reduced the response of the amplifier to frequencies above three vibrations per second in order to suppress the effects of man-made disturbances such as motor traffic.

Most long-period amplifying devices are troubled by a gradual drift of the zero or neutral recording position. Kammer's amplifier [see Fig. 101] obtains long-term zero stability by means of capacity-resistance coupling between the stages. The five-megohm grid leak (damping resistor) across the first of two special 10-microfarad condensers gives the unit a 50-second time constant. Hence it is possible to observe typical seismograms containing vibrations up to a period of 30 seconds.

Gradual changes in the characteristics of vacuum tubes or battery voltages do not occur rapidly enough, according to Kammer, to develop bothersome potentials across the grid resistors. The two 10-microfarad condensers are the only critical parts in the amplifier. They must be of the best quality and have at least 1,000 megohms leakage resistance. Condensers of this type are currently priced at about $10 each. (They are available from Condenser Products Company, Chicago.)

The output stages consist essentially of a bridge circuit similar to those used in vacuum-tube voltmeters. The first tube of the bridge acts both as amplifier and phase inverter — note the one-megohm resistor between the plate of the first tube and the grid of the second — to drive the final tube's grid. This increases the unit's sensitivity. Current to drive the recorder is taken from across the cathodes of the bridge tubes. If desired, voltage can be tapped from across the plates to operate a cathode-ray oscilloscope or other voltage-actuated device. Kammer made his gain control of fixed resistors that diminish by half-value steps from grid to

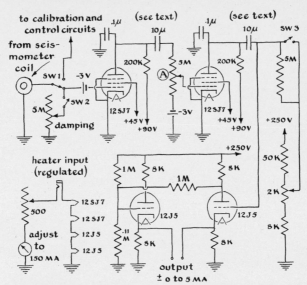

sw1—Transfers seismometer coil to external circuit.
sw2—Removes damping resistor.
sw3—Shortens time constant of grid circuit of first 12 J 5 and permits amplifier to center quickly after changing gain.

Ⓐ— gain control

101
Circuit diagram for the Kammer seismograph

ground, each tapped by a rotary switch. The positive action of the switch generates less noise than the potentiometer which has been substituted, for simplification, in the drawing. The .1-microfarad capacitors, connected between the plates and ground, limit the upper-frequency response of the unit. Without them, nearby vibrations would unduly thicken the trace.

A well-regulated power supply may be substituted for battery operation. The heaters of the tubes are connected in series directly across the high-voltage supply through a dropping resistor which limits the current to 150 milliamperes. Plate and screen voltages for the pentode stages are derived from batteries, even though a power supply is used. Batteries improve the stability of the unit and, since the current drain is small, they will last their rated life.

The arrangement of the amplifier parts is not critical, though Kammer suggests some protection from vibration to eliminate microphonic disturbances originating in the vacuum tubes. In using this amplifier it is important, he warns, to be aware of phase shift introduced by the coupling networks when signals from several seismometers are correlated.

When studying microseisms from simultaneous recordings of three instruments — the so-called "tripartite" arrangement — signals being compared have the same period and hence experience the same amount of phase shift if the amplifiers are nearly identical. This condition, Kammer explains, is easily achieved and can be tested by connecting the inputs of all amplifiers in parallel, driving them from one signal source and comparing the records on separate recorders.

Although this remarkable amplifier was designed to operate from a velocity-type seismometer, it should perform equally well when driven by other long-period voltage sources. It takes little imagination to conceive of seismometers that would produce voltages proportionate to either pendulum displacement or acceleration. Beyond the field of seismometry, the amplifier should find wide application in stellar photometry and in other studies which require the recording of very low frequencies.

4

AN AMATEUR'S SEISMOLOGICAL OBSERVATORY

Some fascinating variations in seismograph design are presented in a review of the instruments built by A. E. Banks of Santa Barbara, Calif. Details are given of the design and construction of each instrument. A remarkable seismograph, largely the handiwork of nature, is described

ONE OF THE MOST comprehensive seismological observatories yet built by an amateur is maintained by A. E. Banks, the proprietor of a stationery store in Santa Barbara, Calif. Banks invested substantially all of his free time over a period of three years in learning how to build simple versions of conventional seismographs. In consequence, he has recently developed a few types not found in the reference manuals.

Because two or more instruments of substantially different types are always on the job at his observatory, he rarely misses an earthquake. The most interesting sections of his record of the big Aleutian quake in March, 1957, which pounded beaches in Hawaii with five-foot waves, appear in Figure 102. The complete record of the quake covers four feet of record paper.

The first section of the record shows the faint and ever-present vibrations known as microseisms, which seem to arise from variations in atmospheric pressure, the pounding of surf and other minor sources of seismic energy. The next section shows the beginning of the quake, which is announced by the first and fleetest of three characteristic types of earthquake waves: the primary or "P" wave. The P wave vibrates in the direction of its travel like an opening and closing coil spring. It travels through the earth at an average speed of about five miles per second. The third sec-

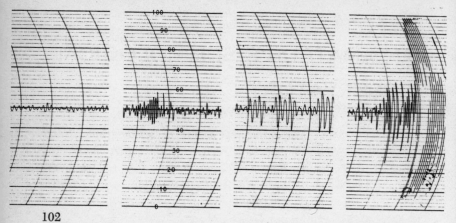

102

Seismogram of March, 1957, Aleutian earthquake recorded by A. E. Banks of Santa Barbara, Calif.

tion shows the arrival of the secondary or "S" wave. This wave travels at an average velocity of about three miles per second; it is often called the "shake" wave because it vibrates at right angles to the direction of its travel like an oscillating violin string. The trace made by S waves on the seismogram is not so jagged as that of P waves; moreover, the height or amplitude of the two are rarely equal. Hence P and S waves can usually be distinguished from each other without difficulty.

The fact that both P and S waves travel at characteristic rates provides a basis for calculating the distance between a quake's point of origin and the recording station. The more distant the quake, the longer the race and the longer the lead of the P waves over the S. The lead of the P waves does not vary, however, in direct proportion to the surface distance between the observing station and the location of the quake. This is primarily due to the fact that the waves take short-cuts through the interior of the earth. The waves are also refracted and reflected by discontinuities in the interior of the earth, and their velocity increases with the depth of their path.

The fourth section of Banks's seismogram shows the final major wave of the Aleutian quake, the long or "L" wave. The L wave always makes a big, dramatic trace and, unlike P and S waves, travels largely through the earth's outer layers. P and S waves are accordingly most useful in investigations of the structure of the earth at great depths, and L waves are most useful in studies of its outer layers. The velocity of L waves is influenced by the character of the terrain but averages about 2½ miles per second.

The seismograph senses earth vibrations by taking advantage of Newton's first law, which states in effect that a body freely suspended and at rest in space will remain at rest until something gives it a push. If an experimenter could float in still air, his position would not be affected by an earthquake, however violent; if a sheet of paper were fastened to the ground, he could make a seismogram simply by reaching down and allowing a pencil to move across it during the quake. Because gravity rules out such ideal suspensions, the designers of seismographs settle for an elastic suspension such as a pendulum or a weight on a spring. A pendulum may be considered an elastic suspension because it behaves as though a spring were stretched between the pendulum bob and the center of the earth.

Galileo was the first to observe two interesting properties of such suspensions. First, they oscillate or swing at a characteristic rate. For example, when an iron ball suspended from a coil spring is pulled down and then released, it bobs up and down at a rate which depends on the mass of the ball and stiffness of the spring. Second, when a pendulum is set in motion by a push it continues to oscillate for a time, the duration of which depends on how soon the energy imparted by the push is dissipated. This is why pendulums have historically been used to measure time. But if this property is prized by clockmakers, it is the bane of those who make seismographs.

The ideal seismograph would respond equally to waves of all frequencies. The seismograph designer, however, must make do with a device which favors some frequencies and discriminates against others. Consider a simple seismometer consisting a heavy iron ball suspended from a spring attached to a framework which rests on the ground.

Let the ball and spring be chosen so that when the ball is disturbed, it bobs up and down once a second. Assume the ball is at rest when an earthquake strikes. If the quake shakes the frame faster than one oscillation a second, the ball will remain at rest while the spring expands and contracts. When the frequency of the shake corresponds to that of the ball and spring, the ball absorbs energy from each oscillation. It starts to bob up and down; the distance of its motion increases with each added oscillation. When the frame oscillates less than once a second, both ball and spring move up and down with it. Earth vibrations are detected by observing the motion of a pendulum bob with respect to its supporting frame. Such motion is accordingly apparent when the frequency of the frame is higher than that of the pendulum. It is almost totally absent when the frequency of the frame is lower.

The most desirable seismograph would thus be one with a natural period of oscillation longer than any earthquake wave. It would require a pendulum capable of swinging only once in several minutes; ideally the pendulum should oscillate once in several hours. Such leisurely pendulums are either difficult to make or impractically large. Moreover, the most interesting earthquake waves have frequencies in the range of about three oscillations per second to one per minute.

Seismological observatories usually record only the lower end of this range, and employ separate instruments tuned to oscillate at two, eight and 15 seconds. The two-second seismometer detects P waves and discriminates against microseisms, which lie in the two- to nine-second range. The eight-second instrument responds strongly to both P waves and microseisms. The 15-second instrument records these plus S and L waves. An instrument of this period is difficult to adjust; thus many amateur seismologists who have only one instrument compromise on a period of 10 seconds.

The second property of pendulums observed by Galileo — their tendency to continue swinging once they are set in motion — is controlled with friction or electrical resistance. This increases the rate at which unwanted energy is dissipated and so counteracts the pendulum's tendency to oscillate excessively at its natural period. It is often accomplished by immersing a vane attached to the bottom of the pendulum bob in a bath of oil. The same result can be achieved by making the vane, or even the bob, out of copper and suspending it between the poles of a strong magnet. Eddy currents induced in the copper are transformed into heat by the resistance of the metal.

Ideally the bob should be damped just enough for the pendulum to come to rest promptly. If the pendulum is damped too much, it will be sluggish and require more than one swing to reach equilibrium. If it is damped too little, it will swing several times before coming to rest. The best compromise, called "critical" damping, lies between these extremes and is determined experimentally for each instrument.

Unless they are in the immediate vicinity, earthquakes move the supporting frame of the pendulum only slightly — a thousandth of an inch or less. For the pendulum to make a useful record this motion must be amplified. The earliest seismographs were equipped with a system of amplifying levers, some of which turned on jeweled pivots. The short end of the first lever was coupled to the pendulum bob, the frame of the instrument providing the fulcrum. The long end of this lever drove another lever fitted with a stylus. The stylus made a trace on a cylinder of smoked paper rotated by clockwork.

The mechanism required a heavy pendulum bob so that enough energy could be transmitted from the frame to the stylus without setting the bob in motion. The modern seismograph usually employs a combination of mechanical, optical and electrical amplifying elements; they are arranged in such a way that the seismic energy merely controls the movement of an electrically powered recording pen.

In essence, then, a seismograph consists of an elastically suspended weight which acts as the sensing element, a device to amplify the motion of the weight with respect to its supporting framework, and a pen or stylus to record the amplified motion. A fully equipped seismographic station employs at least nine sensing elements. Three sense vertical motions and are tuned to periods of about two, eight and 15 seconds. The second set of three, similarly tuned, responds to horizontal oscillations in the north-south direction; the third set, to oscillations in the east-west direction.

A. E. Banks tells how he designed and built his seismographs

I FELT MY FIRST EARTHQUAKE in 1914 while sitting in an Iowa farmhouse. Although that experience touched off my interest in seismology, it was not until September of 1955 that I attempted to build an instrument. I had had no previous experience and so had to start at the bottom and go as far as I could with the information I could dig out of books. Most of them were addressed to the specialist. I soon found that even an amateur seismologist should have majored in physics, geophysics, mechanical engineering and meteorology. Later I discovered that he must also be able to dig a ditch and mix a batch of concrete. A facility with hand tools and electrical circuits also comes in handy. But if the amateur is willing to settle for standards somewhat lower than those of the professional seismologist, the construction and operation of a seismograph turns out to be surprisingly simple.

A so-called "horizontal component" seismometer, one which detects lateral oscillations, can be made in a couple of hours if one has the materials on hand — a few scraps of wood, some screws, a bolt, a bit of strap iron and a small piece of sheet metal. The device essentially consists of a small triangular wooden frame hung like a garden gate from a larger frame [*Fig. 103*]. The upper pivot is made from two pieces of strap iron. As shown in the illustration, one piece is screwed to the hypotenuse of the frame, filed to a point and bent over like a fishhook. The point of the hook fits into an indentation made with a center punch in the second piece, which is fastened to the frame. The bottom pivot consists of a lag screw filed to a point. It fits into an indentation in the end of a stud bolt. The base of the frame is fitted with three leveling screws. These are adjusted so the beam swings to equilibrium in the center of the frame. The stud bolt provides a further means of adjusting the inclination of the beam and thus of altering its natural period.

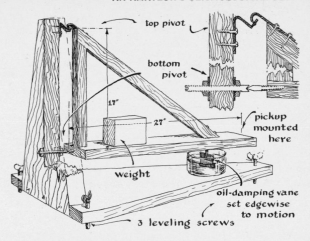

top pivot

bottom pivot

17″

27″

pickup mounted here

weight

oil-damping vane set edgewise to motion

3 leveling screws

103
A seismometer to detect horizontal motions of the earth

The period can also be adjusted over a wide range by placing a weight such as a brick on the beam. The brick serves as a pendulum bob, the period of oscillation increasing both with the weight of the bob and its distance from the pivots. The period is determined empirically by giving the pendulum a push and counting the number of seconds required for the beam to reach the limit of its swing and return.

Finally the pendulum is fitted with a damping vane and housed to shield it from air currents. A piece of nonmagnetic sheet metal two inches square is soldered in the slot of a wood screw and screwed into the bottom of the beam. The vane is immersed in a bath of light machine-oil. The depth of immersion is adjusted until the beam makes about two full swings before coming to rest.

A more elaborate version of essentially the same device is the Wood-Anderson torsional seismometer [*Fig. 104*]. Here the wooden frame is replaced by a heavy metal base and a 14-inch length of half-inch pipe. A 50-gauge wire (diameter .001 inch) is stretched between the bracket at the top of the pipe and the base. The long edge of a rectangular piece of sheet copper — about 1/2 inch wide, an inch long and 1/16 inch thick — is soldered or cemented to the

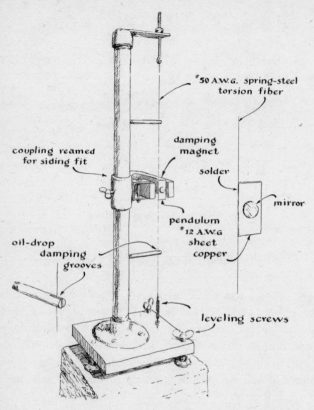

*50 A.W.G. spring-steel torsion fiber

coupling reamed for siding fit

damping magnet

solder

mirror

pendulum *12 A.W.G sheet copper

oil-drop damping grooves

leveling screws

104
A seismometer which detects horizontal motion by twisting a vertical wire

middle of the wire. This serves as the pendulum. The pendulum is damped by a magnet which may be moved to adjust the degree of damping. The wire passes through oil-filled grooves in the ends of two studs supported by the pipe. These studs suppress the vibration of the wire.

If the instrument is exposed to large variations in temperature, a coil spring must be inserted between the wire and its attachment to the base to compensate for differences in the expansion of the wire and its pipe support. Because an ordinary coil spring will twist the wire, it is necessary to use a double spring, one half of which is coiled in one direction and the other half in the reverse direction. Lateral movements of the earth shake the attached side of the vane with respect to its free edge. The wire, which corresponds to a hinge, twists slightly as the vane swings.

Seismometers to sense vertical vibrations usually consist of a pendulum hinged for vertical movement and supported in horizontal equilibrium by a set of springs. One of many possible arrangements is shown in the accompanying drawing [*Fig. 105*]. A mainspring supports the beam of the pendulum by holding it against a knife-edge. A second knife-edge is mounted on a short beam at right angles to the main beam. This knife-edge bears against an anvil linked to a second spring which opposes the force

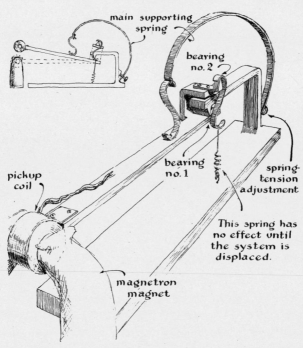

105
A seismometer to detect vertical motions of the earth

of the mainspring, depending upon the position of the pendulum and hence of the alignment of the two knife-edges. Adjustment of the second spring alters the natural period of the pendulum.

Here the pendulum bob is a coil of insulated copper wire which moves between the poles of a war-surplus magnetron magnet. Current induced in the coil is dissipated by a resistance connected across the leads and so damps the motion by an amount which varies with the resistance.

My first instrument was of the garden-gate type. The beam was a 27-inch piece of one-by-four-inch wood; bricks stacked on the beam acted as the pendulum bob. I found that the sensitivity of the instrument varies both with the angle at which the beam hangs and with the amount of damping. If the angle is too steep, the swing is imperceptible. If it is not steep enough, the beam will not return to equilibrium in the center of the supporting frame. The critical adjustment lies between these two extremes. To find it and at the same time find the proper weight and position of a bob which will oscillate at the desired rate requires some tinkering. This does not take long once you get the hang of it.

The beam must of course be coupled to an amplifier. My first one consisted of an arrangement of levers. It worked after a fashion but was so full of friction that it would have taken a 100-pound pendulum to drive it effectively. So I built the electronic system described by E. W. Kammer [see page 236].

Although the system worked perfectly and precisely as described by its designer, seismographs based on this principle make recordings in which the excursions of the pen represent the velocity at which the earth vibrates, so I decided to attempt the design of a displacement instrument utilizing electronic components. The answer was found while browsing in a local radio store. I chanced to spot an inexpensive photovoltaic cell, one of the so-called "sun batteries" used in exposure meters. Why not substitute one of these for the photosensitive paper and drive the amplifier with its output? The principle has been used for years to amplify the deflection of galvanometers. Actually two photovoltaic cells are needed. They are arranged side by side so that the spot of light reflected from the mirror drifts from one to the other.

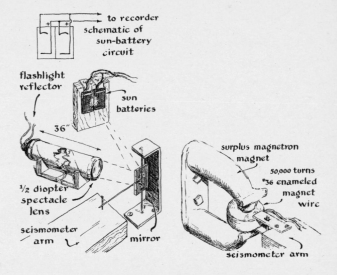

106
Optical and electrical elements for linking seismometers with amplifiers

The difference between the output of one cell and that of the other indicates the amount of deflection. The cells I use are made by the International Rectifier Corporation in El Segundo, Calif. They are called Type B-2-M and sell for $2.50 each. The system works with any convenient light source. A 35-millimeter slide projector works well. You can also make a source out of the reflector and socket assembly of a flashlight, a cardboard mailing tube and a spectacle lens [*Fig. 106*].

Although a mirror silvered on the back surface will do, one silvered on the front surface will yield better results. The mirror can be mounted on two pivots which fit into indentations in a strip of metal bent into a U. The indentations are made with a center punch before the strip is bent. The lever linking the mirror to the pendulum can be a short length of magnetized piano wire. The wire is magnetically attached to and moved by a steel brad in the free end of the seismometer beam.

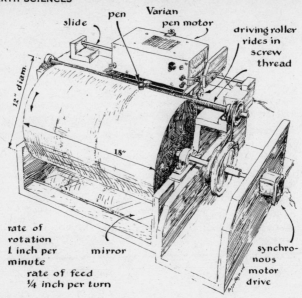

slide — pen — Varian pen motor — driving roller rides in screw thread

12" diam.

18"

rate of
rotation
1 inch per
minute
rate of feed
¼ inch per turn

mirror

synchro-
nous
motor
drive

107
Homemade recording drum for recording earthquake waves on inexpensive wrapping paper

The output of the sun batteries is directly connected to a Varian G-10 graphic recorder. This instrument, made by Varian Associates, Palo Alto, Calif., includes a self-contained, high-gain amplifier with which the sun batteries can easily drive the recording pen to its full deflection. The recorder is manufactured in two units: the amplifier and pen motor comprise one and the chart drive the other. The units may be purchased separately.

Although I have both units, I have replaced the chart drive with a home-made drum [see Fig. 107]. A conventional seismograph can eat up a lot of costly chart paper when it is driven fast enough to show the details of microseisms 24 hours a day. But the drum of my contraption is covered with a piece of common butcher paper 18 inches wide and 38 inches long. It turns two revolutions per hour. The pen is moved across the drum by a screw feed at the rate of 1/4 inch per revolution. Thus if the paper moves slightly more than an inch per minute, a 1,500-foot roll of it will keep the drum in continuous operation for three years! Butcher paper retails at $5 a roll.

I used hand tools to build the whole assembly except for the drum, which must be true within 1/32 inch or the pen will skip. A local machine shop turned out the drum for me at a cost of $13.50 including all materials. The lead screw is a length of pre-threaded rod carried by most hardware dealers as stock for stud bolts. The threads are engaged by a pair of rollers from a Meccano set. The rollers support the plywood carriage on which the pen unit rides. I now have two drum assemblies and an Esterline-Angus chart recorder in operation.

Contrary to the impression this description may create, the construction of a seismograph is neither difficult nor time-consuming. A few days ago I started to build a seismometer at noon; by five o'clock I had used it to bag a quake, the epicenter of which was 5,400 miles away. Incidentally, my recordings are timed by an electric clock checked against station WWV. The second hand of the clock closes a switch once a minute, discharging a two-microfarad condenser through the pen motor and recording a short pip on the seismogram.

The casual observer who wanders into a seismograph station may not be impressed by the opportunities for experiment which these slow-paced instruments provide. Firsthand experience will soon correct that impression. Building, testing and attempting to improve seismographs has kept me away from my television set for many a happy month; more projects are lined up now than when I started.

I am still trying to debug an instrument of the strain type which I put together over a year ago. This instrument, incidentally, is built on two pillars 60 feet apart. Between the pillars is a long piece of half-inch pipe. One end of the pipe is fixed to the first pillar; the other end is fitted with a coil which moves between the poles of a magnet fixed to the second pillar. When a quake alternately compresses and expands the crust of the earth between the two pillars, the coil develops a voltage [*Fig. 108*]. Unfortunately the setup is presently sensitive to wind and the rumble of nearby traffic.

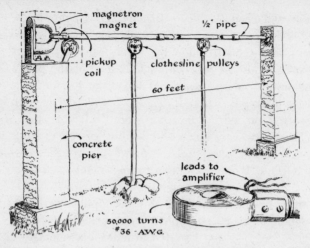

108
A. E. Banks's adaptation of the Benioff strain-seismometer

A well-water seismograph

THE SEISMOGRAPHS constructed by Banks are models of conventionality compared with one operated by Elmer Rexin, maintenance superintendent of the Nunn-Bush Shoe Co., in Milwaukee, Wis. Rexin has named his instrument, aptly enough, a "well-water" seismograph. Earth vibrations in his vicinity set up sympathetic variations in the level at which water stands in an abandoned well. Merely by putting a float in the well and coupling it mechanically to a graphic recorder, Rexin had a seismograph! Although not without precedent, it is the only instrument of its kind being operated by an amateur, as far as I know.

Heavy earthquake shocks often cause water to squirt from the ground in some regions. Small mounds of sand, resembling the craters of volcanoes, frequently mark the spots where underground water has erupted under pressures generated by the quake. The flow of artesian wells and the general level of water in wells in the vicinity are disturbed by these quakes. Many wells have been equipped with apparatus for recording water level, as well as hydrostatic pressure, and some of the resulting records have shown typical earthquake waves.

I am indebted both to Rexin and to *Earthquake Notes*, Journal of the Eastern Section of the Seismological Society of America, for the following account of the Milwaukee well.

Elmer Rexin explains how he turned a well into an earthquake detector

IN 1925 the Nunn-Bush Shoe Company added to its water supply by drilling a well to a depth of 380 feet and clearing it to 400 feet with a shot. The well was used until 1945, when gas contaminated the water. The casing was then plugged. In 1946 the U. S. Coast and Geodetic Survey received permission to install a water-level recorder in the hole. Shortly after the instrument went into operation, groups of closely spaced, vertical lines appeared on the charts.

These lines aroused my curiosity and I consulted the head geologist of the Geodetic Survey of Wisconsin about them. We suspected that earthquakes might cause them. He requested reports from Washington, D. C., and when the cards arrived about three weeks later our guess was confirmed. The reported quakes coincided with the records made by the well. With our curiosity thus satisfied, we dismissed the subject and I paid no further attention to the well.

Then, on the afternoon of May 7, 1947, something happened that was to make a radical change in the way I use my off hours. An official of the company rushed into the maintenance shop at 3:38 and told me that the whole boiler room was shaking and that he had heard a deep, rumbling noise. Within seconds the chief engineer rushed in with the same story. Although I had felt or heard nothing, I wondered if the disturbance could be caused by an earthquake. So the three of us went down to the well, and sure enough there were the lines — big ones! I telephoned our newspaper office and the reporter tried to convince me that the shock came from a big explosion on the southwest side of the city.

But while I was speaking with him another reporter yelled that Father Joseph Francis Carroll, chairman of the department of physics at Marquette University, had just reported a local earthquake. From that day forward I have been an earthquake enthusiast.

The next day I met Father Carroll and told him about the well. He was interested immediately and with his encouragement I decided to equip the well with an improved recorder, one that would make an enlarged chart of the waves. In this new device [*see Fig. 109*] the motion of the water is transferred from the well

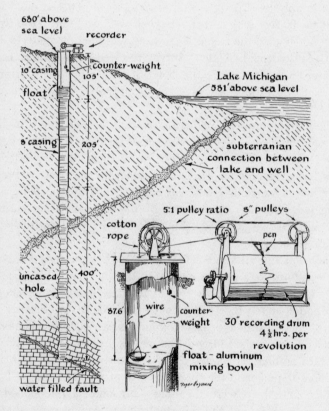

109
A seismograph activated by an abandoned well

to the record sheet by means of a float and a counterweighted line which passes over a pulley above the well. This pulley is belted, in turn, to a pair of matched pulleys that carry an endless belt to which the pen is attached. The oscillation of the matched pulleys causes the pen to move back and forth in a straight line. The record sheet is carried beneath the pen by a motor-driven drum. The drum makes one revolution in about four and a half hours.

The new recorder worked even better than we expected. The first markings to appear were not earthquake waves but extremely long curves, two every 24 hours, in the shape of perfect sine waves. Previously Father Carroll and I had discussed the tides of Lake Michigan, and I now consulted the library of Milwaukee's meteorologist. An early report by the U. S. Army Corps of Engineers showed that in spring the combined lunar and solar tides would amount to about two inches. When I made a check of the well against the predicted tides, and took measurements of them at the beach, all three corresponded.

Then I noticed that other curves were appearing on the graph. I suspected that variations in barometric pressure might be causing some of them. A microbarograph borrowed from the Johnson Service Company of Milwaukee proved that this was a good guess.

On May 29, 1947, the water rose and fell six tenths of a foot over a period of six hours, in addition to changes accounted for by the tide and barometric pressure. The following day I learned that a tidal wave had swept in on this side of the lake with a great loss of property. So I had to add tidal waves to the growing list of events that disturb the well.

Earthquake waves were being impressed on the record right along, of course, and it was necessary to unscramble these other curves in order to interpret the quake records. While learning to do this I first observed a curious effect. As areas of high barometric pressure moved out over the lake, the water level in the well would rise instead of going down. By this time I had learned to distinguish the small seiches caused by abrupt changes in barometric pressure during severe lightning storms. The seiches, tides, tidal waves and changes in barometric pressure at the lake all appeared to operate in reverse of the well. When the water in the lake rose, that in the well fell, and vice versa. Father Carroll and I discussed this with the late Father James B. Macelwane, then head of the Geophysics Technology Institute of St. Louis University. We reached the conclusion that the well is connected with the lake by a natural tunnel of some sort. Hence the effect we observed is the normal functioning of a U tube — with the well forming one arm of the U and the lake the other.

The largest quake registered by the well-recorder during its 12 years of operation caused the water to oscillate 11.9 feet. This was the Assam-Tibet quake of August 15, 1950, 12,000 miles from Milwaukee. This was one of the six greatest quakes ever recorded by seismologists. It took a toll of approximately 5,000 lives and left 5,000,000 homeless. The initial tremors reached Milwaukee at 8:35 in the morning and continued until 9:00 in the evening. The quake in Montana on August 18, 1959, caused a water oscillation of 2.5 feet in the well and its tremors persisted for 2½ hours.

The sensitivity of the well to earthquakes is probably accounted for by a water-filled fault that connects with the well at the 400-foot level, but until now we have not devised an experimental method for checking this theory. If our guess is correct, the action would be much like that of a syringe, with the fault serving as the rubber bulb. Pressure created by quakes would compress and expand the fault, thus forcing water into the well and sucking it out again. As a seismograph, the well is quite sensitive, and I have little trouble distinguishing primary and secondary waves of even low-magnitude quakes.

At present I am interested in setting up apparatus for measuring short-period pressures that may be created in the well. The apparatus will consist of a waterproof microphone which will drive an electrical recorder through a high-gain amplifier. I once sank a microphone to a depth of 160 feet and detected a regular pattern of pressure waves, but the seal broke where the lead entered the water-tight container, and you can guess what the record showed after that.

5

HOW TO TRACK
EARTH SATELLITES

Anyone with access to a piano and a radio set capable of picking up signals from an artificial satellite can measure the satellite's altitude. You can even do it with a set of sticks and a stop watch, although not as accurately

ARTIFICIAL SATELLITES and their associated hardware have opened new horizons for the amateur scientist. Scores of amateurs participated in the Moonwatch and Moonbeam programs sponsored by the U. S. National Committee of the International Geophysical Year. These formal activities marshal the services of advanced amateurs to man elaborate stations which make observations of immediate scientific value. But the amateur does not need elaborate equipment to keep track of a satellite's path, or even to predict with fair accuracy how long a satellite will stay on orbit. Anyone can do it. The amateur who prefers to make observations with a minimum of equipment can get into business with nothing more than three wooden slats and a stop watch.

These techniques require that the observer be outdoors, often before sunrise. For the comfort-loving amateur there is another means of keeping track of satellites, at least so long as they transmit radio signals. Many ordinary radio receivers have built-in converters which enable them to pick up the short waves broadcast by satellites. Even those receivers without converters are easy to adapt to short-wave reception. Converter units, available from dealers in ham radio supplies, are priced at about $50. Those amateurs who prefer to build their own converters will find complete instructions in *The Radio Amateur's Handbook.* Parts for a two-tube converter cost about $15.

Ralph H. Lovberg and Louis C. Burkhardt, physicists at the Los Alamos Scientific Laboratory, have suggested a way in which the amateur can determine the height of a satellite as it passes overhead. Their method is based on the Doppler shift, the apparent decrease of pitch noted when a source of sound, such as a train whistle, rushes past the observer.* Radio-equipped satellites are in effect whistling objects. Their radio transmitters radiate signals at predetermined frequencies. In the case of the first two satellites placed on orbit the frequencies were approximately 20 and 40 megacycles per second.

To measure the distance between the observer and a satellite, the signal from the satellite is tuned in on a radio receiver and mixed with a signal generated by a local oscillator of somewhat higher or lower frequency. The difference frequency is then amplified, fed into a loudspeaker and converted into sound. For example, when a signal of 40 megacycles is mixed with a locally generated signal of 39.997 megacycles, the amplified difference frequency of 3,000 cycles will produce a whistling sound pitched about two octaves above middle C. The period during which the pitch changes may last more than five minutes.

The distance of the satellite is determined by measuring the pitch of the sound at brief intervals during this period, and noting the time at which each tone is identified. The frequency of the sound at each interval can be estimated by comparing it with the notes of a piano or, preferably, by following the whistle down the scale with an accurately calibrated audio-frequency oscillator. Whenever the signal and comparison tone (piano or oscillator) coincide (are in zero beat), the corresponding time should be recorded as read from the second hand of a watch or clock.

---

* It was by this method that Lovberg and Burkhardt learned that the first satellite was coming over Los Alamos at a height of about 170 miles at night and 260 miles during the day. The figures are in good agreement with those released by the Smithsonian Observatory.

Ralph H. Lovberg and Louis C. Burkhardt describe
the radio-piano method of locating a satellite

IN THE CASE of our measurements of the first satellite, we used a conventional Hallicrafter SX-28 receiver at 40 megacycles. The local beat-oscillator was left off and a surplus BC-221 frequency meter was coupled loosely (by means of a twist of insulated wire) to the antenna lead.

The signal generator is set at approximately 3,000 cycles below the satellite frequency when the "little traveler" is first detected. This results in an audible tone in the receiver output. The tone is now fed into a loudspeaker together with the output of an audio oscillator. In a typical run one sets the audio oscillator to a tone lower than that of the satellite, say 2,500 cycles per second, and waits for the satellite tone to drop to the same value. The zero beat between the two tones is first heard as a fluttering sound which diminishes in frequency to a slow swelling and fading of the 2,500-cycle note. At the instant the tone becomes steady, one records the time as well as the frequency (2,500 cycles in this instance) and quickly shifts the audio-frequency oscillator to, say, 2,400 cycles, and waits again for the matching of the tones.

The resulting table of frequencies and times is then plotted as a curve like the one shown in Figure 110. This indicates the passage

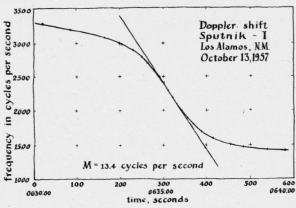

110
Curve for determining the height of a satellite

of the first satellite over the observer. Next we draw a line tangent to the curve at its steepest point. The slope of the tangent line represents the *number of cycles per second that the frequency changes per second* and varies in proportion to the distance of the satellite.

If we call this slope m, then the distance of the closest approach of the satellite is given by the simple formula $d = fv^2/cm$. Here f equals the frequency of the satellite's transmitter (40 megacycles), v equals the velocity of the satellite in miles per second (about 4.9 miles), c is the speed of light in miles per second. The velocity v will vary somewhat from the 4.9-miles-per-second value, depending on such factors as the eccentricity of the satellite's orbit. The amateur may obtain fairly accurate velocity figures from agencies such as the Smithsonian Astrophysical Observatory. These figures are sometimes reported in the daily press.

Sticks and stop watch: an optical method for tracking satellites is suggested by Walter Chestnut, a physicist at Brookhaven National Laboratory

IF AN OBJECT IS in a stable, circular orbit around the earth, one may say that the gravitational force of the earth pulls the object with a force which equals its centrifugal force. The relation may be expressed in mathematical terms in such a way that the object's altitude may be determined by a simple measurement of the number of degrees traversed by the satellite in one second as the object passes overhead. This angular velocity may be measured by timing the transit of the satellite as it passes stars, the positions of which are known.

If the amateur does not have a star chart, the angle can be easily measured by a fixed astrolabe, a triangle of wooden slats nailed together and supported as shown in the accompanying illustration, Figure 111. The astrolabe forms an angle of 10 degrees. The nails serve as sights; they should be painted white so that they will be clearly visible in poor illumination. The construction of the instrument should be as light as possible, because

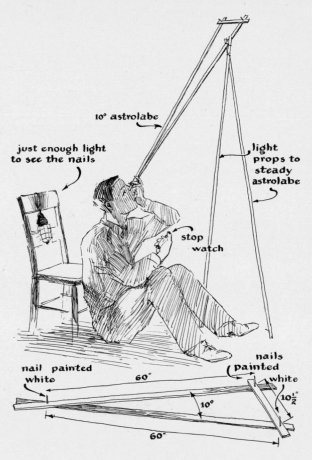

111
A simple astrolabe to measure the speed of an artificial satellite

it must be swung into position quickly when a satellite is spotted. The two outer nails should be placed in line with the satellite's path and held steady. The number of seconds are then counted from the time the object appears to touch the first nail until it reaches the second one. The corresponding altitude in miles can then be read from the accompanying table, Figure 112.

10 DEGREES TRANSIT TIME (SECONDS)	ALTITUDE (MILES)
2	56
3	84
4	112
5	138
6	166
7	193
8	219
9	246
10	273
12	325
14	375
16	426
18	477
20	526
25	650
30	770
35	890
40	1,000
50	1,225
60	1,450
70	1,660
80	1,860
90	2,060
100	2,250
120	2,620
140	2,980

112
Table of artificial satellite transit times and corresponding altitudes

Readers may calculate their own table for astrolabes of other angles by the equation:

$$d_1 = 282 \, t/a \sqrt{1 - .0705 \, t/a}$$

In this equation d_1 equals the altitude of the satellite in miles; t is the time of transit in seconds for an angle of a degrees. For an astrolabe of 15 degrees and a transit time of 60 seconds the altitude would be $(282 \times 60/15 \times \sqrt{1 - .0705 \times 60/15})$, or 1,128 $\times$ .8474 (956) miles. The same calculation is carried out for each value of time desired in the table.

Both the table and the equation assume that the satellite is observed within 15 degrees of the zenith. If the satellite is more than 15 degrees from the zenith, multiply the distance given in the table by the cosine of the angle between the orbit and the zenith. The equation and table also assume that the orbit is a circle. Most orbits, however, will be ellipses. But if one knows the maximum and minimum heights of the satellite, the table (and equation) can be corrected for ellipticity by the equation:

$$C = d_1 \left(\frac{d_e - d_1}{2(4,000 + d_e)} \right)$$

In this equation d_1 is the altitude obtained from the table (or the first equation). C is the distance (in miles) to be added to d_1 if C is positive, or to be subtracted from d_1 if C is negative. The average of the maximum and minimum altitudes of the satellite is represented by d_e. In the case of Sputnik I the maximum and minimum altitudes were respectively 570 and 170 miles; d_e accordingly equals 370 miles.

By following these instructions carefully the amateur can determine the altitude of a satellite with an accuracy of about 20 miles for every 1,000 miles of its height. The limits of error will doubtless be determined more by the accuracy of the observer's measurements than by errors of the method.

We have observed the rocket of Sputnik I on two occasions. The first time we merely wanted to find out if it was really there. On the second look the astrolabe was propped against a convenient tree. As the rocket traveled from one sighting nail of the astrolabe to the other, a transit time of 11.6 seconds was recorded. Unfortunately the tree swayed a little in the stiff morning breeze; this doubtless introduced an error of a few miles. The altitude for an 11.6-second transit, as it is read from the table, is 314 miles.

Timing the orbit of a satellite

WHAT ABOUT METHODS of measuring changes in the time it takes a satellite to make a trip around the world?

As satellites spiral inward toward the earth they speed up. When the orbital time of a satellite decreases to about 87 minutes, the

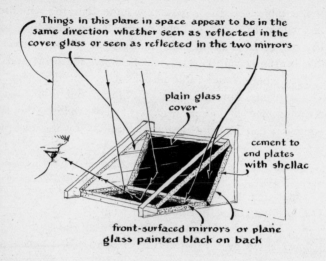

Things in this plane in space appear to be in the same direction whether seen as reflected in the cover glass or seen as reflected in the two mirrors

plain glass cover

cement to end plates with shellac

front-surfaced mirrors or plane glass painted black on back

113
Dipleidoscope to measure the time required for a satellite to orbit around the earth

satellite will be consumed by friction with the lower atmosphere. Thus by timing the passage of a satellite during a few transits, its lifetime can be predicted. If the measurements can be made with good accuracy, two timings are sufficient for an approximate prediction.

A convenient instrument for timing the orbit of a satellite is the dipleidoscope, a device invented about 1860 by an English barrister named J. M. Bloxam. It consists of a pair of mirrors tilted toward each other at an angle of somewhat more than 90 degrees and covered by a sheet of glass as depicted in Figure 113. The three elements may be supported by a pair of end plates, as shown, or simply taped securely. Ideally the mirrors should be front-surface silvered and the cover glass should be silvered so that it reflects 38 per cent of the light striking it and passes the rest. But ordinary back-silvered mirrors (or even plain glass with a back-coating of black paint) will work, and the cover glass need not be silvered at all.

When the dipleidoscope is held at an angle which reflects light from the satellite into the eye, two images will be seen. One image is reflected by the cover glass, the other by the mirrors. As the satellite passes overhead, the two images move toward one another, merge and then pass out of the field of view in opposite directions. The time is recorded at the instant the images merge. The device should be set up in advance of the transit on a firm but easily adjusted support such as the ball-and-socket tripod head popular with photographers.

The axis of the dipleidoscope should be adjusted roughly at a right angle to the anticipated path of the satellite. During one transit the instrument is adjusted so that the two images will merge. On the same transit the time is recorded. The instrument is then left undisturbed for a second observation during the next transit. In the case of Sputnik I observations made 24 hours apart

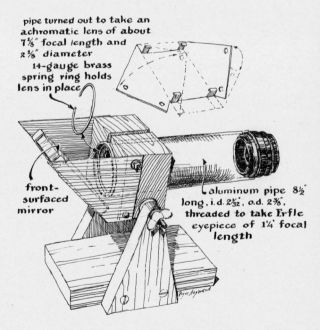

pipe turned out to take an achromatic lens of about 7⅛″ focal length and 2⅛″ diameter

14-gauge brass spring ring holds lens in place

front-surfaced mirror

aluminum pipe 8½″ long, i.d. 2½₃₂″, o.d. 2⅜″, threaded to take Erfle eyepiece of 1¼′ focal length

114
Low-power, wide-field telescope for observing artificial satellites

would show the approximate apparent gain in time for 15 revolutions.

Most satellite observers will also want a good low-power, wide-field telescope. An inexpensive one of the type used by Moonwatch teams is depicted in Figure 114. It is designed for table-top use, the front-surfaced mirror being an anti-crick-in-the-neck feature for those who prefer to look down rather than up. The achromatic objective lens and Erfle eyepiece together retail for about $25.

6

EXPERIMENTING WITH THE EARTH'S CHARGE

Normally the air around your head is some 200 volts positive with respect to the ground under your feet. But what happens when thunderstorms pass overhead? Facts about the earth's electric charge and several experiments for detecting and measuring it

ONE SUNNY MORNING a few years ago a jolt of electricity knocked Fred Ellis, an Ohio radio ham, from the roof of his barn. Fortunately Ellis landed on a stack of straw and lived to tell the tale. "I started to hook a ground wire to a 50-foot antenna tower on the roof," he reported, "when a fat spark jumped from the metal tower to my hand and knocked me off balance. Although the weather was hot and dry there had been no breeze of any consequence for several days. Hence the charge could not have been generated by wind friction. How do you account for it?"

In Minneapolis a steeplejack was badly burned when a similar spark jumped from the base of a metal flagpole and touched off a

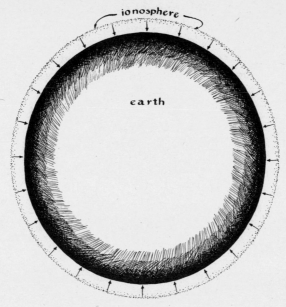

115
Principal components of nature's Van de Graaff electrostatic generator

nearby pile of gasoline-soaked rags. Again the accident occurred on a still day.

A television viewer on a Pennsylvania farm, plagued for months by a strange electrical disturbance which occasionally obscured his picture, finally cured the difficulty when he detected small sparks jumping from the sheet-metal cupola on his house. The trouble was ended by grounding the cupola.

In all three cases the explanation has to do with the sometimes-overlooked fact that the earth is, among other things, the negative electrode of a huge electrical generator of the Van de Graaff type. Many details of this natural generator await explanation; if you enjoy electrostatic experiments, here is a ready-made project and a machine that goes with it.

Nature's generator works on the same basic principle as the man-made Van de Graaff machine but differs remarkably in its geometry and details of construction. The conventional Van de

Graaff employs a pair of spherical electrodes, held apart by a cylindrical insulating column and charged by the action of a motor-driven belt. The arrangement resembles a big dumbbell. The belt "pumps" electrons out of one sphere and deposits them in the other. As the pumping action continues, an electric field builds up between the spheres. The voltage is limited only by the curvature of the collectors and the insulating properties of the column, belt and surrounding atmosphere.

In nature's design, on the other hand, the parts of the generator take the form of concentric spheres. The earth, which is the negative electrode, is at the center. It is surrounded by a hollow sphere of insulating material: the lower atmosphere. The insulator is in turn surrounded by the positive electrode: the ionosphere. A spherical pattern of thunderstorms within the insulator functions as the charging belt. The machine's effectiveness as a generator of high voltage leaves something to be desired because the atmosphere is a relatively poor insulator: its resistance amounts to only 200 ohms. Yet thunderstorms do an astonishingly good job of keeping the electrodes charged.

Lightning, the counterpart of the man-made machine's corona points, carries current amounting to thousands of amperes. On the average 100 strokes of lightning hit the earth every second. You can hear the resulting electromagnetic debris at any hour by hooking a long antenna to the input of an audio-frequency amplifying system and turning up the volume. It makes a sharp, buzzing sound.

The energy output of the 2,000 to 6,000 thunderstorms in progress at any one time is sufficient to maintain an average potential of 360,000 volts between the earth and the ionosphere. This despite a leakage of current through the atmosphere of 1,800 amperes! The intensity of the field diminishes with height, but near the surface it amounts to about 100 volts per yard of altitude. Accordingly we walk around with our heads in air some 200 volts positive with respect to the ground at our feet.

Given sufficient time, conductors insulated from the ground pick up the potential of the surrounding air. A negatively charged body attracts positive ions from the air until its negative charge is

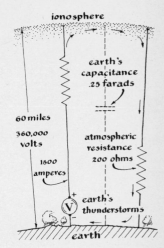

ionosphere

earth's
capacitance
.25 farads

60 miles
360,000
volts

atmospheric
resistance
200 ohms

1800
amperes

earth's
thunderstorms

earth

116
Circuit equivalents of the electrostatic
generator comprised in the earth, atmosphere and ionosphere

neutralized. Conversely, a positively charged body attracts negative electrons. The time required for a body to reach electrical
equilibrium with the surrounding air depends largely on its size
and the concentration of ions naturally present in air.

The amount of electricity that a body can accumulate — its
capacity for holding charge — is also proportional to its size. Ellis's
antenna tower was so big, and had lost so much negative charge
to the surrounding air, that he was knocked off balance by the
swarm of returning electrons. Had he touched a small object, say
a metal ventilator or several hundred feet of wire, the current
would doubtless have been so small he would not have felt it.

Several methods of measuring the intensity of the earth's field
are based on the fact that conductors can reach electrical equilibrium with the surrounding air. These methods lend themselves
to an interesting series of experiments. In principle the measurement
is simple. You merely place a test structure (a few feet of wire
will do) at a given height above the ground, insulate it from the
earth, wait until it reaches electrical equilibrium with the air,
and connect a voltmeter of appropriate sensitivity between the
test structure and the earth. The meter reading is divided by the
height in feet; the result is the field intensity in volts per foot.

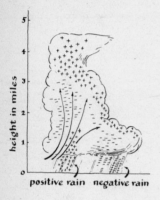

positive rain negative rain

117
Distribution of charge in a thunderstorm

The field intensity varies considerably with location, topography, the hour of day and the state of the weather. Readings made at the top of mountains or steep hills average much higher than those made at sea or in prairie country. Conversely, observations made in valleys average somewhat lower. Usually the charge of the earth is negative, but under the trailing edge of a thunderstorm it is often positive. Here potential differences of 3,000 volts per foot have been recorded. The intensity of the earth's electrical field also varies during the day; this appears to be a consequence of the uneven distribution of the earth's land area.

The number of thunderstorms reaches a peak when the continents of the Western Hemisphere are turned toward the sun; at that time Europe and Africa have just absorbed their daily quota of solar heat. This explanation, like many others concerning the generation and distribution of the earth's electric field, has not been tacked down as neatly as physical meteorologists would wish. More observations of the daily population of thunderstorms, together with corresponding information on the variation in field intensity, are needed.

Although the measurement of field intensity is simple in principle, it is made difficult in practice by the fact that considerable time may be required for a conductor to pick up charge from the surrounding air. Lord Kelvin devised the first method of speeding up the process. He insulated a metal tank from the ground, filled it with water and arranged matters so that water would flow from a spray nozzle at the bottom, where the charge density is greatest per unit area.

He called the arrangement a "water-dropper." The surface of each drop, immediately before it is detached from the stream, is an extension of the surface of the tank. Accordingly the potential difference between the drop and the air is equal to that between the tank and the air. When the drop is detached, it carries charge away. The process continues until equilibrium is established between the tank and the air.

The test conductor need not consist solely of the tank. A relatively small water-dropper can be used for charging a test structure of any desired size. Garden sprays of the type which operate on compressed air supplied by a hand pump will charge a 30-yard length of wire in about 20 seconds. Fine spray is preferred to large drops because the higher ratio of droplet surface to volume not only conserves water but speeds the charging process.

The charging time can also be reduced by enriching the concentration of ions in the vicinity of the test structure. For example, a wire 10 to 15 feet long with a glass insulator at each end is suspended a yard or so above the ground between a pair of posts. A short length of the wire is then wrapped in string or paper that has been soaked in inflammable lead nitrate. When the string or paper is ignited, the flame produces ions in the vicinity of the wire; in a few seconds the potential of the wire will reach that of the ambient air. A torch waved in the vicinity of the wire will accomplish the same result but at some cost in terms of convenience.

Where it is desirable to monitor the field continuously over long periods, radioactive materials may be called into service. A film of polonium electrolytically deposited on a wire will emit alpha particles which strongly ionize the surrounding air.

The practical measurement of field intensity is further complicated by the necessity of using measuring instruments of extreme sensitivity. Test conductors of reasonable size store little energy at low voltages — at most a small fraction of a watt. If a substantial part of that little is consumed in driving the pointer of the measuring instrument, the accuracy of the reading will suffer. Lord Kelvin measured the potential of his water-dropper with a quadrant electrometer.

This instrument consists of a metal vane suspended by a fine wire inside a metal structure which resembles a pillbox cut into four sectors. All the sectors are insulated from the ground, and sectors diametrically opposed to each other are wired together. The two pairs of sectors are then charged in opposite polarity by a battery, and the vane is connected to the test structure under measurement. A small mirror cemented to the wire from which the vane is suspended serves as a pointer; a spot of light reflected from the mirror moves as the mirror turns.

The vane moves in response to the electrostatic attraction and repulsion between its charge and that of the sectors. In the finest quadrant electrometers the wire supporting the vane is replaced by a quartz fiber which has been made a conductor by depositing a film of gold on it. When the vane is charged, it draws almost no current; yet the device is extremely sensitive to changes in voltage. Amateurs who go in for instrument-making will find the construction of such an electrometer a challenging and rewarding enterprise.

Most modern electrometers are built around vacuum tubes of the screen-grid type. The basic circuit is simple. Bias voltage is connected between the cathode and grid of the tube through a high resistance. A microammeter is inserted into the plate lead; a dry-cell battery supplies both screen-grid and plate voltage. The test structure is connected to the grid and the cathode is grounded. The intensity of the earth's field determines the charge on the grid and hence the strength of the plate current. The device is calibrated by connecting a source of known voltage to the grid and noting the resulting deflection of the microammeter.

A number of precautions must be observed or the grid will draw an intolerable amount of current. Some current, for example, is contributed by positive ions which are ejected by the cathode and strike the grid. Another source of current is gas atoms ionized by electrons accelerated between the grid and plate. In addition, some of these electrons strike the plate with enough energy to produce soft X-rays, which in turn dislodge electrons from the grid. Light falling on the grid also ejects electrons from it. Finally, grid current tends to leak along the surface of the bulb.

A number of techniques have been developed for reducing these currents. The production of positive ions can be reduced by operating the cathode at subnormal temperature. The grid can in effect be shielded by charging the screen grid to a higher positive potential (15 volts) than the plate (6 volts). This has the effect of repelling positive ions ejected by the cathode. Reduced plate voltage prevents electrons from acquiring enough energy for ionizing the residual gas in the tube and lowers the production of X-rays. Photoelectrons are eliminated by enclosing the tube assembly in a light-tight box. Surface leakage is reduced by washing the glass envelope with alcohol and dipping the area surrounding the terminal of the control grid in ceresin wax. In applications demanding maximum sensitivity air is evacuated from the light-tight box.

By meeting these circuit requirements and using a tube of special design, such as the General Electric FP-54, it is possible to detect currents of 60 electrons per second. Other special electrometer tubes include the Victoreen 5803 and Raytheon 5886. The RCA 954 and 959 and the Western Electric 259-B types may also be used in all but the most exacting electrometer applications. For maximum sensitivity the grid must be tied to the cathode through a resistance on the order of 100,000 megohms. Such resistors are manufactured by the S. S. White Company, Victoreen and the International Resistance Company.

A third method of measuring the earth's field intensity eliminates the need for highly sensitive instruments by employing a device called a "field mill," which in effect transforms electrostatic charge into alternating current. Alternating current from the mill is amplified electronically and rectified. The output drives low-sensitivity direct-current ammeters, recorders and so on as desired.

In effect, the field mill is comprised of a motor-driven variable capacitor which is connected in series with the capacitor represented by the test structure, the earth's surface and the intervening air. As the capacity of the variable capacitor increases, current flows into it from the test structure. When the current of the variable capacitor decreases, current returns to the test structure. The frequency is made high in relation to the time required for the test structure to assume electrical equilibrium with the surrounding air. Hence the test structure remains substantially at the ambient potential, and energy lost through the weak oscillating current is not significant. Output from the mill is provided by voltage developed across a megohm resistor inserted between the variable capacitor and the test structure.

As usually constructed, the mill takes the form of a capacitor with three plates, two fixed and the third motor-driven. One plate is a shallow cylinder closed at the bottom and open at the top. The other two plates form the lid of the cylinder. Each of these plates looks rather like a two-bladed paddle; it consists of opposing quadrants joined at the apex.

One plate is mounted flush with the open end of the cylinder, but is insulated from it. This plate cover two quadrants of the cylinder, leaving two quadrants open. The open quadrants are closed by the other plate, which is mounted directly above them. This last plate is keyed to the end of a shaft which extends through the assembly to the motor, fastened to the bottom of the box. When the shaft rotates, the blades of the plate alternately cover and expose the fixed plates.

The rotating assembly is mounted on insulators and grounded through the megohm resistor across which the output voltage is developed. The alternating-current output is rectified by a synchronous reversing switch, or commutator, keyed to the opposite end of the motor shaft. By rectifying the output synchronously, both field polarity and intensity can be observed. The mill is calibrated by comparison with a known voltage. It is both rugged and portable. Special designs have been developed for use in aircraft, and have contributed significantly in recent years to this phase of meteorological research.

7

AN ELECTRONIC WEATHER FORECASTER

Douglas A. Kohl, principal engineer of General Mills, Inc., Minneapolis, describes the construction of a device to make accurate short-term forecasts. The instrument continuously displays clues to the meteorological activity responsible for thunderstorms and the local state of the earth's electric charge. Total cost, excluding a graphic recorder: about $100

THE ATMOSPHERIC PROCESSES which we observe as weather give rise to two major electrical effects. One is the 360,000-volt potential that is maintained between the surface of the earth and the ionosphere by the activity of thunderstorms. During thunderstorms the field can locally build up to thousands of volts.

The second effect also has its origin in thunderstorms. A portion of the energy liberated by lightning takes the form of electromagnetic waves called sferics (from atmospherics). These account for the familiar "static" heard on radio receivers. Each lightning stroke radiates at least one sferic, and some 20 million strokes occur on earth every day.

Part of the energy released by these strokes escapes into space, but most of it echoes between the earth and the ionosphere until it is dissipated as heat. Much of the rainfall in the U. S. and many spectacular windstorms stem from thunderstorms or cumulonimbus cloud activity characterized by the separation of electric charge. When the stress of these charges exceeds the dielectric strength of the atmosphere, a discharge occurs that has far-reaching consequences.

The uniform pattern of the electric field is disrupted, and if lightning accompanies the discharge, sferics are radiated. Both the field disturbance and sferics can be detected and measured with relatively simple apparatus, the former over an area of 50 to 200 square miles and the latter for hundreds of miles. The resulting data provide meaningful clues to approaching weather. My initial interest in the electrical aspects of weather has grown into a full-scale avocation which I can recommend to anyone with more than a passive interest in meteorology.

To the eye, lightning appears deceptively simple: merely a big spark which, it is said, never strikes twice in the same place. This impression vanishes when a discharge is recorded with responsive instruments. Strokes from cloud to cloud, from cloud to ground or from the top of a cloud to the bottom are nearly always preceded by complex minor discharges, or leaders, which precede the main arc.

The leaders advance in stepwise fashion, following routes along the most highly stressed regions between centers of opposite charge. These junior discharges trigger the main arc by moving the centers of charge progressively closer. Fields of extreme intensity result, and the final transfer of charge follows the ionized pathways created by the leaders.

The leaders usually begin about a thousandth of a second before the main arc, and often advance in as many as 30 steps. Each step produces an electromagnetic disturbance and an abrupt change in the electric field. Not all leaders end in an arc, particularly when they are associated with rapidly growing cumulonimbus clouds. They can still be detected electrically.

Another characteristic of lightning is the multiple stroke of the main arc. Single strokes are uncommon. Multiple strokes are usually completed within a few millionths of a second; otherwise they extend over several thousandths of a second. Few strokes are of intermediate duration.

Although oscillograms show that no two sferics are alike, all cover a broad spectrum of frequencies. Most of the energy is concentrated in the region below 20 kilocycles.

The sferics are detected by means of a rudimentary radio receiver; the number picked up during a given interval can be counted automatically by equipping the receiver with a register.

In monitoring sferics on three frequencies (430, 2,000 and 5,100 kilocycles) I have observed that the count at each frequency is related both to the distance the sferic is propagated and to the type of discharge from which it is radiated. The ratio of counts among the three frequencies changes characteristically as the storm approaches or recedes.

During late-afternoon storms at a distance of 100 to 200 miles, for example, every 100 counts at 430 kilocycles are accompanied, on the average, by 46 counts at 2,000 kilocycles and 13 counts at 5,100 kilocycles. By the time the storm has moved into the local area, the ratio has changed from 100:46:13 to 100:96:50.

Cold-front advances and storms characterized by a high percentage of cloud-to-ground discharges show considerably less change in ratio. A comparable ratio for long-distance frontal activity would be 100:74:40. Normally one is chiefly interested in the rate of counts at each frequency. It is possible, however, to set up a coincidence-counter to identify sferics that appear simultaneously on two or more frequencies. This counter shows that nearly 90 per cent of those sferics registered on the 5,100-kilocycle channel also appear on the 430-kilocycle channel, thus confirming their common origin.

Recordings made in the vicinity of Minneapolis are almost as dramatic as the lightning which produces them. The 430-kilocycle channel has provided consistent data up to a radius of 200 miles with counting rates frequently rising as high as 150,000 sferics per minute! The current flowing in a main arc, which may register as a single sferic, can exceed 20,000 amperes.

The duration of the arc is of course measured in millionths of a second. But at the rate of 150,000 sferics per minute the average current flowing between the earth and the cloud is on the order of 500 amperes. Other investigators report a mean energy of some 200,000 joules per full-sized lightning discharge. The corresponding energy liberated over the monitored area could thus amount to 30 billion joules per minute, or 500,000 horsepower!

On clear days the distribution of the electric field between the ground and the ionosphere is relatively uniform. But violent changes are observed when a storm passes overhead, and the build-up in charge which results in a stroke of lightning is easily observed. Many such build-ups occur in less than 30 seconds. Interactions in the field are as fascinating as they are complex. A single discharge can warp a relatively smooth field so that another stroke follows in a matter of seconds.

One also observes many polarity reversals in which the normally negative earth swings positive. These changes, like the leaders which initiate lightning, follow a steplike pattern. In most instances the highly stressed field relaxes slowly without evidence of an arc. From this it would seem that the potential electrical energy in a widespread storm may be much greater than is indicated by the record of sferics.

For purposes of weather forecasting, measurements of sferics and field intensity need be combined only with readings from a local barometer and wind-direction indicator. After a reasonable amount of practice in interpreting this information, reliable eight-hour forecasts are easy to make. During the summer of 1947 our method gave only one incorrect eight-hour forecast in 50 attempts. The score of the local Weather Bureau for the same period was less than 50 per cent. The Bureau's forecasts were handicapped, however, by an unusual pattern of weather.

The effectiveness of sferics and field intensity in forecasting lies in the fact that cumulo-nimbus cloud activity provides a sensitive indication of potentially turbulent air conditions during the summer months. An array of these clouds usually appears in late afternoon. They may either develop into thunderstorms or dissipate with the setting sun.

On the basis of visual information alone it is impossible to predict which of these two courses they will follow. In contrast, variations in the strength of the electric field, coupled with a moderate sferics level, nearly always signal the advance of thunderstorm activity into the local scene, even though the visible clouds have not begun the familiar consolidation that marks the first stage of a maturing storm.

The sferics record at any location constitutes the summation of weather activity throughout the area covered by the recorder. The profile shows the consolidations, growth and maturity of various thunderstorm cells. (A typical record made in the late spring of 1956 is shown in Figure 118.) Weather conditions at the time were reported as a stalled front to the north, with high humidity and temperature carried into the region by several days of southerly winds. The heat of the sun caused thunderstorm activity to begin around noon; the thunderstorms were then dissipated as the atmosphere cooled off at night. Full scale on the graph is 200,000 sferics per minute. The rate varied from 21 counts per minute (9:30 a.m. on May 27) to more than 200,000 per minute (after 6 p.m. on May 28). This 10,000-fold increase was intimately related to the weather disturbance.

In this as well as in many other periods of activity one or two fairly intense consolidations take place prior to the change of weather in the area. These are noted at about noon on both days. Apparently in the complex interactions within a region close to major weather landmarks — high-pressure ridges, low-pressure cells, fronts and so on — the advent of one or two thunderstorms will either trigger general regional activity or else the cumulonimbus formations will quickly dissipate.

The sustained activity early in the evening of May 28, shown by the record, persisted as the cold front moved across the area. The southerly flow of air apparently blocked the movement of

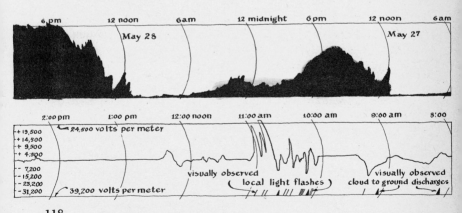

118
Records of "sferics" *(top)* and of disturbances in the intensity of the earth's electric field *(bottom)*

the front a second time; the temperature drop and northerly winds did not materialize until May 31, after local thunderstorms were observed during the night of May 29. Sferic activity from the region west and north persisted during the entire period.

As for the forecast that was based on this record, it should be noted that thunderstorms were not visible in the distance until about 5 p.m. on May 28. In spite of strong southerly winds on May 27 the decrease in sferic activity early in the evening led to the correct prediction that no change in weather would occur in the immediate vicinity during the night and following morning.

A stronger southeast wind appearing at midafternoon the next day, coupled with the rapid increase in sferic activity, led to the forecast that turbulent weather would enter the vicinity within several hours. The nearest storm was seen and estimated to be 12 miles from the sferics station. A slow decrease in sferic level, which occurred during the following morning, added to occasional field disturbances beneath passing clouds and resulted in a further prediction that the weather had not cleared and other storms were imminent. These developed on schedule.

For rapidly moving storm systems the advance indication on the sferic recorder amounts to only a few hours, and reliable eight-hour forecasts are not difficult. As the observer acquires the knack of interpreting the records, he can also make accurate forecasts under more passive conditions.

Observations of the electric field then become particularly useful. Occasionally tremendously impressive cloud formations, including the formidable roll clouds associated with maturing thunderstorms, appear; by conventional standards these would signal foul weather. But when the recorder shows them to be charge-free the observer knows at once that they will be nonviolent. Locally severe storms, on the other hand, are accompanied by violent changes in electric field even though the general sferic level may be fairly low — a clue that the enveloping storm covers a small area.

With the exception of the electrical-pen recorder, the equipment for measuring field intensity and making sferic counts is relatively inexpensive. The sferic detector is essentially a special radio receiver equipped with a means for counting short pulses of current [*see Fig. 119*]. The antenna consists of a bare copper wire at least 20 feet long suspended 10 feet or more above the ground between glass insulators. It serves the dual purpose of picking up sferics and sensing field intensity.

A sferic signal excites the tuned 456-kilocycle transformer, and the resulting oscillations are amplified. The train of amplified oscillations is then rectified and used to trigger a pulse-forming circuit. The output is averaged in a vacuum-tube voltmeter circuit. The antenna should be equipped with a lightning arrester; as a further protection the receiver is equipped with a choke coil designed to block damaging bursts of energy at high frequencies.

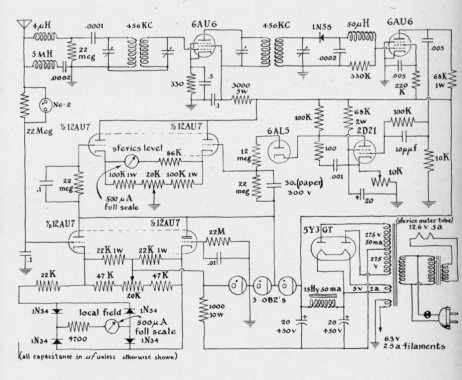

119
Schematic diagram for a sferics counter and field-intensity meter

The radio-frequency amplifier consists of two standard 456-kilocycle intermediate-frequency transformers and a high-gain pentode tube. Incoming signals are rectified by a crystal diode that delivers negative pulses at the output. The negative pulses tend to drive the grid of the 6AU6 tube to cutoff, the point at which no current can flow between the cathode and plate. The output of this tube is fed to the 2D21 Thyratron by way of a resistance-capacitor network designed for a pulse duration of 50 microseconds. Most multiple-stroke lightning discharges are thereby registered as a single count. Corresponding pulses generated by the Thyratron tube persist for 10 microseconds. The sensitivity of the circuit to sferics is controlled by adjusting the bias of the Thyratron. Normally this control is set to register not more than one pulse per hour during the winter or during fair summer weather.

The output of the Thyratron is coupled to a capacitor-resistance "averaging" circuit. This smooths out random fluctuations in the sferics counting-rate, and thus gives meaning to recorded values of 50 counts per minute or less.

As mentioned earlier, the rate at which sferics are detected spans a broad range: from less than 20 sferics per minute to more than 200,000. Hence the scale of the recorder must be compressed as the sferics rate increases to prevent the pen from being carried off the paper. This is accomplished by taking advantage of the grid-cutoff characteristic of the 12AU7 voltmeter tube. As the counting rate increases, progressively higher negative voltage is

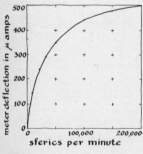

120
Calibration curve for sferics counter

applied to the grid of the 12AU7, thus reducing the response of the meter.

The leakage current of the antenna, which varies with the intensity of the electric field, is measured by another averaging voltmeter circuit which utilizes a second 12AU7 tube. One grid is connected to an averaging resistor-capacitor circuit which is connected in turn to the antenna. Some capacity and resistance are inserted to counteract the effects of abrupt changes in the electric field which accompany local lightning discharges. The antenna is so effective that transient changes in the field can induce potential differences in the circuit as high as 10,000 volts!

To protect the meter a 22-megohm resistance and a .1-microfarad capacitor are connected in series between the antenna and ground, and the grid of the voltmeter tube is tied to the junction between the two. The capacitor requires an appreciable interval to reach full charge through the resistor. This delay protects the meter against abrupt voltage surges. Sensitivity to local weather is lost by the circuit, however, if transients are suppressed completely. The resistor is therefore bridged by a small neon tube.

When the input voltage exceeds the firing potential of the tube (70 to 100 volts), the neon glow short-circuits the resistor and in effect transfers the antenna directly to the capacitor and the grid. The five-millihenry choke and .0002-microfarad capacitor connected between the antenna and ground present a low resistance to slowly varying fields, such as those produced by nearby power lines, and thus prevent these sources of voltage from firing the neon tube.

8

DETECTING THE EARTH'S ROTATION

A century ago, the French physicist Léon Foucault constructed a pendulum for demonstrating the rotation of the earth and thereby settled a classic controversy. Directions are given for duplicating Foucault's results

ONE DAY in the middle of the last century the French physicist Léon Foucault inserted a slender rod in the chuck of a lathe and plucked the free end of the rod so that it vibrated like a reed. When he started the lathe, he observed that the turning rod continued to vibrate in the same plane. Later he tried much the same experiment with a vertical drill-press. From the chuck of the drill-press he suspended a short pendulum consisting of a length of piano wire and a spherical weight. He set the weight to swinging and started the drill-press. The pendulum also continued to vibrate in the same plane. For a time nothing much came of these observations, but in them was the seed of an experiment destined to settle a classic scientific controversy.

In the year 1543 Nicolaus Copernicus had sent a copy of his new book, *On the Revolutions of the Celestial Orbs*, to Pope Paul III with a note containing a historic understatement: "I can easily conceive, most Holy Father," he wrote, "that as soon as people learn that in this book I ascribe certain motions to the earth, they will cry out at once that I and my theory should be rejected." Cry out they did, and some, including a few scientists, were still crying out in 1850, when Foucault was invited to stage a science exhibit as part of the Paris Exposition scheduled for the following year. Being not only a gifted physicist but also something of a showman, he selected as the site of his exhibit the church of Sainte Geneviève, also known as the Panthéon.

From the dome of the Panthéon he hung a pendulum consisting of 200 feet of piano wire and a 62-pound cannon ball. On the floor, immediately below the cannon ball, he sprinkled a layer of fine sand. A stylus fixed to the bottom of the ball made a trace in the sand, thus recording the movement of the pendulum. Great care was taken during construction to exclude all forces except those acting vertically to support the system. Tests were even made to assure symmetry in the metallurgical structure of the wire. Finally the ball was pulled to one side and tied in place with a stout thread. When the system was still, the restraining thread was burned.

The pendulum made a true sweep, leaving a straight trace in the sand. In a few minutes the thin line had expanded into a pattern resembling the outline of a two-bladed propeller. The pattern grew in a clockwise direction, and at the end of an hour the line had turned 11 degrees and 18 minutes. This could be explained only on the basis that the earth had turned beneath the pendulum. Copernicus was vindicated.

It is easy to visualize what had happened if one imagines a pendulum erected at the North Pole. The pendulum is hung, perhaps from a beam supported by two columns, in line with the earth's axis. The supporting structure corresponds to Foucault's lathe or drill-press — or the dome of the Panthéon. So long as the pendulum is at rest the whole affair simply turns with the earth, making one complete revolution every 23 hours and 56 minutes (the sidereal day). The pendulum is now drawn out of plumb and carefully released. The direction of the swing persists, and the earth turns beneath the pendulum.

To an observer on the earth the plane of vibration appears to rotate in a clockwise direction, because at the North Pole the earth turns counter-clockwise. The same effect would be observed at the South Pole, except that there the rotations would be reversed. If the swing of the pendulum appears to turn clockwise at the North Pole and counter-clockwise at the South Pole, what happens at the Equator? Substantially no deviation is observed.

plane of oscillation of a
pendulum at the
earth's pole
appears to
rotate once
a day

plane of
oscillation of
a pendulum at
the Equator appears
to be stationary

121
Foucault pendulums suspended at
North Pole and the Equator

Here the entire system — the earth, the supporting structure and
the pendulum — is transported almost linearly from west to east
[see Fig. 121].

At the poles the rate at which the swing of the pendulum appears to rotate is 15 degrees per sidereal hour; at the Equator it
is of course zero degrees per sidereal hour. The rate varies with
latitude; the higher the latitude, the higher the rate. This neg-
lects certain fine deviations caused by the curvature of the earth's
orbit around the sun and by other perturbations. But it holds for
the gross, easily observed, motion.

With the help of a few simple geometrical concepts it is easy
to see why a pendulum appears to rotate more slowly as it approaches the Equator. Imagine an arc along an intermediate
parallel of latitude through which the earth has turned during
a short interval, say an hour or so [AB in Fig. 122]. The angle
subtended by the arc at the earth's axis increases at the rate of
15 degrees per hour — one full turn of 360 degrees per sidereal
day. Now assume a pair of tangents [AC and AB] to the earth's

surface subtended by the arc which meet on a projection of the axis at a point in space above the pole.

The angle between the tangents increases in size at the same rate with which the pendulum's plane of vibration appears to rotate. The reason it does so becomes clear if one assumes that the pendulum continues to vibrate in the plane of the first tangent as it is transported to the position of the second.

At the pole the two angles are equal; both increase at the rate of 15 degrees per hour. At the Equator the angle subtended by the arc at the earth's axis continues to increase at the rate of 15 degrees per hour. But the pair of tangents subtended by the arc at the Equator meet the projected axis at infinity. The angle vanishes, and its rate of increase does the same. Therefore the pendulum's rate of rotation is zero. Foucault demonstrated that the apparent rotation of the pendulum varies with the trigonometric sine of the latitude at which it is installed. Its rate at points between the poles and the Equator is equal to 15 degress per hour multiplied by the sine of the latitude.

Amateurs who set up pendulums at New Orleans will observe an apparent rotation of about 7 degrees and 30 minutes per hour. They must wait two days for a full revolution. Those in

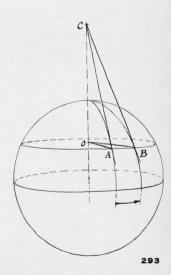

122
The geometry of Foucault pendulum's swing

Manila must wait four days; those on Howland Island in the South Pacific, about 40 days!

About the best way to gain an understanding of the Foucault pendulum is to make one. Like many such enterprises, this seems simple until it is tried. Many amateurs who have felt the urge to set up the apparatus have abandoned the idea because they had no Panthéon in which to hang a 200-foot pendulum and no cannon ball for a bob. This is no problem. Pendulums 10 or 15 feet long can be made to work handsomely with bobs weighing as little as five pounds. The most vexing problems encountered in making a pendulum have to do not with its size but with starting the bob in a true swing, maintaining the trueness of the swing, and supplying energy to the bob.

Foucault's method of starting the bob is still the most elegant. Many starting devices have been tried: mechanical releases, magnetic releases, mechanisms which accelerate the bob from dead rest, and so on. It is generally agreed that burning a thread is the simplest and best of the lot.

Until recent years the problem of making the pendulum swing true resisted some of the world's best instrument makers. It seemed clear that any method of suspension must have radial symmetry such as one would expect of the suspension device depicted in Figure 123. To assure this Foucault and subsequent experimenters took great pains in procuring wire of uniform characteristics and in designing the fixture to which the wire was attached.

Roger Hayward, whose illustrations adorn this volume, tells me that the wire for the Foucault pendulum in the Griffith Observatory in Los Angeles was specially drawn and tied to a long two-by-four beam for shipment from an eastern mill to the West Coast. The designers were afraid that coiling the wire would destroy its symmetry. The pivot to which the wire was attached at first consisted of a set of gimbals with two sets of knife-edges at right angles to each other.

Despite these precautions the completed pendulum insisted on performing figure eights and ellipses. Hayward, who had designed other exhibits for the Observatory, suggested that the wire simply be held in rigid chuck. This invited a break at the junction of

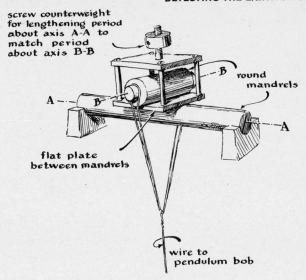

123
Foucault suspension based on principle of crossed cylinders and planes

the wire and the chuck, which could cause the wire to lash into a crowd of spectators. To minimize this hazard a crossbar was clamped to the wire just above the ring-shaped driving magnet. Thus if the wire had broken, the crossbar would have been caught by the magnet ring. Clamping the wire in a chuck cured the difficulty. The wire has now been flexing for more than 20 years without any apparent ill effect.

At about the time the Griffith pendulum was installed a French physicist named M. F. Charron devised a method for maintaining the true swing even when the forces acting on the pendulum are measurably asymmetrical. Charron set out with the objective of designing a vise which would grip the wire rigidly and would also provide a long radius through which the wire could flex. He used a ferrule which at its upper end fitted snugly around the wire and at its lower end flared away from the wire, as shown in Figure 124.

The diameter of the hole at the lower end precisely accommodated the swing of the pendulum. It was observed that, when the

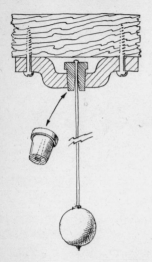

124
Charron pivot for a Foucault
pendulum

125
An amateur's version
of the Charron pivot

pendulum swung true, the wire simply made contact with the
inner surface of the ferrule at the end of each beat. If the pendulum describes an ellipse, on the other hand, and there is sufficient
friction between the ferrule and the suspension wire, then the
lower edge of the ferrule functions for a short interval as the
point of suspension and the bob describes a somewhat narrower
ellipse during this portion of the swing. The same effect is observed during the equivalent portion of the return swing. The
accumulating effect tends to shrink the ellipse without limit,
causing it to approach the desired straight line.

Stephen Stoot, a Canadian amateur, has suggested a modification of the Charron suspension for small pendulums which accomplishes the same result. He fixes a carefully centered washer
around the wire just far enough below the point of suspension
so that the wire touches the washer at the end of each swing,
as depicted in Figure 125.

The third basic problem is how to supply the pendulum with
a periodic push in the precise direction in which it needs to go.

No completely satisfactory mechanical solution has been devised. A variety of electrical drives are in use, however. Most of these feature a ring-shaped electromagnet which acts on an armature carried by the wire near the point of suspension. Power is applied during the portion of the swing in which the wire is approaching the magnet, and is interrupted when the wire moves away.

The arrangement in use at the Griffith Observatory is typical. Current for the ring magnet is supplied through a relay. The action of the relay, in turn, is controlled by a photoelectric cell. A beam of light, folded by mirrors so that the beam crosses itself at a right angle near the wire, actuates the photoelectric cell [see Fig. 126]. When the suspension passes through the center of the ring magnet, a vane on the wire breaks the beam. The relay then operates, and applies current to the magnet. After an appropriate interval, during which the wire approaches the magnet, a time-delay relay breaks the circuit automatically.

In 1953 R. Stuart Mackay of the University of California described in the *American Journal of Physics* a novel method of driving Foucault pendulums. His apparatus consists of a simple coil bridged by a condenser into which power is fed continuously, and over which the bob swings freely. The method takes advantage of phase-shift effects which are essential to the operation of ordinary doorbells and buzzers. It requires no contacts, light beams or other arrangements to interrupt the current.

Here is Mackay, telling how it works.

R. Stuart Mackay of the University of California describes his method of driving Foucault pendulums

IF ONE ENERGIZES A COIL with alternating current and sets an iron pendulum bob swinging immediately above it, the current through the coil will increase or decrease depending upon whether the bob is moving toward or away from the coil. The magnetic property of the iron influences the magnetic field set up by the coil and therefore the coil's inductance.

The inductance, in turn, influences the flow of current. The fluctuations in the amplitude of the alternating magnetic field do

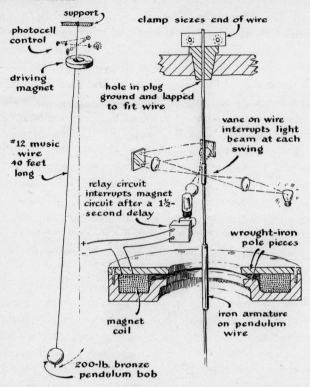

support

photocell control

driving magnet

clamp siezes end of wire

hole in plug ground and lapped to fit wire

#12 music wire 40 feet long

vane on wire interrupts light beam at each swing

relay circuit interrupts magnet circuit after a 1½-second delay

+

wrought-iron pole pieces

magnet coil

iron armature on pendulum wire

200-lb. bronze pendulum bob

126
Conventional electronic drive for a Foucault pendulum, as installed at the Griffith Observatory in Los Angeles, Calif.

not occur instantly. The effect is such that the current, and consequently the attractive force of the coil's magnetic field, is greater when the bob approaches the center of the coil than when it recedes. If the circuit is essentially inductive, enough energy will be transferred to the bob to maintain the pendulum's swing.

The effect can be made stronger by placing a capacitor in series with the coil so that the combination resonates slightly below the 60-cycle frequency of the power line. In effect, the system is then working on one side of the resonance curve, where a given change in inductance causes a pronounced change in current.

Some Foucault pendulums, particularly those set up as public displays, feature bobs of bronze or other nonmagnetic materials. These may also be driven by the coil. One takes advantage of the fact that such bobs can act as the secondary winding of a transformer. The magnetic field of the stationary coil and that set up by current induced in the bob are in opposition. Hence the coil and the bob are mutually repelled. As the bob approaches the coil the flow of current increases in both.

But because of electrical lag in the circuits the current, which starts to rise with the approach of the bob, does not reach its peak until the bob has traveled somewhat beyond the center of the coil. Accordingly the bob is subjected to a greater net repulsive force when it is moving away from the coil than when it is approaching the coil. Energy is thus made available to drive the pendulum.

The forces acting between the coil and a nonmagnetic bob are smaller than those between the coil and a magnetic bob. Moreover, energy dissipated by currents induced in the bob causes greater damping in the system. The effect can be shown easily by substituting a short-circuited coil for the bob. The change of current in both coils, induced by changes in inductance, can be enhanced by resonating each circuit near the power-line frequency, as in the case of magnetic bobs.

When the capacitor of the bob coil is made slightly too large for resonance, the circuit becomes a trifle inductive. The force between the coils is then repulsive; sustained oscillations result. If the capacitor is too small, an attractive force is produced which will not sustain the motion. A circuit diagram of the two coils appears in Figure 127. It is possible, of course, to attach a driving coil tuned for repulsion to the bottom of a nonmagnetic bob.

The first coil I tried was wound with No. 16 wire. It was eight inches in diameter, two inches thick and had a two-inch hole in the center. It was used simply because it chanced to be on hand. The coil resonated at 60 cycles when it was placed in series with a 25-microfarad paper condenser. On the application of 10 volts it drove a three-inch iron bob on the first try. Considerably more power was delivered when the magnetic field was altered by lay-

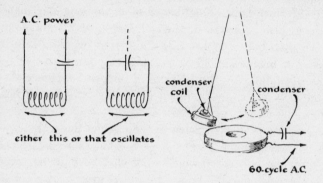

127
One version of the Mackay electrical drive for a Foucault pendulum

ing the coil on a six-inch circle of 1/16-inch sheet iron. Should one wish to enhance the effect further, the coil may be inserted into a cylindrical core of iron, as shown in Figure 128.

Which of the two drive systems is preferable, magnetic or nonmagnetic? A performance analysis indicates little choice either way, though the magnetic bob is probably simpler to make. It is true that over a number of cycles any small perturbing force can produce a marked effect on the swing of a Foucault pendulum, usually resulting in a slightly elliptical orbit. The "plane" of oscillation of a pendulum swinging in an elliptical path will precess in the direction of tracing the ellipse at a rate roughly proportional to its area.

Thus, if one does not take care, a Foucault pendulum can appear to turn at the wrong rate, or even to indicate that the earth is turning backward. It is tempting to suppose that the nonmagnetic bob will tend to avoid the "magnetic potential hill" that it "sees," that is, the repulsive force will tend to deflect the bob to one side if the swing does not pass directly through the center of the magnetic force. In contrast, a magnetic bob might appear to favor the center of the "potential valley" it "sees," even though its normal swing would not necessarily bisect the field of force. Thus in either case one might expect some induced perturbation.

In practice, neither has much effect on crosswise amplitude if a fairly heavy bob is used. Interestingly enough, since the motions in the two directions responsible for the ellipse are 90 degrees out of phase, and since changes in the magnetic field are controlled by the major portion, there is a slight tendency to damp out the minor motion.

The matter of perturbing effects warrants further discussion, particularly from the viewpoint of comparing these systems with the conventional ring-magnet drive. It might seem that driving the pendulum from the top by means of a ring magnet would result in minimum sensitivity to asymmetries, but this is not strictly true. A pendulum is less sensitive to asymmetries at its top. But a greater driving force is also required there. It is the percentage of asymmetry which interests us.

An air-core coil is, of course, simpler to construct, install and maintain than the ring-magnet drive. It must be said, however, that this method of drive does suffer somewhat in comparison with the ring-magnet system in that the whole field is not turned on and off in the course of providing useful drive. The steady useless component of the field is not necessarily symmetrical. Consequently asymmetry may be added to the system continuously.

This means that in this system the magnet must be made more perfect than in a system wherein the field changes the required amount by going fully off. When desired, the magnetic field of the air coil can be trimmed for symmetry with small tabs of magnetic iron.

For the purpose of most demonstrations, however, extreme precision is unnecessary. With reasonable care in alignment the angular velocity of the pendulum's apparent deviation should fall within 15 per cent of the anticipated value.

128
Magnetic core to intensify the Mackay drive

VI.

NUCLEAR
PHYSICS

1

EXPLORING THE ATOM AT HOME

Atoms can be investigated with simple apparatus. Some old tin cans, glass jars, discarded inner tubes, etc., and you are on your way. A practical cloud chamber may be made from a whiskey glass. Nuclear physics, as a hobby, need be neither costly nor hazardous

SOMEONE ONCE SAID that all the equipment a scientist really needs is a pencil, some paper — and a brain. James Clerk Maxwell and Albert Einstein managed to push back the frontiers of knowledge without so much as a synchrocyclotron to their names. But for research in nuclear physics, a pencil and paper are not quite enough. The minuteness of atomic materials puts them beyond the grasp of our senses. You can't toss an electron onto a pan balance and take its weight, or time the spin of a proton with a stop watch. Yet, should you invent a theory about atomic phenomena and hope to tie it to nature, you must somehow make physical contact with the atom, directly or indirectly. Failing this, you must at least measure as many consequences of the atom's behavior as possible.

The problem of learning how the atom is put together and what happens inside it has been likened to that of finding out how an automobile is made without being permitted to see inside the factory. You must reconstruct what happens inside by examining the raw materials that enter the building and the finished product that comes out. There's no rule against blindly probing the interior with a pole or knocking the factory to bits with a cannon ball. You are even permitted to photograph the flying debris, a technique perhaps neither as accurate nor delicate as you might wish. But crude as the technique may be, experience has demonstrated its effectiveness in chipping the outer layer of mystery from the atom.

Thousands of amateurs of all ages and callings have joined nuclear physicists in making just such violent experiments. The "cannon" used by amateurs for bombarding atoms are not so accurate or powerful as those commanded by professionals. Nor are they as imposing or costly to make. The sensitivity of some devices made by amateurs for observing nuclear phenomena is unsurpassed by professional gear, however, and their construction is surprisingly simple. Some years ago, for example, a member of the Corps de Ballet at Radio City Music Hall in New York City made a serviceable cloud chamber from a two-ounce whiskey glass and, to the astonishment of her fellow performers, made a hobby of detecting cosmic rays backstage! (Recently her young son exhibited an identical cloud chamber at his school's science fair.) In contrast, a group of boys in El Cerrito, California, devoted all of their free hours during four years of high school to the construction of a multi-ton cyclotron.

Nuclear physics need be neither a hazardous nor a costly hobby. Radioactive atoms abound in the air we breathe and scores of high-energy particles dart through our bodies every second. Most of these are protons, atoms of hydrogen stripped of their planetary electron by the impact of cosmic rays. Observing such particles calls for nothing more dangerous than a wisp of water vapor. To change the direction of such particles in flight and manipulate them in other interesting ways, you must use electrical methods, but this need not be hazardous if you exercise reasonable care.

As for cash outlay, the apparatus used by the pioneers of nuclear physics can be duplicated in principle from such materials as old tin cans, glass jars, discarded inner tubes, steel shafts, copper wire and a few pounds of dry ice. When properly assembled, these enable you to trap the fundamental particles of nature, measure their speed and mass, observe their disintegration and, perhaps, their formation. Do you like to perform tricks with tops? You will find a top spinning at a fantastic rate inside every atom. You can flip these end-for-end, make them wobble, and even trace pleasing abstractions on a fluorescent screen. The following pages tell you how to proceed.

2

CLOUD CHAMBERS FOR
DETECTING NUCLEAR EVENTS

About C. T. R. Wilson: How the circular rainbows made by clouds in sunlight led to the invention of a powerful instrument for investigating the structure of the atom

WHILE AT THE Ben Nevis Observatory in Scotland in 1894, C. T. R. Wilson, the eminent British physicist, became fascinated by the play of sunlight on clouds surrounding the mountain, particularly by rainbows formed in the cloud which circled the sun. On returning to the University of Cambridge, where he was senior demonstrator in the Cavendish Laboratory, Wilson attempted to imitate the phenomenon in miniature.

His apparatus consisted of three bottles, some tubing and an air pump. He put some water in a large bottle and inside this up-ended a small bottle, also partly filled with water. It was held in place about half way down in the larger bottle. Now the large bottle was stoppered and connected by tubing to an evacuated third bottle. When a petcock was opened, air rushed out of the big bottle into the vacuum chamber. As a result the moist air in the small inverted bottle expanded suddenly, and the air was cooled by the expansion. At the reduced temperature, the air contained an excessive amount of water vapor and was in a state of supersaturation. If dust particles or other nuclei were present, the excess vapor would condense on them and form a cloud.

Wilson's interest centered on the role played by these nuclei. It had long been known that condensation could be induced by factors other than dust. The German physicist R. von Helmholtz, for example, had demonstrated that the condensation of a steam jet was ac-

celerated by the presence of certain chemical reactions or by a
nearby flame. Other workers had induced the same reaction by placing a sheet of zinc near the jet and directing ultraviolet light onto it.

Wilson repeated these experiments, substituting an improved
version of his expansion chamber for the steam jet. This apparatus
consisted of a glass cylinder instead of the nest of glass jars. Expansion was accomplished by the movement of a close-fitting piston.
While experimenting with this chamber Wilson observed two effects
which acted in opposition. Exposure of the chamber to X-rays lowered the amount of expansion required for cloud formation. In contrast, by placing a pair of oppositely charged metal plates in the
chamber he discovered that he could inhibit the cloud formation.
Further, he observed that X-rays induced the formation of fine
drops in immense numbers which could be seen best in the beam of
an intense light. Clouds induced by X-rays vanished the instant
Wilson placed a charge on the plates — clear evidence that each
drop must carry an electric charge. It seemed clear to Wilson that
the droplets derived their charges from the ions on which they condensed. If so, the apparatus could serve as a useful instrument for
investigating ionization phenomena in gases.

It was only a short step from this theory to the application of the
chamber to the study of the known ionizing properties of uranium.
Wilson observed that a minute quantity of this element could induce the formation of clouds in the chamber, even at distances as
great as three feet. During these experiments he noted the abrupt
formation of occasional "tracks" in the chamber, thin trails of vapor
which showed in the light beam as gleaming threads. Ultimately,
these were identified as ionization trails, droplets formed on gas
molecules electrified in the wake of speeding fragments from the
disintegrating atoms of uranium. Thus, from the fascination of rainbows for a gifted man came the invention of a powerful instrument
for attacking the ancient riddle: Of what stuff is the universe made?

Modern versions of Wilson's chamber take many forms. Miniatur-
ized designs, weighing but an ounce or so, have been carried aloft
by balloons to detect cosmic rays in the thin reaches of the upper
atmosphere. At the opposite extreme, chambers resembling the
breech of a cannon and weighing many tons have been built to

study nuclear events in gases compressed to 100 atmospheres and higher.

A simple "peanut-butter jar" cloud chamber

THIS SIMPLE CHAMBER is capable of showing many of the effects observed by Wilson. To construct it, you need little more than a pair of 12-ounce peanut-butter jars, a coffee can, a short length of rubber tubing, some plumbing materials and a toy balloon. The assembly appears in Figure 129.

To make the chamber, cut the jars' tops so as to leave the screw-rims, then butt and solder the two rims together with a disk of fly screening sandwiched between. Next drill a hole, large enough to take a No. 6 machine screw, through the bottom of one of the jars, and drill a larger hole, about 3/8 inch in diameter, in the side of the same jar. Drilling glass is not difficult. Cut several notches in the end of a piece of brass tubing, chuck the piece in an electric drill and rotate the notched end (at about 400 revolutions per minute) against the glass while applying a slurry of No. 120 Carborundum grains in water. Avoid wobbling the drill and go easy on the pressure when the drill cuts through the inner wall.

This first jar will be the expansion chamber. In the wall of the second jar cut a hole 9/16 inch in diameter, and fit it with a short pipe nipple screwed to a "street" elbow — a fitting with a male thread on one end and a female on the other. This piping and the fittings should be of the size known in the trade as 1/4 inch: its outside diameter is 35/64 of an inch and the inside diameter, 3/8 inch. Slip the neck of the balloon over the end of the street elbow and tie it in place. Then insert the pipe assembly through the jar and cement it in place, as illustrated, with a mixture of litharge and glycerin or any of the commercially available rubberized cements.

A circle of 14-gauge bare copper wire is then fastened to the inside bottom of the expansion chamber and secured by a machine screw. Seal it airtight with rubber cement. The remaining hole in the chamber is fitted with a rubber stopper. Now make a solution consisting of equal parts by volume of water and alcohol with ink added (to color the fluid black) and a half teaspoon of salt and,

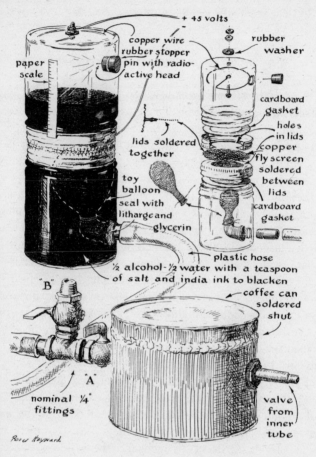

+ 45 volts

copper wire
rubber stopper
pin with radio-
active head

rubber washer

paper scale

cardboard gasket

holes in lids

copper fly screen soldered between lids

lids soldered together

toy balloon

cardboard gasket

seal with litharge and glycerin

plastic hose

½ alcohol-½ water with a teaspoon of salt and india ink to blacken

coffee can soldered shut

"B"

nominal ¼ fittings

"A"

valve from inner tube

Roger Hayward

129
Details of Wilson cloud chamber made from two peanut-butter jars

with a funnel, fill the jars (through the hole where the radioactive pin fits) to approximately the level shown.

Connect the outer end of the pipe nipple with a source of compressed air. The easiest source is a pumped-up automobile inner tube, but you can make a convenient pressure tank of a coffee can of the one-pound size. The valve assembly from an old inner tube will serve as an inlet. Solder a pipe nipple into the tank for an outlet and fit it with a shut-off cock ("A" in the drawing) for admitting air to the expansion chamber. A drain cock ("B") is also provided for bleeding the chamber during the expansion stroke.

In preparing the apparatus for operation, first close both cocks and pump the tank to a pressure of about 10 or 12 pounds. Opening the shut-off cock "A" admits air to the balloon and forces the fluid from the lower jar through the screen (which minimizes turbulence) into the chamber above. This compresses the air trapped above the fluid, and its temperature increases. The warmed air quickly takes up additional moisture from the fluid. Close the shut-off cock and open the bleeder. This relieves the pressure inside the chamber, and air escapes from the balloon through the bleeder valve.

Both the fluid and the temperature drop abruptly, creating a state of supersaturation in the expansion chamber. The action differs from that of Wilson's chamber in that the expansion stroke ends with air at substantially atmospheric pressure, whereas expansion in the Wilson chamber is completed at lowered pressure. The higher working pressure gives the "peanut butter" chamber an advantage because the increased density of the gas betters the chance that a nuclear particle will collide with the nucleus of an atom and thereby produce an interesting event.

Important information for beginners constructing Wilson cloud chambers

BEGINNERS SOMETIMES ATTEMPT to simplify Wilson's apparatus by exhausting air directly from the chamber, thus avoiding the complication of a piston, either liquid or mechanical. Such schemes invariably fail because the turbulence created by the escaping air destroys the tracks. Piston devices confine the motion of the air to the vertical direction. Small eddies are created near the lower walls of the chamber, but they are not serious.

Wilson took special pains to avoid turbulence when constructing his second instrument. This one had a more accessible chamber, consisting of a glass cylinder and piston. The moving parts were fitted with almost optical precision to prevent air from leaking past the piston into the chamber. Lord Rutherford recalled in later years how, during the early stage of construction, he observed Wilson in his laboratory painstakingly grinding the piston into the cylinder. Rutherford, called away from Cambridge, returned some months later to find Wilson still sitting in precisely the same place, patiently grinding away!

Wilson's third and final design featured a clever solution of the problem of access to the interior of the chamber. Essentially this apparatus consists of a steel cylinder equipped with a glass top and a close-fitting, free-floating piston. The assembly stands in a shallow pan of water which acts as a seal. The expansion stroke is made by exhausting air beneath the piston through a vent in the center of the pan extending slightly above the level of the water. The length of the expansion stroke is limited by a rubber stop beneath the piston. To reach the interior of the chamber, you simply lift the assembly from the pan and pull out the piston.

This is the chamber Wilson described in the celebrated paper he presented before the Royal Society in 1912. A tribute to the excellence of the design is the fact that during the remainder of Wilson's long career all his nuclear researches were made with this chamber. It is now preserved in the Cavendish Museum. A few years ago Sir Lawrence Bragg asked Wilson whether the apparatus could properly be labeled "the original." "Why," exclaimed Wilson, "I never made but one!"

Certain requirements must be observed when operating an expansion chamber. The volume and speed of expansion must be maintained, and stray ions must be swept from the chamber. The expansion stroke of the apparatus diagrammed here is completed in about a twentieth of a second, well within the limit required. It can be speeded by increasing the diameter of the tubing.

Early in his experiments Wilson learned that the supersaturation required for showing tracks of negatively charged particles is reached when the ratio of the chamber's volume after expansion to its volume before expansion is 1.25. At this ratio a few drops form in a dust-free atmosphere. Positive ions will not act as condensation nuclei for water vapor until the expansion ratio reaches a value of 1.31. This requirement can be lowered somewhat by adding alcohol to the water. When the expansion ratio exceeds 1.38, a dense cloudy condensation is produced in the chamber even when no nuclei are present. Wilson usually adjusted his apparatus for a ratio between 1.33 and 1.36. The expansion ratio of the peanut-butter chamber is established by the amount of air admitted to the balloon and, hence, by the level reached by the fluid in the expansion chamber during the compression stroke. This level is measured by the paper scale cemented to the upper jar.

The chamber is cleared of spurious ions (and unwanted clouds) by connecting a voltage between the copper electrode in the expansion chamber and the salt solution. It is good practice to sweep the field after each expansion and to maintain the voltage across the chamber until the moment of expansion.

Beginners will discover that the tracks show up best when viewed obliquely in an intense beam of collimated light. The irregular end of a peanut-butter jar has thus far won no laurels in the optical goods industry, and the walls are not much better. Professional chambers are equipped with windows of plate glass. If you want to make good photographs of nuclear tracks, you must of course synchronize the camera shutter with the completion of the expansion stroke. Wilson's exposures were made by discharging two gallon-sized Leyden jars through a mercury spark gap. The exposure time was about a thousandth of a second. If you own one of the electronic-flash outfits now popular with photographers, you will be spared the labor of duplicating Wilson's gap.*

Numerous combinations of common objects can be made to serve as Wilson chambers. Doubtless the simplest arrangement consists in nothing more than a rubber bulb fitted to the neck of an Erlenmeyer flask. The combination is partially filled with colored water and upended. Compression and expansion of the air above the liquid is accomplished merely by squeezing the bulb. The device is satisfactory for visual demonstrations, but trouble is encountered when you try to take photographs of tracks with it. The expansion

---

* Experimenters who construct this chamber, or other versions of it to be described, can procure a speck of radioactive material for study, free of charge, by forwarding a request to the Amateur Scientist Department, SCIENTIFIC AMERICAN, 415 Madison Avenue, New York 17, N. Y. To receive the speck *you must enclose a stamped, self-addressed envelope.*

strokes are difficult to reproduce and all but impossible to synchronize with the camera shutter.

Essentially the same principle has been put to work in the following highly successful chamber.

L. R. Hull, a physics teacher at South Side High School, Fort Wayne, Ind., describes his "rubber-plunger" cloud chamber

THE EXPANSION ELEMENT of this chamber is a rubber plunger of the type used for cleaning drains, more familiarly known as the "plumber's friend." This works into a chamber made of a glass cylinder cut from a quart jar and closed at the top by a disc of plate glass [*Fig. 130*].

To cut the jar you wrap a single turn of iron wire (such as that used for binding brooms) around the jar tightly at the place where the cut is desired, the ends being separated by a small sheet of as-

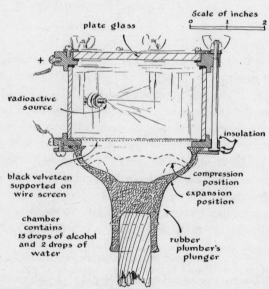

130
Construction details of a cloud chamber actuated by a rubber plunger

bestos insulation where they would otherwise make electrical contact. The loop becomes red hot when you connect it across the six-volt terminals of a transformer or storage battery. After about 30 seconds of heating you remove the wire. Plunge the jar into cold water immediately. The glass will break cleanly at the line where it was heated by the wire. The sharp edges are then rounded with abrasive such as emery or carborundum.

The top of the chamber is closed either by a disk of Lucite (about a quarter of an inch thick) or by a piece of heavy plate glass. Plastic is easy to work with ordinary hand tools. If you decide to use glass but do not own a circular glass cutter, one can easily be rigged from a wheel-type cutter available in hardware stores. Fasten the wheel end of the cutter to one end of a short length of inch-square wood so that the wheel protrudes slightly beneath the lower edge of the wood. Next drive a wood screw through the wood vertically at a distance from the cutter wheel equal to the radius of the desired glass disk. The protruding tip of the wood screw serves as the center point of a compass, the wheel as the other point. Then make an indentation with a center punch in a small scrap of 16-gauge sheet metal.

You place this punched piece of metal on the glass to be cut, backing the metal with friction tape to prevent it from slipping. The punched indentation is centered with respect to the glass. Now you put the protruding tip of the wood screw in the indentation and make a circular cut in the glass with a single, firm rotary stroke of the tool. After this, if you make 10 straight radial cuts from this disk to the edge of the glass sheet, you can break away the outer pieces, leaving a disk the same size as the circular cut. You then smooth the edge of the disk with abrasive.

The glass cylinder, window and plumber's friend are fastened together with metal rings. The ring fittings can be built of thin sections cut from sheet metal and soldered. If a metal cutting lathe is available, you can machine them from a thick slab of stock. Rubber gaskets must be inserted where the metal and glass come into contact. Turbulence in the chamber is minimized by inserting a disk of black velveteen, supported by wire screening, between the cavity of the rubber plunger and the chamber. The radioactive sample is supported inside the chamber by a machine screw inserted through the side wall.

The assembled chamber is supported on a wooden bracket. Its expansion is actuated by a lever mechanism, which is tripped by a motor-driven cam. The chamber is illuminated by a 300-watt slide projector, the beam of which is controlled by a shutter released electromagnetically. The camera is positioned above [*shown in Fig. 131*].

To make the compression stroke you lift the horizontal lever quickly and hook it to the vertical lever. The compression should not exceed about one third of an atmosphere, or the chamber will fill with fog on expansion. After about 30 seconds you start the motor. The cam advances until the metal arm at the top of the vertical lever drops into a notch on the cam. A spring then pulls

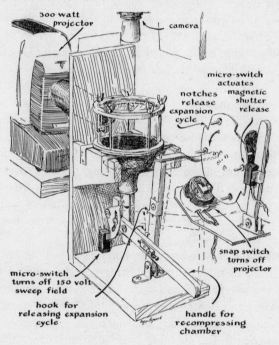

131
The "plumber's friend" cloud chamber equipped with automatic camera for photographing alpha and beta rays

magnetic
shutter
release   rubber
band

132
Details of electromagnetic shutter release

the vertical lever away from the chamber, unhooking the horizontal lever. The plumber's friend then springs to its original shape, accomplishing the expansion stroke.

An electrostatic "clearing" field is applied to the chamber automatically during the compression stroke by a microswitch actuated by the horizontal lever. The field is removed by the switch and the leads to the chamber are short-circuited automatically at the end of the expansion stroke. Similarly, the motor-driven cam is equipped with switches for operating the projector and shutter release in sequence. Exposure time is fixed by the tension of a rubber band hooked to the shutter [see Fig. 132].

The proportion and amount of liquid in the chamber are not critical. Good tracks form with either 180-proof grain alcohol or rubbing alcohol as it comes from the bottle. Performance is influenced by room temperature, however. Above 70 degrees Fahrenheit results are improved by diluting the alcohol slightly with water — say 15 drops of alcohol to two drops of water. It should be kept in mind that fog results from too much liquid as well as from over-expansion. The chamber rarely requires more than 20 drops of liquid. Don't expect to see tracks during the first few expansions. The liquid must have time to evaporate.

Beta tracks, being thin, are more difficult to see than alphas and appear best when the alphas have faded.

The dry-ice diffusion cloud chamber

AN EVEN SIMPLER FORM of cloud chamber than the one described by Hull can be had if you have access to a source of dry ice. You merely fasten a disk of alcohol-soaked blotting paper in the bottom of a jar,* screw on the lid and upend the jar on a cake of dry ice, as shown in Figure 133. Every few seconds a sharp, momentary vapor trail will appear near the bottom of the jar. Most of the trails represent particles from radioactive material in the earth, or fragments of atoms smashed in the atmosphere by cosmic rays. But once in a great while the trail will mark the passage through the jar of a primary cosmic particle from space, perhaps the con-

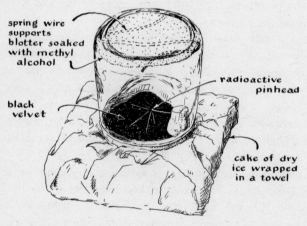

spring wire supports
blotter soaked with methyl alcohol

radioactive pinhead

black velvet

cake of dry ice wrapped in a towel

133
A cloud chamber of the diffusion type made from a peanut-butter jar

* This is, in principle, the same experiment that the ballerina conducted with a whiskey glass.

cluding phase of an event which had its origin millions of years ago in an exploding star.

An apparatus of this type is called a "diffusion" chamber. Its operating principle and construction are described by I. C. Cornog of the University of Pennsylvania's Randal Morgan Laboratory of Physics.

"Suppose that a closed vessel is arranged so that the top is warm and the bottom quite cold, and so that a vaporizing liquid is at the top, inside the vessel. This produces a sharp change of temperature inside the vessel, the liquid at the top being near room temperature, and that at the bottom about 70 degrees below zero centigrade. After a time the vapor formed at the top is found to be continuously diffusing downward, becoming colder and more saturated as it moves. Near the bottom of the vessel it becomes supersaturated, and in that zone the path of an ionizing particle will show up just as it does in the expansion chamber. If these conditions are maintained, and if the sensitive region near the bottom is properly illuminated, radiations entering the vessel will be continuously observable.

"The simplest sort of continuous diffusion chamber consists merely of a large glass beaker. Inside, on the bottom, is a piece of black velveteen to increase the visibility of the tracks. Across the top, inside the jar, is placed a sheet of cardboard, which is kept saturated with alcohol. The jar is set on a cake of dry ice. Tracks appear in the sensitive region near the bottom a short time after the device is placed in operation.

"It is altogether likely that you will not see the tracks at first, even though they are present. You wait and hope for the best. After a time the temperature gradient is established, the dust particles disappear and you begin to see tracks as you look down into the vessel toward the side where the light originates."

Seven clues to a successful diffusion chamber

I HAVE BUILT a number of diffusion chambers based on Dr. Cornog's description and observed beautiful tracks. But many things can go wrong — and they do. The interval between

completing a chamber and the time it starts to work will be shortened considerably if you give some attention to these details:

1. The vessel should be reasonably airtight. A wide-mouthed jar
fitted with a screw top of metal and turned upside down works better than one which merely sits on a metal plate. If the latter arrangement is used, wet the metal plate with alcohol to form a liquid
seal.

2. The importance of side-lighting cannot be overemphasized.
The beam from a home movie or slide projector makes a satisfactory lighting arrangement. The important point is to light the individual droplets brightly in comparison with their surroundings.

3. You must learn to recognize the trails of droplets as they appear. Soon after the apparatus is set up, clouds will form two or
three inches above the bottom of the vessel and "rain" will begin
to fall from them. This micrometeorological phenomenon will be
enhanced if the velveteen carpeting on the floor of the chamber is
moistened with alcohol. The rain is easy to recognize and the tracks
appear as thin, silvery threads in its midst. They remain sharp for
only a second, then drift away like miniature wisps of smoke.

4. If you use an upended jar as the chamber, it is advisable to
cement the alcohol pad to the inner surface at the top and the velveteen covering to the inner surface of the metal lid. The cement
must be allowed to dry thoroughly, else it may contaminate the alcohol and thus ruin the experiment. Another, and better, way to
hold the parts together is to use a wire expansion ring or some similar device.

5. Remember that there must be a sharp difference of temperature between the top and bottom of the chamber. Ordinary ice will
not work. A temperature difference on the order of 150 degrees
Fahrenheit must be maintained between the top and bottom of the
jar. The assembly should rest directly on the block of dry ice. A
metal bottom, because of its superior heat conductivity, works better than one of glass or plastic. The dry ice should stand on some
insulating material such as corrugated cardboard, and the uncovered
portion of the top of the ice should be covered with a bit of cloth
to prevent frozen vapor rising from it from interfering with observation.

6. A well-soaked pad holds enough alcohol to keep the chamber going for about eight hours. As previously mentioned, the metal plate at the bottom should be moistened, but not flooded, with alcohol, as a thick layer of alcohol tends to reduce the depth of the chamber's sensitive region.

7. It is easy to paralyze the chamber with overly "hot" radioactive material. The amount of luminescent material in the minute hand of a Westclox can stop the chamber's activity at a distance of 18 inches! Use only a tiny chip of it. However, in most localities tracks induced by cosmic rays will provide enough excitement to reward the amateur's effort in constructing the device.

A more elaborate diffusion chamber is described by Major Reuben B. Moody of the U. S. Air Force

My brother Jerry and I have spent many enjoyable hours in the construction of cloud chambers of assorted shapes and sizes — some of which worked.

Our first chamber was constructed according to the instructions of Dr. Cornog. For the chamber itself we used a wide-mouthed pickle jar with a metallic screwtop. A synthetic sponge was secured to the bottom of the jar by means of expansion clamps (manufactured from coat hangers), and the sponge was then thoroughly soaked with rubbing alcohol. Across the mouth of the jar we stretched a black cloth over which we screwed the metal lid. The jar was upended on a cake of dry ice. The cloth remaining outside the jar was spread out to cover the ice, thus providing a contrasting background and preventing the dry ice "smoke" from interfering with our vision.

We detected a miniature rainfall almost immediately, and within five minutes we could perceive the threadlike vapor trails. (My wife, who is not overly enthusiastic regarding scientific matters, was disappointed because no lightning flashes were detected during our miniature rain storm.)

Our first cloud chamber remained active for as long as the dry ice lasted — about seven hours. Although we were fascinated and elated with the results of our first endeavor, we began to think of ways to improve our results and to reduce the eyestrain attendant on observing them. In our pickle-jar chamber the sensitive region never exceeded a depth of about one inch. Also, the eyestrain was terrible, due to the ghostlike and short-lived appearance of the tracks and because of light reflections from the glass sides of the jar.

Since metal is a better heat conductor than glass, we conceived the idea that the all-important temperature difference could be improved by constructing a metal cloud chamber. Accordingly, from the kitchen we obtained a coffee can about six inches deep and six inches in diameter. After painting the interior of the tin can with blackboard slating, we cut three horizontal window slits in the can, one above the other.

These windows, designed for observation and lighting purposes, were about one inch high and three inches wide. Over the windows we glued strips of cellophane (we found that scotch tape could not withstand the extreme cold without shrinking and without losing its adhesive properties). To ensure air-tightness we secured the edges of the cellophane windows with strips of plastic tape. On the bottom of the can we placed a cut-to-size disk of velveteen fabric, and to the lid of the coffee tin we glued the synthetic sponge [see Fig. 134].

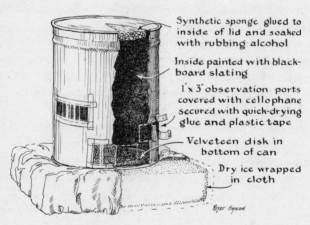

Synthetic sponge glued to inside of lid and soaked with rubbing alcohol

Inside painted with blackboard slating

1" x 3" observation ports covered with cellophane secured with quick-drying glue and plastic tape

Velveteen disk in bottom of can

Dry ice wrapped in cloth

Roger Hayward

134
An improved version of the diffusion or "continuous" cloud chamber

With the coffee-can chamber we obtained much better results. The eyestrain was eliminated; the sensitive region increased in depth to about 2.5 inches, and we were able to observe from 30 to 50 tracks per minute. Again the chamber remained active for as long as the dry ice lasted — this time about 18 hours with a cake of ice about two inches thick.

> *Gareth D. Shaw, an engineer of Baltimore, Md., discusses some theoretical aspects of a chamber he made for identifying atomic particles and measuring their major characteristics*

ALL CLOUD CHAMBERS are based on the fact that ions are created when charged particles move through a gas at high speed. Close encounters between the particle and an atom in its path dislodge an electron from the atom. The process forms two charged particles: the electron itself and the ionized atom, now postive because it has lost a unit of negative charge. Either particle can disturb the delicate balance of electrical forces in a neighboring molecule of alcohol in the vapor state.

On close approach to an ion the molecule acquires on the side facing the ion a charge that is opposite in sign to the charge of the ion. In consequence the molecule and the ion are mutually attracted. Other molecules in the vicinity react similarly. The ion thus acts as a center of condensation. When the temperature of the gas is below the dew point of the vapor, a droplet of alcohol quickly forms. A speeding particle leaves thousands of ions in its wake; the resulting droplets comprise the vapor trail.

The experimenter is interested in the size and shape of the tracks because they provide clues to the identity of the responsible particles. It is therefore important to minimize convection currents in the chamber by filtering as much heat from the light beam as possible. A small aquarium with flat sides makes a good filter. Most 35-mm. slide-projectors come equipped with heat filters and blowers. A pair of projectors may be needed to provide enough light for making photographs. Tracks show up best when viewed at an angle of about 120 degrees with respect to the light sources — each spaced at 120 degrees from the viewing port.

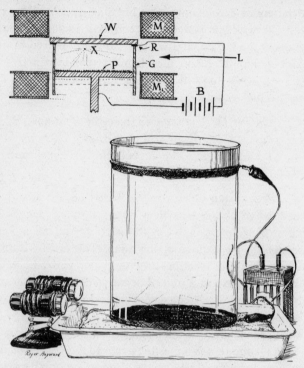

135
Schematic arrangement for applying magnetic field to cloud chamber
(*above*). Chamber with "clearing field' applied (*below*)

Photographs can be made inexpensively with a 35-mm. camera of
$f/3.5$ aperture equipped with an auxiliary lens for close work. Lens
openings range from $f/3.5$ to $f/8$ and shutter speeds from $1/10$ to
$1/100$ second with film rated ASA 200. The photographs reproduced
in these pages were made with Kodak Tri-X film and developed in
Kodak Microdol, a fine-grain developer. When the light source is
relatively weak, a procedure known as "pushing the film" is possible
with this developer. The speed of the film is doubled by doubling
the time in which the film is kept in the developer.

Once the technique of operating the chamber has been mastered,
the experimenter should consider adding a magnetic field to it, as
shown schematically in the accompanying illustration [*Fig. 135*]. A

chamber without a field is like a yardstick without inch marks — interesting but not very useful. When a charged particle moves at right angles to the direction of a magnetic field, it is acted upon by a force at right angles to both its direction and that of the field. If the field extends in the vertical direction, for example, and the particle moves from east to west, the particle is accelerated in the north-south direction.

As a consequence a particle that enters a uniform field follows a circular path [see Fig. 136]. The radius and direction of the path depend on the sign and magnitude of the charge on the particle, on the mass and velocity of the particle and on the strength and direction of the field.

A suitable electromagnet can be constructed inexpensively from scrap steel, available in most communities from local industries or scrap dealers. My magnet consisted of two pole-pieces and a yoke made of a pair of plates separated by two rectangular members [see Fig. 137]. The pole-pieces were approximately five inches long. The upper one was machined to a diameter of nine inches and the lower one to a diameter of seven inches. Both were made of soft-steel shafting. In the upper pole-piece was machined a conical hole, which tapered from two inches at the top to five inches at the bottom. The hole provides a clear path for viewing and photographing the tracks. The lower pole-face was shaped to produce a uniform distribution of magnetic flux through the sensitive region of the chamber. The face of this piece is in the form of a shallow, curved cone. The apex of the cone should be rounded off (1/8 inch radius) to prevent the magnetic flux from bunching at this point. The inner

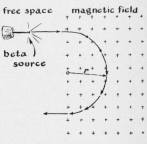

free space   magnetic field

beta
source

136
Path of an electron at right
angles with a uniform magnetic
field

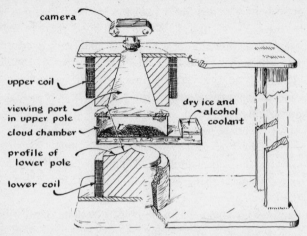

camera

upper coil

viewing port
in upper pole

cloud chamber

profile of
lower pole

lower coil

dry ice and
alcohol
coolant

137
A diffusion cloud chamber equipped with a magnetic field

edge of the upper pole-face coincides with the center of curvature
of the lower pole-face. The radius of curvature in the case of my
magnet is four inches ["*r*" *in the illustration*].

The pole-pieces are welded to the pair of soft-steel plates, each
3/8 inch thick, 10 inches wide and 18 inches long. The plates are
welded in turn to the spacing members, also made of soft steel; each
member is 1½ inches thick, two inches wide and 14 inches long. The
spacers provide an air gap of four inches between the pole-faces.

Each of the two coils for energizing the magnet consists of 1,000
turns of No. 14 enameled copper magnet-wire, wound on wooden
forms and wrapped with insulating tape. The coils require some 60
pounds of wire. The forms were made approximately 1/16 inch
larger than the pole-pieces so that the coils could be slipped over
the poles easily after they are removed from the forms.

The lower coil rests on the yoke plate and requires no fastening.
The upper one is supported by an aluminum ring bolted to the
upper pole. The magnet is energized by a six-ampere direct current
at 100 volts, and is designed for a maximum duty-cycle of 15 minutes. Extended operation at six amperes results in overheating. The
magnet produces a field strength of 1,000 gauss in the sensitive

region of the chamber. Motor-generators of the type used for arc welding are suitable for powering the unit and can occasionally be picked up on the surplus market for a few dollars. An inexpensive power supply can also be assembled from surplus rectifier-units of the silicon-disk type.

The coils must be interconnected so that the current flows in the same direction through each. When they are properly connected, the north end of a magnetic-compass needle will point to one pole-face and the south end to the other. A resistor of 1,000 ohms rated at 20 watts should be connected across the input terminals of the coils to dissipate the energy generated by the collapse of the magnetic field when the magnet is turned off [*see Fig. 138*]. Without this resistor serious arcing will occur at the switch contacts. If a voltmeter or other instrument is connected across the coils, it should be removed before turning off the magnet; otherwise the sharp rise in voltage that accompanies the collapse of the field will damage the meter.

When the magnet is ready for operation, the field strength must be measured in the region to be occupied by the sensitive part of the chamber. The current through the coils is adjusted as accurately as possible to six amperes and a note is made of the voltage at this value of current. The field is then measured (in gauss) with a flux-meter. This measurement is made only once, so a fluxmeter may be borrowed from a local electric-power firm or the physics laboratory of a nearby school. If desired, the magnet may be calibrated for a series of current values.

You will be well repaid in terms of convenience for care taken in constructing the chamber. One good design, which is made principally of sheet metal, provides two compartments. The lower one

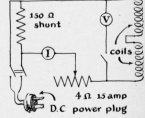

138
Circuit configuration for energizing
magnet of a cloud chamber

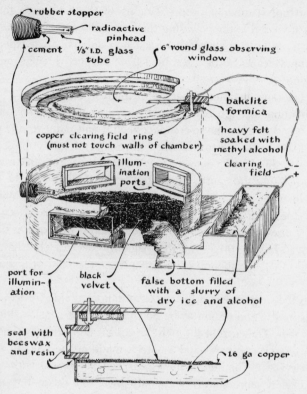

rubber stopper

radioactive pinhead

cement   ⅛" I.D. glass tube

6" round glass observing window

bakelite formica

heavy felt soaked with methyl alcohol

copper clearing field ring (must not touch walls of chamber)

clearing field   — +

illumination ports

port for illumination

black velvet

false bottom filled with a slurry of dry ice and alcohol

seal with beeswax and resin

16 ga copper

139
A diffusion cloud chamber adapted for use with a magnetic field

holds the refrigerant (a slurry of crushed dry ice mixed with alcohol), and also serves as the base for the upper compartment [*see Fig. 139*]. Sheet steel may be used, but copper is recommended at least for the surface between the compartments because of its effectiveness as a conductor of heat.

The upper chamber is closed by a lid that consists of an assembly of concentric rings and a disk of clear glass. The ring assembly supports the glass and includes an insulated ring of copper that serves as one electrode for applying an electric field across the chamber to clear it of old tracks. The ring assembly also incorporates a felt pad from which alcohol evaporates when the chamber is in operation.

As an alternative scheme the wall of the chamber may be lined with a strip of blotting paper arranged so that its lower edge rests in the pool of alcohol at the bottom of the chamber. Fluid is drawn through the paper by capillary attraction, evaporates, condenses and returns to the pool for recirculation. The chamber may be supported within the magnet on a flat wooden platform. A bracket to support the camera in line with the opening should also be provided.

To prepare the chamber for operation, crush enough dry ice into pea-sized lumps to fill the lower container. Do not handle the ice with your bare hands — a frozen finger is quite as painful as a burned one. Alcohol is next added *slowly* to the ice. Violent bubbling may occur until the temperature of the container drops close to that of the ice. Additional ice may be added from time to time as required. Next saturate the pad with alcohol and pour about a tablespoonful of alcohol into the chamber. Place the assembly in the magnet and apply power to the coils.

Some of the trails in the chamber will be curved. If the upper pole of the magnet attracts the north end of a magnetic-compass needle (which indicates that the direction of the magnetic flux is from the lower to the upper pole), electrons will follow a counterclockwise path. Relatively light particles of low energy that carry a positive charge will curve clockwise. The direction in which some particles move can be determined by inspection.

Energy expended in the creation of ions during flight causes the particle to lose speed; more time is thus available for the transfer of energy near the end of flight. The heavier ionization is seen as a thickening of the track. The direction of flight is known, of course, when particles originate in a radioactive material deliberately placed in the chamber. The identity of some particles can also be determined by inspection. Alpha rays make relatively short, thick tracks; electrons and protons, thin ones. Mesons are usually so energetic that their flight is not perceptibly affected by a field of 1,000 gauss. Consequently their tracks appear thin and straight.

It is interesting to analyze photographs of tracks and to calculate the speed, mass and energy of the responsible particles. The accompanying photograph [*see Fig. 141*], for example, shows the circular

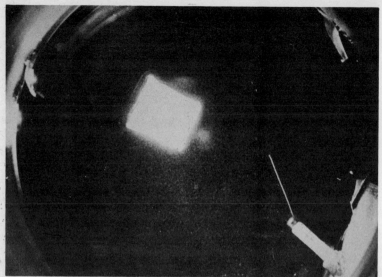

140
Vapor trail *(angling upward at lower right)* of an alpha particle

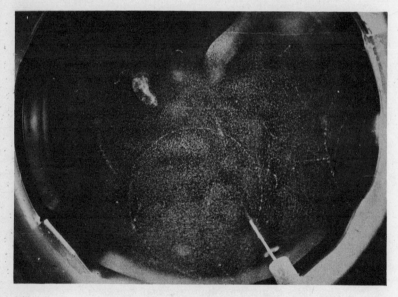

141
Photograph by Gareth Shaw of the circular track of an electron in a magnetic field of 800 gauss. Apparatus used was homemade

path of an electron ejected from a short stub of wire coated with radioactive material. Before the photograph was made, the current of the magnet was adjusted to generate a field strength at the chamber of 800 gauss.

The momentum of the particle, expressed in units of "magnetic rigidity," is equal to the radius of its path multiplied by the field strength. The radius of this particular path is 3.09 centimeters. Thus the momentum of the particle is equal to 3.09 × 800, or 2,472, gauss-centimeters. With this quantity known, the velocity of the particle can be learned by doing just a little more arithmetic. The quantity representing the magnetic rigidity is combined with the electron's charge to its mass (1.7588×10^7 electromagnetic units per gram) and the velocity of light (3×10^{10} centimeters per second) according to the accompanying formula [see Fig. 142]. In this case the velocity turns out to be 2.47×10^{10} centimeters per second. This is equivalent to about 153,000 miles per second, or 82.4 per cent of the velocity of light. The energy of the particle is found (in millions of electron volts) by squaring the ratio of the velocity of the particle to that of light and inserting the result in the second formula. The energy of the electron in this example was .389 million electron volts.

An interesting property of matter can be observed by calculating the velocity and energy of a substantial number of electrons and plotting the result as a graph [see Fig. 143]. Note how the curve bends up sharply as the speed of the particle approaches the velocity of light. This is in accord with the theory of relativity, which states that matter gains mass with velocity, and that the mass becomes infinite at the speed of light. This means that the kinetic energy of a particle, however small it may be, must also increase without limit as it approaches the speed of light, because kinetic energy is the product of mass and velocity.

A similar graph can be drawn to show how the particle acquires mass with velocity. The mass of the electron at rest is known (it is 9.1×10^{-28} gram), and its velocity can be measured by means of the diffusion chamber. To find its mass at any velocity these values are inserted in Einstein's equation for relativistic mass [third formula, Fig. 142]. The rest is simple arithmetic.

$$v = Hr \, \frac{e}{m_o} \sqrt{\frac{c^2 - v^2}{c^2}}$$

where:

v = velocity of electron in centimeters per second

Hr = magnetic rigidity in gauss-centimeters

$\frac{e}{m_o}$ = ratio of electron's charge to mass (1.7588×10^7 emu/gm)

c = velocity of light (3×10^{10} cm per sec)

e = charge of electron (1.602×10^{-20} emu)

$$T = 0.511 \left(\frac{1}{\sqrt{1 - \frac{v^2}{c^2}}} - 1 \right)$$

where:

T = kinetic energy in millions of electron volts

(with other quantities as previously defined)

$$m = \frac{m_o}{\sqrt{1 - \frac{v^2}{c^2}}}$$

where:

m = increased mass of particle in grams

m_o = rest mass of particle

(with other quantities as previously defined)

$$v_\alpha = \sqrt{\frac{2 KE}{m_o}}$$

where:

v_α = velocity of alpha particle in cm/sec

KE = kinetic energy of alpha particle in MEV

m_o = rest mass of alpha particle in grams

142

Formulas for determining the velocity, kinetic energy and mass of fundamental particles from cloud-chamber observations

The curvature of alpha particles is difficult to detect with this apparatus because a magnetic field of 1,000 gauss exerts little influence on their relatively large mass (about 8,000 times that of the electron). The energy of alpha particles can be found by analysis of the tracks, however, because the length of the tracks depends on the rate at which the particles expend energy in ionizing atoms. Curves showing this relationship have been constructed from data acquired

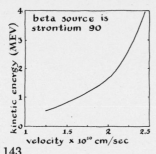

143
Energy graph of beta particles

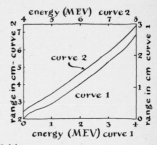

144
Energy-range graph of alpha
particles

by observing numerous alpha-decay processes [*see Fig. 144*]. To
find the energy of an alpha particle, measure the length of its track
in centimeters and refer to the curves. Care must be taken to enlarge the photographs accurately to full scale; errors in enlargement are preserved in the results.

The classical formula for computing kinetic energy ($KE = \frac{1}{2}m\,v^2$)
may be used for computing the energy of alpha particles because their velocity is so low that the relativistic mass effect may be
neglected. This formula expresses energy in terms of ergs. To convert ergs into electron volts multiply by 6.25×10^{11}. The length of
the alpha track depicted in Figure 140 is 3.1 centimeters, which according to the graph corresponds to an energy of 4.65 mev. By arranging the classical kinetic energy formula for velocity, and inserting the value for kinetic energy just found, you will arrive at a
velocity of 1.496×10^9 centimeters per second, or about 9,000
miles per second.

The diffusion chamber invites numerous other interesting experiments. Air can be replaced by other gases, for example. In general
it will be found that the quality of the tracks drops in proportion
as the molecular weight of the gas falls below that of the vapor.
The accompanying photograph of a beta track [*Fig. 141*] was made
in an atmosphere of oxygen.

Gamma rays and X-rays dislodge electrons throughout the gas;
the resulting tracks are characteristically erratic [*see Fig. 145*]. In

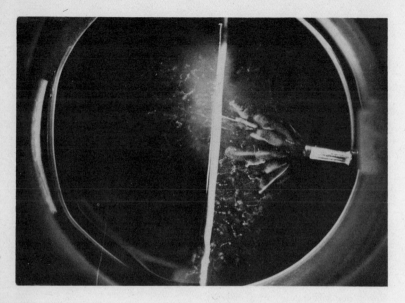

145
Alpha particles *(heavy trails)* and electrons produced both by X-rays
and particle source *(at right)*. Wax barrier crosses center

this case a particle source was included and appears at the right
side of the picture together with a pattern of alpha tracks. The
white strip across the center was made by a wax barrier, inserted to
determine whether electrons could penetrate it. The broad, irregular masses in the vicinity of the alpha particles are wisps of cloud
representing old tracks. These could have been cleared away by
momentarily connecting a potential of from 45 to 90 volts across
the electrodes of the chamber.

3

A SIMPLE
MAGNETIC-RESONANCE
SPECTROMETER

At the center of every atom there is a minute top, the nucleus, which spins on its axis with incredible speed. By subjecting it to crossed magnetic fields that pulsate you can flip it over, make it wobble and, by these effects, identify itself. Here is a simple apparatus for thus experimenting with the nucleus. It was especially designed for amateurs by scientists of the U.S. Air Force

SHORTLY AFTER WORLD WAR II a group of physicists wrapped a coil of wire around a glass tube in which water had been sealed, put the assembly between the poles of a magnet and sent a high-frequency current through the coil. When the frequency was raised or lowered through a critical range, the current flowing in the coil varied sharply. This occurred precisely at the point where the frequency of the oscillating magnetic field set up by the coil resonated with the magnetized nuclei of hydrogen atoms in the water.

Further experiment showed that other atoms as well as molecules of many kinds react in the same way. Of more interest, however, was the observation that the current varies uniquely for each kind of substance sensitive to the test. In the dozen years since these relatively simple experiments were made the technique has given rise to an instrument called the magnetic-resonance spectrometer which rivals the power of the optical spectroscope for investigating the structure of matter.

In the course of applying the new technique to the analysis of biological substances, a group working under Miles A. McLennan in the Bioelectronics Section of the Aero Medical Laboratory at the Wright Air Development Center has designed a simple version of the magnetic-resonance spectrometer that amateurs can make at home. It should serve not only as an introduction to an interesting new field of experimental physics but should also make an attractive classroom demonstration or science-fair project.

According to the "classical" theory of physics, all elementary particles of matter spin on their axes like tops, and those that have an electric charge (e.g., electrons and protons) generate magnetic fields. (The classical picture has now been superseded by the quantum-mechanical view, but it will suffice for the purposes of this discussion.) Particles bound in atoms and in molecules not only spin but also move on orbits. This motion adds to the field generated by the spin. The fields of neighboring particles merge; depending on the structure of the atoms or molecules and on the direction in which the magnetic forces point, the fields tend to cancel in some cases and to reinforce in others. In consequence all atoms and molecules are characterized by unique patterns of interacting magnetic forces.

What will happen to these tiny magnets if they are subjected to the influence of an external magnetic field? It was this question that led to the development of the new technique. In the case of the single-proton nuclei of the hydrogen atoms of water, the magnetic axes normally point in random directions. It might therefore be supposed that an external field would cause the proton axes to line up in the direction of the field. This, however, does not happen. Instead the field causes the protons to precess, or wobble like a spinning top that has been tipped from the vertical.

We might say that each particle now has two axes; it spins on one and precesses around the other. The axes on which the particles precess line up with the external field, but attempts to align the axes on which they spin get nowhere. Increasing the strength of the external field merely causes the particles to precess faster. In fact, the rate of precession varies in proportion to the field strength and is equal to the intensity of the field (expressed in gauss) multiplied by 4,228.5. Thus when a sample of water is placed between the poles of a typical magnetron magnet with a field strength of 1,450 gauss, the hydrogen nuclei precess at the rate of 6,131,325 revolutions per second.

It is possible to disturb the particles, however. They can even be flipped over so their "north" and "south" poles are reversed. This is accomplished by setting up a second external field at right angles to the first and causing it to oscillate or reverse direction precisely in step with the rate at which the particles are precessing. In the case of water in a biasing field of 1,450 gauss the critical frequency is 6.1 megacycles. Energy is absorbed by the particles from the oscillating field during each alteration, just as a tuning fork is set into vibration by the sound waves to which it is resonant.

Resonance between the particles and the oscillating field can be established by adjusting either the frequency of the current through the coil or the strength of the biasing field (which determines the rate at which the particles precess). As the oscillating-field frequency approaches resonance the particles absorb energy. As it recedes from resonance the borrowed energy is emitted, part being returned to the coil and the remainder being shared with neighboring particles.

In most substances the exchange of energy between the particles and the coil is surprisingly sluggish with respect to the speed of most atomic processes. Some particles respond immediately at resonance, but others require intervals ranging from a few seconds to several minutes. This complicates the design of magnetic-resonance spectrometers because their electrical circuits must be made extremely stable and their output must be observed with the aid of pen recorders.

It turns out, however, that the addition of ferric nitrate to water increases the susceptibility of the particles to the outside field and radically decreases the time required for energy exchange without affecting the rate at which the particles precess. According to the Aero Medical Laboratory group, no completely satisfactory explanation for the action of ferric nitrate has been advanced. It may be that ferric ions in solution decrease the magnetic interaction of the particles and thus render them more susceptible to the influence of external fields. Whatever the explanation, ferric nitrate dissolved in water makes it possible to demonstrate the phenomenon of magnetic resonance with relatively simple apparatus.

The experiment consists of placing a test tube containing the solution of ferric nitrate in the pulsating field of a magnetron magnet and, by means of an oscilloscope, observing the exchange of energy at resonance between the sample and a coil around the test tube which is energized by a vacuum-tube oscillator. The energy absorbed during a single flip of the particles is too small for detection by conventional electronic devices. Hence in this experiment the frequencies are brought in and out of resonance 60 times per second. The frequency of the vacuum-tube oscillator is held constant while the rate of precession is varied by modulating the biasing field of the magnetron magnet. This is accomplished by placing a second coil energized by 60-cycle alternating current between the poles of the magnetron magnet; the flux of this modulating coil alternately reinforces and opposes that of the magnet. The rate of precession varies in proportion.

The vacuum-tube oscillator is equipped with two controls, one for adjusting the frequency to the average rate at which the proton axes precess and the other for adjusting the amount of energy fed back from the plate circuit of the vacuum tube to the grid circuit. The latter control regulates the intensity at which the tube oscillates. With this control the oscillator can be put into or out of operation or, when desired, set at the marginal oscillating condition. The modulating coil is wound with a space in the center to admit the test tube, and placed so that its axis is concentric with the biasing field [see Fig. 146].

With the sample in position the oscillator is turned on and adjusted as closely as possible to 6.1 megacycles, the average frequency at which the protons precess. The feedback control is adjusted for the marginal condition at which oscillations are barely sustained. At this critical point current flowing in the plate circuit of the oscillator tube is highly responsive to changes of energy in the coil around the test tube. The amplitude of the plate current is observed by connecting the plate circuit to the vertical terminals

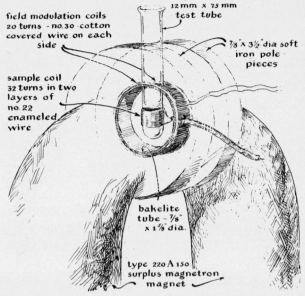

field modulation coils
20 turns - no.30 cotton
covered wire on each
side

12 mm x 75 mm
test tube

⅞" x 3½" dia soft
iron pole
pieces

sample coil
32 turns in two
layers of
no. 22
enameled
wire

bakelite
tube - ⅞"
x 1⅝" dia.

type 220A 150
surplus magnetron
magnet

146
Magnet and specimen assembly of the magentic-resonance spectrometer

of the oscilloscope as illustrated in the complete circuit diagram, Figure 147.

A spot of light will appear on the screen, indicating that a fixed value of plate current is flowing. The modulating coil of the biasing magnet is now energized. If the frequency of the oscillator has been adjusted to the average rate of precession, the spot of light will expand into a vertical line, indicating that the plate circuit is responding to energy exchanged between the coil and the particles. The display can be made more interesting by connecting the horizontal plates of the oscilloscope to the 60-cycle power supply which energizes the modulating coil. Typical magnetic-resonance patterns are shown in Figure 148.

In the apparatus designed at the Aero Medical Laboratory the magnetic biasing field is supplied by a Type 220A 150 surplus magnetron magnet. But any magnet of comparable size and magnetic

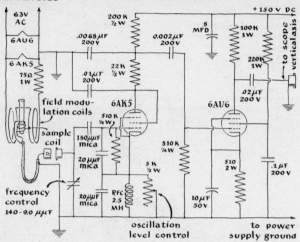

147
Circuit diagram for the magnetic-resonance spectrometer

strength (about 1,450 gauss) will work. The pole faces need only be large enough and spaced far enough apart to take the accessory parts. An electromagnet will work if it is energized by a well-regulated direct current. The pole faces of the magnet were replaced by soft iron disks 3½ inches in diameter and ⅞ inch thick to provide a field over a large area. For maximum response all protons must precess at the same rate, which means that all must be acted upon uniformly by the modulated biasing field. The intensity of the field will vary with the distance between the pole faces. Hence these must be made parallel and free from surface irregu-

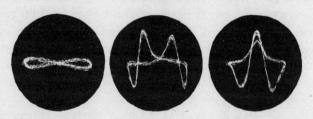

148
Nuclear magnetic-resonance patterns: Non-resonance *(left)*, Out-of-phase resonance peaks *(center)*, In-phase resonance *(right)*

larities. Surplus magnets from magnetrons of the radial-cathode type usually bear a small white dot on the base which gives an approximate figure in gauss for the field strength that may be expected in the air gap.

The magnet used in the instrument constructed at the Aero Medical Laboratory is rated at 1,450 gauss. It was modulated by a coil consisting of 20 turns of No. 30 cotton-covered magnet wire wound on a Bakelite tube 1⅜ inches in outside diameter and ⅞ inch long. Ten turns of the coil are wound at one end of the tube and 10 turns are wound in the same direction at the other end. A hole ⅝ inch in diameter is cut in the center of the coil form to admit the test tube. A second hole ⅜ inch in diameter is made at right angles to the first to admit a length of coaxial cable for linking the oscillator coil to the source of high-frequency current. The modulating coil is energized by the transformer which supplies the tube heaters, and it sweeps the strength of the biasing field 50 gauss above and below its mean value.

The test tube is 12 millimeters in diameter and 75 millimeters long. A two-layer coil of No. 22 enameled magnet wire, consisting of 16 turns per layer, is wound on the straight portion of the test tube as close as possible to the closed end. The test tube and coil assembly are mounted vertically in the Bakelite form on which the modulating coil is wound.

The circuit construction is conventional. The oscillator is designed around a 6AK5 pentode tube. When used with an oscilloscope of high sensitivity, output from the oscillator may be taken at the junction between the 22,000-ohm resistor and the 200,000-ohm resistor in the plate circuit. With 'scopes of lower sensitivity, such as the Heathkit Model O-10, a single-stage amplifier using a 6AU6 pentode is added as shown in the circuit diagram. A variable capacitor, such as the Hammarlund Type MC-140-M, is used for adjusting the frequency of the oscillator.

These components are assembled on an aluminum chassis three inches high, five inches wide and six inches long. Input and output connections are made through an RG 58/U coaxial cable equipped with UG 290/U and UG 88/U terminals.

The test solution is prepared by dissolving .4 gram of ferric nitrate in 100 cubic centimeters of distilled water. Two cubic centimeters of this solution are added to the test tube and placed in the biasing field. Power is applied. After the horizontal-sweep circuit of the oscilloscope has been made synchronous with the 60-cycle modulating voltage, a pattern should appear on the screen. The pattern may resemble a horizontal figure eight, as shown at left in Figure 148. This indicates that the frequency of the oscillator coil lies outside the limits within which the particles are precessing and that resonance is not established.

To search for resonance, set the oscillator capacitor for minimum frequency (the plates of the capacitor meshed fully) and adjust the intensity (feedback) control to the point where the oscillator is on the verge of going out of operation. Then increase the frequency slowly while observing the 'scope. It may be necessary to trim the feedback control occasionally to maintain the marginal oscillating condition.

The procedure can be simplified with the aid of a short-wave radio receiver. If the receiver is equipped for continuous-wave reception, the oscillator signal will be heard as a shrill whistle. If not, it will make a rushing sound, perhaps accompanied by a 60-cycle hum. The receiver is particularly useful in checking the point at which the oscillator goes out of operation when adjusting the feedback control. If the receiver is calibrated, it may be used to calibrate the oscillator. If not, the receiver can be calibrated easily by tuning in on the time signal of Station WWV.

When resonance is established, the display will resemble the center pattern in Figure 148. Usually two peaks appear which are joined at the bottom by loops. This indicates a displacement (phase difference) in the time at which signals arrive at the vertical and horizontal plates of the 'scope. The Heathkit Model O-10 'scope is equipped with a line-sweep switch and a phase control for manipulating the display. When these are properly adjusted, the peaks coincide as shown in the pattern at the right.

What does the display mean? The height of the pattern is proportional to the number of protons resonating with the oscillator; the width of the pattern, to the range through which the particles precess. Accordingly if all of the particles were precessing at precisely the same rate and all flipped over precisely at resonance with the oscillator, the pattern would resemble an inverted "T." The spectrometer could then be said to have perfect resolution. Evidently in this instrument all the particles do not precess at the same frequency.

Part of the explanation lies in the interaction of magnetic forces within the test sample. The fields of neighboring protons merge in such a way that some particles are partially shielded from the influence of the outside field. But in this instrument the breadth of the peaks is largely explained by cross-sectional variations in the strength of the biasing field. Particles in regions of high-field intensity precess at higher rates than those in regions where the field is relatively weak.

These differences are preserved when the field is modulated. Some particles are swept into resonance with the oscillator earlier or later than others, and the displayed peak is broadened accordingly. The width of the peak illustrated is about 20 gauss, which means a difference of some 85,000 revolutions per second in the rate of precession of the slowest and fastest particles.

With an instrument of high resolution many substances show fine multiple peaks. This is due to the complex magnetic interaction between systems of particles and the consequent shielding of the biasing field. Many substances are not sensitive to an external magnetic field because the magnetism of their spinning particles cancels out. But those substances that do respond can be identified by the characteristic pattern which shows up on the 'scope. The resolution of the apparatus described here is not high enough for fine spectroscopic work. As indicated earlier, it is intended to serve as a simple demonstration of the magnetic-resonance effect.

Modifications to adapt the apparatus for limited applications would include the provision of larger pole faces on the magnetron magnet to provide a more uniform biasing field. In contrast with the 20-gauss peak-width displayed by the apparatus, the best instruments made today resolve to a few ten-thousandths of a gauss; this means that irregularities in the biasing field must be kept below this figure. High resolution also requires precise and calibrated control of the intensity, frequency and amplitude of the biasing field. In this demonstration the high sweep-rate of 60 cycles per second is made possible by limiting the experiment to a test solution of ferric nitrate. Few substances are so responsive.

Incidentally, the magnetic-resonance spectrometer can also be used for measuring the strength of magnets. The magnet to be tested supplies the biasing field. It is modulated as described above, and the oscillator is adjusted to resonance. The strength of the unknown field in gauss is equal to the frequency of the oscillator when it is at resonance divided by 4,228.5.

4

A HOMEMADE ATOM SMASHER

For less than the average cost of a set of golf clubs, you can equip yourself for playing with electrons — the minute "spheres" surrounding the atom. With this apparatus you can transmute the elements, alter the properties of some common materials and, incidentally, learn much at first hand about the structure of matter. F. B. Lee, a chemical engineer and faculty member of the Erie County Technical Institute in Buffalo, N. Y., tells how to build and operate the machine. Some safety measures are suggested on page 359

THE PARTICLE ACCELERATOR, more popularly known as the "atom smasher," has about the same relationship to nuclear physics that the telescope has to astronomy. The accelerator probes the microcosm; the telescope, the macrocosm. Like the telescope, the accelerator can open exciting vistas to the amateur. But unlike the telescope, the accelerator has failed to attract a large amateur following. The notion seems to have got around that a small particle accelerator is little more than a toy. But in 1932 the British physicists J. D. Cockcroft and E. T. S. Walton did important pioneer work in nuclear physics with a 150,000-volt accelerator of the electrostatic type which today can be built for less than $100. With it Cockcroft and Walton succeeded in transmuting lithium into unstable beryllium, which then broke down into helium with the release of energy on the order of 17 million electron volts — scarcely the performance of a toy. A beam of particles from a machine of this size is capable of cutting the time of chemical reactions, of inducing mutations in living organisms, of altering the physical properties of organic compounds and of producing scores of other interesting effects.

The beam of the machine to be described is brought outside of the apparatus for irradiating targets of substantial area in the open air. The energy of the particles spans a relatively wide range. It is, therefore, of principal interest to the amateur chemist. The physicist usually requires a closely collimated beam in which all particles have about the same energy, whereas the chemist is satisfied with a more diffuse beam in which the energy of the particles varies considerably. Since the targets irradiated by the chemist are usually rather thick, it is almost impossible to provide all sections of the irradiated material with electrons of uniform energy even if this were desirable. Fortunately it is usually satisfactory to have a large percentage of the electrons penetrate the target completely.

The ions produced within the target by the beam are largely independent of the energy of the beam, but the permissible thickness of the target increases with the accelerating voltage. Electrons accelerated to an energy of 250,000 volts will penetrate metallic aluminum to a depth of about .25 millimeter; polyethylene, to a depth of some three millimeters; air, to a depth of some two meters. The depth of penetration is roughly inversely proportional to the density of the target material and to the square of its atomic weight.

With the machine I shall describe amateurs can perform endless experiments based on the ionization of target materials by electrons. In the case of hydrocarbon targets numerous hydrogen atoms are dislodged from their sites in the molecule by the stream of fast-moving charged particles. Some of the atoms promptly combine into molecules of hydrogen (H_2) and escape as gas. Pairs of carbon

345

atoms so stripped can then combine to cross-link the hydrocarbon molecules.

Such cross-linking has a profound effect on the physical properties of the irradiated substance. For example, when molecules of the plastic polyethylene are cross-linked by irradiation, the plastic becomes much harder and melts at a higher temperature. The field is new and full of opportunities for the amateur.

The electrostatic accelerator may be thought of as a highly developed two-element electronic tube. It consists of an evacuated tube fitted with a source of electrons or protons at one end, an accelerating electrode at the other end, and a high-potential electric field between the two. If the accelerating electrode is made positive and the source is either a filament, a radioactive or photoelectric surface, or even a sharp point of metal, the resulting beam will be composed of electrons. If the accelerating electrode is made negative and a tiny amount of hydrogen is admitted to the tube, the gas will ionize and the beam will consist of hydrogen nuclei (protons).

The major requirements for constructing a linear accelerator are a source of high potential and a vacuum system capable of reducing atmospheric pressure (760 millimeters of mercury in a mercury manometer) down to .00001 mm. of mercury. The high potential may be generated by a Van de Graaff machine such as those described in Section IX. A machine capable of delivering 20 millionths of an ampere (20 microamperes) at a potential of 500,000 volts can be built for less than $30.

The tube for my accelerator was constructed from a junked piece of Pyrex pipe two inches in diameter and about three feet long. A 24-inch length would have been preferable, but the dimensions are not critical. A hardwood plank eight inches wide, two inches thick and five feet long serves as a common base for the accelerator and vacuum pumps.

The accelerator tube is mounted vertically near one end of the base, as shown in the accompanying drawing [see Fig. 149]. The cathode fitting, which closes the lower end of the tube, was machined from a piece of brass 2½ inches in diameter and one inch thick. A hole is drilled in one wall to receive the half-inch copper pipe which connects the tube to the vacuum pumps. Another hole,

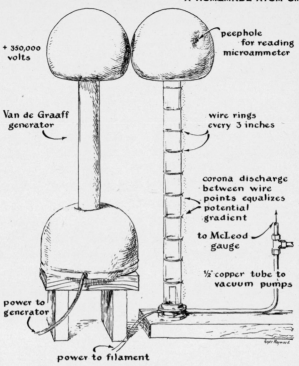

+ 350,000 volts

peephole for reading microammeter

Van de Graaff generator

wire rings every 3 inches

corona discharge between wire points equalizes potential gradient

to McLeod gauge

½" copper tube to vacuum pumps

power to generator

power to filament

Roger Hayward

149
An electrostatic particle accelerator with a Van de Graaff generator as its power supply

in which an eighth-inch pipe thread is cut, receives a standard quarter-inch compression fitting which serves as a gland for the filament assembly.

The filament assembly is comprised of a quarter-inch rubber rod about half an inch long, through which two No. 18 enameled copper lead wires are run to support a half-inch length of No. 30 Nichrome wire. The lead wires were coated with vacuum grease before they were forced through the holes in the rod. The rod was then greased lightly and slid into the compression fitting, after which a collar of rubber tubing was slid over it. Finally the compression nut was run home to seal the assembly. Details of the gland

347

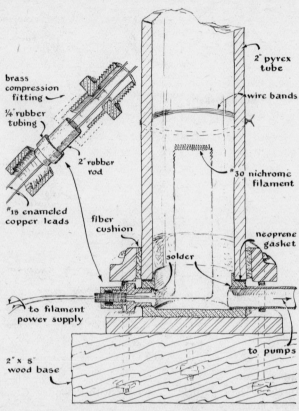

brass
compression
fitting

¼″ rubber
tubing

2″ rubber
rod

#18 enameled
copper leads

fiber
cushion

2″ pyrex
tube

wire bands

#30 nichrome
filament

neoprene
gasket

solder

to filament
power supply

to pumps

2″ x 8″
wood base

150
Filament assembly and base seal of electrostatic accelerator tube

are shown at upper left in Figure 150. The entire unit is vacuum-tight, easy to assemble and has given no trouble.

With the Van de Graaff machine suggested, the tube develops a beam of only 10 to 20 microamperes, and the filament operates at a proportionately low temperature. The optimum filament-temperature must be determined experimentally. The temperature is controlled by a rheostat in series with the power supply, which may be a simple doorbell transformer. When the temperature is too high, excessive emission lowers the resistance of the tube and consequently the voltage of the Van de Graaff machine. Lowered tube-voltage of course means lowered beam-energy.

In contrast, low filament-temperature results in scanty filament-emission, which lowers the beam current and increases the tube resistance. Thus at low filament-temperature the tube develops maximum voltage, and proportionately higher energy is imparted to individual particles in the beam. This compensates somewhat for the lower beam-current. For this reason downward departures from the optimum value of the filament temperature are preferable to upward departures.

The electron beam is restricted to the axis of the tube by a symmetrical electrostatic field established by a series of rings spaced at three-inch intervals along the tube. The rings consist of four turns of 26-gauge bare copper wire. The ends of the wire are twisted tightly enough to hold the coil in place on the glass and are spread about half an inch apart. The points so formed act as corona electrodes and pick up charge from the surrounding air until electrical equilibrium is established between the air and the rings. In larger tubes, fixed resistors are substituted for the corona points. This, however, is not necessary in machines operating at 500,000 volts or less.

The upper end of the accelerator is closed by a window of aluminum foil through which the beam passes into the air. To prevent the foil from rupturing under atmospheric pressure, it is supported by an aluminum grid made of quarter-inch aluminum plate. The plate is drilled with 37 holes 3/16 of an inch in diameter and arranged in a hexagonal pattern [see Fig. 151]. Approximately 50 per cent of the grid area is thus open. The grid is cemented to the upper end of the tube with vacuum wax. The foil window, which should not exceed .001 inch in thickness, is similarly cemented on top of the grid.

High-vacuum equipment is sealed with special waxes which have a low vapor-pressure, i.e., they evaporate so slowly that their vapors exert very little pressure. These include de Khotinsky wax, which has a vapor pressure of one micron of mercury; Dennison waxes, with a pressure of .01 micron; and Picein and Apiezon-W waxes, with a pressure of .00001 micron.

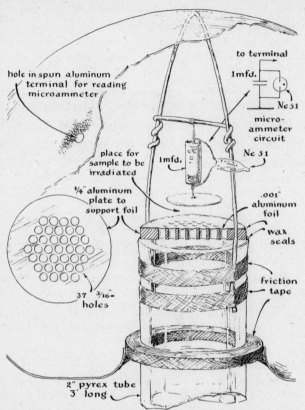

151
Details of anode window and microammeter for the accelerator

The experimental physicist John Strong recommends a wax made by melting together equal parts of beeswax and rosin. The vapor pressure of this mixture approaches that of Picein and Apiezon-W. It is applied smoking hot with a medicine dropper, and though it adheres well to cold surfaces, it is good practice to warm the glass or metal parts on which it is spread.

I used Picein, which chanced to be available. The parts were heated to the softening point of the wax, after which the joints were rubbed with the wax until a thin coating adhered. The pipe and grid were then pressed together until the wax set. Next the side face of the grid was coated, and the foil was pressed in place. The seal was completed by applying a thin bead of wax around the outside edges of both joints.

A loop of 12-gauge brass wire was then attached to the top of the tube by friction tape as a frame to support the 12-inch spherical terminal. A simple microammeter, which consists of a high-resistance capacitor of one microfarad bridged by a 1/25-watt neon tube, is also supported by the frame. The input terminal of the microammeter is a 1½-inch disk of 12-gauge sheet aluminum supported by one axial lead of the capacitor at a height of 3/4 inch above the aluminum window. The remaining lead of the capacitor is soldered to a cross wire attached to the brass loop [see Fig. 151].

The electron beam enters the disk and eventually charges the capacitor to the firing potential of the neon tube, which then flashes and discharges the capacitor. A current flow of one microampere causes the tube to flash at 15-second intervals, the flashing rate being proportional to the intensity of the beam current. A dimple roughly two inches wide and half an inch deep is made in the spherical terminal opposite the neon tube, and a quarter-inch peephole is drilled at the bottom of the depression.

The dimple prevents the concentration of a strong electrostatic field at the sharp edge of the hole and the loss of current through corona discharge. The neon tube can be observed safely at a distance of about two feet. The positive terminal of a 350,000-volt Van de Graaff generator is placed in contact with the accelerator terminal as the source of accelerating potential. Samples of material to be irradiated, such as hydrocarbon compounds or seeds, are placed on a carrier of thin polyethylene sheet between the aluminum-foil window and the disk electrode of the microammeter.

The accelerator tube must be evacuated to pressure on the order of .01 micron of mercury to prevent excessive collisions between the accelerated particles and molecules of gas. Molecules ionized by such collisions are accelerated toward the filament as positive ions, collide with other molecules and at high pressures create still more ions until the resulting avalanche of charged particles paralyzes the tube. At a pressure of .01 micron, gas molecules have a mean free path of 15 feet or more, and collisions are accordingly infrequent.

A vacuum of this quality requires elaborate pumping equipment and extreme care in eliminating leaks. The most inexpensive commercial equipment capable of attaining the desired pressure is priced at about $200; hence there is substantial inducement beyond the mere challenge of an interesting problem to use a home-built substitute — such as the compressor units from old refrigerators.

A rough vacuum of 20 millimeters or so is easily pumped either by a water aspirator or a refrigerator compressor (connected backward). Higher vacuums may be attained by connecting two refrigerator compressors of the rotary type in series to make a two-stage unit. Compressors of the piston type are not satisfactory unless they are modified, because the inlet valve which is actuated by gas pressure stops working when the system has been pumped down to a pressure of about 30 millimeters.

It is possible to make a 50 per cent improvement in the performance of piston compressors by bypassing the inlet valves. Rotary compressors, such as are used in the Frigidaire, have no valves and are easily adapted to multistage use. My system uses two second-hand units, one of the piston type and the other of the rotary, as "roughing" pumps. These were purchased from a local dealer in used iceboxes for $5 each, including the motors.

The intake valve of the piston unit was bypassed by drilling a hole in the side of the cylinder just above the low point of the piston's travel. A short length of copper tubing was brazed to this port as the new intake. The piston covers the port as it ascends, thus eliminating the need of gas pressure to actuate the inlet valve. The intake of this unit is connected by a hose to the discharge port of the rotary compressor. A system of pipes and valves permits the discharge from the rotary compressor to be connected either to the intake of the piston unit or to a two-gallon vacuum reservoir.

A similar system of pipe- and valve-connections permits the intake of the rotary compressor to be connected either to the outlet of a diffusion pump or to the reservoir. Connected in tandem and exhausted into the air, the pumps will reduce the pressure to about one millimeter. But by exhausting into the two-gallon reservoir (previously pumped to a pressure of one mm.) it is possible to obtain a final vacuum of about .1 mm.

Special oils of low vapor-pressure must be used for lubrication. The pumps are first drained of conventional oil, then filled with about half a pint of paraffin oil, operated for 10 minutes and drained. If the paraffin oil shows traces of the old oil, the pumps are again flushed with paraffin oil.

They are now filled with vacuum oil. Some volatile fractions may still remain. These can be removed by several hours of operation. Unlike conventional vacuum pumps, refrigerator compressors have large areas of contact between the oil and gas on the discharge side of the pump and are accordingly susceptible to volatile fluids.

My vacuum reservoir consists of a pair of one-gallon glass jugs connected with the pumps by half-inch copper pipe inserted through rubber stoppers coated with vacuum grease. The reservoir is first exhausted by the tandem pumps. The pinchcocks are operated to switch the reservoir to the output of the rotary compressor. If the system does not liberate too much gas, one pumping of the reservoir will last many hours.

The final pressure at which the tube works is achieved by means of a diffusion pump. A half-gallon reservoir is connected between the inlet of the rotary pump and the exhaust of the diffusion pump. Pressure in both reservoirs is indicated by a manometer connected as shown [see Fig. 152]. When the pressure of either reservoir rises above three millimeters, it is reconnected to the inlet of the rotary unit and pumped down to one mm.

My attempt to make a mercury diffusion pump from spare pipe-fittings did not succeed. I must confess, however, that I did not try very hard. The project should not be difficult for those with access to machining facilities. Diffusion pumps of various designs and capacities are available on the market from $30 up, but a local glass blower turned out one for me at $15. He is willing, for the time being, at least, to supply amateurs with duplicates at this price, plus packing and shipping charges. I will be glad to make the necessary arrangements with him on request. Small pumps require about three pounds of mercury, which costs about $12. A heating unit ranging from 100 to 300 watts must also be provided for vaporizing the mercury. My pump [see Fig. 153] was made to operate against a back pressure of about four millimeters. Judging by the literature,

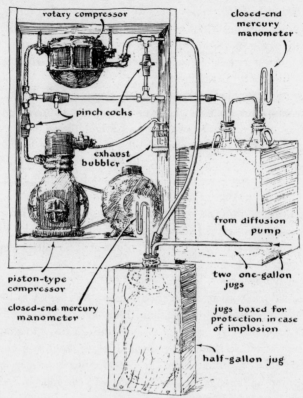

152
"Roughing" pump and reservoirs for vacuum system of the accelerator

many commercial pumps require a back pressure of .3 mm. or less. In general, the rate at which diffusion pumps remove gas from the system varies inversely with the back pressure against which they operate.

The ultimate pressure they produce depends on the vapor pressure of the pumping fluid, which includes various oils in addition to the mercury. Vapor pressure, in the case of mercury pumps, establishes a lower limit of one micron (.001 millimeter) unless the system is equipped with a trap to prevent the mercury vapor from entering the evacuated vessel. A cold trap made by refrigerating

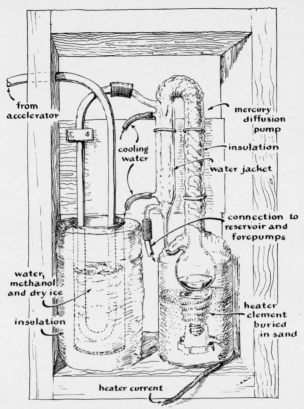

153
Mercury diffusion pump and cold trap for the vacuum system

part of the plumbing between the diffusion pump and the accelerator tube enables the pump to achieve a pressure of .01 micron if the temperature of the trap is maintained at minus 40 degrees centigrade.

My trap consists of a U-shaped section in the half-inch copper line. The section is inserted in a tin can insulated by a half-inch layer of cardboard covered by aluminum foil. The cooling mixture consists of equal parts of water and wood alcohol to which crushed dry ice is added as required. The trap is not chilled until the system has been pumped to one or two microns. This procedure prevents the formation of ice in the trap which will subsequently release water vapor as low pressures are attained, and thus increase the pump-down time substantially.

The mercury is vaporized by a unit from a radiant heater to which an extra winding was added to reduce its rating to 150 watts. The heater is mounted in a tin can and buried in sand up to the top of the ceramic cone. Heat radiated from the center of the cone is sufficient to energize the pump. A 150-watt incandescent lamp would doubtless work as well. In selecting a site for the apparatus keep in mind that most diffusion pumps require a supply of cooling water.

Once the vacuum system is complete, the easy part of the job is ended. One then locates and seals the leaks. This tedious procedure can consume days or weeks depending upon the experimenter's luck and the efficiency of his leak-detection gear.

At least three closed-end mercury manometers should be provided. These consist of quarter-inch glass tubes about 24 inches long. If soda-lime glass is used, one end can be sealed over a Bunsen burner. A short section six inches from the closed end is then heated to softness and bent 180 degrees so that it lies parallel to the long portion of the tube. The long portion is then heated at the point opposite the closed end and similarly bent 180 degrees. The result is a flat "S."

Enough mercury is introduced into the tubing to fill the closed leg of the "S" and about 20 per cent of the center leg. This can be accomplished by placing the tube in a reclining position and rocking it as the mercury is introduced into the open end. The closed leg must be completely filled without a trace of bubbles. One manometer is inserted in each of the reservoirs and another is temporarily connected to the accelerator tube.

The roughing pumps are now started. If the mercury has not separated from the closed end of the manometer at the end of 15 minutes, the tube may be tapped gently. If this does not cause separation, check the pumps for faulty operation. After the pressure has been reduced to about one millimeter, the individual elements of the system should be isolated by closing all pinchcocks.

The pumps are then stopped. The manometers may be provided with cardboard scales calibrated in arbitrary units. Manometer readings are recorded at the end of the pump-down and compared with a second set of readings made after an interval of 12 to 24 hours. Each section of the system will doubtless show a rise in pressure. Vacuum grease is then applied to all joints where a leak is suspected and the procedure is repeated. Ultimately the system will appear to be tight. A run can then be attempted with the diffusion pump in operation.

In my system a pressure of one micron is achieved at the end of about 30 minutes, and a usable vacuum in the accelerator tube is attained about eight hours later. The roughing pumps are used for about an hour or until the tube pressure drops to .5 millimeter, after which they are valved off and shut down. The half-gallon reservoir on the outlet of the diffusion pump has sufficient capacity to receive the exhaust for several days of continuous pumping.

Most experimenters will want at least one high-vacuum gauge of the McLeod type to check leaks too slow to show on the manometers. The McLeod gauge operates on the principle of trapping gas in a chamber of substantial volume and then compressing it by a column of mercury into a closed capillary tube. The pressure of the compressed gas is then compared with that in the vacuum system by observing the difference in height to which a column of mercury rises in a matching capillary connected to the system. One of my gauges is shown in Figure 154.

It was made of discarded laboratory pipettes that had broken tips but were otherwise usable. Readings made with it are accurate down to about 10 microns, but gas released from the rubber connections prevents measurements at lower pressures. A second gauge made by my local glass blower detects .1-micron pressures. The instruments require about three pounds of mercury. Dibutylphthalate ($1 per pound) has been substituted for mercury as an economy measure; I have also tried salad oil and olive oil. These are usable if they are boiled for a few minutes at one millimeter of pressure, but they absorb volatile materials easily and in time become erratic.

Several hazards should be noted. First, a large evacuated glass

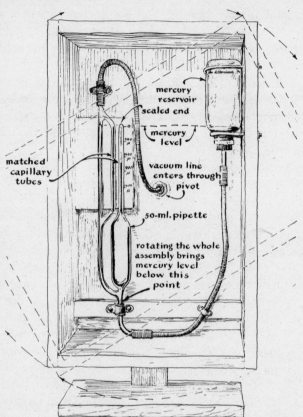

mercury
reservoir
sealed end

mercury
level

matched
capillary
tubes

vacuum line
enters through
pivot

50-ml. pipette

rotating the whole
assembly brings
mercury level
below this
point

0
100 μ
400 μ
900 μ
1600 μ

154
McLeod gauge for measuring low pressure in the vacuum system

vessel can, if it breaks, scatter glass at high velocity over a large
area. It is essential that the glass reservoirs be enclosed in wooden
or metal containers.

Second, keep in mind that the accelerator is a close relative of
the X-ray tube. The penetrating power of X-rays is determined in
part by the atomic weight of the target bombarded by electrons.
X-radiation emitted by light elements such as aluminum is readily
absorbed by glass, thin metal or even air. But heavy metals, such as
copper, generate penetrating and dangerous radiation. It is im-

portant, therefore, to expose only materials of low atomic weight to the beam.

Third, the inexperienced worker should observe care in handling mercury, particularly when it is confined in glass tubes. If air is admitted abruptly to a manometer of the closed-end type, it is astonishing what damage the "water hammer" (in this case mercury hammer) can do. Enclose the manometers in transparent plastic bags. Just having a few pounds of mercury around constitutes a substantial hazard because the vapor pressure of mercury is high enough to worry about even at temperatures as low as 80 degrees Fahrenheit.

Fourth, although the voltage of the Van de Graaff generator is not necessarily hazardous in itself, an unexpected shock can throw one off balance and thus lead to an accident.

I will be glad to provide assistance in locating supplies. Letters addressed to F. B. Lee, 230 Hampton, Kenmore 17, N. Y., will be answered as promptly as possible.

Some hazards and precautions

JAMES H. BLY of the High Voltage Engineering Corporation in Burlington, Mass., recommends a change in the design of the particle accelerator.

"In general, I think it is fair to say that we like F. B. Lee's design approach to this machine very much. However, we are somewhat concerned over the hazards involved. We agree wholeheartedly with his comments concerning the hazards of glass breakage and the use of mercury. We feel strongly, however, that there is inadequate discussion of the potential hazards due to X-rays and electrons. Even though the experimenter restricts himself to targets of low atomic number, there will inevitably be some generation of high-energy X-rays when using electrons of 200 to 300 kilovolt energy. If currents as high as 20 microamperes are achieved, we are sure that the resultant hazard is far from negligible. In addition, there will be substantial quantities of scattered electrons, some of which will inevitably pass through the observation peephole. Although it is conceivable that it would be safe to look through this peephole from a distance of two feet, we are very doubtful that this is in fact the case. We believe the machine would have been improved considerably if these hazards had been more thoroughly explored."

The apparatus described has been tested exhaustively for radiation hazard. Lee might well have pointed out, however, that one invites trouble by remaining near particle accelerators when they are in operation, or even by staying in the same room with them during prolonged periods of operation. Lee does not share Bly's concern about the hazard of scattered electrons from the peephole. As a precaution, however, the peephole may be covered on the inside by a small piece of window glass which will plug the hole completely for electrons. As an alternative the neon tube can be cemented in the peephole and connected with its circuit through a pair of contacts (an arrangment that would permit the high-voltage terminal to be removed when desired). The lamp could then be observed at a distance with the machine in operation.

5

THE MILLIKAN OIL-DROP EXPERIMENT

Suspend a drop of oil in mid-air by means of electrostatic attraction, and you can accurately measure the charge on a single electron. In effect, the oil drop becomes a balance capable of responding to a force on the order of a trillionth of an ounce

WHILE WORKING with a Wilson cloud chamber in the spring of 1909 Robert A. Millikan, then professor of physics at the University of Chicago, learned how to make a drop of water hang in mid-air like Mahomet's fabled coffin. The drop was poised so delicately between gravity and a counteracting electric field that it would respond easily to a force on the order of a trillionth of an ounce — a force some 10,000 times smaller than the smallest that could be detected with the best mechanical balance of the day. With his technique Millikan proved the existence of the electron, measured its charge and thereby helped touch off the revolution in physics that has continued up to the present.

At the turn of the century many physicists held to the notion that electricity behaves like a fluid, that the amount of charge on an electrode can be altered by any desired amount. But some argued otherwise. For example, the emission of electrically charged particles by zinc exposed to light (the "photoelectric effect"), and the production of ions in a gas-discharge tube, supported the notion that electricity comes in tiny particles. The British physicists C. T. R. Wilson and H. A. Wilson had independently attacked the question by observing the response of a cloud of water droplets to X-rays and an electric field. Millikan decided to sharpen the experiment by concentrating on the behavior of individual drops instead of the whole cloud.

To form the drops he set up a modified version of C. T. R. Wilson's cloud chamber: a glass cylinder equipped with a piston. When the piston was pulled down quickly, expansion lowered the temperature of humid air inside the cylinder and caused a cloud of water droplets to form. Millikan fixed electrodes inside the chamber at the top and bottom and connected them to a 4,000-volt storage battery. He lighted the droplets from the side with an arc lamp and observed them through a small telescope.

When the chamber was expanded and the field applied, most of the droplets drifted to the bottom under the influence of gravity. Some of the droplets, however, picked up electric charge during the expansion; most of these promptly darted toward one electrode or the other, depending upon the sign of their charge. A scattered few of the droplets hung in space for a second or two, their tendency to fall being precisely balanced by the upward tug of the electric field. Then evaporation would reduce their weight enough to upset the balance and start them moving toward the upper electrode. It was these droplets that caught Millikan's interest. He soon learned how to compensate for the evaporation by gradually lowering the voltage across the electrodes.

Occasionally he found it possible to make a drop stand still for as long as a minute. Now and again he observed that one of these stationary drops would take off abruptly toward one or the other of the electrodes. Moreover, a drop that had started to move in this manner would occasionally pick up speed during its flight, or stop in its tracks. Millikan therefore suspected that the drops must be picking up or losing elementary charges, perhaps the "atoms of electricity" for which the British physicist G. J. Stoney had suggested the name "electron" in 1891.

"This experiment," Millikan later wrote in his book *The Electron,* "opened up the possibility of measuring with certainty, not merely the charges on individual droplets as I had been doing, but the charge carried by a single atmospheric ion. By taking two speed measurements on the same drop, one before and one after it had caught an ion, I could obviously eliminate entirely the properties of the drop and of the medium and deal with a quantity that was proportional merely to the charge on the captured ion itself."

In the fall of 1909 Millikan undertook a new series of experiments with a modified apparatus. The cloud chamber was replaced by a simple container fitted with windows and a pair of flat metal plates spaced about 5/8 inch apart. Light oil was sprayed into the top of the chamber by an ordinary atomizer. Some of the droplets found their way into the space between the plates through a pinhole in the middle of the upper plate.

These droplets were lighted and observed by the same technique used with the water drops. The oil drops reacted like the water drops to an electric field established between the plates, but did not evaporate perceptibly during the period of observation. By manipulating the field to compensate for charges picked up from the air, it was possible to keep a selected drop under observation indefinitely.

Within a matter of months the new apparatus enabled Millikan not only to prove the existence of the electron but also to measure its charge with fair accuracy and, incidentally, to measure the number of atoms in a gram of hydrogen. Before the series of experiments had ended he had independently established the approximate mass and size of the electron, confirmed Albert Einstein's explanation of the photoelectric effect and derived the value of Planck's constant experimentally! Few experiments have been more productive — or more fascinating to those who have repeated it.

The construction of an oil-drop apparatus: George O. Smith, an electronics engineer of Rumson, N. J., describes a simplified version of Millikan's apparatus which you can easily make at home

IT MAY COME as a pleasant surprise to a generation accustomed to thinking of atomic research in terms of cyclotrons and other complex apparatus that Millikan's equipment is easy to reproduce yet precise enough to challenge the most advanced instrument-maker.

The experiment is based on the principle of balancing against the force of gravity the electric force acting on a small drop of oil. The electric force is determined by the interaction of the charge on the drop with the charge on the electrodes of the apparatus. The charge on the electrodes can be measured directly with a voltmeter. But the charge on the drop must be determined indirectly by the speed with which the drop moves through the air.

The speed varies with the intensity of the charge and the size of the drop, so the size of the drop must be found. This can be done by observing the maximum speed, or "terminal velocity," of a drop in free fall through the air. The terminal velocity of a drop is reached when the force set up by friction between the drop and the air equals the force of gravity. The two forces act in opposite directions and cancel, with the result that the speed of the drop remains constant.

Since the force of gravity is known, and the terminal velocity can be determined by timing the drop in free fall through a known distance, the size of the drop can be calculated by means of a

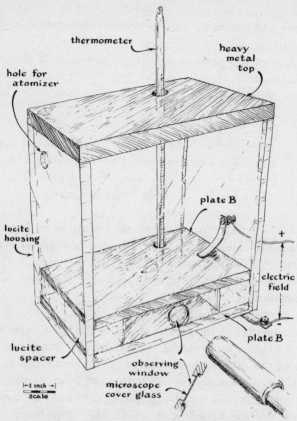

thermometer

heavy
metal
top

hole for
atomizer

plate B

+

lucite
housing

electric
field

−

plate B

lucite
spacer

observing
window

microscope
cover glass

|← 1 inch →|
scale

155

Vapor chamber used in Millikan oil drop experiment showing thermometer well and the electrode assembly. Telescope *(lower right)*

simple formula that takes certain properties of the air into account. The charge on the drop can then be calculated by inserting the known values in another simple formula and doing the arithmetic.

The accuracy of the method depends on the care taken in the construction of the apparatus. The electrodes are enclosed in a housing that can be rectangular [*see Fig. 155*], or cylindrical. The sides of the housing can be made of glass, Lucite or any similar transparent material. Lucite is easier to work than glass, but has no functional advantage.

The dimensions of the enclosure are not critical. The model depicted in the illustration measures some seven centimeters wide, 10 centimeters long and 15 centimeters high. The space between the electrodes should not be more than about an eighth of the height. The electrodes should make a loose fit with the inner walls of the housing so that they can be removed easily for cleaning. The fit should not be so loose, however, that air can circulate freely between the compartments of the housing.

The upper electrode is supported by a pair of lucite blocks. These may be cut from a slab of lucite about a centimeter thick. In addition to acting as spacers between the electrodes, the blocks serve as windows through which the drops can be lighted from the side. The ends of the blocks should make an easy fit with the walls of the box. Their width is not important. Their outer and inner sides must be polished sufficiently to permit good light transmission.

The rough faces can be first smoothed against successively finer grades of garnet paper supported on a flat surface, then polished against crocus cloth until all scratches disappear, and finally finished against wrapping paper charged with rouge of the sort used to polish glass. The optical quality of the polished surfaces need not be better than that of window glass.

Plates for the electrodes can be cut from any kind of metal. Brass is preferred. The facing surfaces of these plates must be flat to better than a hundredth of a millimeter. The upper plate must be thick enough to prevent sagging. The facing surfaces can be smoothed against crocus cloth supported on a flat surface, and finished against wrapping paper charged with rouge.

The corners and edges may be rounded slightly by grinding them against the finest grade of garnet paper. A pinhole approximately a millimeter in diameter is drilled in the center of the top plate and the burs removed. The use of heavy stock will be appreciated when the apparatus goes into operation, because the weight of the upper plate holds the electrode assembly together. (The experimenter will spend a good part of his time cleaning oil from the apparatus. He is therefore advised to resist the temptation of drilling, tapping, screwing and othewise fastening the apparatus together in a solid but time-wasting structure.)

The heavier the plate is made, the less it is likely to be displaced during an experimental run. Electrical contact with both plates is made through flat springs as shown. The box is closed at the bottom by the lower electrode and at the top by a third metal plate.

An observation port is drilled in front of the box at the level of the electrode space and fitted with a microscope cover-glass. The glass is held in position by a retaining ring of piano wire. A hole for the atomizer is drilled near the top of the box; holes are also drilled through the metal cover and the upper electrode for a thermometer. The bulb of the thermometer should be located as far as possible from the pinhole in the center of the upper electrode. The scale of the thermometer should also be kept away from the oil spray to avoid fogging.

After the assembly is completed, the space between the electrodes must be measured. Any distance on the order of a centimeter that chances to come out in the construction is satisfactory. But this distance, whatever it may be, must be determined to the extreme limit of the experimenter's ability, because the charge on the electron cannot be determined to greater accuracy than that with which the distance is known.

The magnifying telescope may be improvised from a microscope, from the small telescope of a war-surplus bombsight, from a telescope gunsight, from half a binocular or from any similar instrument that provides a tube and an eyepiece. The objective lens should have a focal length on the order of 50 millimeters, depending upon the distance between the observation port and the axis of the pinhole in the upper electrode. The lens from a 35-millimeter camera will do. As an alternative, the focal length of the telescope objective may be shortened by adding an auxiliary lens.

The diameter of the objective lens is unimportant. Any combination of objective and eyepiece that can resolve light reflected by a sphere .006 millimeter in diameter is adequate. The eyepiece must be equipped with a reticle capable of spanning a vertical distance of at least a millimeter on the axis of the pinhole midway between the electrodes.

Once the telescope has been adjusted so that drops falling through the pinhole are in sharp focus, it should be clamped in position. The optical system must then be calibrated. A target ruled with accurately spaced hairlines is placed vertically on the axis of the pinhole, and the image of the lines is noted with respect to those on the reticle. The calibration must be made with the greatest possible care. Microscope slides ruled with hairlines spaced in fractions of a millimeter are available from optical-supply houses. A similar target may be made by ruling hairlines on a metal plate by means of a height gauge of the type used by toolmakers.

Power for charging the electrodes may be derived from a conventional vacuum-tube rectifier [*see circuit diagram, Fig. 156*].

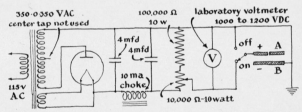

156
Circuit diagram of the power supply for the Millikan apparatus

Electrolytic capacitors are not manufactured for voltages in this range, and oil capacitors rated at 1,000 volts are costly. The ripple current and load are low, however, so if one is willing to risk an occasional blowout, oil capacitors of 400-volt rating may be used. (I have had a bank of 600-volt oil capacitors across 2,000 volts for longer than I care to remember. On the average, I lose one about every two years.)

The field voltage should be held as constant as possible during an experimental run. This is best accomplished by inserting a variable transformer such as a Variac in the power line. A 10,000-ohm variable resistor in series with the 100,000-ohm bleeder resistor is next best. The field voltage should be monitored constantly with a good laboratory voltmeter during a run.

Do not turn off the power supply to observe drops in free fall; use the switch shown in the diagram. This switch not only cuts off the voltage but simultaneously grounds and short-circuits the electrodes, thus killing the field completely.

A 35-millimeter slide projector makes an adequate light source when arranged as shown in Figure 157. Contrast will be improved by covering the rear wall of the enclosure at the level of the space between the electrodes with a swatch of black velvet. The drops should appear as brilliant points of light against a jet-black field.

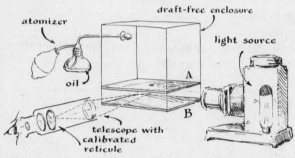

157
Semi-schematic drawing of apparatus for measuring the minute charge on a single electron

One note of caution: Never forget that you are working with lethal voltage. Resist the temptation to grope for the field switch or other controls while squinting through the telescope. Finally, provide writing materials, a stop watch and a good barometer.

To make a run, fill the atomizer with a light, nonvolatile oil. Do not use watch oil, which reacts chemically with lucite. Check to assure that the field voltage is off, then spray the smallest possible amount of oil into the upper chamber. (Excess oil accomplishes nothing beyond increasing the frequency of cleanups.) Then relax for 10 minutes or so. Interesting drops in free fall cover about three millimeters per minute, so they require an appreciable interval to find their way through the pinhole into observation space. In the meantime a table may be ruled, headed like the one made by Millikan [*see table, Fig. 158*]. Now light the region beneath the pinhole with the slide projector. When the telescope shows drops in the field, switch on the field voltage momentarily to eliminate drops carrying heavy charges.

Now enter the barometric pressure and the temperature of the chamber on the table just prepared. Apply the field again and search for a drop that rises slowly. (This assumes that the telescope is equipped with an erector system. If it is not, the motion will appear reversed.) Permit the drop to rise about a millimeter above a selected graduation on the reticle. Then switch off the field and time the drop in free fall. Permit the drop to move a millimeter beyond the terminal graduation. Record the reading on the table under "free fall." Then switch the field on and time the return transit.

If the field is heavily populated by drops, it may be difficult to keep track of a selected drop while looking away to record the transit time. This difficulty can be overcome either by learning to make entries on the table while keeping one eye on the drop, or by enlisting a helper to do the recording while you call out the observations.

Occasionally a drop will collide with an ion and change speed. Record the transit and go right on tabulating. You can throw out the questionable entry later. Try to record 50 or more transits before shifting to another drop.

For the experiment to have meaning the drop must collide with at least one ion while under observation; the more ions it collides with, the better. Such collisions may become infrequent as the run continues, because ions created by the injection of oil tend to recombine and therefore to decrease in number. The experiment will proceed much more rapidly if the supply of ions can be replenished by irradiating the space between the electrodes with X-rays. An X-ray machine of the type described in Section IX is inexpensive and easy to make.

The extreme hazard of working with X-rays must not be overlooked. The X-ray tube must be shielded by a container of lead at least three millimeters thick. A hole equal in diameter to the space between the electrodes of the oil-drop chamber is drilled in the

DISTANCE BETWEEN ELECTRODES	.7135 CENTIMETER
DISTANCE OF RISE AND FALL	.145 CENTIMETER
POTENTIAL OF ELECTRIC FIELD	735 VOLTS
BAROMETRIC PRESSURE	74.26 CENTIMETERS OF MERCURY
TEMPERATURE	21.5 DEGREES CENTIGRADE
DENSITY OF OIL	.893 GRAMS PER CUBIC CENTIMETER
VISCOSITY OF AIR	.0001817

TIME OF FREE FALL (SECONDS)	TIME OF RISE WITH FIELD (SECONDS)	AVERAGE TIME OF RISE (SECONDS)	CALCULATED CHARGE ON DROP (ELECTROSTATIC UNITS)	NUMBER OF CHARGES ON DROP	MAGNITUDE OF INDIVIDUAL CHARGE $(10^{10} \times e)$
34.4	28.6				
33.9	28.5				
34.5	28.6				
34.3	28.7				
34.0	29.0				
34.4	29.1				
34.2	29.1				
34.3	28.4				
33.9	28.9				
33.8	29.0				
34.2	29.1	28.77	4.79×10^{-10}	1	4.79
	28.6				
	28.7				
	28.3				
	28.6				
	28.7				
	29.1				
	28.9				
	29.0				
	28.6				
	28.8				
	10.1				
	10.2				
	10.5				
	10.3				
	10.2				
	10.2	10.31	9.45×10^{-10}	2	4.725
	10.6				
	10.2				
	10.5				
	10.4				
	10.2				
	6.1				
	6.0				
	6.2				
	6.1	6.11	14.43×10^{-10}	3	4.81
	6.2				
	6.1				
	6.1				
	4.5				
	4.6				
	4.4				
	4.4				
	4.3	4.47	18.93×10^{-10}	4	4.73
	4.5				
	4.5				
	4.6				
	4.4				

158
A typical table of observations from Millikan's oil drop experiment

tube end of the X-ray shield. The fan-shaped pattern of radiation from the hole is directed into the observation chamber through the lucite spacer opposite the light source. Stand well behind the X-ray unit when it is in operation. An exposure of a second or two will provide a good supply of ions.

After the times of free fall and rise have been tabulated, the constant values are recorded. These are the distance in centimeters between the electrodes, the distance of rise and fall, the field potential, the oil density (the reciprocal of the weight, in grams, of one cubic centimeter of oil), the temperature, the barometric pressure and the viscosity of air.

The rest is plain arithmetic. First run off the average time of free fall for all the drops observed. Note that Millikan's table lists only 11 observations of free fall. This compares favorably with the number of rise times observed for each state of charge on the drop. The figures are therefore about equally good. The rise times for each state of charge are then averaged and entered on the table. The distance of rise and fall is now divided by the average times to give the speed of the drops in centimeters per second. (On Millikan's table the average time of free fall through .145 centimeter is 34.17 seconds. This converts to a velocity of .00424 centimeter per second.) The computed value is entered as the terminal velocity (V) in the formula for the radius of the drop (r) given in the table on page 372 [*Fig. 159*]. The remaining values required by the formula are taken from the table and from a reference text such as *Handbook of Chemistry and Physics*.

The radius of the drop is then computed and entered in the formula for electric charge (q), also given in the table. After inserting the other constant values required by the formula, the charge is computed for each of the rise times and entered on the table under "Calculated Charge on Drop (Electrostatic Units)."

Determine the difference between each of the tabulated charges by subtracting the lower value from the next higher for all computed tabulations. A certain minimum difference will be found. The total charge on each drop will be some integral multiple of this minimum, which should approximate 4.8×10^{-10}. Dividing the calculated charge on the drop by this minimum gives the num-

$$r = \frac{-\dfrac{b}{P} \pm \sqrt{\dfrac{b}{P^2} + 4\,\dfrac{9V\eta}{2g(\rho-\rho_m)}}}{2}$$

where:
r = radius of drop in cm
V = terminal velocity of drop
in cm/sec
g = acceleration of gravity
in cm/sec²
ρ = density of oil in gm/cm³
ρ_m = density of atmosphere
in gm/cm³
η = viscosity of atmosphere
b = .000 617
P = barometric pressure in
cm of mercury

$$q = \frac{4\pi r^3 g(\rho-\rho_m)}{3E} \cdot \frac{V+V_1}{V}$$

where:
q = electronic charge in
electrostatic units
V = terminal velocity (downward)
of drop in cm/sec
V_1 = terminal velocity (upward)
of drop in cm/sec
r = radius of drop as computed
E = electric field in volts/cm

(all other units as previously
defined)

159
Formulas for calculating radius and
charge of oil droplet from its observed velocity

ber of charges on the drop. (The quotient must be rounded off to
the nearest whole number.) The calculated charge of the drop is
then divided by the number of charges. This quotient is entered
in the final column ("Magnitude of Individual Charge") and compared with the most recent determination for the charge on the
electron: $4.8029 \pm .0001 \times 10^{-10}$ electrostatic units.

The significance of the oil-drop experiment

SOME APPRECIATION of the far-reaching consequences
of the experiment suggested by Mr. Smith can be gained by considering its influence upon the theory of the photoelectric effect.
All substances emit electrons under the influence of light. By
placing a negative electrode close to the substance and connecting a battery between the two, a voltage can be found that is
just sufficient to stop outward-bound electrons. It turns out that

the stopping voltage depends solely on the color of the light and not at all on its intensity.

Einstein explained this in 1905 by supposing that all the ejected particles carry an identical charge, which when multiplied by the stopping voltage just equals the product of a certain quantity h (which Max Planck had derived to explain the radiation of energy from a "black body") and the frequency of the light minus the amount of energy required by the particle to break free of the substance. This theory made no sense to most physicists of the day, because it required the light to be radiated in chunks of a size determined by the constant h, which Planck apparently had pulled out of thin air.

"At the time it was made," wrote Millikan, "this prediction [by Einstein] was as bold as the hypothesis which suggested it, for at that time there were available no experiments whatever for determining anything about how the potential necessary to stop the discharge of the negative electrons varied with the frequency of the light or whether the quantity h to which Planck had already assigned a numerical value appeared at all in connection with photoelectric discharge. We are confronted, however, by the astonishing situation that after ten years of work at the Ryerson Laboratory this equation of Einstein's seems to us to predict accurately all of the facts which have been observed!"

VII.

MATHEMATICAL MACHINES

1

A PUZZLE-SOLVING MACHINE

It attacks the classic problem of the farmer, the fox, the goose, and the corn — and signals when it gets into trouble

IF YOU ARE IN THE HABIT of rummaging in war-surplus stores that stock electrical parts you may have wondered why the piles of used relays have largely disappeared. Who has bought these bits of junk and for what purpose? A little checking will disclose that most of these components have been picked up by science enthusiasts who go in for the new hobby of building "thinking" machines — elementary computers, as well as some not so elementary.

My introduction to the hobby came during lunch hour some months ago when I spotted a fellow leaving a surplus store with an armload of relays and asked what he intended doing with them. "Why," he explained, "I'm going to use them in my thinking machine." He thereupon went into details so intriguing that I wound up that evening by having dinner with Paul Bezold, a businessman who has long made a hobby of inventing puzzles and now has even more fun expressing them in terms of electrical circuits.

"A lot of people will tell you that machines can't think," Bezold said, "and perhaps they are correct. But it seems to me it is largely a matter of what you mean by the word 'thinking.' Some of the purists say that if a machine can do it, you can't call it thinking. Whether it is thinking or not, I have made several machines which do a number of things that human beings do with their brains, and so have many other amateurs."

Bezold points out that you do not have to be an electrical wizard to build these machines, nor do you need any mathematics beyond arithmetic. It helps a lot if you enjoy puzzles, and a knowledge of circuit symbols is handy. You can memorize the symbols in a few minutes. Perhaps the most novel idea the beginner will encounter is the use of switches, relays, lamps and other circuit elements to express words and logical relationships.

The two positions of a simple switch, for example, can mean more than "on" and "off." They can also symbolize yes or no, true or false, or the digits 1 or 0. A relay is not much more than a glorified switch, operated electrically. One part consists of a bar of soft iron surrounded by a coil of insulated wire [*see Fig. 160*]. When current flows through the coil, the bar becomes a magnet which attracts a similar bar called the armature. The motion of the armature is transmitted through insulators to one or more flat springs that carry contact points. These serve as switches. Current flows through the relay's coil; the contact springs are flexed by the armature, and so the switch is operated. When the current stops, everything snaps back to normal.

Offhand it may seem that putting a relay in a circuit is the hard way to go about flipping a switch. But in thinking machines

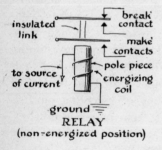

RELAY
(non-energized position)

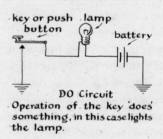

DO Circuit
Operation of the key does something, in this case lights the lamp.

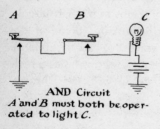

AND Circuit
A and *B* must both be operated to light *C*.

160
Basic circuit elements used in digital computers and logic machines

most of the switches must flip automatically, usually by current flowing through other switches also operating automatically. Thus one or more input pulses can proceed through complex networks of relays as a spreading chain reaction, modified or conditioned en route according to the requirements of the designer. This, incidentally, is the way the human brain works, with the neurons acting much like relays. In thinking machines the end of the reaction is always the same: an output circuit closes or opens, thus lighting a lamp or putting it out, starting or stopping a motor, or causing some other registering device to work. Essentially the reaction consists in the manipulation of logical relationships.

Thus far Bezold has used only five basic circuits in variations and combinations. With these five, he says, an amateur can build automatic devices to solve almost any puzzle than can be stated precisely in words. In addition to a simple "yes-no" circuit, the designer will need one expressing an "and" relationship. Such a circuit consists of two switches connected in series so that current must flow through first one, then the other to effect closure. The circuit is completed when both switch A *and* switch B are operated [*see Fig. 160*]. Equally useful is the "or" circuit. This has two switches connected in parallel so that operation of either one permits current to flow. Closing switch A *or* switch B makes the connection [*see top diagram, Fig. 161*].

The fourth basic circuit expresses the logical relationship of "if, then" [*second diagram, Fig. 161*]. It requires a two-way or transfer switch in which the switch blade operates between two contacts, connecting with one in the "on" position and with the other in the "off" position. The first of these is called the "make" contact and closes when the switch is operated. The second is called the "break" or "back" contact, and it passes current until the switch operates, whereupon it opens or breaks the circuit. Relays can be equipped with several sets of contact springs of both kinds. By connecting the make and break contacts of one relay to the switch arms of following relays, the designer can build up a branching pyramid of transfer circuits. With only five relays, for example, such a "transfer tree" can switch the input circuit to

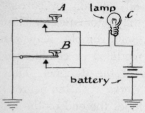

EITHER-OR Circuit
'Either'*A* 'or'*B* will light *C*.

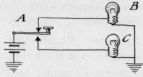

IF, THEN Circuit
'If'*A* is depressed 'then' *C*
lights, 'if' not 'then' *B* lights.

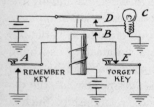

REMEMBER-FORGET Circuit
A closes relay, *B* locks it
and *D* lights *C*.
E restores circuit to normal.

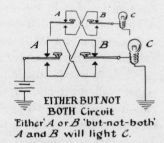

EITHER BUT NOT
BOTH Circuit
'Either' *A* or *B* 'but-not-both'
A and *B* will light *C*.

161
Additional circuit elements for digital computers and logic machines

any one of 32 output circuits. Every relay added to these five will double the number of output choices available.

If the machine is to do any sort of advanced thinking, it must have a memory. This is easily contrived by wiring a make contact so that it will connect the coil of its relay to a source of current whenever the relay is operated. When operated by an incoming pulse, the relay will then remain "locked down" by its own internal circuit. To make the relay forget, it is only necessary to insert a break contact in series with the locking circuit. Usually the break contact is actuated by a part of the machine which calls on the memory for information. After the stored information has been delivered, the break contact operates. The relay returns to normal and thus "forgets" in preparation for the next incoming signal [*third diagram, Fig. 161*].

Bezold has put a selection of these basic circuits to work in a machine which can solve the old puzzle of the farmer faced with the problem of moving a fox, a goose and a bag of corn across a river in a boat large enough to hold only the farmer and one of the three objects. The fox cannot be left alone with the goose or the goose with corn, for obvious reasons.

The problem is to design a combination of circuits which expresses the logical relationships posed by the farmer's dilemma and which will raise an alarm when the person working the puzzle makes an error. Each of the four principals — farmer, fox, goose, corn — is represented by a pair of switch keys, one on each side of the river [*see diagram, Fig. 162*]. When you press the key next

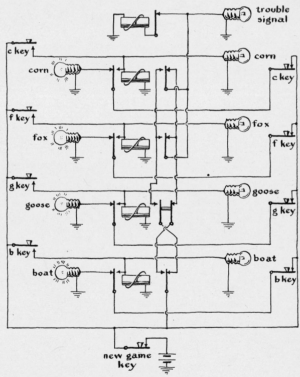

162
Logic circuit of farmer-fox-goose-corn puzzle

to one of the principals, a signal lamp lights, showing that the member has moved across the river. A relay is assigned to each of the four.

An analysis of the logical propositions discloses what form the switching circuit shall take. First, it is seen that a safe situation exists whenever the farmer is where the goose is. Things are equally safe when the goose is alone. But trouble threatens whenever the goose is with the fox, with the corn or with both. Obviously the goose needs the most watching. The farmer and goose play opposite roles, the presence of one making for safety, the other for trouble. They act like a pair of switches or relays, one of which is the negative of the other, *i.e.*, one is a make contact and the other a break.

The fox and the corn also spell trouble. Relays representing them should, therefore, be of the same type as that for the goose.

Suppose, now, that a relay with a make contact is assigned to the farmer. In terms of logic it stands for "not farmer." Its contacts close whenever the farmer crosses the river in the boat, so that the farmer symbol may be contained in the boat. Hence break contacts are assigned to the other three characters.

How shall the four relays be interconnected? The situation is always safe when the farmer is present; it is unsafe when he is absent *and* the goose is present *and* the fox *or* the corn is present. Hence the farmer's relay should be connected in series ("and" circuit) with that of the goose. To indicate the opposite roles of the farmer and goose, the interconnection between them is crossed. The goose's relay in turn is connected in series with one side of a parallel connection ("or" circuit) between the fox and corn relays. If a lamp and battery are now connected in series with this circuit, nothing will happen unless the farmer-boat relay is operated, indicating that he has crossed the river. But when he crosses, power is transferred from the *break* to the *make* contact. This completes the circuit through the unoperated *break* contacts symbolizing the goose, fox and corn. Trouble is thereby signaled.

This takes care of the situation on the near side of the river. A second circuit must be constructed to represent events on the other side, one which functions in a negative sense compared with the first. This can be accomplished by setting up a series of *make* contacts which corresponds with the *break* contacts of the first circuit.

An investigation of the complete circuit network (all contacts on the right side of the relays shown in Figure 162) will disclose that their operation in unison conforms to every logical requirement of the puzzle and that they accurately respond to every combination of events within the logical limits of the situation.

This portion of Bezold's machine could be constructed with four simple toggle switches and corresponding sets of make-break contacts. But such a machine would not be very convenient as a parlor game, because the player would have to throw the farmer's switch and one of the other three at precisely the same instant or the alarm would flash. Hence Bezold made a fancy affair in which each relay also functions as a memory element. He confesses that the gadget's apparently extravagant use of contacts would make a switching engineer very unhappy. "The extra contacts shown in the left side of the circuit diagram were on the relays," he explained, "so I just wired them into the arrangement shown for the fun of it."

An interesting variation of the logic circuit built by Bezold can be designed for signaling an error made by malfunctions within the machine itself. Bezold's arrangement signals positive trouble by lighting the lamp and sounding the buzzer when the goose and corn, for example, are placed alone on either side of the river. But such indications are given *only if the machine is working properly*. Trouble will not be signaled if the lamp has burned out, or if the battery is exhausted. All machines are subject to failures of this kind and, in the case of large computers used for solving scientific problems, automatically navigating aircraft or guiding missiles, such errors can lead to serious consequences.

Fortunately, it is not difficult to make computers "self-checking," capable of disclosing internal malfunctions. In the case of the boat-goose-corn-fox machine the self-checking feature can be provided by adding two more circuits, each a complement of the two utilized in Bezold's machine. The second pair function in a negative sense, compared with the first pair. In effect, for

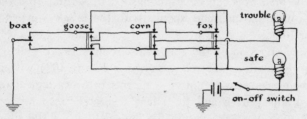

163
Farmer-fox-goose-corn puzzle circuit provided with self-checking feature

each set of *make* contacts in the first pair a set of *break* contacts is provided in the second as shown in the circuit diagram, Figure 163. A second signal lamp is connected into these circuits as diagrammed. One lamp or the other must light for every switch position or the operator knows that the machine is malfunctioning. In other words the machine states positively that the situation is safe or that it is not safe. This device can be built for $2 or less from four double-throw toggle switches, two flashlight lamps and a dry cell.

2

A TICKTACKTOE MACHINE

Noel Elliott, an amateur of Kellogg, Idaho, comments on the machine he constructed

THE DESIGN OF THIS MACHINE closely resembles that of all electrical calculating devices, although on a much simpler scale than most. It can remember, calculate and transfer information from one circuit to another. The calculation and transfer, however, occur as soon as the information is received rather than in a timed sequence, such as takes place in a big calculator. This is possible because of the simple nature of the information. The operator informs the machine of his move by throwing a switch, and the machine, after carrying out its calculation, makes its reply move by lighting a pilot lamp in the appropriate space on the playing field.

The machine has two basic functions: to prevent its human opponent from occupying three spaces in a row, and to prevent him from establishing a fork — the threat of making three-in-a-row along either of two lines. The work of design began with the classification of all possible moves.

Since there are nine spaces on a ticktacktoe playing field, there are nine possible first moves. The moves are of three types: center, corner and side. Statistics show that the best move against a center opening is a corner, and against any outside opening, the center. The circuits that carry out this strategy consist of "or" switches in all outside positions and a direct connection between the center switch and a lamp in one of the corners.

After the opening move and the reply, the human player has a choice of seven remaining spaces. This means that for his first two moves he has a total of 63 possible combinations. The machine's replies to these are handled by an "and" circuit, with current from the battery flowing through the first-move switch and the second-move switch to the lamp. Circuits that respond to subsequent moves are designed in the same way, although in some of them provision must be made against setting up duplicate paths and thus causing more than one lamp to light. Conflicts of this type are avoided by equipping the circuit with memory relays interconnected so that operation of one switch automatically opens the circuit of another which would otherwise interfere.

3

SOME COMPUTER THEORY

Puzzle machines are not merely entertaining gadgets. They offer insights into mathematical problems — and the working of digital computers

NEITHER BEZOLD NOR ELLIOTT has constructed a digital computing machine so far. These require too much apparatus for the average amateur's pocketbook if their capacity for numbers goes beyond a couple of digits. But Bezold has set up small circuits for the basic operations of arithmetic. A set of relays equipped with transfer and lockdown contacts, for example, can easily be interconnected to count pulses.

Two relays are needed for each digit. A pulse (in the form of a momentary ground connection) enters the transfer contact of the first relay and energizes the coil of the second relay. The second relay locks down and simultaneously applies energy to a lead connecting with the coil of the first relay. But since the transfer contact of the first relay also is connected to this lead, thus grounding it during the pulse, no current can enter the coil of the first relay. When the ground connection is removed at the end of the pulse, the first relay operates, locks down and thereby transfers the input connection to the next pair of relays, where the second incoming pulse causes the cycle of operation to be repeated. The train of relay pairs may be extended indefinitely to count as many pulses as desired. One or more break contacts can be inserted along the line, of course, to unlock previously operated pairs.

Two relays may also be interconnected in such a way that each responds to alternate pulses, the incoming pulses causing one relay to lock down and the other to release in seesaw fashion. Such a pair in effect divides incoming pulses by two. Like the counting relays, these can be cascaded, each succeeding pair dividing the output of its predecessor. Such "flip-flop" circuits find extensive application in computing machines that work with binary numbers — in which all quantities are expressed by combinations of 1 and 0. In the binary system 1 plus 1 equals 0 with 1 to carry. The first relay of the flip-flop pair symbolizes the binary digit. If it is holding a digit when the pulse arrives, the circuit flip-flops, thus restoring the first relay to 0. The second relay then sends a pulse to the next succeeding pair, the first relay of which operates and thus stores the digit 1. The two sets of relays then stand at 10 — which in binary notation means 2. The machine has, in short, performed an addition. Its capacity to add is limited only by the number of relays built into it.

Designing and building these entertaining gadgets combines the age-old fascination of puzzle solving with that of performing electrical experiments. Those who have taken to the new hobby are quick to point out, however, that its satisfactions go beyond the mere production of ingenious playthings. You gain an insight into the nature of games and puzzles which acts as a powerful stimulus to the imagination. The theory of equations, probability, topology, the infinitesimal calculus — all these, as Edward Kasner and James R. Newman pointed out in their book *Mathematics and the Imagination,* have grown out of problems first expressed in puzzle form.

Essentially puzzle solving involves discovering a logical relationship among terms which has been buried beneath an ingenious pattern of rhetorical statements. The solution can be made easier by restating the puzzle in simple language. When this is done, certain key words generally stand out. These include: "and," "or," "yes," "no," "either but not both," and "but not." Such words can be represented by patterns of electrical keys, relays, diodes and related parts common to switching systems. The first steps in designing a puzzle circuit, or "pircuit," therefore, consist in restating the puzzle in simple terms, arranging the elements in logical sequence and substituting electrical counterparts for the key words — as follows.

4

HOW TO DESIGN A "PIRCUIT" OR PUZZLE CIRCUIT

Harry Rudloe of New York City describes three pir-cuits he designed at 16. The first: his battle-of-numbers game

THE FIRST PROJECT I attempted was the design of a circuit to represent the "battle of numbers" game. As this game is usually played, opponents take turns picking up matches from a pile of 13. A player may pick up one, two or three matches at a time, and the one forced to pick the last match loses.

In my machine a row of 13 signal lamps is substituted for the matches [*see Fig. 164*]. Push-button keys control the lamps. At the beginning of a game all 13 lamps are lighted. The machine's opponent opens the game by flipping a toggle switch which gives either himself or the machine the first move. The player makes his move by depressing the key which turns off the number of lights he chooses, that is, the one he presses and all those to the left. When he releases the key, the machine registers its move.

An analysis of the game discloses that a win can be forced by the player who moves second. Consider the first 12 lamps (left to right) as consisting of three groups of four lamps each. If, after the first player has put out one, two or three lamps, the second player puts out the remainder in each group, he cannot fail to win, because only the 13th lamp will remain lighted after all the lamps in the three groups have been extinguished in this sequence.

Thus, if the machine is designed with built-in instructions to follow this strategy, it will always win when the opponent elects the first move. It will also win even when it is required to make the first move if the opponent fails to figure out the winning strategy and carry it out without a mistake; if any lamps in a

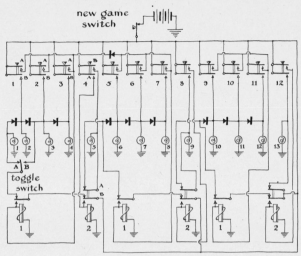

164
Circuitry for "battle of numbers" game

group remain lighted after the opponent has made his move, the machine will invariably seize the advantage. The opponent can win only by electing to make the second move and playing a perfect game.

Each group of four lamps is controlled by a circuit identical with the others. The diagram here denotes by the letters A and B some of the possible opening moves. Consider first a game in which the machine wins. The toggle switch has been thrown to position A, indicating that the machine's opponent moves first. He can put out one, two or three lamps by operating the first, second or third key, respectively. Contact spring A on the operated key transmits an impulse to relay 1 (associated with group 1). The relay locks down, because its winding receives power through the lower contact from its spring (connected to the battery through the upper contact and spring of relay 2 of group 1).

This cuts off power to some of the lamps in the first group of four. The lamp associated with the key and those to its left will go out — but not those to the right of the key. Observe that "but-not" elements, utilizing rectifiers of the dry-disk type and wired

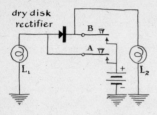

165
Circuit elements symbolizing
"but not" situation

as shown in Figure 165, are inserted between each pair of lamps in each group. Contact B of the key now transmits power to the lamps at the right of the key but not to those at its left. This completes the opponent's play. He now releases the key — which initiates the machine's play. Contact B opens, cutting off power from the alternate "but-not" circuit to all remaining lamps of the group. This registers the machine's move.

Now consider a game in which the machine has the losing side. The toggle switch is operated to position B. This cuts off power to the first two lamps and constitutes the machine's first move. The opponent gains the advantage by depressing key 4 and thus extinguishing the remaining lamps in this group. The contact spring A on this key transmits an impulse to the winding of relay 2 in group 1, and the relay locks down through its bottom contact (by means of power supplied through spring B). Spring B of relay 2 acts as an "either-or" element, supplying power either to the first group of four lamps or to its lockdown contact. This prevents power from entering the first group of lamps for the remainder of the game. Spring A on relay 2 cuts out the first lamp in the second group of four. Contact B on key 4 continues to supply this lamp with power, however, until the key is released.

The machine could be designed so that this play would put out either the first, second or third lamps of group 2. It could not, however, capture the advantage by any of these plays. Hence in the interest of keeping the circuit as simple as possible I confined the machine's choice of play to the first lamp. This tactic also gives the opponent the maximum choice of plays — and the maximum opportunity for making an error! The opponent can now preserve his advantage by operating key 8. This extinguishes the

remaining lamps in the second group. The machine will reply by
putting out lamp 9. The opponent then operates key 12, putting
out the remaining lamps in the final group and forcing the machine to lose by putting out lamp 13. None of my friends has yet
discovered the simple winning strategy of this game, although a
few have won by accident.

Two more-complicated river-crossing puzzles

IN THE 16TH CENTURY Niccolo Tartaglia, the Italian
mathematician and inventor, suggested a somewhat more elaborate version of the farmer-goose-fox-corn puzzle. Three lovely
brides and their jealous husbands must cross the proverbial river
in the small boat holding only two people. Each husband insists
that the crossing must be so arranged that his wife is never in
the company of another man unless he, the husband, also is present.

A circuit representing this situation is developed by following
the same elementary rules of symbolic logic as in the simpler
farmer problem. Your friends will find the machine more interesting if you install signal lamps to indicate the location of each
character as play progresses. A convenient circuit for accomplishing this employs a relay equipped with front and back contacts
(an "either-or" arrangement) and a pair of double-pole, single-
throw keys — the arrangement shown at the left of the relays in
Figure 162 and, in simplified form, in Figure 166. This "transfer"
circuit is identical for all characters in this as well as in other
puzzles. All the contact springs are assumed to be connected to
the battery unless otherwise indicated. Operation of the "cross"

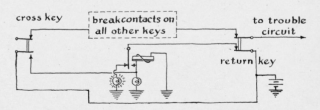

166
Convenient circuit for effecting the transfer of an action

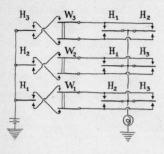

167
Complete circuit for "jealous husbands" puzzle

key closes the bottom contact of the relay and thus energizes the relay's coil. The armature accordingly locks down through the bottom contact of the "return" key. In effect the arrangement constitutes a memory circuit and relieves the player of the need to keep account of his moves or reconstruct them by inspecting the position of the toggle switches (or relays, whichever are used for constructing the trouble circuit). Operation of the return key releases the memory relay. The "break" contacts of all keys may be wired in series to supply power to the trouble circuit. When the player wishes to send a pair of characters across the river, he operates the key representing one character and, before releasing it, operates the other key. Power is thus prevented from entering the trouble circuit until the move is completed.

As in the boat-goose-fox-corn problem, the trouble signal operates whenever any husband is on the opposite side of the river from his wife and she is in the presence of either or both of the other husbands. The logic portion of the circuit is shown in Figure

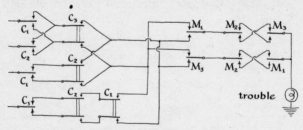

168
Cannibals-and-missionaries puzzle circuit (battery connects to unterminated C_1, C_2 and C_3 switch arms at left)

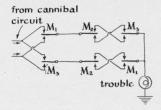

169
Circuit configuration for "missionary" portion of puzzle circuit

170
"Cannibal" configuration of puzzle circuit showing presence and location of two characters

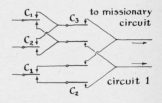

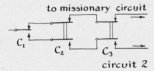

171
"Cannibal" configuration of puzzle circuit showing presence and location of three characters

167. Although the diagram omits mechanical linkages, it is understood that all the switches associated with the same character, H_1, for example, operate in unison and in the same direction. They may be linked mechanically (toggle switches) or electromagnetically (relays). For simplicity relay coils have been omitted from the diagram of the logic circuit.

In a still more complex version of this puzzle, the husbands and wives become missionaries and cannibals — three of each. Same river, same two-passenger boat. All the missionaries can row. Only one cannibal can row. If the cannibals on either side of the river outnumber the missionaries at any time — into the stewpot go the missionaries!

Outnumbering may occur in these combinations: three to two, three to one and two to one. The complete logic circuit is shown in Figure 168. Its action is easier to follow if you divide the circuit into three parts and examine them one at a time. The missionary configuration [*Fig. 169*] will register trouble if proper cannibal circuits are closed when any two missionaries are opposite the third missionary. Circuit 1 [*Fig. 170*] conducts when any two or three cannibals are on one side of the river. It also shows which side they are on. Circuit 2 [*Fig. 171*] similarly indicates when all three cannibals are on the same side of the river and which side they are on. In combination, the three configurations register all the possible trouble situations: (1) when all three cannibals are on the same side with just two, any two, missionaries, (2) when any two or three cannibals are on the same side with a lone missionary.

5

AN ELECTRONIC MOUSE
THAT LEARNS
FROM EXPERIENCE

Harry Rudloe describes his variation on Claude Shannon's celebrated robot. Rudloe's mouse can scarcely be called a thinking creature, but it demonstrates that, with a few hand tools and junk parts, the amateur can design and build a machine capable of exercising choice and profiting from experience

AFTER CONSTRUCTING a variety of games and puzzles with built-in "intelligence," I became interested in the problem of designing a machine with the ability to learn from experience and apply its acquired knowledge in avoiding future mistakes. Claude Shannon's famous "mouse," which investigates a maze and learns how to avoid blind passages by trial and error, fascinated me and I decided to have one of my own.

His mouse is a simple bar magnet enclosed in a mouse-shaped covering and equipped with copper whiskers which "ground" the mouse upon contacting the brass walls of the maze. It is moved by other magnets concealed beneath the maze. Its "brain" is located outside the maze. I wanted a self-contained mouse — even if that meant building him the size of a jack rabbit.

I could not find any published circuit information on Shannon's mouse, but after consulting a few books on switching systems I finally succeeded in designing and constructing a mouse which can learn any maze with the following properties: (1) the correct passage leads to a fork; (2) every fork leads into two passages, one of which is a dead end; (3) there are no more than three forks and dead-end passages [see Fig. 172].

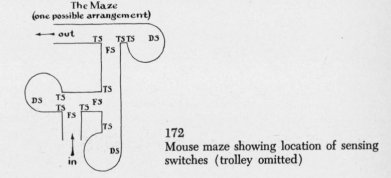

172
Mouse maze showing location of sensing switches (trolley omitted)

This last limitation was imposed by the size of my pocketbook, for the cost goes up with the complexity of the maze and the necessary increase in the mouse's memory capacity. Cost also prevented my mouse from being completely self-contained; its power supply and brain are located outside the maze.

The mouse is powered by two motors, each driving a front wheel, as shown in Figure 173. Its rear is supported by two contact shoes which slide over a pair of electrically independent metal strips fastened to the floor of the maze. One strip serves as a ground return. The other strip supplies juice to one of the motors; the second motor gets its power by way of a trolley fastened

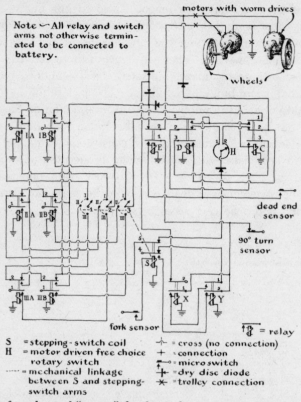

173

Circuit of mechanical "mouse" that learns by experience to run maze

to the ceiling of the maze. Information is transmitted from the brain to these motor "muscles" through the conducting strips.

Steering is accomplished by cutting off power to one or the other of the driving wheels, as in the case of tread-equipped tractors and bulldozers. Friction against the sides or walls of the maze is reduced by mounting rubber wheels on each side of the mouse. They also help the mouse negotiate dead-end passages. These dead ends terminate in circular or "cheesebox" walls which force the mouse through a 270-degree turn. By pivoting an additional 90 degrees the mouse can leave the dead-end passage and continue to the next fork without reversing its motors.

If it is to profit from experience, the mouse must be fitted with some means of sensing its environment, of storing this information and of drawing upon it for subsequent use. As a minimum, the creature must be able to count the forks as it proceeds through the maze and remember where it went wrong in the sequence; for instance, if a right turn at fork 2 led to a dead end during the exploratory run, it must remember and go left at the same fork the next time.

This information is sensed by means of three "organs," all composed of microswitches. The first group of microswitches is distributed along the ceiling of the maze — one at the entrance of each fork. This sequence of switches advises the brain whenever the mouse comes to a fork. The second set of switches, mounted on the walls, signals the mouse whenever it arrives at a dead end. The third group of switches, also wall-mounted at the entrance to each straightaway passage, informs the brain that power should be restored to both motors. All switches of each group are wired in parallel.

The mouse's brain consists of three basic elements: "neurons" for remembering (in the form of two relays for each fork), an associative device (a stepping switch) and an element enabling the mouse to choose a fork at random when it does not know which is correct. The heart of the latter element is a motor-driven rotary switch which is alternately conducting and nonconducting.

When the mouse first enters the maze, both of its driving motors receive power through a master relay. The mouse accordingly proceeds to the first fork. Here an impulse from the fork sensor signals the brain. As a result: (1) the master relay cuts off power to the motors; (2) a secondary relay then supplies power to one or the other of the motors, depending upon the position of the rotary switch at the moment; (3) the stepping switch advances to the first set of contacts through which the memory relays are actuated. The mouse, powered by one motor, turns to the right or the left as the chance position of the rotary motor has selected. Now the straightaway sensors advise that a straight passage lies ahead, actuate the master relay and restore power to both motors. The mouse proceeds through the passage.

If the mouse reaches a fork at the end of the passage, the cycle of operation repeats. The mouse has learned nothing. If the passage leads to a dead end, however, the memory relays come into action. The dead-end sensor transmits a pulse through the appropriate spring of the stepping switch and thus locks down either a "right-turn" or "left-turn" memory relay. With this information stored, the mouse negotiates the circular wall of the dead end and proceeds to the next fork. The mouse thus learns only from *hard* experience. Chance may lead it through the maze successfully on the very first run. In that case the mouse emerges from the experience as ignorant as though the run had not been made. On the other hand, chance may cause it to explore every dead end in the course of a single run. If it does, the mouse has learned all there is to know: it will never make a mistake again!

The mouse's memory works this way: When it reaches the first fork on a second run, the fork sensor transmits an impulse which advances the stepping switch to the first set of contacts and trips the master relay, cutting power to both motors. If neither relay is locked down, the mouse chooses at random. But if one relay is locked, its break contact inactivates the random-choice circuit, and a set of "make" contacts on the same relay feeds power to the motor that turns the mouse in the correct direction.

6

COMPUTERS AND THE TERROR OF MATHEMATICS

DESPITE THEIR FASCINATION with science, many amateur scientists shudder at the thought of having to use mathematics. Doubtless the rush to embrace the new hobby of building electrical computers may be attributed in part to this aversion to direct mathematical methods. Many who build these machines firmly believe they are working with nonmathematical methods and go to extremes in inventing ingenious methods apparently involving no advanced mathematics to determine such quantities, for example, as the area of a flat surface with an irregular boundary. Not all enthusiasts confine their inventive efforts to electrical devices, of course. Numerous mechanical, chemical and even optical gadgets can be adapted as problem solvers, as pointed out in the following discussion.

7

THE PLEASURES OF MATHEMATICS

F. W. Niedenfuhr, Professor of Engineering Mechanics at Ohio State University, lures the amateur scientist into an encounter with integral calculus

IT MAY COME as something of a surprise to amateurs to learn that they often skate dangerously close to the edge of integral calculus. Integral calculus is not nearly so formidable as it sounds. It is a study, at least in part, of the problem of measuring area. In view of the fun that can be got out of mathematics, and of the understanding of advanced work in science which it can afford, it is unfortunate that more amateurs do not devote some of their time to the subject. Experiments with problems of area can make an interesting starting point. I will give an example of a difficult problem later on, but first let us look into an easier case.

Imagine that we have drawn a simple closed curve on a sheet of writing paper. (Simple means that the curve does not cross itself.) This curve marks out an area on our paper. How many ways can you think of to find this area?

The problem is interesting to me because I like to watch the ways in which students at various stages of sophistication attempt to solve it. A third-year college student may begin by trying to write the equations of the curve. A mature mathematician will ask: "How accurately do you want to know the area?" A graduate student in mathematics will sometimes protest that he is not sure he understands the problem, and that anyway it probably cannot be solved. An engineer may admit that he once knew how to find the area but has now forgotten, or he may produce a machine called a planimeter and proceed to measure the area for you. Usually he will not know why this machine works, but he is pretty sure that it does. But don't press the poor fellow — he has another job to do.

I saw a very clever (and most significant) solution to this problem at a model-airplane meet some years ago. The contest rules required that the models have a fuselage whose cross-sectional area was not less than a certain minimum. This area was easy to check in the good old days when all the models had rectangular cross sections, but with the advent of more stream-lined shapes the judges began to have trouble making sure the rules were being followed.

They finally decided to find the required area by first having an accurate drawing of it, and then cutting out the drawing and weighing it. Since the weight per unit area of the paper was known, the area of the cut-out drawing was easy to obtain. Now this solution to the area problem is a splendid example of applied integral calculus. It is a little surprising, then, that people who have actually studied calculus will laugh at the method, or dismiss it as impractical. Yet when an accurate balance or scale is at hand it is the quickest way to determine an area. (How many ways can you think of for improvising a balance to "weigh areas"?)

Another obvious way to find an area is to draw the figure on graph paper and count the number of little squares inside the simple closed curve. Then if we know the area of each square we find the total area by multiplying the area per square by the number of squares enclosed by the curve. Of course near the edges of the figure we will have to count partial squares, and some error will be introduced each time we estimate the size of such a square.

But the total error will generally be small for two reasons. First, we will sometimes overestimate and sometimes underestimate the area of a partial square, and our errors from this source will tend to cancel out. Second, the human eye is an excellent judge of the relative sizes of small areas. This process is not so tedious as might be imagined, because on the interior of the figure we can count great blocks of squares at once, rather than each square individually. I find that making drawings on 8½ × 11-inch paper with quarter-inch squares printed on it provides excellent accuracy and is not too time-consuming.

A variation on the system of counting squares is the Monte Carlo method. You might like to try this one experimentally. Draw the area on a piece of paper again, and put your finger down at random. One of four things will happen: (1) your finger will come down on the paper inside the unknown area, (2) it will come down outside the area, (3) it will come down on the boundary of the area, or (4) it will miss the paper entirely. Now on a separate tally sheet keep track of the results as follows: In the first case (your finger lands inside the area) write "Yes" on the tally sheet. In the second case write "No" on the sheet. In the third and fourth cases do not write on the sheet at all. After a large number of tallies have been made you can find the unknown area by multiplying the total area of the paper by the number of "Yes" tallies divided by the number of "Yes" plus "No" tallies. The accuracy of the answer will depend on two things. First, the number of tallies must be large; second, you must put your finger down in a random manner each time. Obviously if you always put your finger down outside the given area, you would have no "Yes" tallies, and the formula given above would indicate that the unknown area is zero.

Pursued by hand, the Monte Carlo method will only lead to bruised thumbs and poor estimates of the area, but it does appear to be a useful method when automatic machines can be devised to make and record a large number of tallies. Machines have been constructed which integrate (calculate areas) by this method, but they are handicapped by the difficulty of providing random numbers which tell the machine how to "put its finger down."

Any mechanical device to produce random numbers will be subject to wear, and this wear introduces a bias in favor of a particular number. For a time it was thought the sequence of digits in *pi* (3.14159 . . .) would be random, but this is not the case. There still is no completely satisfactory way to produce random numbers. In spite of this practical difficulty, the Monte Carlo method of integration holds great promise.

There is still another way in which the original problem can be solved. Suppose our unknown area has been divided up into a large number of narrow strips by equally spaced vertical lines drawn on the paper [*Fig. 174*]. By itself each strip differs little from a long, narrow rectangle. Suppose we have numbered each strip for identification purposes and measured its length. If the lengths of the strips are L_1, L_2, L_3 and so on, the following is an obvious formula for the area:

$$\text{Area} = (L_1 + L_2 + L_3 \ldots) \times B$$

B is the width of the strips. Now the ends of each strip will not be rectangular but tapered or cut on the bias. If a strip is rather wide, you may have difficulty in deciding its length, and the accuracy of the final result will depend on how well you define the length of each strip. If the strips are narrow, however, it will be easy to decide the length. Imagine, for instance, that each strip is as narrow as the thickness of the paper. If the strips were literally cut apart, we could measure the length of a number of threads. This would be tedious but not difficult. Thus the accuracy of the formula increases as B becomes very small, and as the

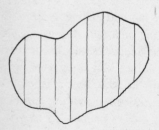

174
Division of irregular area into strips of uniform width

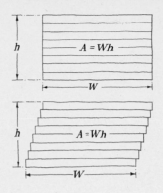

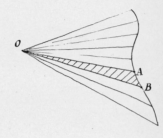

175
Laminated area *(top)* does not change
in size when canted *(bottom)*

176
Irregular area divided by rays of equal
angle

177
Element of irregular area divided
by rays of equal angle

number of strips increases. The "fundamental theorem" of integral
calculus is based on this formula.

The area given by formula will not be changed if the strips
are moved with respect to one another. This explains why the
areas of the parallelogram and the rectangle in the accompanying illustration [*Fig. 175*] are the same. The parallelogram is just
the rectangle with its strips pushed over a little. The pushing
process does not change either the length or width of a strip.

Another process for finding areas is to divide the unknown area
into a large number of triangles, find the area of each triangle,
and add up the areas. We split the area by drawing rays, each
of which has the same angular relationship to the others [*Fig. 176*].
Now look at a typical element of this area [*Fig. 177*]. Let C be
the center of AB, and R be the distance from O to C. Imagine

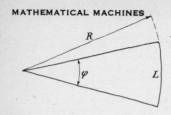

178
Angle measured by graphic method

that we swing an arc of radius R (OC) between the lines OA and OB. If the angle AOB is very small, this arc will appear to be practically a straight line of length W. The area of the triangle is then one-half $R \times W$.

If the angle AOB is denoted by the symbol $(d\varphi)$, you see that the two lengths R and W determine the angle. In fact, we may say by definition that $(d\varphi) = W/R$. You are familiar with measuring angles in degrees, but this new method of measuring angles is generally more useful in mathematics. The units of this measurement are called "radians." For instance, if in the above example $R = 3$ inches and $W = .3$ inch, then $(d\varphi)$ is an angle of .1 radian, which is equivalent to just under six degrees.

Measurement of larger angles in radians may be done by drawing a circular sector [*Fig. 178*]. Let R be the radius of the sector, and L be the length of the arc. The angle φ, expressed in radians, is $\varphi = L/R$. If we keep increasing the angle φ, the sector opens up into a circle [*Fig. 179*], and the angle φ becomes 360 degrees.

How many radians is this? The "arc length" L has become equal to the circumference of the circle which is $2_\pi R$. Then $\varphi = L/R =$

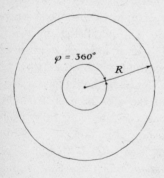

179
Sector opened to make angle of
360 degrees

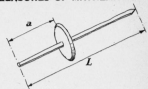

180
Basic element of planimeter

$2\pi R/R = 2\pi$. Thus 2π radians equals 360 degrees. The advantage of using the radian measure for angles lies in the fact that if we say "angle equals arc length over radius," we may also say "arc length equals angle times radius."

Back to our little triangle. Since $(d\varphi) = W/R$, or $W = R\,(d\varphi)$, the area of the little triangle is $\frac{1}{2}RW = \frac{1}{2}R^2\,(d\varphi)$. Let R_1, R_2, R_3 ... be the radii of the small triangular "slices" of the big area. Then, since each "slice" has the same central angle $(d\varphi)$, the big area is given by the formula:

$$A = \frac{1}{2}(R_1{}^2 + R_2{}^2 + R_3{}^2 + \ldots)\,(d\varphi)$$

This represents the sum of the areas of the little triangles. This formula too is very close to a calculus formula. Its accuracy will increase as $(d\varphi)$ decreases and the number of terms increases.

You now have enough information to build a machine to measure areas (a planimeter). Imagine a straight bar which serves as the axle of a knife-edged wheel [*Fig. 180*]. Now imagine that this bar moves a small amount parallel to the plane of the paper, while the wheel rolls and slides on the paper. Let the bar move from BC to $B'C'$ [*Fig. 181*]. This motion could be accomplished by first moving the bar parallel to itself from BC to $B'C''$ and

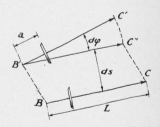

181
Geometry of planimeter action

then rotating it about B' until it reaches $B'C'$. How far would the wheel roll during this motion? In moving from BC to $B'C''$, the wheel rolls (and slides sideways a little) a distance (ds), and in moving from $B'C''$ to $B'C'$ the wheel rolls a distance $a \, (d\varphi)$. [Here again $(d\varphi)$ is measured in radians, and is a small angle.] So the total distance the wheel rolls is (dp), where $(dp) = (ds) + a \, (d\varphi)$.

What area did the bar sweep out? In moving from BC to $B'C''$ the area covered was $L(ds)$, and in moving from $B'C''$ to $B'C'$ the area covered was $\frac{1}{2} L^2 (d\varphi)$, so if the total area swept out is called (dA):

$$(dA) = L \, (ds) + \frac{1}{2} L^2 (d\varphi)$$

Combining the last two equations:

$$(dA) = L \, (dp) - La \, (d\varphi) + \frac{1}{2} L^2 (d\varphi)$$
$$= L \, (dp) + (\tfrac{1}{2} L^2 - La) \, (d\varphi)$$

Now you should know, if you have not already guessed, that in the notation of calculus if x is any quantity, the symbol (dx) stands for a little bit of x. For instance, if A is an area, (dA) is a very small "slice" of that area. If p is a distance, (dp) is a short step along the way.

Having mastered this much calculus, we may now play a trick on our little wheel and axle — or tracer arm, as it is properly called. We attach another bar to it at point B. This second bar is called a polar arm. The polar arm has one end hinged to the tracer arm at B, and one end fixed (but free to pivot) at point O [Fig. 182].

Now trace around the circumference of an area with the tracer point C. The area swept out by BC will be the area we are attempting to measure plus the area hatched in the illustration. But the hatched area will be covered twice, once with the wheel rolling forward and once with the wheel rolling backward, so it cancels out. If we consider the total area swept out by the tracer arm

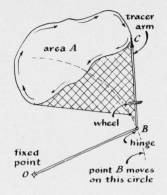

182
Demonstration of integration by use
of the planimeter

as being the sum of a large number of very small areas (dA), as
described above, we may write:

$$A = (dA)_1 + (dA)_2 + (dA)_3 + \ldots$$
$$= L\,[(dp)_1 + (dp)_2 + \ldots] +$$
$$(\tfrac{1}{2}L^2 - La)\,[(d\varphi)_1 + (d\varphi)_2 + \ldots]$$

Now we must interpret each of these sums. The total distance
(p) through which the wheel rolled is:

$$p = [(dp)_1 + (dp)_2 + \ldots]$$

The total angle through which the tracer arm BC turned is:

$$\varphi = [(d\varphi)_1 + (d\varphi)_2 + \ldots]$$

But since the polar arm forced the tracer arm to return to its
exact starting point, the total angle turned is zero. Thus $A = Lp$
(p, again, is the distance the wheel rolled). This is easily obtained from scale markings on the rim of the wheel.

The little instrument we have been discussing is called a polar
planimeter [*Fig. 183*]. There are several models on the market
— all rather expensive for beginners, I fear. You can have more
fun constructing your own. An accurate polar planimeter is a
precision machine. If you are not quite up to fine mechanical

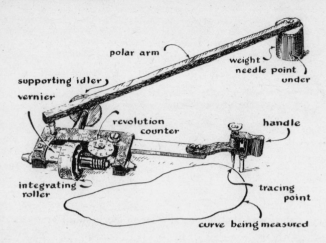

polar arm

weight
needle point
under

supporting idler

vernier

revolution
counter

handle

integrating
roller

tracing
point

curve being measured

183
Practical form of the planimeter

work, there is another way out. Your pocketknife can be used
as a satisfactory, if approximate, planimeter. Open both blades
as shown in the upper portion of the accompanying drawing
[*Fig. 184*]. Make sure that blade *B* makes contact on the cutting
edge, and that blade *C* makes contact at its point when the opened
knife is held upright on a table. Determine the distance *L*.

Now pick an area to be measured. The longest diameter of the
area should be considerably shorter than *L*; say, no more than
half as long. Locate the center of the area approximately. Draw
a straight line (to be used as a reference line) outward from the
center of area [*see lower diagram, Fig. 184*]. Now hold the knife
so that point *C* is at the center of area, and *B* is on the reference
line. Holding blade *C*, push the knife along the reference line
until the point of *C* is on the boundary of the curve. Then, keeping the knife upright, guide point *C* completely around the area,
tracing out the boundary line, and finally pull it back to the
center. Meantime the supporting blade *B* will have been riding
freely on the paper. When you return to the starting position,
blade *B* will no longer be on the reference line, and the line of
the knife, *BC*, will make an angle with the reference line. Call

184
The jackknife in position for use as a
planimeter *(top)*. Irregular area to
be measured together with reference
line at bottom

this angle φ (measured in radians). The area you have traced
around is then given approximately by the formula $A = L^2\varphi$.
This is so easy to do that it is worthwhile trying it on a few known
areas just to see how good your pocketknife really is.

If it is inconvenient to measure the angle directly in radians,
measure it in degrees, multiply by 2π and divide by 360, in accordance with the definition of a radian given above. This sliding type of planimeter is often called a "hatchet planimeter."

Now for the more difficult problem I promised earlier. It would
seem natural, in view of all the foregoing, to seek the area of a
curved surface by enclosing the surface in a polyhedron of many
sides and then adding up the areas of the faces of the polyhedron.
For example, the area of a cylinder can be obtained approximately by adding up the areas of the faces of an octagonal box
in contact with the cylinder [*Fig. 185*]. The result would be more
accurate if instead of an octagonal box we used a box with
many more sides. Just to show that this is not always such
an easy process, consider the following. Cut the cylinder along
a vertical line and unroll it into a flat sheet. The area of this sheet

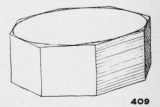

185
Area of cylinder approximated by
octagonal box

186
Cylinder analyzed into rectangles and triangles

is the same as the area of the cylinder. Divide the flat sheet into rectangles and triangles as shown [*Fig. 186*].

Now roll up this sheet to form a cylinder again. Let each vertex of each of the triangles stay on the surface of the cylinder. By connecting these vertices with straight lines we form a polyhedron with a large number of triangular faces which is inscribed in the cylinder. The sides of the triangles are not on the surface of the cylinder, but run inside it from one surface point to another. It is tempting to assume that the area of the polyhedron more and more closely approximates the area of the cylinder as the number of triangles is increased, that is, as the grid of rectangles and triangles becomes finer and finer.

This is in fact not true. If the grid is chosen properly, the polyhedron can be made to approach a kind of Japanese-lantern shape [*Fig. 187*]. The area of such a polyhedron can be made very much *larger* than the area of the circumscribing cylinder. The reason for this is that the planes of the triangles slant in and out with respect to the surface of the cylinder. If the number of vertical divisions is very large as compared to the number of horizontal divisions, the triangles become almost perpendicular to the curved surface. Thus the area of these triangles bears no particular relation to the area of the cylinder.

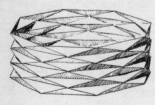

187
Cylinder of indefinitely large surface area
unrelated to its volume

VIII.

AERODYNAMICS

1
LOW VS. HIGH

*A note about the charms of low-speed aerodynamics —
strangely neglected in contrast to rocket problems*

THE TWO GROUPS of hobbyists who build and fly model
craft present a strong contrast. The newborn fraternity of rocket
enthusiasts follows rigorous scientific methods and displays a deep
interest in theory. But the tens of thousands who sail boats, fly kites,
and make model airplanes seem to be content with rule-of-thumb
methods and classical designs. Almost without exception the craft
they sail or fly are slavish copies of models long standardized or
some variation based on a hunch. If more than ten amateurs have
during the past 30 years made a serious attempt to investigate the
origins of forces responsible for the behavior of their low-speed
models and vehicles, I have yet to learn about them.

Yet fascinating problems in this area (neglected by professionals
as well as amateurs) await solution on every side — in air pollution
control, space heating, air conditioning, ventilating systems and
even in the design of meteorological instruments. The performances
of all these systems and mechanisms are influenced by micro-ounce
forces set up by the low-speed flow of air, forces susceptible to
measurement and scientific control. Yet all these mechanisms have
been fashioned by rule-of-thumb techniques.

Perhaps the professional neglect of this basic science can be explained in terms of dollars and cents: it may be felt that the small
results would not be worth the time spent.

But this explanation can scarcely apply to amateurs. Time is the
amateur's chief stock in trade. Many boys (aged 8 to 80) spend
endless hours building and flying kites. Still, with few exceptions,
the kites they fly are aerodynamically no improvement over those
flown 3,000 years ago. Even the Navy continues to use the classical
and grossly inefficient box kite to haul aloft the radio antennas of

its emergency life rafts. It is true that some of these are fancy affairs with aluminum tubing and fabric substituted for sticks and paper. But aerodynamically the Navy's kites are a thousand years old. Even more surprising is the lack of active interest in low-speed aerodynamics by the multimillion-dollar model-airplane industry. A significant percentage of its estimated 100,000 enthusiasts are gifted laymen, professional pilots and others who hold degrees in science and engineering. Each year these energetic hobbyists build and fly tens of thousands of model aircraft. Yet the miniature wings they construct are still inappropriately patterned on large-scale airfoils designed for speeds above 50 miles per hour or on models put together by cut-and-try methods.

Some of the curious effects caused by the motion of air can be demonstrated with simple household objects. Suspend two apples by strings, like a pair of pendulums, so that the apples are close together. When you blow between them, they will move toward each other, instead of flying apart as might be expected.

Take a piece of paper an inch or so square, stick a pin through it and drop it on the end of a spool with the pin in the spool opening. You will find it difficult to dislodge the paper by blowing through the other end of the spool.

Set an electric fan on the floor and let its air stream blow toward the ceiling. If you drop an inflated rubber balloon into the air stream, it will not be blown away but will stay in the air stream and hover over the fan, even when the fan is tilted at a considerable angle.

All these effects are accounted for by a common property of moving air — one which explains why airplanes fly and how it is possible for a good baseball pitcher to throw a slight curve. Less pressure is exerted on a surface by air in motion than by air at rest. Airplane wings are shaped so that air flows faster over the upper surface than the lower one; this reduces the pressure above the wing and produces a lifting force. The effect was first described in precise terms by Daniel Bernoulli, of the celebrated family of Swiss mathematicians, in 1737.

Another interesting property of air is its stickiness. It clings to objects, "wets" them and thus tends to retard their motion through it. In general these drag forces, as well as those of lift, increase with increasing velocity. At speeds from about 50 to 400 miles per hour, the thin film of air that clings to the surface influences the forces in significant ways. At higher speeds the forces change: at the speed of sound, for example, moving objects literally rip the air apart, compressing that in front and creating a vacuum in the wake. The professionals today are largely occupied by the effects that lie beyond what was once called the "sonic barrier."

But no one appears to be in the least concerned with the equally interesting effects in what may be called the region of the gentle breeze. Just before the beginning of World War II a group of amateurs in Boston, headed by Captain W. C. Brown of the Army Air Force, decided to explore the behavior of aerodynamic forces set up by velocities under 10 feet per second. Several members of the group were majoring in aerodynamics at the Massachusetts Institute of Technology. The group spent many months building a precision wind tunnel for low-speed investigations. Unfortunately the tunnel was in operation for only a brief period before the war started, and the group completed only two studies. They plotted the characteristics of a family of airfoils worked out mathematically for indoor airplane models, and investigated the effect of streamlining the structural elements associated with these profiles. After Pearl Harbor most of the group went into military aviation, and that ended the project. But the few prized scraps of information that emerged from it continue to be published, from time to time, all over the world.

Following World War II the Department of Aerophysics at Mississippi State University undertook a series of exhaustive studies of the behavior of air at velocities between 15 and 40 miles per hour, and a few amateurs have also made some experiments in the lower portion of this range. Representative examples of this work are described in the following pages.

At the other extreme, amateur rocketeers by the tens of thousands are now devoting most of their hobby hours to the investigation of the forces which determine the behavior of their models. Usually, the rockets are products of cooperative effort directed by professional advisers. The individual members of rocket groups tend to specialize, some helping with airframe design, others the propulsion unit, launching mechanisms, testing facilities, guidance and telemetry systems and evaluation. Six months of effort may go into the design and construction of a rocket which will spend less than a minute in flight. But data collected in those few seconds will occupy the group for many additional months. As one consequence of this approach to the hobby, rocketeers have accumulated an impressive amount of firsthand knowledge in the field of high-speed aerodynamics, propellants, instrumentation, preflight testing and launching techniques — as attested by the rapidly growing literature of amateur rocketry. An account of the pioneering activity of one group concludes this section.

2

A LOW-SPEED WIND TUNNEL

The most accurate apparatus ever made for investigating the micro-ounce forces developed by the slow movement of air was designed and built by a group of amateurs in Boston, Mass. Some details of its construction are discussed, together with the results. Many fascinating problems await exploration by this technique. The tunnel is described by W. C. Brown, a member of the group

ONE OF THE FAILURES of the past 35 years of aviation has been the inability of man to conquer the low-speed field. The slow autogiro and helicopter represent two of the few successful innovations in conventional design since aviation became a fact. Who can predict what other discoveries in this field may revolutionize present design?

Before the war several attempts were made with various types of equipment to gather data in the low-speed aeronautical field. One notable project was a tunnel of about three feet diameter with the air stream driven by an ordinary fan. The famous B-7 airfoil came out of this work. Another project, more ambitious, was a tunnel in the Midwest which produced some interesting tests, although numerous corrections had to be made. But the Boston instrument continues to hold the record as the largest and most accurate low-speed wind tunnel ever constructed, and it could serve as a model for further work in this field today.

John P. Glass, in those years a student at M.I.T., started it all, and to him goes much credit for the tunnel's design. Glass's design was executed by members of the Jordan Marsh Aviation League. William H. Phillips, also a former M.I.T. student, started designing the balances about a year after work was begun on the tunnel proper.

The Boston tunnel was 18 feet long with a standard diameter of five feet at all points. The air was forced through the tunnel, instead of being sucked as in most high-speed tunnels. (Roger Hayward's drawing, Figure 188, shows the general arrangement.) This method was dictated largely by economic considerations. A tunnel of the conventional sucking type would have required an entrance

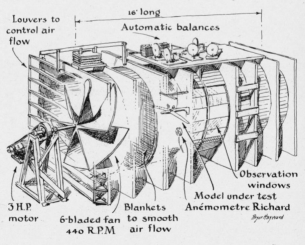

188
Partial cutaway of a low-speed wind tunnel

cone about 18 feet in diameter and a length of 60 feet to get a smooth air flow. Even so, air flow at the low speeds contemplated by the designers would doubtless have been disturbed by eddies originating outside the tunnel. By compressing the air at the propeller end of the instrument and permitting it to seep through blanketing layers of fabric into the test chamber, the tunnel achieved a smooth air flow with a structure of reasonable size. The pressure drop through the blanket, about three pounds per square foot, overcame any irregular pressures arising from turbulence created by the propeller and kept out of the test chamber eddies caused by persons moving about in the room.

The tunnel was driven by a propeller five feet in diameter with six overlapping blades connected through a belt to a direct-current motor of 440 revolutions per minute and three horsepower. The velocity of the air stream could be varied between 2 and 12 feet per second by means of a shutter placed between the propeller and the blanket. This system of control offered a distinct advantage over regulating the speed of the motor, because it tended to offset slight velocity changes caused by variations in power line voltage, belt slippage and related factors.

Air speed through the tunnel was measured by two gauges: a calibrated pendulum vane and an anemometer of the Richard type. Pressure in the tunnel during the calibration period was measured by a manometer arrangement, built by Phillips, which utilized a pair of milk bottles. It was extremely accurate but was abandoned after it was found too sensitive to temperature changes for prolonged use.

The test models were suspended from an airfoil balance. The first balances, intended for use with outdoor models, could weigh a force up to four ounces and were sensitive to three-hundredths of an ounce. They were of the automatic spring type. It was found that a different type would be required for work with indoor models, because the forces to be measured were so infinitesimal. This problem was by far the most difficult encountered during the tunnel's design and construction. A successful design was developed after much work by Phillips [see Fig. 189]. The new balance, of the automatic torsion type, was sensitive to one-thousandth of an

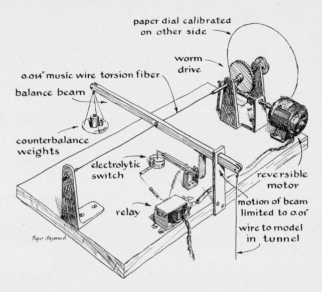

paper dial calibrated
on other side

worm
drive

0.014" music wire torsion fiber

balance beam

counterbalance
weights

electrolytic
switch

relay

reversible
motor

motion of beam
limited to 0.01"

wire to model
in tunnel

Roger Hayward

189
Torsion balance and electrolytic switch for low-speed wind tunnel

ounce and had a capacity of one-tenth of an ounce. It achieved its
extreme sensitivity by using an electromechanical amplifier, incor-
porating the feedback principle, whose main features were derived
from an instrument used at M.I.T. for measuring the surface tension
of liquids. Any force tending to disturb the equilibrium of the balance's master beam was, in effect, counteracted by an equal force
derived from a reversible electric motor actuated by a set of contacts carried by a secondary beam.

The Boston tunnel employed five of these balances. One measured the vertical force, or lift, acting on the airfoil under test, and
two others measured the drag forces. The two remaining balances
measured pitching, rolling and yawing.

The test objects investigated by the Boston group consisted of a
series of rectangular airfoils 30 inches long by five inches wide.
They were not true wing sections, like those of an aircraft, but
merely thin sheets, bowed like a wind-filled sail. The curve was
stiffened by a set of lateral ribs. Starting with the arc of a circle as

the curve of the basic airfoil, the experimenters derived mathematically a family of related curves in which the peak of the curve was progressively shifted aft from the leading edge. The curves are described by the N.A.C.A. system, in which the diameter of the airfoil, or "chord," is taken as unity and the remaining dimensions are expressed as a percentage of this length. Five numerals define the curve: the first digit gives the highest point reached above the chord; the second and third give the distance of this maximum height from the leading edge, and the last two specify thickness.

The experimenters found that the most successful airfoil aerodynamically was the one in which the peak of the curve (8 per cent) was located 40 per cent aft of the leading edge [*see top chart, Fig. 190*]. Because this airfoil has no thickness (being formed of a single sheet of material), it is designated 84000. (For convenience the last two zeros are frequently omitted.) A two-surface airfoil of the same shape with a thickness of 15 per cent is designated 84015.

The basic objective of these investigations is to measure two characteristics of a given airfoil: how variations in the speed of the air stream and the angle at which the airfoil meets the stream affect its lift and drag. The airfoil, or if desired a complete model of the airplane, is suspended in the test section of the tunnel from a T-shaped

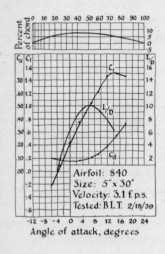

190

Aerodynamic characteristics plotted from wind-tunnel measurements structure which in turn is coupled with the balances. After a series of readings at a predetermined range of air-stream velocities, the tunnel is shut down and the angle of attack is increased. A second set of forces is then recorded. The procedure is repeated through any range of attack angles desired.

The forces so observed are recorded in thousandths of an ounce. The observations are transformed by simple equations into coefficients of lift and of drag (usually designated C_l and C_d) and plotted as a set of curves, one showing the lift coefficients, another the drag coefficients and the third the "L/D" ratio of the two through a range of angles of attack. The main chart [*Fig. 190*] shows a set of these curves derived for the 84000 airfoil.

The Boston tunnel of course can investigate the aerodynamic behavior of test objects of any shape. The instrument also opens boundless opportunities for the exploration of jet effects at low speed and of the drag effects of various surface textures.

3

HOW TO MAKE THE FLOW
OF AIR VISIBLE

When the neglect of low-speed aerodynamics was called to the attention of Scientific American's *readers, a number of professional aerodynamicists were moved to respond. One of the most interesting letters came from the Department of Aerophysics at Mississippi State University*

Sirs: Possibly the explanation of why this aspect of aerodynamics fails to attract amateurs may be found in the invisibility of air itself. Perhaps the solution to the problem lies in making the flow of air visible. The words "I don't see" have become synonymous with "I don't understand." And surely with understanding comes interest.

If so complicated a device as a cloud chamber, which renders cosmic-ray tracks visible, can be reduced to the simple apparatus shown in your pages, surely aerodynamics likewise can be simplified.

The aerodynamic smoke tunnel has long been used to gain a better understanding of various flow phenomena. Alexander Lippisch has made extensive use of the smoke tunnel in designing delta-wing aircraft. The Forrestal Research Center at Princeton University has several smoke tunnels in operation. This aerodynamic tool, the smoke tunnel, is well suited for experiments by amateurs.

I recently constructed a small smoke tunnel which was designed to make use of an ordinary tank-type vacuum cleaner for its source of power [see Fig. 191]. The smoke for the tunnel is obtained from cigarettes.

The tunnel itself is made of two-by-twos and Masonite. The pieces were assembled to form a duct approximately one foot high and two feet long. One end of the duct, the entrance, was flared out to a width of about six inches. The rest of the duct has a width of 1½ inches. One face was then covered with a pane of window glass. A "screen door" made of fine screening (a couple of layers of window screen will do) was made to cover the entrance so as to smooth out the entering air. Toward the other end of the tunnel a hole was cut in the back wall to allow the air to be exhausted by the vacuum cleaner. The cover from a two-inch spool of adhesive tape makes the fitting to attach the vacuum cleaner tube.

The smoke is introduced into the tunnel through a "rake" made from several pieces of ⅛-inch copper tubing attached to a pipe about half an inch in diameter [Fig. 192]. To this rake is attached, by means of rubber tubing, the smoke generator. The smoke generator is made of two narrow cans and some balsa plugs. I started off with a generator that "smokes" a single cigarette but soon worked up to a "three-holer" for a denser smoke. From the other side of the generator another rubber tube is led to the exhaust side of the vacuum cleaner to produce the pressure differential necessary to burn the cigarettes.

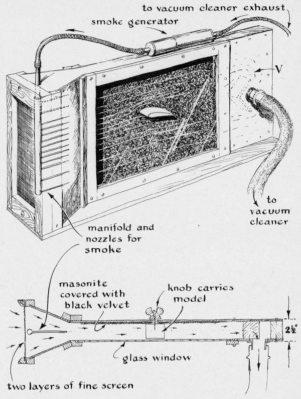

to vacuum cleaner exhaust

smoke generator

V

to
vacuum
cleaner

manifold and
nozzles for
smoke

masonite
covered with
black velvet

knob carries
model

2½"

glass window

two layers of fine screen

191
Suction-type smoke tunnel

After sealing all joints and corners with plastic wood and smoothing the inside of the duct, I painted everything except the glass
with flat black paint.

Wonder of wonders, the thing worked on the first try. However,
later I became dissatisfied with the smoke filaments and found that,
as in mirror grinding, the product improves with attention to detail.
I found that the smoke filaments were sharpest when the tubes of
the rake were lined up accurately with the center line of the tunnel
and when no air leaked in but all the flow came in by the front
door. With only a little care sharp, crisp smoke lines were obtained.

423

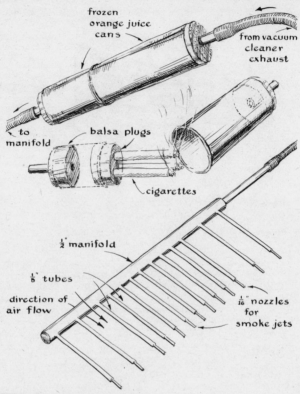

frozen
orange juice
cans

from vacuum
cleaner
exhaust

to
manifold

balsa plugs

cigarettes

$\frac{1}{2}"$ manifold

$\frac{1}{8}"$ tubes

direction of
air flow

$\frac{1}{16}"$ nozzles
for
smoke jets

192
Smoke generator and nozzle assembly

Models to be tested are mounted in the middle of the tunnel behind the glass face. With a knob projecting from the back of the tunnel I control the angle between the model and the flow. For best results the models should be big enough to span the 1½-inch tunnel and should be about three or four inches long.

It might be mentioned that the use of cigarettes as the smoke source has the advantage that the exhaust from the tunnel need not be conducted out-of-doors, as in the case of smokes from burning rotten wood or vaporized kerosene, often used in the larger tunnels. Even after a long evening of running, my kitchen is no worse off than after an evening with several cigarette-smoking guests. Supplying the tunnel with three cigarettes at a time has cut down on my own smoking, incidentally.

Photographing the flow patterns obtained in the tunnel is one of the most interesting aspects of this hobby. When you have pictures of the flows, you can study the details at your leisure and compare different conditions. The black background and white smoke streams form contrasting patterns which are easily photographed. If you make pictures, you must pay some attention to lighting and reflectivity. The back wall of the tunnel must be almost absolutely flat black for the best results. Ordinary rough black paper such as is used in photograph albums is not quite black enough to get good contrast, as it reflects about 10 per cent of the incident light. Black velvet or velveteen reflects less than 1 per cent.

The models should be painted so that they show up in the pictures. At first I painted the models all white, but this reflected too much light. Later I found that if the models were given a coat of white paint, then a coat of black paint, and then some of the black paint was scraped away around the edges, the white paint that showed through outlined the model very well.

I used two 200-watt bulbs in reflectors placed at 45 degrees to the glass to light the smoke lines. The camera was a pre-World War I Kodak, *circa* 1905. I used plus-X film and a setting of $f/8$ at one quarter second.

The pictures [*see Figs. 193, 194, 195 and 196*] show the effects on wind flow of an inclined flat plate, a cylinder and an airfoil section. The airplane model shows how the lift on the wings of an airplane causes the flow to curl up into wing-tip vortices as it streams past the wing. Of course other experiments can be performed. I have done some preliminary work on boundary-layer control, both by suction and by blowing, in the tunnel. The problems of laminar separation and boundary-layer transition are readily studied.

The speed of this tunnel is on the order of two to eight feet per second may be regulated by choking off the flow out of the exhaust end of the vacuum cleaner. Incidentally, a V-shaped baffle should be installed in the exhaust end of the tunnel [*see Fig. 191*] to prevent the flow pattern from necking down into the exhaust

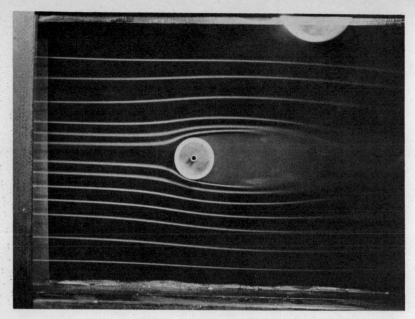

193
Airflow around a cylinder

194
Reaction of airstream to inclined plane

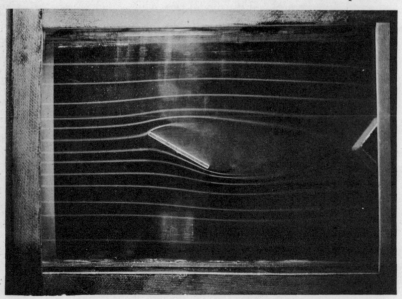

195
Flow around airfoil at angle of stall

196
Reaction of airstream to aircraft in normal flight

427

hole. The speed is best measured at the exhaust hole, and the speed in the test section is computed from the ratio of the area of the test section to that of the exhaust hole.

Although not very fancy and certainly not expensive (less than $3, exclusive of the vacuum cleaner and camera) this smoke tunnel can afford many an hour of entertainment. Model airplane builders have used mine to test new airfoil sections. There are doubtless many other uses.

J. J. CORNISH

Department of Aerophysics
Mississippi State University
State College, Miss.

4

AN AMATEUR-BUILT
SMOKE TUNNEL

Dushan Mitrovich, a high-school student of Chestnut Hill, Mass., submits the design of a smoke tunnel he built at home. Cost: less than $15

A SMOKE TUNNEL capable of quickly evaluating the relative merits of various aerodynamic forms can be put together in a few evenings from materials which should cost no more than $15 in most communities. The design I adopted [see Fig. 197] provides an observation chamber measuring six inches high, eight inches long and an inch wide. The tunnel proper, which features a bell-mouthed air inlet, is made of four pieces of balsa wood. The entering air is straightened by a grid of 23 thin brass vanes, each two inches long and spaced at quarter-inch intervals. The diffuser, made of quarter-inch plywood, starts as an oblong rectangle and gradually becomes an octagon at the exhaust end.

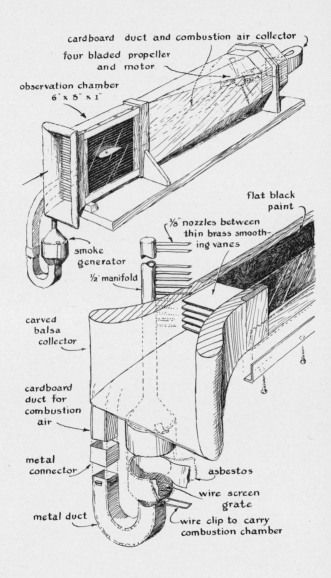

cardboard duct and combustion air collector

four bladed propeller and motor

observation chamber 6" x 8" x 1"

flat black paint

⅛" nozzles between thin brass smoothing vanes

smoke generator

½" manifold

carved balsa collector

cardboard duct for combustion air

metal connector

asbestos

wire screen grate

metal duct

wire clip to carry combustion chamber

197
Details of aerodynamic smoke tunnel with self-contained power plant

The air is drawn in by a pair of crossed, nine-inch propellers notched front and back so they fit into each other and rotate in the same plane [*Fig. 198*]. They are housed in the octagon at the exhaust end and driven by a 15-volt, direct-current motor of the kind used in model trains. The propeller-motor assembly is supported in a brass tube, two inches long, which is held in the center of the octagon by four streamlined struts. A spinner on the propeller and faring aft of the motor streamline the whole power plant.

The smoke generator, located below the air inlet, consists of a cylinder four inches in diameter and two and one half inches long. The funnel-shaped top feeds smoke to a half-inch manifold fitted with 24 smoke nozzles. The nozzles are made from eighth-inch tubing flattened slightly into ovals at the point of discharge. They enter

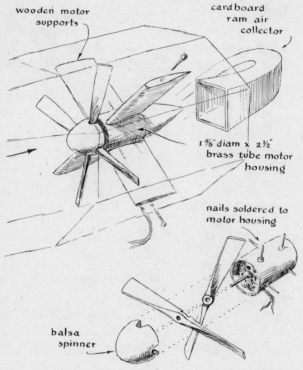

198
Mitrovich motor and propeller assembly for powering smoke tunnel

the inlet at an angle of 45 degrees and end flush with the inner wall halfway between each of the smoothing vanes.

Construction details of the smoke generator are obvious in the drawing. I burn joss sticks (available in Chinese stores) to generate the smoke; they work better in this tunnel than cigarettes, which produce too much heat, or titanium tetrachloride, which is corrosive and clogs the nozzles. The joss sticks, cut to a length of about one inch and impregnated with a few drops of lighter fluid, are placed on the wire mesh, which serves as a grate. To provide enough air to keep them burning, the propeller must be running when the generator is put in place. The pile is ignited, permitted to burn for a few seconds and then blown out. It continues to deliver a dense smoke.

Air speed in the experimental chamber can be varied between 4 and 15 feet per second by adjusting the input voltage to the motor. The rear wall of the chamber is painted flat black. Illumination for photography is supplied by two 25-watt tubular bulbs equipped with cardboard reflectors. They are placed about three inches from each side of the chamber. To counteract reflection from the glass front of the chamber, I place a sheet of flat-black cardboard in front of the tunnel and photograph through a hole cut in the center for the lens. My models are made and tested by the procedures recommended by J. J. Cornish.

5

KITCHEN-SINK AERODYNAMICS

Equipped with a sheet of glass, some balsa wood and a source of running water, the amateur can investigate the forces set up by wind on objects of various shapes. The experiment utilizing the Hele-Shaw apparatus is described by Francis W. Niedenfuhr, Department of Engineering Mechanics, The Ohio State University

THE PROBLEM OF SHAPING A SURFACE to some desired contour occupies amateurs in many fields. Where the basic design is firmly established, as in telescope making, the problem is mainly one of craftsmanship. It may not be easy to make a telescope mirror of high precision, but the maker knows in advance exactly what shape he must try to achieve. In what follows we are going to consider a type of project in which the object is to discover the best or most efficient shape.

This problem applies whenever one sets out to build a racing sloop, an airplane or even a kite. Any boy can make a kite that will climb a hundred feet or so. But to design one which will fly higher than all competitors with a given length of string is a challenge of astonishing sophistication. The performance of a kite, like that of a glider, an airplane or any other vessel in a fluid medium, depends critically on the shapes of its working parts.

Two types of force are of prime interest to those who must design hydrodynamic and aerodynamic shapes. One is summed up in the aerodynamic term "lift." Here the major effect acts at right angles to the motion of the fluid. It accounts for the rise of a kite or an airplane and for the ability of a sailboat to tack against the wind. Generally shapes which create forces perpendicular to the streamlines manage in one way or another to cause the fluid (air, steam or water) to flow at greater velocity on one side of the object than on the other. This differential motion causes a drop in pressure on the side of higher velocity, and the object tends to move in that direction. If you hold a sheet of paper horizontally and blow over its upper surface, the sheet will not bend down but will jump up momentarily, because of the reduction of air pressure on top. The effect explains why gusts of wind sometimes lift the roofs off houses, why ships traveling close together may be sucked together and why it is dangerous to stand near the edge of a railway platform when a train speeds by.

The second interesting force, exerted in the direction of the flow, is called "drag." The air drag on the tail of an ordinary diamond-shaped kite is partly responsible for keeping it heading into the wind. A box kite will rise higher both because it is lighter and because there is less drag on its surfaces. The force of drag is due to friction between adjacent air layers of different speeds around the airfoil. Anything that promotes turbulence in the air layers increases drag. At a speed of 200 miles per hour an airplane's wings with protruding rivet heads and lap joints show almost 50 per cent more drag than when the wings are perfectly smooth.

An impressive array of devices, ranging from mile-long towing basins to yard-long shock tubes, has been devised for investigating the forces of fluid flow. Most of them are beyond an amateur's resources.

But the Hele-Shaw apparatus is not.

Sir George Stokes first proved that when a thin layer of viscous fluid such as water is made to flow between a pair of parallel plates, the streamlines approximate those of a theoretical nonviscous liquid. Ludwig Prandtl subsequently pointed out that air behaves as a nonviscous fluid outside the boundary layer. H. J. S. Hele-Shaw constructed an apparatus based on Stokes's observations and made useful measurements concerning the flow around ship hulls. Although the proofs presented by Stokes apply to flow between two parallel plates, Hele-Shaw found that good results can be obtained by letting water flow in a thin sheet over one plate, leaving the top surface of the water free. The device is useful for investigating the performance of airfoils, because the air flow over a long narrow wing is essentially two-dimensional except near the tips.

In the Hele-Shaw apparatus a thin sheet of water flows very

slowly over the surface of a glass plate around a cross-section model of an airfoil, a set of sails or a ship's hull [*see Fig. 199*]. The streamlines are made visible by means of a dye, such as potassium permanganate. They can easily be photographed for close study, and the flow lines will yield quantitative results concerning the pressure distribution over the model.

It is obvious that when an obstruction reduces the area through which a given amount of fluid flows, the velocity of the flow must increase. Where the streamlines flow around the model, they will be crowded into a narrower area. By measuring the distances between streamlines (marked by filaments of dye) at various points along the flow channel, we can get an idea of the relative velocities and pressure distributions at these points.

The construction of the Hele-Shaw apparatus is not difficult. The plate over which the water flows can be a piece of plate glass about

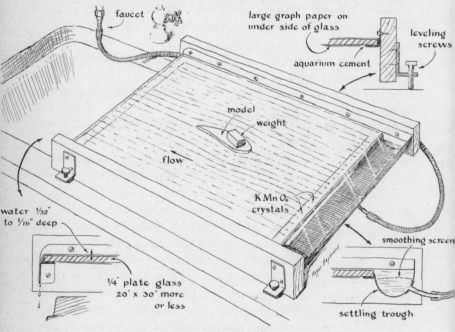

199
The Hele-Shaw apparatus with a model in place

30 inches long and 20 inches wide. To enclose the sides of the channel a metal angle along each side, sealed to the glass with aquarium cement, will serve. The plate is leveled by means of leveling screws in the frame which supports it. A film of water is fed onto the plate from a settling trough fitted with a smoothing screen.

When the plate has been set up and leveled, water is made to flow very slowly over the surface in a film of uniform thickness. The plate should first be thoroughly washed with soap and rinsed with strong ammonia water so that its whole surface will be wetted to make the film uniform. A small squeegee or an automobile windshield wiper will help in the cleaning job.

The model to be placed in the stream can be made from a sheet of balsa wood a quarter of an inch thick. If the model is to represent a sail, it will need to be thinned to a section one sixteenth of an inch thick. After cutting the model, sand its lower surface as flat as possible and waterproof it with two coats of dope. The model can be held in place on the plate either with cement or by a weight on it. If you put a large sheet of graph paper beneath the glass plate, it will be easier to make measurements of the distances between streamlines.

When the film of water has assumed a uniform flow, place a crystal of dye directly upstream from the model, so that the filament of color will flow around it. At what is called the "stagnation" point, just in front of the model, the streamline splits in two, one half flowing around each side of the obstruction. The two halves of the filament come together again at the trailing edge and re-form a single filament. The split streamline defines the boundary layer of flow around the model.

Now if you place other crystals of dye at uniform intervals (say every quarter inch) in a row along the starting edge of the plate, they will generate filaments which will flow in parallel lines downstream until they come to the region where the model diverts the flow. There the parallel filaments will curve and be pushed closer together or farther apart, depending upon the shape of the model.

Now a couple of simple formulas enable us to calculate the comparative velocity of flow and the pressure at various points around the model. These quantities can be computed simply from the distance between the filaments, or streamlines, at those points. Where the stream is flowing freely and uniformly, before it reaches the model, the average velocity between one streamline and the next, multiplied by a certain constant, is equal to the reciprocal of the distance between the streamline: *e.g.*, 1/¼ when the distance is ¼ of an inch. The general formula is VC = 1/D, with C standing for the constant and D for the distance between streamlines. At a point upstream from the model the distance between streamlines may be expressed by "*a*" [*see Fig. 200*]. The equation then reads VC = 1/a. At a point A on the model, where the distance between the surface of the model and the first streamline is *b*, the equation is V_AC = 1/b. Now we can eliminate the C by division and get the ratio V_AV = a/b. In other words, the ratio of the original distance between filaments to the distance between filaments at a given point on the model is a measure of the change of velocity of flow at the

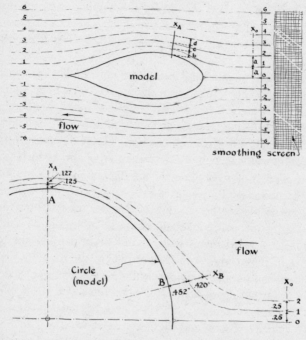

200
Streamlines around an airfoil (*above*) and a cylinder (*below*)

model. When the distance between filaments narrows, the flow speeds up in proportion to the reduction of the distance.

Similarly we can calculate the change in pressure at a given point on the model by another formula. The difference between the pressure in the free stream and that at a point on the model is equal to $k[(V_A/V)^2-1]$, the letter k standing for a constant.

Let us illustrate the method with a specific problem. The model is a circular obstruction [*see lower diagram, Fig. 200*]. At the starting line of the flow the streamlines are a quarter of an inch apart. At point B on the leading side of the circle the distance has widened so that the first streamline is .482 of an inch from the surface of the model. Thus $V_B/V = .25/.482$, or .518. This means that the velocity of flow between the model and the first streamline at point B is .518 of the original velocity. The change of pressure there is $k(.518^2-1)$, or $-.732k$. The minus sign corresponds to the fact that the pressure is inward.

At point A on the model the distance to the first streamline narrows to an eighth of an inch, and $V_A/V = .25/.125$, or 2, meaning that the velocity of flow is double that in the free stream. The pressure here falls by 3k.

By plotting the pressure distribution at various points over the surface of a model, you can compute the lift that will be exerted on a given shape at a given angle to the direction of the stream flow.

Another and quite different project which may interest you is the study of the flight dynamics of flexible model aircraft. Small wooden gliders are adaptable to this study.

When an airplane flies through a gust of wind, it may nose up and down slightly with an oscillation of a certain frequency. The airplane's fuselage, being elastic, also bends at a characteristic frequency. When the two modes of vibration chance to coincide, the airplane begins to gallop through the air, bending and pitching in an oscillation of growing amplitude.

The phenomenon can easily be demonstrated with a model glider. To make the usual stiff model sufficiently flexible, you can introduce springs consisting of piano wire into the structure of the frame. With a little ingenuity you may also discover how to produce wing flutter in the craft by inserting elastic hinges at appropriate places

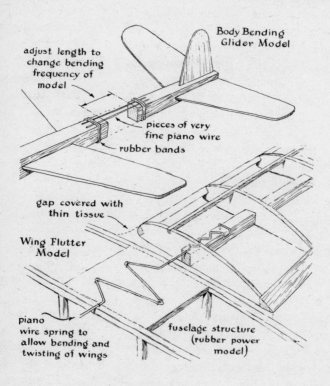

adjust length to
change bending
frequency of
model

Body Bending
Glider Model

pieces of very
fine piano wire

rubber bands

gap covered with
thin tissue

Wing Flutter
Model

piano
wire spring to
allow bending and
twisting of wings

fuselage structure
(rubber power
model)

201
Flexible airplane models for demonstrating oscillation effects

in the wings [*see Fig. 201*]. To demonstrate the classic flutter effects the wing should be allowed to bend upward and twist about its center at the same time.

As airplanes have gone to higher speeds and lighter structure, the problems of flutter and aeroelasticity have become very important to the aircraft industry.

6

BATHTUB AERODYNAMICS

With slight modifications that anyone can make, minia-
ture plastic airplanes will behave in water much as big
planes do in air

Thousands of airplane crashes take place in the
U. S. every pleasant weekend without getting into the newspapers.
Nobody gets hurt in these accidents. But they do cost the fliers a
pretty penny — a total somewhere in five figures. The perilous sport
to which these statistics refer of course is the building and flying of
model airplanes.

In the U. S. there are now some 100,000 enthusiasts who build
and fly miniature aircraft. The group includes commercial airline
pilots as well as cub scouts. Needless to say, these hobbyists wish
they could find some way to test their designs scientifically and inexpensively beforehand to cut down the high accident rate when
they submit their craft to the hazard of flight.

Discussing the techniques of aerodynamic research, a famous airplane designer once said: "If we could only see the splash, our
troubles would end!" George Davis, an aeronautical engineer of
Teaneck, N. J., recently made a related comment: "If someone hit
on the secret of keeping models within arm's reach during test
flights, I would pay him a million dollars for exclusive rights to the
idea!"

David Raspet, a 13-year-old amateur, thought he had the answer.
His method? Fly the models in a water model of the air! By using
water he compresses the scale: miles per hour become inches per
second, and the geometry of the flying field shrinks to the proportions of the family bathtub. It may be argued that data derived from
hydrodynamics do not necessarily hold for aerodynamics. Within
limits the argument has substance. Still, our knowledge of the laws
of streamline flow obeyed by aircraft is based in part on the study

of hydraulics. Lessons learned in the bathtub actually can be applied to the design of a model plane.

> *At 13, David Raspet "flew" model airplanes in water, assisted by his father, the late August Raspet, of the Aerophysics Department, Mississippi State College. They wrote this report on their project.*

DURING A RELUCTANT SESSION in the bathtub one wintry Saturday evening the senior author of this account (the son) happened to find a small plastic airplane model beside the tub. It seemed more interesting than the brush and soap, and he occupied himself with certain experiments. While attempting to sail the plane under water, he noticed that it stalled from a normal glide. To improve its balance he trimmed the model with a few tacks stuck with soap into the nose. The result was a surprisingly good slow-speed glide.

Interestingly enough, this kind of underwater experiment provides a good study of slow-speed motions of airplanes. After many such fascinating experiments, the senior author and his father (the junior author) decided to write this report and thereby communicate the pleasure to their fellow enthusiasts of aviation.

The nice thing about the technique that will be described is the ease with which it may be carried out. The very elegantly molded plastic models, usually only something to look at, can actually be made to fly without a motor — under water. These flights are reasonably similar to real flights in the air in that they show stalls, spins, pitching on the nose and whip stalls. All this can be observed in slow motion without expensive high-speed motion picture photography. Measurements of glide angle and flying speed can easily be made. In addition it is possible to study the nature of the boundary layer (the thin layer of air that surrounds the surface of the whole plane) and of the wing-tip vortex, and to investigate the influence of stall on the tip vortex and the nature of wing-root interference. In other words, here is an entertaining and instructive technique which requires only a simple plastic model and a bathtub. If you don't have a bathtub, go to your local swimming pool or to a pond and conduct your underwater aerodynamics there.

You can buy a cheap plastic model for 10 cents at most dime stores. We have used the Spitfire and P-40 of this type. The wing span of the models is four inches. Next in size and price come such models as Olin's Howard Pete or Mooney Mite, which have a span of 6½ inches and sell for 25 cents. In the more realistic class are the F-51 made by Hawk, a model of 9½-inch span, and the Grumman F9F and the 10-inch F-90, both made by Aurora. All of these models cost less than a dollar.

For those fortunate enough to have war-surplus recognition models, we suggest the Gotha 242 glider as an ideal performer. It has a 13¼-inch span and is a little big for the average bathtub, but it would be a fine size for a swimming pool. These recognition models sold for several dollars. In the field of exact-scale plastic models the Allyn models are excellent. Their prices run from $1.79 to $2.79.

The 10-cent models require only a little weight added to the nose to achieve stable flight. We used one or two small tacks stuck into soft soap molded into the open bottom of the nose to get balance on these models.

Most of the more expensive plastic jobs have hollow fuselages which must be filled with water. You must make sure that there are no air bubbles inside the model for bubbles will move back and forth as the model pitches, thereby changing the center of gravity and affecting the stability as badly as shifting ballast will in a large airplane. Quite a few test pilots have met with accidents due to shifting ballast.

When the model is completely free of bubbles, it can be "flown" in the tub and its trim can be checked. Usually a little lead or a nail is needed in the nose or spinner to get longitudinal balance. The model will behave exactly as models in the air except that the flight will be very slow. If the model pitches its nose up and stalls, more weight is needed in the nose. When correct balance is obtained, a smooth, straight flight results.

On jet-type models the jet intakes need not be closed, for when the model is filled with water the water merely flows through the jets at slow speed.

On the recognition models it may be necessary to drill two holes (at the top and bottom of the fuselage) to be sure of filling the fuselage with water. You can make tests at different wing loadings: for a low wing loading fill the fuselage with wax; for a heavier loading, with a heavy liquid.

When a model which is slightly tail-heavy is launched in a normal glide, it will pull up to a stall. If the model is perfectly symmetrical, it will recover by nosing down in a normal manner, but if it is slightly asymmetrical, it will fall off into a slow-motion spin. This is really a fascinating maneuver to observe.

A research-minded modeler may well find that he wants to go beyond experiments with planes of conventional construction. We suggest that you cut off the horizontal tail and then try to trim the model for stable flight. On swept-back models such as the F-90 it is quite easy to achieve stable flight without the horizontal tail.

The function of a vertical tail can easily be seen when a model with and without the vertical tail is flown in a tub. Without the vertical tail stable flight is impossible: if you stall the model it cannot recover, and it spins to the bottom.

When a model properly trimmed for straight flight is launched in a sideslip, the model usually recovers in a very short distance. But if it is slightly tail-heavy, it will emerge from the slip in a spiral dive.

These are only a few of the stability tests that can be made. You can test the model's response to gusts of wind by agitating the water with your hand just as it flies by. You can even reproduce a rising thermal by letting the tub faucet run; a column of water moves up around the falling stream. When a model hits this gust of water it will react exactly as it would in the air. Just as a sailplane, bird or model soars on an atmospheric thermal, a small model will gain a few inches of altitude as it flies into the tub "thermal."

One of the really nice features of underwater testing of models is that the water ordinarily is quiet and free of turbulence. For this reason glides made underwater are truly a measure of the performance of the model. The method of making measurements is quite simple. Make two marks about 36 inches apart on the bottom of the tub, either with a wax pencil or some adhesive tape. Then release the model from a point in the water above the first mark so that it glides to the bottom at the second mark. The glide ratio is easy to calculate: it is 36 divided by the altitude in inches at which the model is released. Quite consistent results can be obtained if you take a little care to launch at the correct glide and with the model's normal flight speed. Enterprising modelers may wish to time the flight speed with a stop watch. From this speed and the wing loading, engineers are able to compute the lift coefficient. Using the lift coefficient and the glide ratio, it is possible to compute the drag coefficient.

You can even hold flight competitions in the bathtub. The authors had such a competition, using 10-cent models of a P-40 and a Spitfire. The object was to see who could get the better glide angle out of his model by cleaning it up. The hollow fuselages were filled with wax, the props filed off, the spinners smoothed with sandpaper, the landing gear removed, all sharp corners rounded and rough edges filed down. The canopy was filled flush with wax and the under camber of the wing also filled with wax (modeling clay may be used instead). When all this was done, the glide ratio was improved from two to one to three to one — a 50 per cent gain. The Spitfire won the competition with a glide ratio of 3¼ to 1.

The same process of drag reduction can be applied to the larger plastic models. Propeller-driven models should have the propeller blades removed and the spinner filed smooth. All joints should be smooth and the leading edges nicely rounded. Embossed insignia should be filed off or sanded smooth.

Another really fascinating and instructive experiment is to make the flow of water around the model visible. In a wind tunnel this is done by injecting smoke into the tunnel. In the bathtub you merely attach a small crystal of potassium permanganate to the model with soft soap. As the model flies, the permanganate dissolves, leaving a clearly visible trail of purple. If you place the crystal of permanganate on the very end of the wing tip you will see the trail curl up into the tip vortex [see the top of illustration, Fig. 202]. If you launch the model so that it will stall, you will note the first indication of loss of lift in the weakening of the tip vortex. When the model recovers from the stall, the tip vortex again rotates strongly. The lift is directly proportional to the strength of the tip vortex.

443

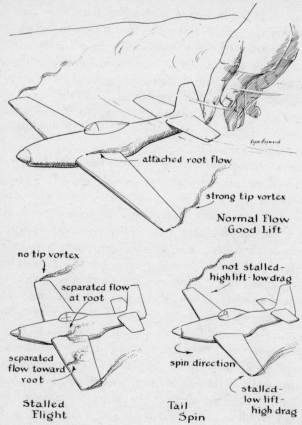

attached root flow

strong tip vortex

**Normal Flow
Good Lift**

no tip vortex

separated flow
at root

not stalled-
high lift-low drag

separated
flow toward
root

spin direction

**Stalled
Flight**

**Tail
Spin**

stalled-
low lift-
high drag

202

Aerodynamics of model airplane demonstrated by underwater "flight"

Place a crystal of permanganate in the wing root on the top side at the leading edge. Now fly it under water, preferably with the water a little warm in order to get a more dense purple color in the flow line. You will notice that as the model approaches a stall the flow line separates from the surface of the model [*lower left, Fig. 202*]. The lift in a region which has a separated flow is very much weaker than when the flow is attached. On large models in wind tunnels or in full-scale flight tests, the regions of separated flow are commonly indicated by tufts of wool attached in the right places.

You can see what happens when a plane approaches a stall by placing a crystal in the middle of the wing on the upper side. In the stall the flow there is inward toward the fuselage. This shows that the pressures on a stalled wing are lower on the root than toward the tip.

You can also observe the effect of surface disturbances on the flow around a wing. If you place a wire on the upper surface of the wing, lying spanwise near the 25 per cent point of the chord, you will see an early separation. If you put the wire on only one wing, you will force the model into a spin, for the wing with the wire will lose lift earlier than the other. The wire acts as a lift spoiler. A wire placed ahead of the wing will make the flow over the wing turbulent. The flow line will spread like a diffuse jet. But you will notice that the flow does not separate as early as it does on a plain wing. A turbulent boundary layer does not separate as soon as a laminar one does.

In these days of high technology even in modeling, one must know something about the regime in which his flight tests are taking place. One thing you want to know is the Reynolds number, which is a measure of the boundary-layer flow around the plane at a given speed. At a Reynolds number of about 60,000 (in the air) most model airplanes perform poorly because of the increase in drag. If your model flies slightly below this number, you can improve its performance by adding a wire or by roughening the leading edge to increase turbulence.

In the air the Reynolds number is the speed in miles per hour times the chord in feet times 10,000. In water the Reynolds number is found by multiplying the speed in miles per hour by the chord in feet by 150,000; that is, the number is 15 times higher in water than in air. But of course the models fly much more slowly under water than in the air.

You can easily compute the Mach number of their underwater flight. The Mach number is simply the ratio of the speed of the flight to the speed of sound in the medium. In water the speed of sound is 5,000 feet per second. Thus when your model flies at one foot per second (*e.g.*, the Grumann F9F), the Mach number is 1/5000. You do not have to worry about the sound barrier or shock effects!

Although motorless flight is fascinating enough, you will want before long to try some propulsion on your water model. You can easily equip the plastic P-51 with a suitable motor: Install a small thrust bearing on the spinner, drill the prop spinner for a prop hook of piano wire, thread a double strand of ⅛-inch rubber through the fuselage and hook it to the rear with a wire clip. Now wind up your motor and release the model — preferably from the bottom of a swimming pool. You will get a nice flight, in some cases even reaching the "ceiling" (pool surface) from a depth of six feet. Don't be surprised if the model pops to the surface, but if by any chance the model should take off in the air, let us know!

For jet propulsion of a jet model, place a few pieces of dry ice inside the jet, seal the jet intakes with scotch tape, fill the fuselage with water and then launch the model. The carbon dioxide gas evaporated from the dry ice emerges under pressure from the jet exhaust and thus gives propulsion.

The authors wish you many pleasant and interesting evenings with bathtub aerodynamics. Archimedes long ago made a famous discovery in a bathtub. You may not make any great discoveries, but you will learn some aerodynamic fundamentals and find a lot of entertainment — which has proved challenging enough to interest a number of scientists, professional and amateur. Perhaps you will even invent some new variations on these fascinating experiments.

7

AMATEUR ROCKETRY

The men who send today's rockets deep into outer space gained their initial experience a generation ago as amateurs. Then, as now, they looked forward to setting foot on the moon. Today thousands of laymen experiment with rockets. Elbert G. Barrett and John H. Granger of the Reaction Missile Research Society give detailed instructions for building and launching two research rockets.

IF, DURING A WEEKEND DRIVE in the country, you should happen to see a thin trail of white smoke shoot 100 feet into the air, you may well find a group of scientific amateurs near the bottom of it. They will be equally proficient in handling explosive chemicals, differential equations, and machine tools. In short, they are amateur rocket experimenters. Occasionally they dream of setting foot on the moon, and people who live nearby wish they would — or at least that they would move away! Sometimes the roar of their rocket motors can be heard night and day. But if amateur rocket experimenters are short on local popularity, they are long on enthusiasm and persistence. They have been at it for at least 30 years, and have given rise to nearly all the leading professional rocket workers.

Rocketry is not an avocation for the lone amateur; it requires more in the way of resources than he can usually provide. Rocket experimenters pool their talents and their cash. That they can do so successfully is indicated by the substantial number of amateur rocket groups scattered across the U. S.

Scare headlines to the contrary, these groups are not composed of irresponsible, unqualified, thrill-seeking children bent on self-destruction. It is true, of course, that accidents have occurred. We live in a dangerous age. But a serious injury has yet to be reported when the methods advocated by the following account have been practiced.

The modern hobby of rocketry was initiated in Germany in 1927, with the formation of a group which included Willy Ley, Max Valier and Johannes Winkler. By 1931 the German amateurs had built a liquid-fuel rocket that could rise to a height of about a mile. Wernher von Braun, Hermann Oberth and many others joined the group; at one time it had nearly 1,000 members. When the Nazis came to power, the society was disbanded and its equipment and experimental results were seized.

Another pioneer group was the American Interplanetary Society, formed in 1930 by seven men in New York City. The early years of the group were fraught with difficulty, chiefly because of the lack of a permanent proving ground. Upon the completion of a test firing on borrowed ground, the group would load its gear into cars and light out for home, often just ahead of the police. But the Society persisted. Finally, through the use of static test stands, as distinguished from flight tests, a rocket engine that performed reliably and consistently was developed by James H. Wyld. He and three other members ultimately succeeded in raising enough money to form what has since become a well-known manufacturing enterprise: Reaction Motors, Inc. Some of their engines have chalked up impressive firsts: they have powered the *Bell X-1,* first plane to pass the sonic barrier, and the Martin Viking rocket, long the holder of the altitude record for single-stage rockets of 158 miles. In 1933 the American Interplanetary Society changed its name to the American Rocket Society; since 1940 the group has not engaged in experimental work because its members are widely scattered and many of them have become professionals.

A third pioneer group is the British Interplanetary Society. The day when man will achieve space flight has doubtless been substantially retarded because the law in England forbids laymen to experiment with rockets. The British Society's gifted members have, however, continuously published a fine journal devoted to space flight and allied subjects.

The outbreak of World War II interrupted the work of all rocket societies. Then, in 1943, George James of Glendale, Calif., founded the Southern California Rocket Society, later renamed the Reaction Research Society. At about the same time the Chicago Rocket Society was organized. These turned out to be vigorous groups, and interest in rocketry has been growing ever since. The Reaction Research Society staged a number of successful mail flights by rocket in an effort to emphasize the peaceful use of the art. The lack of adequate space for testing prevented the Chicago group from undertaking comparable experiments. Nonetheless an impressive number of ideas and much useful data have come out of its program of theoretical work.

Representative groups formed since 1943 include the Pacific Rocket Society, the Philadelphia Astronautical Society, the M.I.T. Rocket Research Society, the Intermountain Rocket Society, the Boise Rocket Research Society, the Society for the Advancement of Space Travel and the Reaction Missile Research Society, Inc. All are affiliated with the American Astronautical Federation, formed as a national organization to collect and distribute information and to promote space flight.

Amateur rocketry has a variety of attractions beyond the spectacular but short-lived flight of the rocket. The design and construction of the missile, its launching apparatus and instrumentation pose many intriguing problems. The rocket must be aerodynamically stable both before and after burnout; this problem of stability can be attacked in many ways and invites endless designs and tests. The design of small motors and special propellants can challenge a sophisticated knowledge of mathematics, physics and chemistry. Because of space limitations the instrumentation of small rockets calls for great ingenuity; it should appeal to radio amateurs, particularly those interested in miniaturization. Similarly, amateur photographers always find a ready-made welcome in rocket societies because pictures are needed of take-offs, flight paths, instrumentation records and the apparatus before and after firing. Being a member of a team that coordinates so many fields of interest in carrying a program through to the climax of firing a rocket with instrumentation gives one a feeling of pride in accomplishment with few parallels.

Members of amateur rocket societies have no illusions that true space flight will be achieved through their efforts. They have neither the funds nor access to the necessary materials. But they can acquire first-hand information concerning the nature of the problems now awaiting solution. By exchanging information and undertaking certain types of experiments beginners can learn the basic facts of rocket flight.

Barrett and Granger's instructions

A RELATIVELY elementary project undertaken by our Reaction Missile Research Society illustrates the sort of experimental work appropriate for beginners and points up some of the tribulations which the amateur rocketeer learns to take in stride and enjoy. Our project was conceived by Walter La Fleur, who was then doing graduate work in mathematics at the New Mexico College of Agriculture and Mechanical Arts. The purpose of the project was to record information on the trajectory of a rocket by means of a light source carried in the missile. Incidentally, amateurs enjoy naming their rockets. La Fleur's was to carry a flashing light, so the idea of calling it *Firefly* was proposed. It turned out that another group had used the same name, so we dubbed ours *Photuris,* a classical word for firefly. Our "A" series was a low-cost program, each missile setting us back about $9. Series "B" involved electronic instrumentation and each rocket cost $50. In order to record the flight information under the best photographic conditions, all firings were made on moonless nights.

The *Photuris* A basically consisted of a thin-walled steel tube of 1¼ inches inside diameter to which a 2-inch aluminum tube was attached by means of a reduction fitting. The steel section carried the fuel and was fitted with a convergent-divergent nozzle and fins, as shown in Figure 203. The aluminum tube housed the rocket's instruments and was closed at the top by a wooden nose-cone. A compartment at the top of the instrument section was charged with fusee powder, which burns with a brilliant red light. The powder was ignited electrically by passing a heavy current through a fine Nichrome wire buried in it. The lower compartment of the instru-

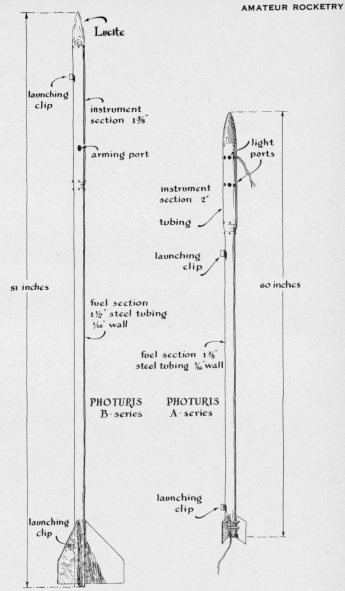

Lucite

launching
clip

instrument
section 1⅝"

arming port

81 inches

fuel section
1½" steel tubing
1/16" wall

PHOTURIS
B-series

launching
clip

light
ports

instrument
section 2"

tubing

launching
clip

60 inches

fuel section 1⅜"
steel tubing 1/16" wall

PHOTURIS
A-series

launching
clip

203
Solid-fuel rockets equipped with optical and electronic instrumentation

451

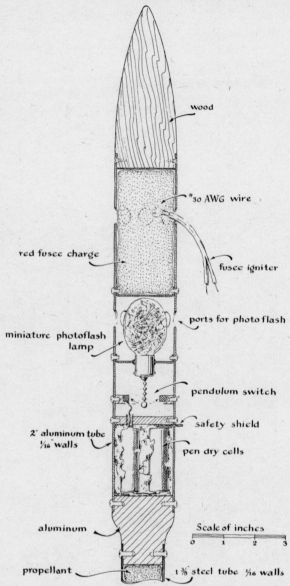

wood

#30 AWG wire

red fusee charge

fusee igniter

ports for photo flash

miniature photoflash
lamp

pendulum switch

safety shield

2" aluminum tube
1/16" walls

pen dry cells

aluminum

Scale of inches

0   1   2   3

propellant

1 3/8" steel tube 1/16" walls

204
Instrumentation section of the Photuris-A rocket

ment section was fitted with a miniature photoflash lamp, a pendulum switch and a battery supply. The principle of the switch was being tested as a possible means of releasing a parachute in future missiles. The switch was designed to close when the missile turned over at the top of its trajectory. A record made by the photoflash bulb would prove or disprove the merit of the idea.

Both the "A" and "B" rockets employed zinc dust mixed with powdered sulfur as a propellant. First we thoroughly stirred a mixture of 85 per cent zinc to 15 per cent sulfur (by weight). Then we used one of two methods of loading the propellant. In the first method we poured the powder into the nozzle of the steel tube in small amounts, lightly tamping each added amount by jouncing the rocket. In the second method, which is more effective but less convenient, the powder is packaged in small cardboard cylinders, the ends of which are closed with tissue paper. These cartridges, each of which contains the same weight of powder, are loaded into the combustion chamber end to end. The second method has the advantage that every rocket loaded in this way has nearly the same thrust. It has the disadvantage that the nozzle must be removed during loading. In both methods of loading the powder is set off by an electrical ignition unit embedded in the last batch of powder to be added.

Both "A" and "B" rockets were lauched from a tower made of angle sections and strap iron. Clips attached near the top and bot-

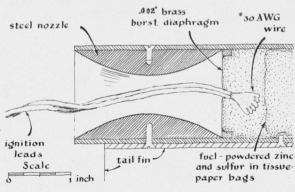

205
Details of rocket nozzle

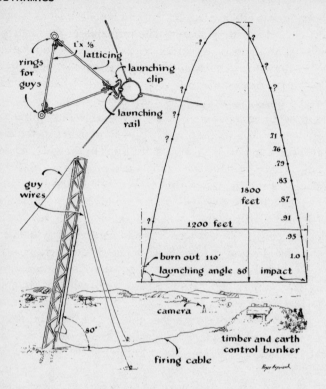

rings for guys

1' x ⅛ latticing

launching clip

launching rail

guy wires

burn out 110'

launching angle 80°

1200 feet

1800 feet

.71
.76
.79
.83
.87
.91
.95
1.0

impact

camera

80°

timber and earth control bunker

firing cable

206
Launching tower and trajectory of the Photuris-B rocket

tom of the missile ride on a launching rail welded to a corner of the tower. The rockets were fired by remote control from an observation bunker located 50 yards from the tower. The bunker [*Fig. 206*] was constructed of heavy timbers and covered by several feet of earth; observation slits were cut in the wall facing the tower. All firings were conducted in a rural mountain area. None of the missiles functioned perfectly in every respect; some were downright failures. This is the usual situation in amateur rocketry.

In the case of *Photuris 1-A* the motor did not function properly. At "fire" the fuel ignited and burned for about 10 seconds. The rocket left the launcher slowly, climbed about 30 feet, nosed over and struck the ground with the motor still burning. Subsequent inspection disclosed that two hot spots had developed in the combustion chamber, and that about a pound of propellant had failed to burn. Reasons advanced for the malfunctioning included the suggestions (1) that the fuel had not been packed properly, (2) that during transportation to the test area the propellant had moved away from the walls of the chamber, causing erratic burning, (3) that the constituents of the propellant had not been mixed in proper proportion and (4) that the burst diaphragm had not been strong enough. The burst diaphragm temporarily closes the combustion chamber so that pressure can build up within it. The diaphragm thus establishes the rate at which the propellant burns. If the diaphragm bursts too soon, the burning rate will be slow at the outset and the rocket will not rise from the launcher promptly. Because the tail fins of the rocket will not stabilize it effectively at low speed, the rocket will thus be aerodynamically unstable during the early part of its flight. The next morning we ran two static tests which proved that the burst diaphragm had in fact been at fault. A thin diaphragm employed in the first static test resulted in a performance identical with that of the previous night: slow burning and a remainder of unburned fuel. A heavier diaphragm used in the second static test resulted in perfect burning. Experimenters should start with a brass diaphragm made of so-called "shim stock" about .002 of an inch thick.

Photuris 1-A not only had motor trouble; its instrumentation section also behaved badly. The signal flare did not ignite properly, the lower end of the wooden nose-cone burned away (although supposedly protected by a layer of asbestos insulation) and the ports provided for flare exhaust appeared to be too small. The pendulum switch apparently worked. Two observers reported seeing a flash as the missile turned over at the top of its trajectory.

Following our tests *Photuris 2-A* was fitted with a stronger burst diaphragm. A low-current relay system was installed to improve the ignition of the signal flare. The flare section was provided with larger exhaust ports, and both the top and bottom of the flare compartment were fireproofed with a thick layer of plaster of Paris.

The time required for these changes, other activities of the Society and unfavorable weather delayed the next test for about two months. Finally the big night came and we threw the switch. The motor refused to fire. Investigation revealed that the propellant in contact with the ignition filament had fused into hard pellets. The combustion chamber was emptied, repacked and fitted with a new ignition element. At the second firing the burst diaphragm ruptured and released a short tongue of flame. The missile did not move from the launcher. Suddenly the wall of the combustion chamber near the exhaust nozzle became red hot and the red area moved slowly toward the nose of the rocket. Subsequent chemical analysis of residue within the combustion chamber disclosed an excess of zinc in the propellant. We changed the fuel mixture to 75 per cent zinc and 25 per cent sulfur (by weight).

Photuris 3-A was fired successfully one week later. The instrumentation was the same as that in previous tests. We did not, however, attain our objectives. The flare went out during acceleration, doubtless because its powder had not been properly mixed. The flash bulb failed to operate when the rocket turned over; a subsequent check showed that its supposedly "new" batteries were dead. As a final contribution to our dismay the rocket shed its fins after three quarters of a second at an altitude of about 75 feet! The total burning time was about one second. The main body of the missile landed 300 feet short and north of the predicted impact area a quarter of a mile away. The divergent section of the exhaust nozzle was badly eroded.

Despite these failures the group felt it had acquired enough experience with zinc-sulfur propellant to risk the construction of a larger missile with more elaborate instrumentation. Accordingly we began to work on the first of the *Photuris B* missiles. The propulsion section was made of steel tubing 1/16 inch thick, 57 inches long, and with an inside diameter of 1⅜ inches. It was equipped with three parallelogram-shaped fins with a 60-degree angle of sweepback. The rocket weighed 8.75 pounds empty and 15.4 pounds fueled, a mass ratio (empty weight to fueled weight) of 1:1.8. The fuel mixture was 75 per cent zinc dust and 25 per cent sulfur. The exhaust nozzle was a 30 degree convergent-divergent double cone of steel.

The instrumentation consisted of a high-brilliancy xenon strobe lamp, a power supply and an associated electronic timing-circuit designed to trigger the lamp at a rate of five flashes per second. Photographs of the flashes, which were bright enough to record on film from a distance of three quarters of a mile, were meant to chart not only the flight path but also to enable us to compute the missile's velocity, its total flight time, its acceleration at any point on its trajectory and so on.

Providing a direct-current source of 300 volts and .008 ampere for the lamp in the small space available turned out to be a major headache. Because batteries of the desired voltage and current rating were not available, we decided to use flashlight batteries and step up their voltage by a vibrator power-supply of the type used in automobile radios. A series of tests were first run to ascertain if the flashlight batteries could deliver enough power to drive the lamp and associated circuitry for the estimated flight time. A large number of three-minute, high-current tests were run on four brands of flashlight batteries available in local stores. We learned in these tests that although the small batteries used in pen-sized flashlights have about a 20th the volume of the largest flashlight batteries (size D), they deliver half as much energy. Another interesting fact came out of the tests: Inferior cells always show a characteristic drop in voltage during the first 10 seconds following the application of a heavy load. As a result we set up a standard testing procedure which required that all cells to be used in the missile deliver voltage within prescribed limits during a 10-second test interval. As finally assembled, the battery consisted of 14 size-912 cells wired in series parallel. It delivered 10.5 volts and occupied 1¾ vertical inches of the instrument section.

The timing circuit consisted of a 2.2-megohm resistor through which a .1-microfarad capacitor was alternately charged by the power supply and discharged by an NE 48 gas-diode tube. Because the supply voltage tended to vary beyond tolerable limits, a voltage-regulating circuit was added. This consisted of two NE 48 gas diodes in series with a 470,000-ohm resistor [see circuit diagram, Fig. 207]. The timing circuit worked well and continued to function even when the voltage dropped below the value at which the strobe lamp would fire.

The problem of triggering the strobe lamp was initially difficult

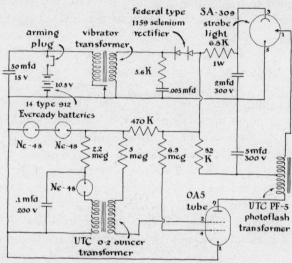

207
Circuit details of Photuris-B electronic instrumentation

but was finally solved by the use of a trigger tube of the OA type which actuated a photoflash trigger transformer. The trigger tube was in turn triggered by the timing circuit through a transformer of the microphone-to-grid type.

A hollowed block of clear plastic was cast and machined to size to serve both as the nose-cone of the missile and the housing of the strobe lamp, an arrangement which afforded an unobstructed view of the lamp. The circuit components were mounted in a cylindrical chassis which fit snugly inside the nose-cone.

The circuit was switched on by inserting a small short-circuiting plug into a port in the instrument section. This connected the plus side of the battery to the body of the missile (which acted as a common ground return for the various circuit components). Bench tests of the circuit proved that the lamp would operate reliably for three minutes.

The gadget behaved normally — that is, it refused to work when installed in the missile. The difficulty stemmed from the vibrator assembly in the power-supply unit. The reeds of the vibrator were mounted on the side of the transformer, which was attached to the body of the missile. Stresses set up when the transformer was screwed into place disturbed the contact adjustment and function of the reeds. It was apparently necessary to readjust the contacts following the assembly of the missile. Because this problem had not been foreseen, the design of the missile had made no provision for access to the reeds. To correct this shortcoming would have meant rebuilding the rocket, so we decided to settle for an approximate adjustment and proceed with the firing.

The rocket was launched at the same angle as that of the *Photuris A* series: 88 degrees with respect to the horizontal. The missile reached an altitude of 1,800 feet and landed squarely at the predicted point of impact 1,200 feet away. The motor functioned perfectly [*see photograph, Fig. 208*].

The trajectory was photographed from a distance of about a third of a mile by a special camera placed at right angles to the flight path. Because the missile passed out of the camera's field, we lost the top part of the trajectory. The missing section of the trajectory was extrapolated from the section that had been photographed, and is shown in Figure 206.

The strobe lamp did not operate during the first part of the flight, doubtless because of the effects of acceleration on the vibrator assembly, but worked well during the last part. The photograph did not come up to expectations; images of the flashes on the plate, although quite definite once located, were tiny and hard to find.

The instrument section was destroyed so completely on impact that not a single component could be salvaged. Thus the group decided, for reasons of economy, to delay additional firings pending the development of an adequate parachute system. In the meantime the idea has been advanced of installing a continuous light source in the missile and providing timing by means of a rotary shutter in front of the camera.

More advanced projects currently under way include the development of a nozzleless, finless missile of high mass ratio, a device to

208
Take-off of Photuris-B

measure range by short-wave radio and a data-recording system. The mass ratios of conventional rockets rarely exceed three to one. The projected missile will have a mass ratio of nine to one. A small cone at the tail of the rocket will replace the conventional fins. Results of wind-tunnel tests on pilot models indicate that a cone should provide better stability than fins.

A number of rocket societies are investigating both solid and liquid propellants. Our group, however, prefers to concentrate on instrumentation. Liquid fuels are challenging and give spectacular performance, but they are costly. Some of them, like hydrogen peroxide and fuming nitric acid, can get out of hand. Amateurs without experience in rocketry will find excitement enough in the zinc-sulfur mix. In contrast with black gunpowder and other solid propellants, the zinc-sulfur fuel can be used with relative safety even in large rockets. Its burning rate is high — on the order of five linear feet per second regardless of tube diameter. Its density is also high, yet danger from explosive pressures is low.

WARNING:

Even so, this fuel mixture, like all rocket propellants, is potentially dangerous and must be used with extreme care. NEVER PERMIT FIRE IN ANY FORM — EVEN A LIGHTED CIGARETTE — IN THE LOADING OR LAUNCHING AREA. During countdown and launch everybody must either take cover behind a solidly constructed bunker or leave the launching and target areas.

Should you feel the urge to take up rocketry as a hobby, you will be well advised either to join with others in your community who are similarly inclined, or become a member of an established group. Few individuals have the time and skills required for the design and construction of a successful, well-instrumented rocket, and none can be in enough places at once to fire and adequately observe the performance of one. Even if he could, he would be cheating himself of the rich satisfactions which come only through participation in a group project.

IX.

OPTICS,
HEAT AND
ELECTRONICS

1

AMATEUR MICROSCOPY

The many diversions and challenges that await the amateur. How to make a powerful microscope from a glass stirring rod. A typical microscope project. Microphotography

ADAM'S LACK OF FORESIGHT when he named the creatures of the earth (Genesis 2:19) certainly made things difficult for his scientific descendants. If he had made a list of the animals as he named them, how easy it would now be, for instance, to label a microscope slide! As it is, the rediscovery and renaming of the world's organisms has been slow, painful work. Aristotle knew about 520 animals and Theophrastus could identify approximately the same number of plants. Today, thanks largely to Linnæus and to the invention of the microscope, our catalogue has grown to about a million species of animals and 336,000 species of plants. But the census of life on the earth is far from complete; no one knows how many thousands of species remain to be discovered and identified.

The quest to complete the roundup of organisms and to name them is one of science's most rewarding challenges. And for amateurs in science it offers a sport second to none. You can engage in it simply by acquiring a microscope, since the biggest remaining field for exploration is in the world of small organisms.

Amateur microscopy has other lures besides the discovery of new organisms. According to Harry Ross of New York City, an amateur who became so fascinated with the microscope that he abandoned a successful career in electrical engineering to deal in optical supplies, "the microscope and its applications cut across the field of nearly every science — any one of which can become a lifetime avocation."

Ross points out that it is possible to make a workable microscope at home in less than an hour, and that one does not need to look far for material to study. "The saliva from your own mouth," he says, "will provide enough varied specimens to keep you going for months on end. The more organisms we find and identify, the more, it seems, await discovery."

In microscopy the problem is not so much finding things to study as developing the will to stick with one thing. We are constantly tempted to embark on a Cook's tour of every avenue opened by the instrument. Suppose, for instance, that someone upsets the salt and its crystals attract your attention. You get to thinking about crystallography. Within arm's reach you can find material enough to keep your microscope busy for hours as you examine the cubic form of salt, the glittering structure of sugar. A particle of dirt from the edge of your shoe provides a comprehensive collection of mineral crystals — quartz, mica, silica, calcite. You chip a flake of ice from the cube in your glass, put it on the slide and look quickly. The needle-like crystals almost instantly become a gleaming sphere. Check the resulting drop of water for purity. Does it hold specks of suspended matter, perhaps dormant organisms? Examine a few grains of pepper. Has its strength been cut, as is sometimes the case, by the addition of starch? If so, you instantly spot the oval-shaped grains. Are you interested in fats? Contrast the appearance of a smear of butter with a bit of grease from whatever meat the cook served. After fat, something else attracts attention. Thus within minutes you may be lured from your initial interest in crystals!

Historians are not sure who invented the microscope. Like many products of technology, the instrument seems to have evolved from many tidbits of accumulated knowledge as intertwined and difficult to trace as the roots of a thousand-year-old redwood tree. The oldest magnifying lens so far discovered was found in the ruins of Ninevah by the British archæologist Sir Austen Layard. It was a crudely polished planoconvex lens of rock crystal which magnified rather well. Pliny the Elder in 100 B.C. mentioned the "burning property of lenses made of glass." But the science of optics in the modern sense did not begin until about the 13th century.

Roger Bacon seems to have been the first to suggest its principles. His writings predicted the telescope and the microscope, and he can probably share credit for the invention of spectacles. Bacon taught the theory of lenses to a friend, Heinrich Goethals, who visited Florence in 1285. From Goethals the information found its way through a Dominican friar, Spina, to one Salvina D'Armato. D'Armato's tomb in the church of St. Maria Maggiore today carries the inscription: "Here lies Salvina D'Armato of the Amati of Florence, Inventor of Spectacles. Lord pardon him his sins. A.D. 1317."

The simple microscope — the single lens — must have been used as soon as spectacles were invented, or perhaps it even preceded them. Who was the first to use it we do not know. But the first to make any important discoveries with it was the Hollander Anton van Leeuwenhoek, born in 1632. After examining some common materials through a simple, single-lens instrument he had made himself, he wrote excitedly to the Royal Society in London about all the seemingly unbelievable objects it revealed.

He discovered "wigglers" and "worms" in water taken from the canal of his native Delft and in scrapings from his teeth. Perhaps his greatest contribution was the observation of red corpuscles in blood. Leeuwenhoek not only identified the red cells but made accurate drawings of their shape and forwarded them, along with measurements of their approximate size, to the Royal Society.

A "Leeuwenhoek" microscope made out of a glass rod

ANYONE WITH A LITTLE TIME to spare can make a duplicate of Leeuwenhoek's microscope and enjoy a thrill now 300 years old. It is easy to make and will give the beginner valuable experience in preparing and handling specimens.

For materials you need only a small length of thin glass rod, a piece of 20-gauge iron or brass one inch by three inches, two machine screws with nuts, a tube of quick-drying cement and a bit of cellophane.

For the glass rod a clear "swizzle stick" of the kind used for

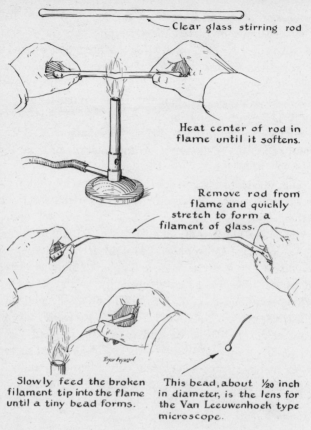

Clear glass stirring rod

Heat center of rod in
flame until it softens.

Remove rod from
flame and quickly
stretch to form a
filament of glass.

Slowly feed the broken
filament tip into the flame
until a tiny bead forms.

This bead, about ¹⁄₂₀ inch
in diameter, is the lens for
the Van Leeuwenhoek type
microscope.

209
How to make the glass-bead lens of a Leeuwenhoek microscope

stirring drinks will do. First you hold the center of the rod in the
flame of a Bunsen burner or a burner of the kitchen stove. The
rod is introduced into the flame gradually to avoid the breaking
stresses set up by abrupt heating. The center of the rod will
quickly reach red heat and become plastic.

Withdraw the rod from the fire quickly and stretch it. The
plastic center will pull into a hairlike filament about two feet
long. After the rod has cooled, break off a convenient length, say

six inches, from the middle section of the filament. Then slowly bring one end of this thread into contact with the flame. The tip will reach incandescence almost at once, and a tiny bead will form. Keep on feeding the filament into the flame until the bead grows to a diameter of approximately one sixteenth of an inch [see Fig. 209].

The lens of your microscope is now finished. This little bead, if it has been made carefully, will yield a magnification of approximately 160 diameters. (The power of such a lens is roughly equal to the number 10 divided by the diameter of the bead in fractions of an inch.) The quality of the lenses made by this primitive method is far from uniform; hence several should be made and the best selected.

A bit of the glass filament may be left attached to the bead and used for mounting the lens to its base. Leeuwenhoek mounted his lens in a sandwich of two brass plates with a hole for the lens. But I find it more convenient to drill a hole in a single plate and fasten the glass piece to the plate by its stem, with the bead over the hole. The hole should be slightly smaller than the bead, so no light will leak past the lens and thus dilute the contrast of the image. The glass is fastened to the plate with quick-drying cement.

The focal length of this tiny lens is of course very short. This means that the stage on which a specimen is mounted must be close to the lens, sometimes nearly touching it. For focusing his microscope and moving the specimen into its field Leeuwenhoek used a set of interacting screws, manipulating a metal point as the stage [see Fig. 210]. In my version of his instrument I substituted a bit of cellophane for the point and fastened it to the adjustment mechanism with cement. Specimens are cemented to the cellophane.

Unfortunately Leeuwenhoek's microscope lacks the viewing comfort of modern instruments. To see the enlarged image you must bring the lens very close to your eye. Roger Hayward has drawn a larger model which employs a conventional slide as the stage, a mirror for controlling the light and a more convenient focusing adjustment. This arrangement adds to the instru-

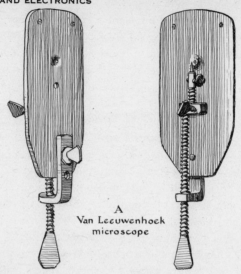

A
Van Leeuwenhoek
microscope

210
A Leeuwenhoek microscope

ment's convenience but does not eliminate the necessity of bring-ing the eye close to the lens [*see Fig. 211*].

Considering its primitive design, Leeuwenhoek's microscope reveals an astonishing amount of detail. Leeuwenhoek is sup-posed to have worked successfully with smaller beads, which gave higher magnification, but he quickly learned to value resolu-tion over magnifying power and to work with the lowest power possible. A big fuzzy image has no advantage over a small fuzzy one.

Leeuwenhoek handed down at least one other fundamental lesson — the importance of preparing objects carefully for micro-scopic examination. As the 18th-century mathematician Robert Smith wrote in his *Compleat System of Optiks,* "Nor ought we to forget a piece of skill in which he [Leeuwenhoek] very particu-larly excelled which was that of preparing his objects in the best manner to be viewed by the microscope; and of this I am per-suaded anyone will be satisfied who shall apply himself to the examination of some of the same objects as do remain before

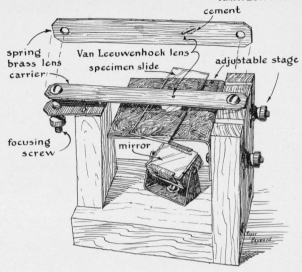

211
Leeuwenhoek's microscope adapted for modern slides

these glasses. At least I have myself found so much difficulty in this particular, as to observe a very sensible difference between the appearances of the same object, when applied by myself and when prepared by Mr. Leeuwenhoek, though viewed with glasses of the very same goodness."

Since Smith's day generations of slide makers have developed techniques for the preparation of specimens which are almost as fascinating as the operation of the microscope itself. Some relatively huge specimens, such as the dry root of a hair or a dried flea from a dog, require no more preparation than being attached to a slide with a dab of Canada Balsam or some other slide cement and covered with a thin glass. Minute objects such as red blood corpuscles can be viewed with reasonable satisfaction if they are merely smeared on a slide and protected with a cover glass. But others which are thick and opaque, or transparent, or contain water in their structure, require special treatment.

If the interior of a specimen is to be studied, either its top must be cut away or, if it is translucent, it must be lighted from below. Some specimens must be cut into extremely thin slices. There are slicing machines called microtomes which can cut frozen tissue or tissue embedded in wax into sections almost as thin as a single wavelength of light. In addition to solving the lighting problem, thin sectioning simplifies the image, for the microscope magnifies in all dimensions. You do not need an elaborate cutting machine. A safety razor blade will do for many kinds of specimens.

When an organism is completely transparent, it may have to be dyed or embedded in a light-refracting substance. The staining process is an art in itself, because staining always produces a chemical change in the organism. Some stains affect one part of the cell and not another. By using different chemicals you may dye the nucleus one color and the surrounding cytoplasm of the cell another color.

Many bacteria can be distinguished from one another only by the way they take a stain; this is the basis, for example, of the classification of "gram positive" and "gram negative" bacteria.

The preparation of slides for the microscope has developed its own special literature, with whole volumes devoted to such subjects as techniques of desiccation; cleaning; bleaching to remove pigments which obscure the view; methods of floating objects in liquid cells; the selection of cover glasses with optical properties matching those of the instrument; the polishing and etching of metal surfaces to reveal crystal structure — processes almost as numerous and varied as the objects that go under the instrument's objective lens. Like all other scientific avocations, the prepartion of specimens for the microscope invites the amateur to plunge in as deep and stay down as long as he likes.

After building and using a Leeuwenhoek instrument you may very well decide to go further. A conventional compound microscope will save a lot of squinting. It should be an instrument of good quality, capable of showing fine detail. Its power should match the ability of the beginner. High-power objectives invariably prove disappointing to beginners, because their successful use calls for skill.

A typical miscroscope project, ideal for beginners. It is described by Joseph F. Burke, a member of the New York Microscopical Society. Its subject: the minute plants called diatoms

DIATOMS GROW wherever there is light and moisture. This means that they can be collected in nearly every part of the world. They can be found on the beach, among the plankton at sea, on the mud bottom of ditches, on the stems of water plants, in the scum on stagnant pools, even in desert sands, for their silica shell remains as a fossil after they have died. A formation of living diatoms usually has a brownish tint, caused by a pigment which obscures the plant's cholorphyll. Deposits of fossilized diatoms, laid down on the bottom of ancient seas, are mined as diatomaceous earth, valued for its mild abrasive action. Many silver polishes are rich in fossilized diatoms — a convenient source the beginner should not overlook.

For live collecting the amateur should equip himself with a few wide-mouthed jars, a spoon and an ordinary coffee or tea strainer of 40 or 50 mesh. As specimens are taken in the field, the collector records the date, time and location along with other data that will assist in the subsequent identification of the material.

To prepare diatoms for mounting, the amateur will need: technical sulfuric acid, technical hydrochloric acid, hydrogen peroxide, powdered potassium bichromate, distilled water, strainers of 40 to 50 mesh, two Pyrex beakers holding 30 cubic centimeters, a Pyrex custard dish, a conical flask of 125 c.c., an assortment of pint and quart jars, glass stirring rods, half-ounce storage bottles with caps, and clean pipettes.

The collected material should be transferred to a large jar. Filtered water is added and the material is thoroughly beaten with a glass stirring rod to dislodge the diatoms from foreign objects. The organisms should then be strained and permitted to settle; allow an hour per vertical inch of solution. Living diatoms should be processed in a darkish place, because their metabolic processes release tiny bubbles of oxygen which cause the organisms to rise to the surface. Having settled, the diatoms will form a brown layer on the bottom of the jar. The water should then be poured off without losing the specimens. This washing process should be carried out three or four times, particularly when the diatoms are salt-water species. Distilled water should be used wherever the local water supply carries a heavy content of lime.

Part of the material is then transferred with the pipette to the Pyrex beaker to form a layer about an eighth of an inch thick. The beaker should be placed in the custard cup. The excess water is removed with the pipette, leaving the specimens moist but not wet. Next powdered potassium bichromate, approximately one third the bulk of the diatoms, is stirred into the mixture. Then comes an operation which must be performed outdoors or in a window with a strong outward draft, as the reaction produces poisonous fumes. Slowly add approximately five c.c. of technical sulfuric acid to the diatom-bichromate mixture. A violent reaction will follow. Beat down the resulting bubbles with a stirring rod. Should the heat of the reaction break the beaker, the custard cup will prevent the loss of the specimens.

The material is then transferred to a quart jar and washed with distilled water five times, allowing about an hour of settling time for each vertical inch of water. The diatoms are now ready for separation according to size. This is accomplished by the familiar process of elutriation. The material is transferred to the first of a series of uniform glass containers. Water is added, and after a certain interval, say half an hour, the water is poured off carefully into the second jar of the series. Again at the end of the predetermined interval, the second jar is poured off into the third. This is repeated until the diatoms are separated into the desired sizes. The diatoms are now ready for individual storage bottles, to which a few drops of hydrogen peroxide may be added as a preservative.

For mounting diatoms, select a cover glass of 12-millimeter diameter and a thickness of .11 to .20 mm. The slide itself should have a thickness of 1 mm. (A supply of cover glasses, slides and mounting cement or "medium" is available at most optical shops.)

Clean the slide and cover glass thoroughly with soap and water. Select a storage bottle containing diatoms and shake it until they are in suspension. With the pipette place a drop of distilled water in the center of the cover glass. If the glass has been cleaned properly, the water will spread to the edge but not overflow. Next add a drop from the storage bottle which holds the diatoms in suspension. The diatoms will spread evenly and settle on the glass. Allow the water to evaporate overnight. Protect the glass from dust.

You will next need a small hot plate and a bottle of medium. I prefer Hyrax for mounting diatoms. Warm the slide on the hot plate and place a drop of Hyrax on the slide's center. Then remove the slide from the hot plate and place it on a wooden support to prevent rapid cooling. With sharp pointed forceps, pick up the cover glass, invert it so that the diatom side is down and press it gently onto the medium until the fluid reaches the edge of the cover glass. The slide is then returned to the hot plate and the Hyrax is brought to a state of vigorous bubbling. As the bubbling slows down, remove the slide to the wooden support. Experience will teach the proper moment of transfer.

After cooling, the slide is placed under the objective and examined. If the washing and mounting have been performed carefully, the amateur is in for a thrill he will long remember. Diatoms have been called "nature's jewels," and man has yet to fashion anything more exquisite. Although more than 10,000 species of diatoms have been recorded thus far, the list continues to grow.

Burke recommends that the beginner equip himself with a reference book on the subject. He will find it essential for classification. He can then experience the satisfaction of labeling his first slide.

Microphotography

WHILE BRUSHING UP on the theory and practice of microscopy you can have a lot of fun, and incidentally pick up much useful optical lore, by purchasing a low-power objective lens

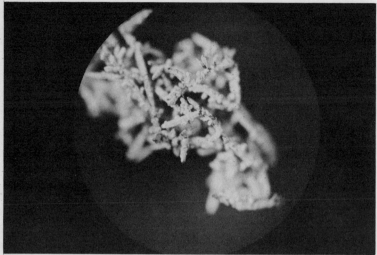

212
Photomicrograph of copper crystals. Magnification: ×100

213
Natrolite crystals (hydrous sodium aluminum silicate) as seen under a magnification of 80 diameters

and making a camera for microphotography. Many beginning amateur microscopists tend to shy away from microphotography, doubtless because this aspect of scientific work, like so many others, has come to be associated in the public mind with the fearfully difficult — something to be undertaken only by learned men garbed in white cloaks and surrounded by a forest of chemical glassware. Nothing could be further from the truth. At magnifications up to 200 diameters, microphotography is about as difficult as snapping pictures with a box camera.

Recently I built a camera, borrowed some micro-mineral specimens from a friend, shot a set of pictures and made the prints shown in Figures 212, 213 and 214 in the course of a single afternoon — and on the very first try! The objective lens was merely fitted into a crude wooden lens-board. A 4- by 5-inch plate holder and ground glass from a 1905 vintage camera served as the back. These were closed in with cardboard sides as shown

214
Gold nugget, magnification 50 diameters

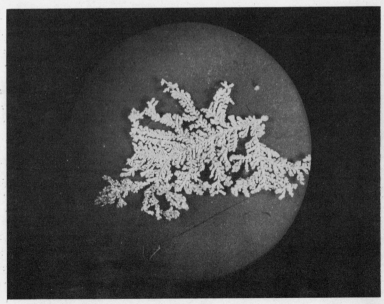

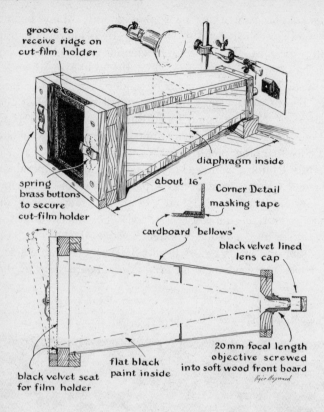

groove to
receive ridge on
cut-film holder

diaphragm inside

about 16"

Corner Detail
masking tape

spring
brass buttons
to secure
cut-film holder

cardboard "bellows"

black velvet lined
lens cap

20 mm focal length
objective screwed
into soft wood front board

flat black
paint inside

black velvet seat
for film holder

215

Details of homemade camera for making photomicrographs. With 20-
millimeter objective magnification equals about ×20

in Figure 215. The shutter was simply a velvet-lined cap, also
homemade. Focusing was achieved by moving the specimen toward the lens until a sharp image appeared on the ground glass.
The exposure was determined experimentally. With a floodlamp
(100 watt) located 14 inches from the specimen, an exposure of
45 seconds was required, on the average, with Plus X film. The
exposure time could have been shortened by using more light.
But the longer interval gives you better control — more time for
uncovering and covering the lens.

2

HOMEMADE ELECTROSTATIC GENERATORS

Some historic and modern machines for the generation of static electricity. The world's first electrostatic machine. Basic principles. Detailed instructions for building a 100,000-volt Van de Graaff generator for less than $5. Some suggested experiments. A note of warning concerning million-volt Van de Graaff machines

NEAR THE CLOSE of the 17th century Otto von Guericke, the amateur physicist of Magdeburg, invented the world's first electrical machine — an electrostatic generator. He wrote down these instructions for building one:

"Secure one of the glass globes which are called phials, about the size of a youngster's head; fill it with sulfur, ground in a mortar and melted by the application of a flame. After it refreezes, break the phial, take out the sulfur globe and keep it in a dry place, not a moist one. Perforate it with a hole so that it can spin upon an iron axle. Thus the globe is prepared.

"To demonstrate the power developed by this globe, place it with its axis on two supports in the machine — a hand's breadth above the baseboard — and spread under it various sorts of fragments such as bits of leaves, gold dust, silver filings, snips of paper, hairs, shavings, etc. Apply a dry hand to the globe so that it is stroked or grazed two or three times or more. Now it attracts the fragments and, as it turns on its axis, carries them around with it.

"When a feather is in contact with the globe, and afterwards in the air, it puffs itself out and displays a sort of vivacity . . . and if someone places a lighted candle on the table and brings the feather to within a hand's breadth of the flame, the feather regularly darts back suddenly to the globe and, as it were, seeks sanctuary there."

After describing numerous other experiments, in some of which the globe produced light and sound, von Guericke concluded: "Now many other mysterious facts which are displayed by this globe I shall pass by without mention. Nature often presents in very commonplace things marvelous wonders which are not discerned except by those who through insight and innate curiosity consult the oracle of experimentation."

Ten generations of experimenters have consulted the oracle since von Guericke's day. So fathomless are the mysteries of his sulfur ball that its "marvelous wonders" continue to charm and sometimes baffle experimenters, whether they twiddle the controls of a Van de Graaff accelerator or merely stroke the hairs on a cat's back. But electrostatics has remained chiefly a curiosity. Most people are acquainted with it only in the form of the crackling shock you get when you touch a metal doorknob after walking across a thick carpet in winter. Those who go in for amateur radio grumble that "static is something you cuss, not study!"

Static electricity has never become economically important, probably because nature has been more generous in supplying effective conducting substances and magnetic materials than she has in providing good insulators. Our electrical technology is based on electromagnetic devices; our electrical power is generated by magnets and moving conductors. Electrostatic machines have been harnessed for only a few specialties, such as generating high voltage for laboratory experiments, producing high-energy X-rays, and sterilizing drugs in medicine.

Some engineers believe that electrostatics has big technological possibilities. One of them is John G. Trump, professor of electrical engineering at the Massachusetts Institute of Technology. He points out that the forces resulting from the presence of electric charge are the most direct and powerful in nature. He and his colleagues at M.I.T. are conducting certain investigations which may produce an electrostatic power generator that one day will compete with the electromagnetic generator.

Professor Trump illustrates how the power-generating capacity of electrostatic machines may be stepped up by asking you to consider two metallic plates, 100 square inches in area, facing each other and separated by an insulator. If a potential difference amounting to 300 volts per centimeter is applied between them, the plates will be attracted to each other with a force of one 2,000th of a pound. Increase the electric field to 30,000 volts per centimeter and the attraction becomes half a pound. Now immerse the plates in a high vacuum — a good insulator, though one difficult to maintain — and increase the field to three million volts per centimeter. The force of attraction jumps to 5,700 pounds! "Force of this order," says Trump, "has more than passing interest for power engineers."

Trump and his associates are working on the problem of developing a practicable system of vacuum insulation which would make possible a field intensity of millions of volts per centimeter in a large machine. If they succeed, an electrostatic power generator will become a reality. The working parts of such a machine would look like an oversized variable capacitor with intermeshing leaves. Only the rotor would move. The machine could be constructed of light metal. A generator of this type, about the size of a hall bedroom and weighing only a few hundred pounds, could deliver 7,500 kilowatts of power. Its efficiency would be impressively higher than that of an electromagnetic generator.

Some pioneering experiments in electrostatics

THE HISTORY OF ELECTROSTATICS began with the discovery of Thales of Miletus that rubbed amber attracted other objects. Through the centuries experimenters like von Guericke explored the "marvelous wonders" of static electricity with a succession of ingenious machines which you may enjoy building.

One of the most important historically was Alessandro Volta's *elettroforo perpetuo*, now known as the electrophorus [*see Fig. 216*]. Volta wrote to Joseph Priestley of the Royal Society on June 10th, 1775: "I hereby draw your attention to a body that,

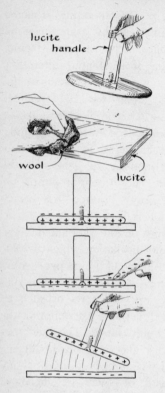

lucite
handle

wool

lucite

216
A modern version of Alessandro Volta's
electrophorus

after being electrified by a single brief rubbing, not only does not lose its electricity but retains obstinately the indications of its active force in spite of being touched repeatedly any number of times."

The electrophorus consists of two working parts: (1) a rectangular block of insulating material such as Lucite or, preferably, polyethylene, and (2) a metal disk fitted with an insulating handle. When the Lucite is wiped with a woolen cloth, electrons are removed from the cloth and deposited on the lucite — in much the same way that a dirty rag smears a clean sheet of glass. Early experimenters (who used sealing wax, hard rubber or other resinous substances instead of plastic) said that the insulator thus stroked had been "electrified by friction." They failed to observe that the cloth took on an equal and opposite charge.

When electrons rub off from the wool to the Lucite (because, as it happens, some of the atoms in wool hold electrons less tightly than those in lucite do), the atoms that have lost electrons become positively charged ions. Accordingly the surface of the wool is peppered with tiny areas of positive charge while the Lucite has similar areas of negative charge. The charges are static — bound at the places where they are deposited — because in an insulator electrons cannot move freely about in the substance.

Ever since Benjamin Franklin named the "positive" and "negative" ends of the electric field, the field has been thought of as originating at the positive end. He might have prevented confusion if he had assigned the names the other way around, because we now have to say that the current "flows" from positive to negative, although actually the electrons flow from negative to positive!

Be that as it may, the field between a pair of opposite charges is often pictured as a pattern of curving lines that radiate into space from a region deficient in electrons and converge on one where they are in excess. The field can be thought of as a bundle of stretched rubber strands, illustrating that there is a force of attraction between the charges of opposite sign.

Von Guericke demonstrated that an electrified insulator would communicate its charge to one that is electrically neutral. We now know that it accomplishes this by sharing its excess electrons with the uncharged body at points where the two touch. Von Guericke also showed that a body can become temporarily electrified merely by entering a field of charge, without touching the charged surface. He wrote: "If a linen thread supported from above is brought near the globe and you try to touch it with your finger or any other body, the thread moves away and it is difficult to bring the finger near the thread."

This was an important discovery. It demonstrated that charging by induction does not exhaust the charge on the body initially electrified, and also that charges of like sign repel each other.

Charging by contact involves the sharing of electrons between two bodies, and each contact diminishes the number remaining on the charging objects. Charging by induction, in contrast, makes no demand on the free electrons but only on the field set up by them. The field causes the electrons of the uncharged substance to veer slightly from their normal orbits. This displacement sets up an "induced" charge in the previously uncharged substance. When the inductively charged body is removed from the exciting field, everything returns to normal and the induced charge disappears.

Induction can give a conductor a permanent charge, in the sense that the charge will remain on the conductor until it leaks off or is otherwise dissipated. All modern electrostatic generators are designed on the principle of inductive charging. And the charging process involves the transformation of mechanical energy into electrical energy. The principle is nicely demonstrated by the electrophorus.

When the metal disk is placed over the charged Lucite, the Lucite's negative field opposes that of the electrons near the lower surface of the disk. These electrons move away to the upper surface of the disk. Consequently the lower surface becomes positively charged and the upper surface negatively charged. If, while the top of the metal is thus charged, you touch the top with your finger, the excess electrons will flow into your body — where, electrically, things are not so crowded. Now if you take your finger away and then lift the metal disk by the insulating handle, a net positive charge is trapped in the disk.

This method of charging removes no electrons from the Lucite, nor does it draw on the Lucite's energy. Yet the metal disk is now energized with positive electricity (many protons have been denuded of their neutralizing electrons and hence their positive fields extend out into surrounding space). The disk will now attract other bodies just as the charged lucite does. Moreover, a spark will jump between the charged disk and your finger— which you can easily observe in a darkened room. The energy expended in the spark came from your muscles when

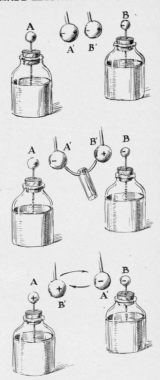

217
A primitive induction electrostatic
generator

you lifted the metal from the Lucite. The spark was created by
electrons colliding with molecules of air in their headlong rush
from your body back into the disk.

A more effective arrangement for generating electrostatic
energy by induction uses two Leyden jars [see Fig. 217]. One
jar, A, has a tiny positive charge. When its positively charged
terminal is brought close to a brass ball, A′, electrons in the
ball are attracted to the side of the ball nearest the terminal.
Similarly the terminal on another jar, B, with a small negative
charge, drives away electrons in the ball B′, making the near
surface positive.

If the two balls are now connected by a metallic rod [middle
drawing], electrons in B′ (repelled by the field of B and at-

tracted by that of A) will flow to A'. Removal of the rod traps the charges — just as the removal of your finger trapped those in the disk of the electrophorus. Now suppose we change the positions of the balls, moving A' toward B and B' toward A [*bottom drawing*].

To do this we must expend work, because A', for instance, is repelled by B and attracted by A. This work is transformed and stored as potential electrical energy as soon as we touch A' to B and B' to A. The excess electrons in A' flow into B, raising negative charge to that of A', and A similarly acquires an increase of positive charge. The cycle can be repeated indefinitely. In theory the amount of energy stored in the jars (capacitors) can be increased without limit. In practice, the storage is limited by the fact that electrons leak away more and more rapidly as the charge increases.

Various induction machines have been designed for performing just this sequence of operations automatically and with considerable speed. In these machines the "carriers" take the form of thin metallic sheets instead of balls, and the capacitors also are metal sheets, called field plates.

The Varley electrostatic generator

AN EARLY FORM of the machine, patented in 1860 by C. F. Varley of England, is easy to construct [*see Fig. 218*]. It consists of a pair of field plates cemented to a square slab of lucite surmounted by a rotating disk of lucite to which six or more sectors of aluminum foil are cemented. Two brushes (of tinsel) momentarily connect opposite sectors, the carriers, with their respective field plates as each carrier enters the region of its plate.

A similar pair of brushes again make contact with opposing pairs of carriers as they move from the region of the field plates. A pair of "corona" combs — quarter-inch metal rods fitted with steel phonograph needles spaced half an inch apart — graze the carriers at positions intermediate between the two sets of brushes. The machine's electrical output flows from the combs to a pair

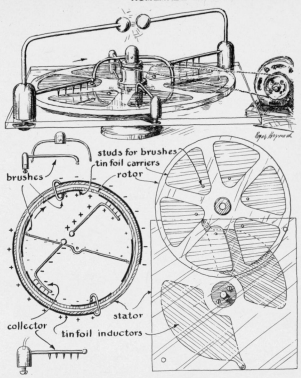

studs for brushes
tin foil carriers
brushes
rotor

collector

stator

tinfoil inductors

218
Varley's induction generator

of spheres an inch or so in diameter which comprise a spark gap.

The lower left diagram illustrates the action. Assume a charge on the field plates [*outer solid segments*]. Electrons flow into the carrier at the left, leaving the right-hand carrier with a positive charge. Work is now expended in moving the carriers "up the potential hill" to the opposite field plates.

Here they make contact with the brushes and part of their newly acquired energy flows into the field plates; electrons enter the field plate [*top of drawing*] from the negatively charged carrier, while the opposite carrier withdraws electrons from the lower plate. The succeeding action of all carriers is similar. After a short period of operation the combs reach ionizing potential, and energy flows from the carriers to the gap, where vigorous sparking occurs.

The machine is not very efficient. This can be demonstrated by observing its operation in a dark room. The rotating carriers appear as a blurred disk of phosphorescence in colors ranging from greenish-blue through violet, while the field plates are outlined sharply in purple. Corona discharge at the combs is brilliant. This display means that electrons are streaming from the thin, sharp edges of the foil and the points of the comb carrying negative charge and into those parts carrying a positive charge. Considered as an electrical "pump," the machine is leaky and thus wastes energy.

The corona effect is explained by the geometry of the machine's conducting parts. Unless distorted by another charge, the electric field radiates into space uniformly in all directions from a point charge. If the charge is enclosed by a conductor, the lines of force always emerge perpendicular to its surface. In the case of a spherical conductor (in effect, an enlarged point) the lines are, therefore, distributed uniformly over the surface. When the sphere is distorted to an egg shape, however, the lines bunch up at the little end and thin out at the big end — because they must emerge everywhere at a right angle to the surface. Crowding at the little end becomes more pronounced as the radius of the "point" is made smaller. This is another way of saying that the intensity of the field, or the potential gradient, increases inversely with respect to the radius of the conductor; in theory it would approach infinity at the point of a perfect needle.

Even in practice, finely made points can concentrate fields of astonishing intensity. The exquisite needles used in field-emission microscopes create field intensities of 750 million volts per inch in the immediate vicinity of the point — although the instrument operates from a power supply of only 5,000 volts! At this field intensity electrons are literally ripped from the metal point and ejected radially into space. Gas, if present in the tube, becomes heavily ionized. The collecting combs of the

Varley machine similarly ionize adjacent air, negative charges being carried by dislodged electrons and positive charges by the ions.

In the early years of this century the Wimshurst generator, similar in basic principle to the Varley but carrying one or more pairs of disks that rotate in opposite directions, was a favored source of power for X-ray machines and other devices requiring relatively small amounts of current at high voltage. The largest machines carried as many as 12 pairs of disks seven feet in diameter and delivered potentials on the order of 200,000 volts.

The Wimshurst and other electrostatic generators of this era could not reach the million-volt range. By 1920 they had been largely replaced by electromagnetic induction coils and transformers as sources of high-voltage power.

The Van de Graaff electrostatic generator

THE MODERN era of electrostatics began in 1929. In that year Robert J. Van de Graaff, a young Rhodes scholar from Oxford University who was working at Princeton as a National Research Fellow, invented the electrostatic belt generator which is now known around the world by his name. He was interested in developing a steady constant-potential voltage with which to accelerate atomic particles to bombard nuclei in order to obtain information about their internal structure.

Today the Van de Graaff accelerator can be found in nearly every large nuclear laboratory in the world; it is the work horse for precision research in this field. The accelerator has attained a particle energy of more than eight million volts, and this figure may soon be more than doubled. In smaller sizes the machine has found a wide variety of applications, particularly as the power source for the high-voltage X-ray treatment of disease.

One of the nicest features of the Van de Graaff generator is its relative simplicity and low cost. Robert W. Cloud of the High Voltage Research Laboratory at M.I.T. has designed a small version as a special construction project for amateurs [see

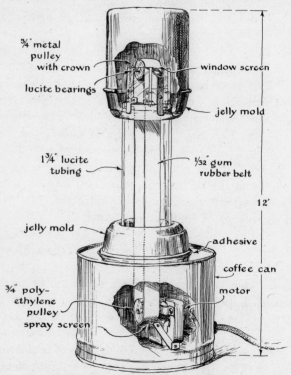

¾" metal
pulley
with crown

lucite bearings

window screen

jelly mold

1¾" lucite
tubing

1/32" gum
rubber belt

12'

jelly mold

adhesive

coffee can

¾" poly-
ethylene
pulley
spray screen

motor

219
A low-power Van de Graaff machine made of old tin cans, jelly molds,
a piece of Lucite tubing and a toy motor. Voltage: 50,000

Fig. 219]. Its action is as simple as its design. A motor developing 3,000 revolutions per minute is housed in a coffee can. It
drives a gum-rubber belt which passes over an insulated pulley
inside the upper terminal. Spray screens, counterparts of the
Varley machine's collecting combs, are situated close to the
surface of the belt at each end of its run, and each connects
with its respective terminal.

As the machine goes into operation, frictional contact removes
electrons from the belt at the driving end and deposits them
on a plastic pulley. Positive charges resulting at the sites on the
belt which have thus lost electrons are then carried by the belt

to a metal pulley at the other end above. Electrons flow from the metal pulley onto the electron-deficient belt. As the machine continues to run, heavy charges build up on both pulleys.

After a few seconds or minutes, depending on the humidity of the air, the field originating at the pulleys reaches ionizing intensity in the vicinity of the spray screens. Electrons are then withdrawn from the upper terminal and sprayed on the belt at the beginning of its downward run. Similiarly electrons en route down the belt come within the region of ionization at the lower spray screen and flow by way of its supporting bracket into the lower terminal.

Through this pumping action the belt continuously exhausts electrons from the upper terminal and discharges them into the earth through the lower one. This leaves the upper terminal with a net positive charge which, because of mutual repulsion of the positive "holes," distributes itself uniformly over the ter-

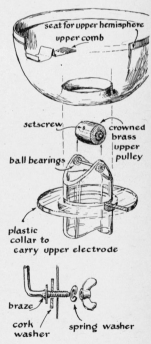

220
Variation in design details of upper terminal assembly for small Van de Graaff generator

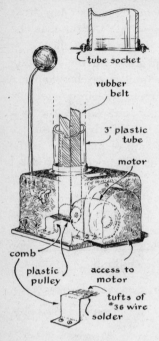

tube socket

rubber
belt

3" plastic
tube

motor

comb

plastic
pulley

access to
motor

tufts of
#36 wire
solder

221
Construction details of lower Van de
Graaff pulley assembly and motor ar-
rangement. Note design of comb unit

minal's outer surface. Accordingly the inner surface carries no
charge. In theory, voltage across the upper and lower terminals
increases without limit.

As in the case of the Varley and the Wimshurst machines,
however, the charge is limited in practice by the quality of the
insulation. At about 100,000 volts charge leaks as corona from the
upper treminal and as conduction current down the insulating
column at a rate equal to the two microamperes which the belt of
this machine is able to carry into the terminal. Although 100,000
volts is an impressive value, the machine creates no shock hazard
because the capacity of the upper terminal to store charge is small.

If a well-rounded object is brought within an inch or so of
the high-voltage terminal, a spark will jump. In this type of
discharge the air is rapidly changed from a good insulator to
a conductor and the spark completely discharges the terminal.
Reduction of the terminal voltage permits the air to regain its

insulating strength, and the terminal is recharged by the belt. If an object with sharp edges is brought near the terminal, it steadily drains charge by corona and decreases the potential. Such a device, with adjustable spacing, is often used in Van de Graaff generators to maintain a constant terminal potential.

A continuous source of high direct-current voltage invites endless experiments. One of the most amusing is the "jumping ball" demonstration. A half dozen small balls made of pith or similar material are given a conducting surface of soot or graphite. They are placed in a cage, which may be made of a strip of transparent plastic rolled into a cylinder and capped with tops from peanut-butter jars. The caps are connected to the terminals of the Van de Graaff. As the machine goes into operation, the electrostatic field from the upper cap attracts the balls. They hop up to it, deliver their load of electrons, fall back and repeat the cycle as long as power is supplied.

Support a sewing needle by an insulator and connect it to the machine's upper terminal. Molecules of ionized air will rush from the point as though they were streaming from a jet under pressure. They easily blow out a match or candle. This electric wind can be made to drive a simple motor. Cut a swastika, with sharply pointed tips, from aluminum foil and indent its center with the pointed end of a pencil. Pivot the indentation on the point of a pin which has been thrust up through a supporting base of cardboard. The swastika will then be free to rotate on the pin point. It will do so vigorously if the pin is connected with the high-voltage terminal of the Van de Graaff. Ionized air streaming from the four points sets up the reactive force of a jet engine.

The power capacity of the Van de Graaff is enough to charge a person to about 50,000 volts. This is 20,000 volts above the ionizing point of air at atmospheric pressure. It is also enough to make the experimenter's hair stand on end. To demonstrate this effect, stand in or on a large glass bowl or a wooden platform supported by four square milk bottles. Touch the high-voltage terminal. After a few seconds your hair will slowly rise. Incidentally, the body adds capacity to the terminal, and so a somewhat larger charge than normal accumulates. When you step down or touch a grounded object, you will experience a slightly painful shock — but it is not dangerous to a person in normal health.

Fluorescent lamps will light up brilliantly where they are touched to the high-voltage terminal. If the room is not too brightly lighted, filament-type lamps also will glow in various colors depending on the kind of gas they contain. You can even manufacture a miniature aurora borealis by boiling water in a thin flask until the air is displaced by steam and then stoppering it immediately. After the steam has condensed, the rarefied air inside will glow greenish and pink when the flask is brought in contact with the Van de Graaff.

Those who own equipment for pumping good vacuums may want to try their hand at assembling and operating a linear accelerator and related apparatus used for nuclear research. Such projects are on a par with amateur-built cyclotrons and, like marriage, are not to be entered upon lightly. They are, nevertheless, well within reach of amateur resources, particularly for groups. [See "A Homemade Atom Smasher," Section VI].

To power such an apparatus you will require a larger version of the Van de Graaff [see Fig. 222]. It differs from the low-power design in a number of important particulars. The spray points for charging the upward run of the belt are supplied by a potential of 5,000 to 10,000 volts from a transformer-rectifier combination. The high-power machines employ metal pulleys at both ends of the belt, the upper one being insulated from the high-voltage terminal.

Charge is sprayed onto the belt as it passes through the corona between the lower points and the grounded driving pulley. A similar set of points, located just inside the upper terminal, removes charge from the upward belt run and conducts it to the upper pulley. After a short period of operation the upper pulley acquires a high charge and current flows to the upper terminal through a current-regulating resistor. This circuit may also include a corona gap near the inner surface of the terminal. A second set of spray points (charging rod), connected directly

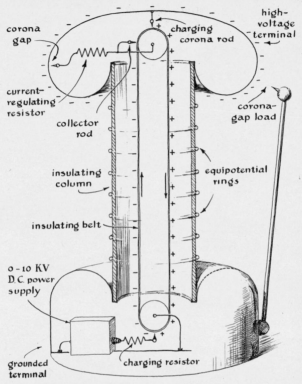

corona gap

charging corona rod

high-voltage terminal

current-regulating resistor

corona-gap load

collector rod

insulating column

equipotential rings

insulating belt

0 - 10 KV D.C. power supply

grounded terminal

charging resistor

222
Semi-schematic representation of high-power Van de Graaff machine

to the high-voltage terminal, is situated at the top of the pulley. The difference in potential between the upper pulley (made "live" by the voltage drop across the current regulating resistor and corona gap) and the high-voltage terminal causes these points to spray a charge of opposite sign onto the downward run of the belt. The value of the current-regulating resistor is chosen so that both sides of the belt work equally. The value of the current-regulating resistor can be computed roughly by Ohm's law. (In small machines it is usually on the order of 40 megohms.) Belts for high-power machines are usually made of rubberized fabric and run at speeds of 4,000 to 6,000 feet per minute.

The capacity of the upper terminal to store charge varies with its size. Its ability to hold charge varies with shape. The ideal terminal would be spherical. Unfortunately this ideal cannot be realized because provision must be made for the entry of the belt. The shape must be such that the intensity of the field at the high-voltage terminal is always less than the value at which spark or corona discharge occurs. Hence the aperture of the terminal must have re-entrant edges and the facing sides of the upper and lower terminals should be identical. Such terminals are commonly made of aluminum spinnings.

Large Van de Graaffs in the million-volt range, intended for scientific and industrial purposes, are now nearly all mounted within a steel tank containing Freon, carbon dioxide or a similar gas at many atmospheres of pressure. The high pressure serves to increase the insulating property of the gas and thus increases both the voltage and current capacity of the machine. Such machines are marketed by the High Voltage Engineering Corporation.

When Van de Graaff machines are designed for potentials above 200,000 volts, the distribution of charge along the insulating column (and even along the belt runs) becomes important. The columns of air-insulated machines using belts more than four inches wide should be fitted with equipotential rings spaced along the insulating column at intervals of about two inches.

WARNING! Anyone undertaking the construction of a high-power Van de Graaff generator should remember that he is building no toy. These potentially lethal machines can reveal "marvelous wonders" beyond von Guericke's most inspired imagining, but, unlike his sulfur ball, they pack the wallop of lightning!

Some tips on Van de Graaff design from F. B. Lee of Kenmore, N. Y.

TWO IMPORTANT PIECES of information for the designer of Van de Graaff machines, are, first, approximately 50 square inches of belt per second passing over the pulleys will produce one microampere of current; second, the maximum potential developed by the machine will be equal to 70,000 times the smallest radius of curvature of the collector in inches.

Thus a perfect sphere 12 inches in diameter will have a theoretical limiting potential of 420,000 volts. Holes made in the sphere to admit the belt assembly alter the pattern of the field and reduce the theoretical maximum. The most effective compromise with the ideal shape for a practical collector is a spheroid slightly flattened at the bottom, with minimum radius of curvature located at a reasonable distance from the insulator to discourage sparking along the insulator surface.

The designer's choice of maximum voltage determines the size of the collector. To realize a large fraction of the theoretical limiting potential, the collector must be at least two or three diameters removed from other metallic parts. The distance should be greater if sharp-edged metal parts are present, and may be somewhat less if all parts are covered by a rounded metal shield of large radius of curvature. The opening which admits the belt to the collector ought not to be much larger than half the diameter of the collector and should be smoothly curved inward, using a generous radius of curvature.

Although a high polish adds to the attractiveness of the collector, it is not essential. Minor surface imperfections, if well rounded, limit the maximum voltage only slightly. Sharp edges or burrs must be ground down. Lint and dust particles will reduce the voltage to 40 per cent of the theoretical maximum if they protrude from the surface as much as 1 per cent of the radius.

Unpolished commercial aluminum spinnings, free of lint and dust, will collect about 85 per cent of the theoretical maximum. A high polish will increase the voltage another 1 per cent. The concentration of charge around the hole through which the belt enters accounts for the remaining 14 per cent, a quantity which varies, of course, with the size of the hole and its distance from other conductors.

The hemispheres from which my collectors have been assembled were procured from a local metal-spinner who, if not too busy, will turn them out for $4.50 each, a reasonable price considering the fact that he pays $2 for the 14-gauge blanks.

I had to furnish the wooden die on which the parts were spun. They would otherwise have cost on the order of $25. Incidentally, I will be glad to supply any number of 12-inch hemispheres at cost plus postage plus 75 cents per pair for handling, boxing and so on. Write to me at 230 Hampton Boulevard, Kenmore 17, N. Y.

Selection of the desired current output determines the size of the belt and the speed at which it must run. Meeting this specification is not so simple as it might seem offhand, because the properties of the materials used for the belt and its driving assembly enforce speed limits on both the belt and the shaft bearings. For maximum current one should in theory use the highest possible belt speed. But there are disadvantages in running belts faster than about 100 feet per second.

Higher speeds aggravate the tendency of belts to fray at the edges and to come apart at the splices. At high speeds, particularly in the case of small pulleys, extreme tension must be maintained; this leads to bearing problems. Lubrication difficulties limit the shaft speed of sleeve bearings to about 5,000 revolutions per minute. The noise level of ball bearings becomes annoying above this speed unless special steps are taken to minimize it. At belt speeds above 100 feet per second appreciable amounts of power are lost through air friction. Finally, part of the charge appears to be "blown" off the belt at excessive speeds — a phenomenon which I do not wish to be called on to explain.

Belts may be made of almost any insulating material: paper, cloth, rubber, plastic and so on. Rubber, because of its poor resistance to ozone, has a limited life, but with used inner tubes costing so little the inducement to improve on it is slight. Rayon, nylon, Dacron and cloth (made into belts with acetone cement) are almost as good. Incidentally, when these materials are substituted for rubber, the position of the corona-collecting combs must be shifted. Cloth belts are more durable than rubber, are quieter and require less driving power, but tend to fray at the edges. This is easily remedied by a coat of lacquer. All things considered, I find that belts of neoprene joined with a diagonal splice are a good compromise.

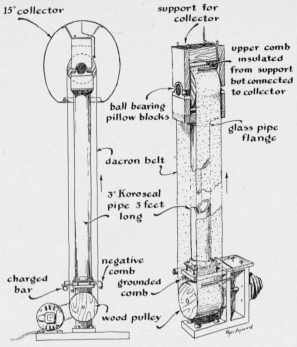

15" collector

support for collector

upper comb insulated from support but connected to collector

ball bearing pillow blocks

glass pipe flange

dacron belt

3" Koroseal pipe 3 feet long

negative comb grounded comb

charged bar

wood pulley

223
Van de Graaff generator with external belt and internal excitation

The upper pulley must be made of a material which is a good electrical conductor, such as wood or Bakelite. Surprised? At such voltages these materials are very good conductors for the small currents involved. Scrap plywood may be glued together to make a highly satisfactory wooden pulley. The lower pulley should also be electrically conducting if a separate 5,000 to 10,000-volt d.c. power supply is used for spraying charge onto the belt.

If the machine is to be self-excited (that is, if the belt is to be energized by friction), the lower pulley should either be coated with or constructed of a material of extremely high resistivity. A 1/32-inch thickness of polyethylene makes a splendid covering for small wooden pulleys. The pulleys should be turned with a slight crown, the edge making a snug fit with the inside of the polyethylene tube. The tube may be made by cutting the ends off a round squeeze bottle. The tube is simply pushed over the wooden core.

The choice of pulley and belt material for self-excited machines determines the polarity of the collector charge. A rubber belt running on a lower pulley of polyethylene or polystyrene will usually pump electrons from the collector and hence charge it positively.

The belts may run on either the inside or the outside of the insulating support. Economy, simplicity and high currents favor running them on the outside. Appearance and neatness of construction require them to be on the inside. The former arrangement permits the use of a small, relatively inexpensive insulator with low current leakage and minimum deterioration due to corona discharge (the source of ozone). It also permits use of the widest belt possible for a given opening in the collector. Problems arising from unequal potentials throughout the insulator are similarly minimized.

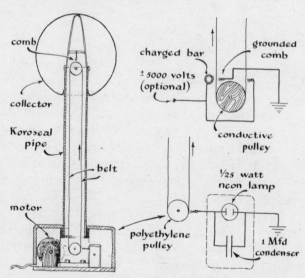

224
Van de Graaff generator with internal belt and external excitation

All hygroscopic or fibrous materials should be avoided in the selection of the insulating column because they invite leakage through the moisture which forms on the surface. The material must also be selected with an eye to its mechanical properties: strength, stiffness and toughness. Finally, it should be ready available at a reasonable price.

Tubing of polyester glass-fiber laminate or polyvinyl chloride meets these requirements and is available in standard pipe sizes. In the three-inch (diameter) size, it costs $2.60 per foot. Polyvinyl chloride is the less hygroscopic of the two and may be flanged or formed to other contours by heating it to its softening point in hot paraffin.

Combs or corona points for applying charge to the belt may be contrived in great variety. Often a common pin or a single phonograph needle can be as effective as the most elaborate comb. A tuft of wire, bound at one end and sheared like a broom at the other, makes a satisfactory comb, as does a small rectangle of wire screening.

Care must be taken to avoid spraying areas of the belt with unwanted charge. This may happen if charges are permitted to mix on the front and back of the belt near the pulleys. The problem is met by mounting the combs on fixtures which provide easy adjustment over a wide range of positions, and by selecting comb sizes which restrict the areas that are sprayed with charge.

3

AN INEXPENSIVE
X-RAY MACHINE

From an old radio tube, some copper wire, and other inexpensive materials — total cost: roughly $20 — you can construct an X-ray machine that will make good pictures through an inch of wood. SAFETY MEASURES THAT YOU MUST OBSERVE. Notes on Röntgen's invention. Highlights of X-ray theory

HARRY SIMONS OF 118 WINDSOR STREET, Kearny, N. J., is a lonely amateur scientist. "For 23 years," he writes, "I have been dabbling in the X-ray portion of the electromagnetic spectrum without once coming across a fellow amateur. Thousands of enthusiasts can be found in the region of radio waves, of light and of gamma rays. But none of them come to play in my back yard. If the prospect of exploring fresh electromagnetic territory sounds interesting to any of these amateurs, I can promise good hunting in the 10^{-8}-centimeter region — and for a total investment of less than $20."

As a lure Simons offers the collection of radiographs reproduced in Figures 225, 226, 227 and 228. He takes special pride in the one which shows screws embedded in an inch-thick block of wood. This shot resulted from his first experiment with X-rays and illustrates what can happen when a fellow with a sharp eye follows a happy hunch.

During a rainy weekend back in 1933 Simons was fiddling with an Oudin coil. This almost-forgotten gadget, a close relative of the Tesla coil, can step up low voltages 1,000 times or more. High voltage generated in this way has an advantage for the amateur experimenter in that it is relatively harmless. In the course of stepping up the voltage the Oudin coil also in-

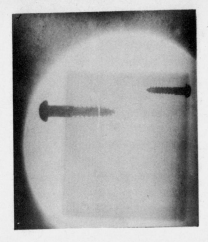

225
Simons's radiograph of two screws imbedded in inch-thick block of wood

226
Radiograph of the plug from an electric flatiron

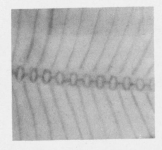

227
Bones of fish revealed by homemade X-ray machine

228
Effectiveness of Simons's X-ray machine in penetrating the steel leaves of a thickness ranging from .002 to .010 of an inch thick

creases the frequency of the current, so that it tends to flow through the skin and away from vital organs such as the heart.

"My original Oudin coil," Simons recalls, "was part of an ultraviolet lamp with which I tested mineral specimens for fluorescence. For no particular reason I decided to replace the evacuated quartz bulb, which produced the ultraviolet rays, with an old radio tube of the 01 type. The glass envelope of these tubes is coated inside with a silvery film of evaporated magnesium — the so-called 'getter' which helps clear the tube of stray gas during the evacuation process and absorbs any that may be liberated by the glass walls or metal parts after the seal-off. I simply held the 01 in my hand and touched its prongs to the high-voltage terminal of the coil.

"Instead of filling with a lavender glow, like the quartz bulb, the inside of the tube remained dark but the glass in contact with the magnesium lighted with a pale greenish fluorescence that reminded me of the glow emitted by old style X-ray tubes of the gas type. Was the radio tube producing X-rays?

"To obtain the answer to this question I put a narrow band of tinfoil around the top of the tube and grounded it — as a substitute for the electrode previously represented by my hand. I then fished a small block of wood, which happened to have two screws in it, from the trash box and placed it on a sheet of photographic film wrapped in black paper. The combination was exposed to the energized tube for 15 seconds at a distance of seven inches. When I had developed the film, I discovered a wonderful radiograph of the screws — plus a lifetime hobby that should appeal to anyone interested in physics."

Why has Simons's hobby failed to catch on? One reason is that commercial X-ray equipment is costly. Even tubes of relatively low power are priced at $100 and up. Many other commercial X-ray parts are also expensive and difficult to procure. The apparatus supplying high voltage to conventional tubes, while no more complex than the power supply of a husky radio transmitter, calls for special rectifying devices, transformers and other components which are not regularly stocked by dealers in electrical supplies.

Moreover, X-rays have earned a bad reputation as playthings. No distinction can be drawn between the danger of exposure to a high-powered X-ray machine and the fallout of an H-bomb. It is a danger that extends not only to the experimenter but to his potential progeny. Human evolution is the result of mutations caused by, among other agents, cosmic rays and the radiations of radioactive elements in the earth's crust. Any radiation added by man alters the rate of mutation, and is rightly a cause of deep concern.

Simons has solved the problem of equipment cost. Protection against exposure to the rays is not difficult to arrange. With these two considerations out of the way, X-rays open a range of experiments equaled by few other phenomena of physics. In addition to providing a source of X-rays for radiographs, a generator of X-rays in combination with accessories enables you to measure the charge of the electron, to study the structure of crystals, to observe the wave-particle duality of matter and radiation, and to probe other microcosmic corners.

Like visible light, X-rays are a form of radiant energy. Their ability to penetrate substances opaque to visible light, however, is neither unique nor particularly unusual. Many substances opaque to light are transparent to other electromagnetic waves. For example, long electrical waves, as well as the shorter ones of radio, pass freely through dry wood, plaster and other substances that do not conduct electricity and are opaque to light. If this were not so, all radio and television receivers would need outdoor antennas.

On the other hand, a thick sheet of flint glass, which transmits radio waves and light with no appreciable loss, stops X-rays. The ability of X-rays to penetrate substances like flesh and bone is merely their most publicized property. However, this property provides a striking case of the immediate application of a scientific discovery. Within weeks of the description of X-rays by Wilhelm Konrad Röntgen in 1895, surgeons heralded them as a tool of the first importance.

They are characterized chiefly by extremely short wavelength — about one ten-thousandth the length of visible light waves.

Like light waves, X-rays can be reflected, refracted, diffracted and polarized. The techniques by which they are manipulated differ from those employed with light, just as light techniques differ from those of radio. The longest X-rays are indistinguishable from ultraviolet rays; the shortest are identical with gamma rays. The distinction between the two is largely a matter of definition. When the emission accompanies the disintegration of a radioactive substance such as radium, it is called gamma radiation. Identical waves generated by electronic means are called X-rays.

All radiant energy, including X-rays, has its origin in a disturbance of electrical charge. Consider a point charge — an electron — surrounded by a symmetrical electromagnetic field and moving through space at constant velocity. What happens to the motion of the field if the central charge is speeded up or slowed down? Experiments indicate that the field reacts much like a mass of jelly. When the central charge is accelerated, the disturbance is communicated radially through the field as a wave motion — the outside parts of the field requiring an appreciable time interval to catch up with the center. Work expended in accelerating the central charge is carried away by the wave as radiant energy, at a velocity which depends on the nature of the "jelly."

In a vacuum the wave attains a maximum velocity of slightly more than 186,000 miles per second. The length of the wave depends upon the abruptness with which the central charge is either disturbed or made to change direction. Violent disturbances require the investment of more work than gentle ones, and result in proportionately shorter and more energetic waves. The waves radiated by electrical power lines, in which a stream of electrons changes direction only 60 times a second, measure about 3,200 miles from crest to crest.

It is possible to subject electrons to much faster oscillations. Military radars, for example, are constructed around magnetron oscillators, small copper chambers that have been called electrical counterparts of the familiar police whistle. The cavities are electrically tuned to frequencies on the order of four billion cycles per second, and streams of electrons forced into the cavities vibrate at this rate. The resulting electromagnetic waves measure some three inches from crest to crest.

As the cavities are made progressively smaller, the pitch goes up and the wavelength goes down in obedience to the principle that the smaller the whistle, the shriller its note. Where, then, can a "whistle" be found that will accelerate charges rapidly or abruptly enough to create electromagnetic waves a mere 25 thousandths of an inch long — the wavelength of visible light? Nature provides such systems in the form of molecules and atoms.

The normal, stable atom emits no radiation unless it is acted upon by an external source of energy. If a fast-moving electron encounters an atom in its normal state, the interloper may collide with one of the planetary electrons in the outer orbital shell of the atom. The impact may cause the electron in the atom to jump to an orbit still more remote from the center of the atom. A sufficiently energetic electromagnetic wave impinging on the atom can accomplish the same end, the requirement being that the frequency of the wave coincide with the period of the outer electron's orbital motion.

In either case the atom gains energy from the encounter and thus becomes unstable. The normal state is soon restored when the electron hops back into its "home" orbit. This represents the shifting of a center of charge, and the excess energy is radiated into space by the accompanying electromagnetic wave. The abruptness of the jump, and hence the length of the wave, depends upon the attraction of the positive nucleus for the planetary electron. When weakly bound electrons occupying an orbit remote from the nucleus make such jumps, the length of the radiated wave measures on the order of 25 thousandths of an inch — the wavelength of light.

This same mechanism accounts for the origin of one kind of X-ray. When a free electron, accelerated to a velocity of some 18,000 miles per second, collides with an electron occupying an inner shell of the atom, both the interloper and the inner-shell electron may carom into space, as shown in the upper diagram of Figure 229. The vacancy thus created is immediately

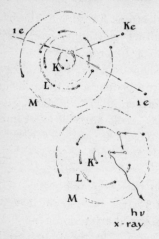

229
Classical representation of X-ray origin in excited atom

filled by an electron from a shell more remote from the nucleus. The attraction of the nucleus for this electron is much greater and the jump accordingly more violent. The resulting wave measures on the order of 250 millionths of an inch — an X-ray.

This initial jump does not end the display. A vacancy has been created in the adjacent orbit by the electron that moved inward. Hence a series of jumps follow as electrons from orbits still more remote from the nucleus move in to fill the succession of gaps [*see lower diagram, Fig. 229*]. In the end the atom must capture a new electron to complete its outermost orbit. In the meantime the atom has emitted a series of waves at progressively lower frequencies, beginning with X-rays and extending through ultraviolet radiation and visible light to heat.

The pattern of forces acting between the nucleus and orbital electrons responsible for the radiation is unique for each kind of atom. Measure the radiation emitted at each frequency and you have an identifying tag for the atom. This is the basis of spectroscopy. The fundamental particles of the atom move in their orbits at rates fixed by these same forces. In effect the atom is "tuned," much as a group of radio receiving sets might be pretuned for a group of broadcasting stations.

Atoms low on the periodic table, such as carbon, hydrogen,

oxygen and nitrogen — the stuff of living matter — are far out of tune with X-rays of extremely high frequency. When such waves impinge on protoplasm, they ignore the barrier and sail right through.

X-rays of the highest frequency, those used for making most radiographs and for the treatment of disease, are liberated when the bombarding electron crashes into the massive nucleus of a target atom. The precise nature of such encounters is not fully understood, but it appears that when the bombarding electron collides with the nucleus head-on, and is stopped dead in its track, the onrushing field may consume the entire mass of the arrested particle and, in effect, transform the electron into an X-ray of very high energy and frequency.

Other electrons strike the nucleus glancing blows, and are thus decelerated. The deceleration is accompanied by the emission of an X-ray of proportionate wavelength and energy. Hence when a stream of bombarding electrons plays on a target composed of massive atoms, the emission of radiant energy includes: (1) X-rays liberated by the acceleration of planetary electrons, characteristic of the kind of atoms comprising the target, and (2) X-rays that span a continuous band of frequencies from the ultraviolet range to those of almost infinitesimal wavelength.

It was this continuous or "white" X-radiation, arising from the bombardment of silicon nuclei in the glass of a Crookes tube, that led Röntgen to his discovery. While studying the green fluorescence that appears at one stage in the evacuation of the energized tube, Röntgen observed a bright fluorescence among some nearby crystals of platinocyanide. The crystals continued to glow even after he covered the energized tube with black paper. He concluded that the tube was emitting a previously unobserved form of radiation.

The Crookes tube consists of a pear-shaped glass bulb that is partially evacuated and fitted with a cathode at the small end and an anode at the large end. When a direct-current potential of about 20,000 volts is connected across the electrodes, positive ions, accelerated by the electric field, bombard the cathode and dislodge electrons from the metal. Most of these are attracted to the anode, but some overshoot the mark. The latter electrons continue to the end of the tube, where they collide with the glass target.

Soon after Röntgen's discovery, the mechanism of white X-ray production was explained by experimental investigation that paved the way for improvements in the tube. By shaping the cathode in the form of a paraboloid, for example, the electron stream could be focused sharply on the metallic target composed of atoms more massive than silicon. X-rays liberated at the spot were more energetic and cast sharper shadows than those from the broad expanse of glass.

Electrostatic machines for the production of accelerating voltages grew in size until some featured a spinning disk of plate glass seven feet across, capable of generating 200,000 volts and currents up to five milliamperes. All the early tubes contained some gas, the atoms of which were needed as a source of electrons. The gas imposed an upper limit on the accelerating voltage.

The limitation was removed in 1913 when W. D. Coolidge of the General Electric Company succeeded in making ductile filaments of tungsten, which he substituted for the cold cathode of the gas tubes. With this independent source of electrons, tubes could be evacuated to the limit of pumping techniques. Accelerating potentials of 300,000 volts and more became practical. Such power levels created another problem; the heating of the anode or target. This problem was first tackled by using tungsten, with its high melting temperature, at both ends of the tube, then by cooling the target with water, and finally by focusing the bombarding electrons in a small spot near the edge of a motor-driven disk made of tungsten.

Although Simons's tube is not in the class with large X-ray tubes of the modern Coolidge type, it performs impressively well. A number of years ago Simons shipped his first machine to George L. Clark at the University of Illinois who, after testing it, reported to the journal *Radiology:* "Simons's apparatus proves that X-rays can be produced for experimental purposes by a unit which can be built for a very small fraction of the cost of an installation of standard commercial equipment. The machine, when in operation, will produce a beam of X-rays easily detected for a distance of several feet in all directions. With 'r' meter measurements we determined the intensity of the rays to be three fourths of a Röntgen unit per minute at a distance of three feet."

The explanation of this copious radiation, compared with that of a Crookes tube, appears to lie in the magnesium coating.

Unfortunately the old 01 and tubes of similar construction are currently in short supply because magnesium is no longer favored as a material to remove gases, except in certain types of mercury-vapor rectifying tubes which are unsuitable for X-ray production. For this reason (plus the fact that he is an inveterate experimenter) Simons now designs his own tubes and has them manufactured by a local glass blower. They cost about $15 each. He rarely makes two alike, for the same reason that amateur telescope makers seldom build two identical instruments. Each design is a new and exciting experience.

One of Simons's latest designs is illustrated in Figure 230. This tube is equipped with a disk-shaped cathode of molybdenum and a magnesium target. It is evacuated to a barometric

230
X-ray tube designed and constructed
by Simons

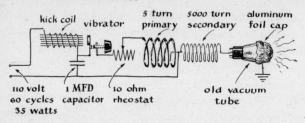

231
Circuit diagram of Simons's X-ray apparatus

pressure of .0001 millimeters of mercury. The over-all length
of the tube is about seven inches. Its emission is substantially
greater than that of the 01 tube. Simons's radiographs, with
the exception of the one showing the screws in a block of wood,
were made with it. Such tubes can be made with a wide variety
of target materials and cathode shapes.

Almost any source of high voltage can be used for energizing
X-ray tubes, including Van de Graaff electrostatic generators
of the type described in this section. Simons prefers to stick
with Oudin coil. It is easily constructed with hand tools. The
job is simplified if you can lay hands on a vibrator of the type
used in the spark coil of a Model-T Ford. As shown by Roger
Hayward's diagram, Figure 231, and the general view in Figure
232, the vibrator consists of a core of soft magnetic iron equipped
with an armature of soft magnetic iron and a set of breaker points.

The core of the vibrator is wound with 3,800 turns of No. 24
magnet wire and connected in series with the breaker points
as shown. When bridged with the one-microfarad capacitor and
connected to the power line, the self-inductance of the coil is
sufficient to charge the capacitor to a potential of several hundred volts when the breaker points are adjusted to open at the
peak of the current cycle. The capacitor discharges through
the five-turn primary winding of the Oudin coil. The primary
is wound with five turns of ¼-inch copper tubing on a 2¼-inch
plastic form three inches in diameter.

The secondary winding consists of 5,000 turns of No. 32 enameled magnet wire wound on a ½-inch rod of clear plastic. Each

layer of wire must be carefully insulated with a layer of varnished cambric that extends well beyond the end of the coil. When the winding is completed, the secondary coil must be thoroughly doped with high-grade insulating varnish. Both ends of the coil are insulated with a tube of varnished cambric.

The assembly is then slipped inside the plastic form on which the primary was wound. The outside end of the secondary is brought out through a small hole in the form and soldered to one end of the primary winding. The inner end of the secondary

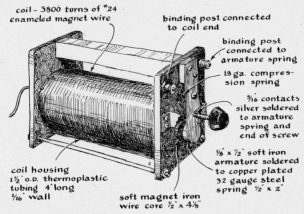

coil - 3800 turns of #24 enameled magnet wire

binding post connected to coil end

binding post connected to armature spring

18 ga. compression spring

3/16 contacts silver soldered to armature spring and end of screw

1/8 x 1/2" soft iron armature soldered to copper plated 32 gauge steel spring 1/2 x 2"

coil housing 1 1/2" o.d. thermoplastic tubing 4' long 1/16" wall

soft magnet iron wire core 1/2" x 4 1/8"

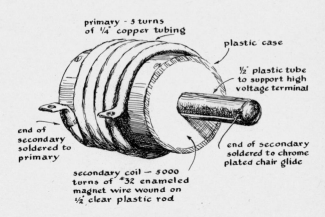

primary - 5 turns of 1/4" copper tubing

plastic case

1/2" plastic tube to support high voltage terminal

end of secondary soldered to primary

end of secondary soldered to chrome plated chair glide

secondary coil — 5000 turns of #32 enameled magnet wire wound on 1/2" clear plastic rod

232
The source of high voltage for Simons's X-ray machine

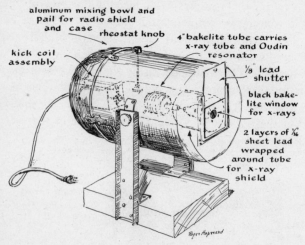

aluminum mixing bowl and
pail for radio shield
and case rheostat knob

4" bakelite tube carries
x-ray tube and Oudin
resonator

kick coil
assembly

⅛" lead
shutter

black bake-
lite window
for x-rays

2 layers of ¹⁄₁₆"
sheet lead
wrapped
around tube
for x-ray
shield

233
X-ray machine built by Harry Simons of Kearny, N. J.

is threaded through a four-inch length of ½-inch plastic tubing
and soldered to the inner face of a chromium-plated chair glide,
which serves as the high-voltage terminal. The ends of the primary form are then closed with disks of ¼-inch plastic and secured in place with screws at the edge. A ½-inch hole in the
center of one disk admits the tube support for the high-voltage
terminal.

The chair glide is lifted temporarily and enough transformer
oil or potting compound poured through the ½-inch tube to fill
the interior. When wired according to the diagram [*Fig. 231*] and
connected to the power line, the coil will produce some 50,000
to 75,000 volts continuously. The power consumption at 110 volts
and 60 cycles is 35 watts.

As shown in Figure 233, all this apparatus must be housed
in a well-grounded metal container. The X-ray tube must be
enclosed in an inner compartment of lead sheet at least ⅛-inch
thick. An opening in the end of the double housings opposite
the tube provides a window for the X-rays.

WARNING! *You must take these precautions*

FIRST, OUDIN COILS are notorious emitters of radio waves that take the form of ragged noise. They can black out radio and television reception for miles around. Federal regulations prohibit the operation of such devices unless they are thoroughly shielded. If any stray radiation can be detected on a nearby radio or TV receiver after the apparatus is assembled as described, it will be necessary to insert a low-pass filter at the point where the power cord enters the housing. The design of such filters is available in standard radio reference texts.

Whenever the machine is in operation, *the experimenter must wear a lead apron and stand well behind the orifice through which the rays are emitted.* Never turn your back to the machine so that you are between it and the apron! It is also advisable to place a few exploratory samples of film around the room while the apparatus is in operation. When developed, these will show the pattern of radiation and protective lead shielding can be installed accordingly. Finally, resist the temptation to make X-ray examinations of the bones in your hands or other body parts. A frozen fish makes a much safer test object.

4

THE "HILSCH" VORTEX TUBE

With nothing more than a few pieces of plumbing and a source of compressed air, you can build a remarkably simple device for attaining moderately low temperatures. It separates high-energy molecules from those of low energy. George O. Smith, an engineer of Rumson, N. J., discusses its theory and construction

THE 19TH-CENTURY BRITISH PHYSICIST James Clerk Maxwell made many deep contributions to physics, and among the most significant was his law of random distribution. Considering the case of a closed box containing a gas, Maxwell started off by saying that the temperature of the gas was due to the motion of the individual gas molecules within the box. But since the box was standing still, it stood to reason that the summation of the velocity and direction of the individual gas molecules must come to zero.

In essence Maxwell's law of random distribution says that for every gas molecule headed east at 20 miles per hour, there must be another headed west at the same speed. Furthermore, if the heat of the gas indicates that the average velocity of the molecules is 20 miles per hour, the number of molecules moving slower than this speed must be equaled by the number of molecules moving faster.

After a serious analysis of the consequences of his law, Maxwell permitted himself a touch of humor. He suggested that there was a statistical probability that, at some time in the future, all the molecules in a box of gas or a glass of hot water might be moving in the same direction. This would cause the water to rise out of the glass. Next Maxwell suggested that a system of drawing both hot and cold water out of a single pipe might be devised if we could capture a small demon and train him to open and close a tiny valve. The demon would open the valve only when a fast molecule approached it, and close the valve against slow molecules. The water coming out of the valve would thus be hot. To produce a stream of cold water the demon would open the valve only for slow molecules.

Maxwell's demon would circumvent the law of thermodynamics which says in essence: "You can't get something for nothing." That is to say, one cannot separate cold water from hot without doing work. Thus when physicists heard that the Germans had developed a device which could achieve low temperatures by utilizing Maxwell's demon, they were intrigued, though obviously skeptical. One physicist investigated the matter at first hand for the U. S. Navy. He discovered that the device was most ingenious, though not quite as miraculous as had been rumored.

It consists of a T-shaped assembly of pipe joined by a novel fitting, as depicted in Figure 234. When compressed air is admitted to the "leg" of the T, hot air comes out of one arm of

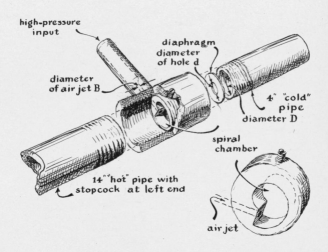

234
Cutaway view of Hilsch tube showing relation of spiral chamber to central pipe-coupling. Detail of spiral at lower right

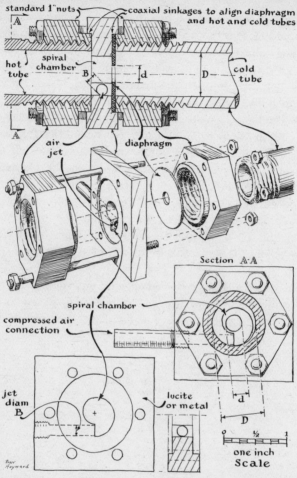

standard 1" nuts

coaxial sinkages to align diaphragm and hot and cold tubes

A

hot tube

spiral chamber

B

d

D

cold tube

A

air jet

diaphragm

Section A-A

spiral chamber

compressed air connection

jet diam B

lucite or metal

d

D

0   ½   1
one inch
Scale

235

Version of Hilsch tube designed by Roger Hayward of Pasadena, Calif.,
for construction by amateurs. Note scale, lower right

the T and cold air out of the other arm! Obviously, however,
work must be done to compress the air.

The origin of the device is obscure. The principle is said to
have been discovered by a Frenchman who left some early experimental models in the path of the German Army when France

was occupied. These were turned over to a German physicist named Rudolf Hilsch, who was working on low-temperature refrigerating devices for the German war effort. Hilsch made some improvements on the Frenchman's design, but found that it was no more efficient than conventional methods of refrigeration in achieving fairly low temperatures. Subsequently the device became known as the Hilsch tube.

The Hilsch tube may be constructed from a pair of modified nuts and associated parts as shown in Figure 235. The horizontal arm of the T-shaped fitting contains a specially machined piece, the outside of which fits inside the arm. The inside of the piece, however, has a cross section which is spiral with respect to the outside. In the "step" of the spiral is a small opening which is connected to the leg of the T.

Thus air admitted to the leg comes out of the opening and spins around the one-turn spiral. The "hot" pipe is about 14 inches long and has an inside diameter of half an inch. The far end of this pipe is fitted with a stopcock which can be used to control the pressure in the system [see Fig. 236]. The "cold" pipe is about four inches long and also has an inside diameter of half an inch. The end of the pipe which butts up against the spiral piece is fitted with a washer, the central hole of which is about a quarter of an inch in diameter. Washers with larger or smaller holes can also be inserted to adjust the system.

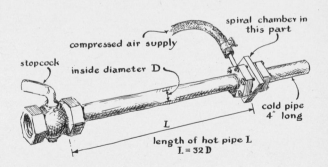

236
Relative lengths of hot and cold tubes of Hilsch device

Three factors determine the performance of the Hilsch tube: the setting of the stopcock, the pressure at which air is admitted to the nozzle, and the size of the hole in the washer. For each value of air pressure and washer opening there is a setting of the stopcock which results in a maximum difference in the temperature of the hot and cold pipes [*see Fig. 237*]. When the device is properly adjusted, the hot pipe will deliver air at about 100 degrees Fahrenheit and the cold pipe air at about —70 degrees (a temperature substantially below the freezing point of mercury and approaching that of "dry ice"). When the tube is adjusted for maximum temperature on the hot side, air is delivered at about 350 degrees F. It must be mentioned, however, that few amateurs have succeeded in achieving these performance extremes. Most report minimums on the order of —10 degrees and maximums of about +140 on the first try.

Despite its impressive performance, the efficiency of the Hilsch tube leaves much to be desired. Indeed, there is still disagreement as to how it works. According to one explanation, the compressed air shoots around the spiral and forms a high-velocity vortex of air. Molecules of air at the outside of the vortex are slowed by friction with the wall of the spiral. Because these slow-moving molecules are subject to the rules of centrifugal force, they tend to fall toward the center of the vortex.

The fast-moving molecules just inside the outer layer of the vortex transfer some of their energy to this layer by bombarding

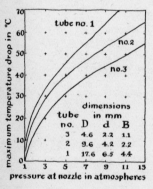

237
Graph of performance for three tubes made by Rudolf Hilsch. The tabulated dimensions "D" "d" and "B" refer to Figure 238

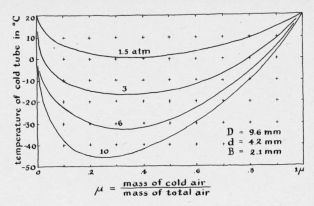

238

Performance graph of Hilsch tube showing effect of hot-tube stopcock adjustment for various input pressures

some of its slow-moving molecules and speeding them up. The net result of this process is the accumulation of *slow-moving, low-energy* molecules in the center of the whirling mass, and of *high-energy, fast-moving* molecules around the outside. In the thermodynamics of gases the terms "high energy" and "high velocity" mean "high temperature." So the vortex consists of a core of cold air surrounded by a rim of hot air.

The difference between the temperature of the core and that of the rim is increased by a secondary effect which takes advantage of the fact that the temperature of a given quantity of gas at a given level of thermal energy is higher when the gas is confined in a small space than in a large one; accordingly when gas is allowed to expand, its temperature drops. In the case the Hilsch tube the action of centrifugal force compresses the hot rim of gas into a compact mass which can escape only by flowing along the inner wall of the "hot" pipe in a compressed state, because its flow into the cold tube is blocked by the rim of the washer.

The amount of the compression is determined by the adjustment of the stopcock at the end of the hot pipe. In contrast, the relatively cold inner core of the vortex, which is also considerably above atmospheric pressure, flows through the hole in the washer and

519

drops to still lower temperature as it expands to atmospheric pressure obtaining inside the cold pipe.

Apparently the inefficiency of the Hilsch tube as a refrigerating device has barred its commercial application. Nonetheless amateurs who would like to have a means of attaining relatively low temperatures, and who do not have access to a supply of dry ice, may find the tube useful. When properly made it will deliver a blast of air 20 times colder than air which has been chilled by permitting it simply to expand through a Venturi tube from a high-pressure source. Thus the Hilsch tube could be used to quick-freeze tissues for miscroscopy, or to chill photomultiplier tubes. But quite apart from the tube's potential application, what could be more fun than to trap Maxwell's demon and make him explain in detail how he manages to blow hot and cold at the same time?

Incidentally, this is not a project for the person who goes in for commercially made apparatus. So far as I can discover Hilsch tubes are not to be found on the market. You must make your own. Nor is it a project for the experimenter who makes a specialty of building apparatus from detailed specifications and drawings. The dimensions shown in the accompanying figures are only approximate. Certainly they are not optimum values. But if you enjoy exploration, the device poses many questions. What would be the effect, for example, of substituting a divergent nozzle for the straight one used by Hilsch? Why not create the vortex by impeller vanes, such as those employed in the stator of turbines? Would a spiral chamber in the shape of a torus improve the efficiency? What ratio should the diameter of the pipes bear to the vortex chamber and to each other? Why not make the spiral of plastic, or even plastic wood? One can also imagine a spiral bent of a strip of brass and soldered into a conventional pipe coupling. Doubtless other and far more clever alternatives will occur to the dyed-in-the-wool tinkerer.

5

A HOMEMADE INTERFEROMETER

Many of the material conveniences we take for granted depend on the optical effect that imparts color to soap bubbles and blueness to the bluebird. An application of the effect is the interferometer, most elegant of yardsticks. The principle is explained in the following pages and a design appropriate for amateur construction is suggested

WHEN TWO RAYS OF LIGHT from a single source fall out of step (say after they have taken different paths and met at a common point), their waves reinforce or counteract each other, just as out-of-phase waves in water do. This effect accounts for the blueness of the bluebird, the fire of opals, the iridescence of butterfly wings and the shifting colors of soap bubbles. It also accounts indirectly for the accuracy of watches, the control of guided missiles, the quality of high-test gasoline and myriads of other achievements of technology which would not be possible without precise standards of measurement.

All measurements, in the final analysis, depend upon one standard — length. Nowadays the length of the meter is calibrated in terms of wavelengths of light. The most commonly accepted standard for determining the length of the meter is the wavelength of the red light emitted by glowing cadmium in the vapor state. By interferometer methods this wavelength has been measured to high precision and comes out to be 6,438.4696 ± .0009 Angstrom units (an Angstrom unit is one 10-billionth of a meter). The meter is 1,553,164.60 ± .22 times this wavelength.

The interferometer, the most elegant of yardsticks, is a singularly finicky and frustrating gadget. A scientist once remarked: "Without a doubt the interferometer, particularly the version of it developed by Michelson, is one of the most wonderful instruments known to science — when it is operated by A. A. Michelson!" In Michelson's hands the instrument certainly established an impressive row of scientific bench marks. It was he who measured the wavelength of the red cadmium line given above.

Making measurements with instruments capable of yielding precision of this order is not easy. One can fiddle with the controls of the interferometer for hours without seeing the fringes, or bands of interfering light, that serve as the graduations of length. No amateur would dream of making the instrument primarily for the purpose of using it regularly as a tool of measurement. But in constructing an interferometer and mastering the art of using it, one can learn a great deal about optics — as well as the technique of making accurate measurements, the art upon which all scientific advances are founded.

You can begin by repeating an experiment first performed by Isaac Newton, which demonstrates the basic principle. Simply press a spectacle lens against a glass plate and look directly into the light reflected by the combination from a wide source of light. If you use a magnifying glass, you will see several rainbow-colored rings, surrounding a tiny black spot about 1/64 of an inch in diameter at the point where the lens touches the plate, as illustrated in Figure 239.

The same effect can be observed with two sheets of ordinary window glass. An irregular pattern of interference fringes will

239
Newton's Rings — seen by placing convex lens against plane glass. (Rings are greatly magnified in this illustration)

surround each point at which the surfaces of the glasses touch. The pattern will be more distinct if the light source has a single color, e.g., the yellow flame produced by holding a piece of soda glass (say a clear glass stirring rod) in a gas burner. If the glass sheets are squeezed even slightly during the experiment, the pattern of fringes will shift, indicating the minute change in distance between the inner faces of the sheets.

Thomas Young, an English physician, and his French colleague Augustin Fresnel demonstrated in the latter part of the 18th century why interference fringes appear. In so doing they established the wave nature of light. They explained that if two rays of light emitted from the same source encounter reflecting surfaces at different distances from the source, the two sets of waves will end up somewhat out of step, because one has traveled a greater distance than the other.

To the extent that the trough of one wave encroaches upon the crest of the other the waves interfere destructively, and the reflected light is dimmed. At various angles of view the apparent distance between the reflecting surfaces will be greater or less, and the intensity of the reflected light will appear proportionately brighter or dimmer, as the case may be. The total energy of the incident light remains unchanged by the interference. It is only the angles at which the energy is reflected that change. Hence the positions of the fringes with respect to the reflecting surfaces appear to shift when the observer moves his head.

Similarly, the apparent position of the fringes depends on the length of the waves. Long waves of red light may appear to annul one another completely in a certain zone, while the short waves of blue light may appear reinforced. In that case the zone will appear blue, although the light source may be emitting a mixture of both long and short waves. If the source is white light, a blend of many wavelengths, some of the colors are annulled and others are strengthened at a given angle of view, with the result that the fringes take on rainbow hues.

Similarly changes in the distance between the reflecting surfaces cause the fringes to shift, just as though the position of the eye had changed. That is why the fringes move when enough pressure is applied to bend two sheets of glass not in perfect contact.

Another interesting simple experiment is to place an extremely flat piece of glass on another flat piece, separating the two at one edge with a narrow strip of paper, so that a thin wedge of air is formed between them. When the arrangement is viewed under yellow light, the interference fringes appear as straight bands of yellow, separated by dark bands, which cross the plates parallel to the edges in contact. The number of yellow fringes observed is equal to half the number of wavelengths by which the plates are separated at the base of the wedge.

When the paper strip is removed and the plates are brought together slowly at the base, the fringes drift down the wedge and disappear at the base, the remaining fringes growing proportionately wider. By selecting relatively large plates for the experiment, it is possible to produce a fringe movement of several inches for each change of one wavelength at the base. A version of the interferometer is based on this principle.

In short, any change which modifies the relative lengths of the paths taken by two interfering rays causes the position of the resulting fringes to shift. A change in the speed of either ray has the same effect, because the slowed ray will arrive at a distant point later than the faster one, just as if had followed a longer path. Any material medium will slow light to less than its speed in a perfect vacuum. Air at sea level cuts its speed by about 55 miles per second, short waves being slowed somewhat more than long ones.

If two interfering rays are traveling in separate evacuated vessels and air is admitted into one of the vessels, the interference fringes will shift, as if that path had been lengthened. From the movement of the fringes it is possible to determine by simple arithmetic the amount by which the speed was reduced. The ratio of the velocity of light through a vacuum to its velocity through a transparent substance is called the refractive index of that substance. The interferometer is a convenient instrument for measuring the refractive indices of gases and of liquids.

Eric F. Cave, a physicist at the University of Missouri, has designed a simple interferometer which will demonstrate many of these interesting effects and enable even beginners in optics to measure the wavelength of light. With suitable modifications the instrument can be used for constructing primary standards of length, measuring indices of refraction and determining coefficients of expansion.

E. F. Cave describes the construction of the Cave interferometer

THE DESIGN PRESENTED HERE is intended to serve primarily as a guide. Most amateurs will be capable of designing their own instruments once the basic principles are understood. Optically the arrangement is similar to that devised by Michelson. A source of light, preferably of a single color, falls on a plate of glass which stands on edge and at an angle of 45 degrees with respect to the source. This plate serves as a beamsplitter.

Part of the light from the source passes through the plate. This portion proceeds to a fixed mirror a few inches away, where it is reflected back to the diagonal plate. The other part of the original light beam is reflected from the surface of the diagonal at a right angle with respect to the source. It travels to a mov-

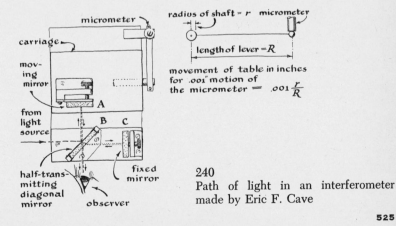

240
Path of light in an interferometer made by Eric F. Cave

able mirror, located the same distance from the diagonal plate as the fixed mirror, and it too is reflected back to the plate. Part of this ray passes through the plate to the eye. Here it is joined by part of the ray returned by the fixed mirror [*see Fig. 240*].

By adjusting the positions and angles of the two mirrors relative to the diagonal plate it is possible to create the illusion that the fixed mirror occupies the plane of the movable mirror. Similarly, by adjusting the angle of either mirror slightly, it is possible to create the optical effect of a thin wedge between the two mirrors. Interference fringes will then appear, as if the two reflecting surfaces were in physical contact at one point and spaced slightly apart at another. A change in the position of the movable mirror toward or away from the beam-splitter is observed as a greatly amplified movement of the fringes.

Beginners may expect to spend a lot of time in coaxing the instrument into adjustment. But careful construction will minimize the difficulty.

The base can be made of almost any metal, although amateurs without access to shop facilities are advised to procure a piece of cold-rolled steel cut to specified dimensions. The instrument can be made in any convenient size. The base of mine is nine inches wide and 14 inches long. You will also need two other plates of the same thickness and width but only about a quarter as long. They become the carriage for supporting the movable mirror and the table on which the diagonal plate and fixed mirror are mounted.

The carriage moves on ways consisting of dowel pins attached to its underside [*see Fig. 241*]. The ways are made of commercially ground drill rod, which can be procured in various sizes from hardware supply houses. Each way consists of a pair of rods, one set being attached to the carriage and the other to the base. The ways can be fastened in a variety of arrangements. I fitted them into a milled slot. Flat-headed machine screws will serve equally well as fastenings if you do not have a milling machine.

The bearing for the drive shaft can be a block cut with a V-shaped notch. If no shop facilities are available for machining

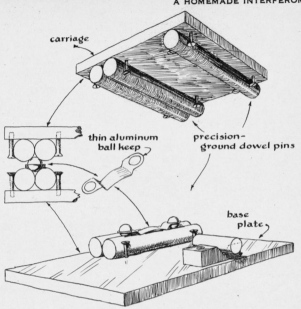

carriage

thin aluminum ball keep

precision-ground dowel pins

base plate

241
Details of the interferometer carriage assembly

it, you can drill four shallow holes in the base as retainers for four steel balls and simply let the shaft turn between the two sets. The height of the block or ball supports should be chosen so that the top of the carriage will parallel the top of the base when the machine is assembled. The ways move on two steel balls fitted with a ball-spacer made of thin aluminum as shown. In operation the carriage is driven back and forth by turning the drive shaft.

The shaft may be rotated either by a worm and wheel arrangement or by a "tangent screw." The latter consists of a screw pressing on a bearing in a lever arm, the other end of which is attached to the shaft [*see Fig. 242*]. A tangent screw permits only a small amount of continuous travel, but it is less expensive than a worm and wheel.

The lever arm should be rectangular in cross section. One end is drilled for the shaft, split as shown and fitted with a clamp-

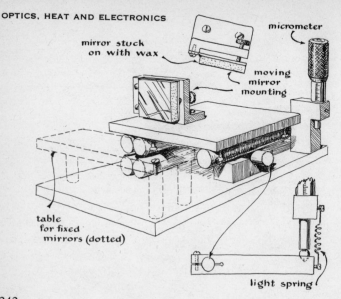

242
Details of the interferometer base assembly showing micrometer-controlled carriage-translation lever

ing screw. The other end is drilled with a shallow hole for the steel ball bearing. The screw may be a machinist's micrometer mounted on a bracket as shown. The ball bearing is held in close contact with the micrometer by a spring. The length of the lever and the diameter of the drive shaft determine the amount by which the carriage will move when the micrometer is turned.

It should be possible to control the movement of the table smoothly through distances equal to at least one wavelength of the light under investigation. The wavelength of the yellow light emitted by glowing sodium is about one 50,000th of an inch. The tangent screw must therefore provide a geometrical reduction to distances of this order.

When the machinist's micrometer is turned one division, the screw moves the outer end of the lever arm a thousandth of an inch. By adjusting the effective length of the lever arm (the distance between the center of the ball bearing under the screw and the center of the shaft) with respect to the radius of the shaft, the relative movement of the carriage can be reduced by any proportion desired. The reduction is equal to the radius of the shaft divided by the effective length of the lever arm. Thus a 10-inch arm coupled to a ¼-inch shaft yields a reduction of 80 to 1, and a turn of one micrometer division produces a carriage translation of .0000125 of an inch.

The quality of the optical parts will largely determine the experiments possible with the instrument and the extent to which it may be worth while later to add accessories and otherwise modify the design. Advanced telescope makers will doubtless prefer to grind and figure the three flats required. Those less skilled in figuring glass may order them from an optical supply house. All three elements should be flat to about a tenth of a wavelength or the resulting fringes will show serious distortion. Small squares can be cut from plate glass and tested for flatness by the method outlined in *Amateur Telescope Making* by Albert G. Ingalls.

If the instrument is to be used for testing lenses, mirrors, prisms and so on, the faces of the pieces of glass should be strictly parallel to one another. Both the fixed and the movable mirror should be silvered or aluminized on the front surface, and for best results the face of the diagonal plate also should be silvered slightly, so that it will reflect about as much light as it lets through.

Mounting brackets should support the optical elements perpendicular to the plane of the base after assembly. They should provide for finely controlled angular adjustment of the mirrors around the horizontal and the vertical axes. In the illustration shown in Figure 243 the movable mirror is mounted with wax, but for anything more than an initial demonstration this is not good practice, especially if the supporting member is subject to flexure. The diagonal plate and fixed mirror are mounted on a rectangular table fixed to the base, and are located so that the center of the beam of light from the source strikes the center of the diagonal plate and is reflected at right angles to the center of the movable mirror.

Two important conditions must be fulfilled if the instrument is to function properly. The light must originate from an ex-

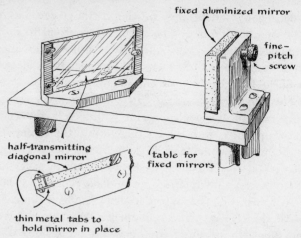

fixed aluminized mirror

fine-
pitch
screw

half-transmitting
diagonal mirror

table for
fixed mirrors

thin metal tabs to
hold mirror in place

243
Details of the interferometer beam-splitter and fixed-mirror assembly

tended source several feet away, and it must be monochromatic. The yellow flame obtained with soda glass is not strictly monochromatic, because most of the light comes from the brilliant spectral doublet of sodium, but it is adequate for demonstrating the instrument.

When in operation the instrument should rest on a solid, vibrationless support. The movable mirror is placed as precisely as possible at the same distance from the beam-splitter as the fixed mirror. Preliminary adjustments are then made with the aid of a point source of light — e.g., the highlight reflected from a small polished steel ball 1/16 of an inch in diameter, placed about 10 feet away. The ball should be lighted with a concentrated beam such as that provided by a 300-watt slide projector.

The ball is located to the left of the observer when he faces the movable mirror and in line with the center of the beam-splitter and fixed mirror. When you look at the movable mirror through the beam-splitter, you will see two images of the source. You change the angles of both mirrors by means of the adjusting screws until the images of the source coincide.

Now you substitute the sodium source of light for the ball.

If the distances of the mirrors from the beam-splitter are essentially equal, you should see a number of concentric circles in orange and black like those of a rifle target. The orange color is characteristic of the sodium doublet, while the black circles mark zones of destructive interference between beams reflected by the two mirrors. Remember that you are making exquisite adjustments requiring patience.

To measure the wavelength of sodium light, first note the precise position of the micrometer and then turn it slowly while counting the number of times the bull's-eye of the target changes from orange to black and back to orange again. From orange to orange or black to black is a half wavelength. Count, say, 100 of these color changes. The carriage has then moved 100 times the half wavelength of sodium light. Read the micrometer setting and subtract it from the first reading. This difference, when divided by the geometrical reduction provided by the tangent screw, is equal to 50 wavelengths of the light.

In reality we are working with the sodium doublet, of course. The wavelength of one of the sodium lines is .000023188 of an inch and the other is .000023216 of an inch. If your experiment comes out correctly, therefore, your instrument will show the average of the two, or .000023202 of an inch. The fact that you are dealing with light of two close wavelengths may cause poor contrast between the orange and dark fringes at certain positions of the carriage. A slight displacement of the carriage from this position will produce maximum contrast.

This design is intended merely to whet an appetite for interferometry. The instrument and theory discussed here are mere introductions to the subject. Before the instrument can yield results comparable with those achieved by Michelson, it must be provided with a monochromatic source, such as the light emitted by the red line of cadmium. Advanced instruments are provided with a small telescope for viewing the fringes. In addition, Michelson inserted a second diagonal plate in the path between the beam-splitter and the movable mirror. It is unsilvered but otherwise identical with the beam-splitter. This plate equalizes the thickness of glass traversed by the two beams and prevents the short waves in one beam from being retarded more than those in the other.

Interferometers can be equipped with accessories for measuring the physical constants of solids, liquids and gases. Glass containers provided with optically flat windows can be introduced into the beams. When the air in one is slowly displaced with a gas, the fringes will drift across the field just as if the carriage were being moved. A count can easily be reduced to the index of refraction of the gas. The coefficient of expansion of a solid with respect to changes in temperature can be determined by clamping the specimen, fitted with a thermometer, between the carriage and base. A count of the fringes is then converted into the dimensional change of the specimen. This information, together with the temperature difference, enables an experimenter to compute the desired coefficient.

6

A PIEZOELECTRIC CLOCK

When connected in an appropriate electronic circuit, a wafer cut from crystalline quartz will vibrate with extreme constancy because of the piezoelectric effect. Moreover, it will control the frequency of the current. When powered by such current an electric clock keeps remarkably good time. W. W. Withrow, a radio ham of Teague, Texas, explains how to build and operate the apparatus

LIKE MOST AMATEURS who make a hobby of science, particularly of those branches which have to do with physics, I have long wanted a good clock. Ordinary electric clocks do for most purposes and nearly everyone takes it for granted that they keep good time. But do they? The accuracy of electric clocks depends on the care with which the operator at the power station maintains constant frequency on the mains. The Texas town in which I live has an excellent city-owned power plant. But its operators have little reason to maintain frequency as closely as they would if the plant were part of a network of stations which must be synchronized. I found that our clocks sometimes vary as much as a minute from one day to another.

The principal element in a timing system is the one which, in effect, counts the units of time. This may be entirely mechanical, as in the pendulum clock. It may be electronic, as in the gas-absorption clock. It may be a combination of the two, as in the Marrison, or piezoelectric-crystal, clock. In each of the three some resonant element must have a highly constant natural period of vibration which can be coupled to an indicator, usually a clock face, for indicating the passage of time with respect to an arbitrary starting instant such as 0000 Greenwich mean time.

When fed with electrical pulses from a vacuum-tube oscillator, a properly cut and mounted quartz crystal vibrates continuously at a rapid and remarkably constant rate. I knew that the National Bureau of Standards uses a crystal clock. But I had dismissed the idea of building a version of it because the Bureau's clock face is driven by a 1,000-cycle motor. Electrical-appliance dealers in my town stock only 60-cycle clocks. Still, I wanted a good clock and could not down the idea of tackling a crystal one, perhaps because electronics has a way of getting tied in with most of my projects whether they are essentially electronic or not.

I decided to try a simplified version of the Marrison clock, using a quartz crystal cut for 120 kilocycles per second. It seemed likely that a clock could be built around a 120-kilocycle crystal without the complication of such accessories as an oven for maintaining the unit at constant temperature, or a special 1,000-cycle clock motor. The frequency of the crystal could be subdivided to 60 cycles by a highly unstable vacuum-tube circuit called a multivibrator and then amplified as desired for driving the clock mechanism.

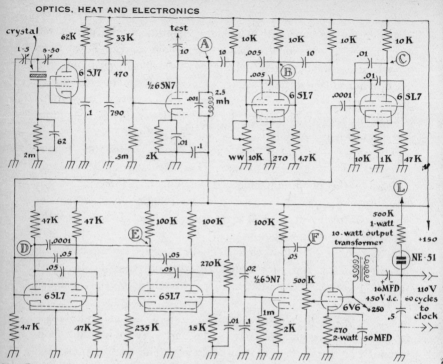

Note: Resistors ½ watt unless marked. Capacitors: MFD denoted by decimals, MMFD by whole numbers.

244
Circuit diagram of quartz-crystal clock

Except for the crystal, the clock was built entirely of standard radio parts plus parts from an old radio plus a spare electric clock. The crystal was made by the Northern Engineering Laboratories of Burlington, Wis. At the time I purchased mine in 1957 the Model T-9D crystal was priced at $14, which represents my principal outlay of cash for the clock. The crystal comes mounted in an evacuated bulb with a pronged base that fits a standard vacuum-tube socket. It is driven by a conventional vacuum-tube oscillator [*see Fig. 244*]. The 120-kilocycle output of the oscillator is boosted by a single-stage resistance-coupled amplifier and reduced to 60 cycles by a series of four multivibrators which respectively operate at 6,000 cycles, 1,200 cycles, 240 cycles and 60 cycles. The output of the last of these multivibrators is fed to a preamplifier, which in turn drives the power amplifier [*see block diagram, Fig. 245*].

Multivibrators, I learned, are tricky gadgets – if you try to make them divide by more than a factor to two or four, as I finally succeeded in doing. It took a long series of experiments to find working values for the resistors and capacitors that finally gave the desired performance. In principle the multivibrator is a two-stage resistance-coupled amplifier in which the output of each tube is coupled to the input of its companion [*see Fig. 246*]. On the application of power to the unit, a mild pulse of current flows in each of the plate circuits.

Pulses also appear as a charge on the respective grids. There is a somewhat stronger pulse on one grid than on the other because multivibrator circuits cannot be made perfectly symmetrical. A heavy flow of current promptly builds up in the plate circuit of the tube receiving the stronger pulse. The grid of the companion tube, being coupled to the plate of the conducting tube, is driven strongly negative and soon reaches the point of blocking the flow of electrons from the cathode of the conducting tube to its plate. The tube is said to have passed the cutoff point. The negative charge on this grid (and on its associated coupling capacitor) then leaks off through a resistor connected between the grid and cathode. The time required for

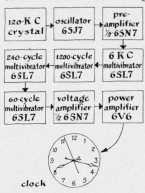

245
Block schematic diagram of quartz-crystal clock

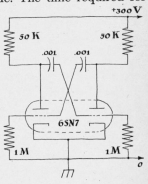

246
Circuit diagram of a multivibrator. Frequency is determined by values of grid capacitors and resistors (1M and .001 in this case)

the leaking process depends on the size of the coupling capacitor and the resistor. As the charge leaks away, the potential of the grid rises toward the cutoff point (beyond which the tube can conduct).

When this critical point is reached, the tube promptly conducts. The resulting pulse drives the grid of the companion tube (through the coupling capacitor) strongly negative and it in turn cuts off. Thereupon the series of events repeats. The negative charge leaks off the grid and a new cycle is initiated. The seesaw action continues — each tube being cut off and cutting off its companion in return. One grid or the other is always negative and one always positive. Alternately one tube conducts and the other tube does not.

The frequency at which a multivibrator performs this automatic flip-flop can be increased somewhat without changing the size of the coupling capacitors or grid-leak resistors. If, as either grid approaches the point at which conduction is about to be resumed, a pulse is applied to the grid from an external source, conduction will be initiated early. An external pulse of proper sign (positive) will neutralize the remaining negative charge and push the grid "over the top." The multivibrator owes its action as a frequency divider to this effect.

Frequency division is accomplished by setting the multivibrator's natural or free-running frequency close to but slightly lower than the desired submultiple of signal frequency and then introducing the signal or controlling frequency to the grid of one of the two multivibrator tubes. The multivibrator then locks in step at the desired submultiple of the signal frequency, because one and only one pulse of the signal can arrive at the critical moment the triggering grid is approaching the cutoff point.

Other signal pulses arrive while the grid is either strongly negative or (during alternate half-cycles) when it is charged positively. Thus if a controlling signal of 120 kilocycles is coupled to one grid of a multivibrator which is adjusted for a natural period of slightly less than 6,000 cycles, the first nine cycles of the signal occur while the triggering grid is substantially below the point of conduction. The 10th cycle, however, arrives just in time to push the grid over the top and initiate conduction. During the next 10 signal pulses the triggering grid is positive and the signal has no effect.

At the end of this interval the companion tube conducts automatically and drives the triggering grid negative in preparation for the next cycle of events. Thus each 20th pulse of the signal triggers the controlled tube into conduction, and the multivibrator accordingly oscillates at a 20th of the signal frequency.

The output of one multivibrator can trigger another. Four properly adjusted units can thus reduce the frequency of a 120-kilocycle oscillator in steps of 6,000, 1,200, 240 and finally 60 cycles. In the case of my clock the 120-kilocycle signal is derived from the stable crystal oscillator. The 60-cycle output of the final multivibrator is filtered and amplified to 110 volts to drive the electric clock.

It must be confessed at this point that the free-running period of multivibrators is influenced by many factors: the voltage of the plate supply, cathode temperature, humidity, atmospheric pressure and even, I have had reason to suspect, the state of one's ulcers. The 6,000-cycle unit is so sensitive to triggering influences that it is apt to lock in step with every disturbance that chances along. It has a revolting way, for example, of deciding to count every 19th pulse or every 21st instead of the desired 20th. This does not mean that multivibrators are too tricky for the beginner. But it seems humane to suggest that prospective builders of the clock should lay in an extra supply of aspirin.

I should mention again, however, that these difficulties can be largely avoided by using a few more vacuum tubes — multivibrator stages — and thus accomplishing the desired frequency division in smaller bites. But like many amateurs, I enjoy doing things the hard way, especially when it holds down out-of-pocket costs. Even so, any amateur with patience enough to make a parabolic mirror will find this project less exacting. One can make major changes in the components at any point, or even start from scratch again without losing anything but time. After all, what fun would one get out of making a piece of gear which behaved well on the first try?

The layout of the parts on the chassis is not critical. The second tube of the line-up, the 6SN7 twin triode, should be installed with some care. This tube plays a dual role, half of it acting as the preamplifier for 120 kilocycles and the other half as the preamplifier for 60 cycles. Hence it may well be placed next to the oscillator, where it can be fed with short, direct connections. The 60-cycle half can be fed without ill effect by any convenient length of wire. Any method of wiring is satisfactory, provided it does not complicate the task of changing resistors and capacitors in the various multivibrators. The multivibrator circuits must be tailor-made. The values of the resistors and capacitors [*specified in the circuit diagram*] are only approximate. They work in my clock, but may not in someone else's.

When the chassis has been wired, checked and the tubes installed, it is necessary to set the 150-volt regulator tube under load for a current of 25 milliamperes. One safe method is to place a temporary 100-ohm resistor in series with the ground side of the regulator tube and adjust the variable 20-watt resistor (beginning at about 2,000 ohms) until a voltage of 2.5 is read across the 100-ohm resistor. This method sidesteps the possibility of damaging a milliammeter, should the circuit be accidentally shorted during adjustment. The output control in the grid of the 6V6 power amplifier should be set at minimum while the multivibrator stages are being tamed.

It is possible to adjust the free-running period of the multivibrators by ear. A headphone (connected through an isolating amplifier) would enable you to hear the tone and judge the frequency of their respective outputs. But a cathode-ray oscilloscope is by far the best tool for the job. If you do not own an oscilloscope, you may be able to interest a nearby television repairman in the project sufficiently to get the use of one — or even persuade the repairman to try the adjustment.

The oscilloscope is used to examine the wave forms, and hence the relative frequencies, of two sources of oscillation at a time. Before the tests are begun, one lead of a 1-megohm resistor (of the quarter-watt size) is tightly wrapped to the tip of each of the oscilloscope's two test-probes, one of which causes vertical deflections to be displayed and the other horizontal deflections. The free end of the resistors are thereafter used as probe tips.

The tests are based on the pattern presented by the 'scope when its inputs are fed with frequencies related in integral ratio, such as 4 to 1, 20 to 1 and so on. When the frequencies are in exact integral ratio, the resulting pattern is one of the well-known Lissajous figures. If the horizontal swing of the 'scope makes one complete oscillation, for example, while the vertical deflection makes two or more, the pattern may look like a misshapen crown: there are a number of vertical teeth around its upper edge. If the teeth drift a little, the ratio of the two frequencies under observation is nearly but not precisely integral.

The testing and adjustment procedure may be a bit tedious, but it is not difficult. The probes of the 'scope are applied to a pair of frequency sources, the pattern is observed and the circuit modified as dictated by thep attern. The sources of frequency to be examined are designated by lettered test points.

The testing routine begins with the 6,000-cycle multivibrator. First place the vertical test-probe of the 'scope on point A, the output of the 120-kilocycle oscillator, and the horizontal probe on point B, the output of the 6,000-cycle (we hope) multivibrator. Remove the 6SL7 tube from the succeeding 1,200-cycle multivibrator. Adjust the gain controls of the 'scope for a pattern of convenient size. Now rotate the variable-grid resistor (10 K) of the 6,000-cycle multivibrator to produce a stationary pattern on the 'scope.

Several such points will doubtless be found. Select one for examination. Adjust the gain control of the 'scope for full deflection and count the teeth in the pattern. With luck, the count will be 20 [see Fig. 247]. If the count is higher or lower, select another of the stable points and count again. If none of the settings yields the desired count of 20, the value of the 4.7-K resistor in the grid circuit of the second multivibrator tube must be altered. Remove the 4.7-K resistor and substitute a rheostat for it. (One made of a 100-K potentiometer will do.) Now set the 10-K variable grid resistor of the first tube to its midpoint and vary the rheostat. Increased resistance will lower the multi-

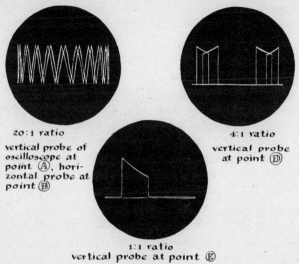

20:1 ratio

vertical probe of
oscilloscope at
point Ⓐ, hori-
zontal probe at
point Ⓑ

4:1 ratio

vertical probe
at point Ⓓ

1:1 ratio
vertical probe at point Ⓔ

247
Lissajous figures of multivibrators, as displayed on the face of cathode
ray oscilloscope, aid in adjusting circuit of clock

vibrator frequency, causing more peaks to appear; decreased
resistance will do the opposite.

A setting will be found which yields the 20 stationary peaks
desired. Measure the value of the rheostat with an ohmmeter,
select a corresponding fixed resistor close to this value and substitute it for the rheostat. Replacing the rheostat with the fixed
resistor will alter the circuit enough to change the count, but a
setting of the variable 10-K resistor should be found that will
restore it to 20.

Replace the tube previously removed from the 1,200-cycle
multivibrator and remove the corresponding tube from the 240-
cycle unit. Put the vertical probe on point C and the horizontal
one on the ungrounded side of the heater circuit at any convenient point. This feeds the horizontal sweep of the 'scope with
the frequency of the power line. If the second multivibrator is
oscillating at the desired 1,200 cycles, the 'scope pattern will
again show 20 teeth.

A slow rotation of the pattern will doubtless be observed, indicating that the power-line frequency is not a precise multiple of the crystal frequency — not quite the 60 cycles customarily advertised. If, in contrast, the pattern shows a pronounced vertical deflection and moves rapidly, substitute the rheostat (just removed from the 6,000-cycle multivibrator) for the 10-K resistor in the grid circuit of the first tube of the 1,200-cycle multivibrator. Again verify the frequency of the 6,000-cycle unit. Now vary the rheostat to produce the 20-tooth pattern, with perhaps the slow rotation mentioned (the vertical probe of the 'scope being on point C and the horizontal one on the ungrounded heater circuit).

Measure the value of the rheostat setting which yields a count of 20 and replace the rheostat with a fixed resistor of this value. Again verify the operation of all units of the assembly to this point. The adjustment procedure is similar for the remaining units. In each case, while a unit is being adjusted, the first tube of the following unit must be removed from its socket. The horizontal probe of the 'scope remains on the ungrounded side of the heater circuit while the 1,200- 240- and 60-cycle units are adjusted. The vertical probe is placed at point D (the output of the 240-cycle unit) and the 47-K grid resistor adjusted until the pattern shows *four* peaks.

Similarly, with the vertical probe at point E (the output of the 60-cycle unit), alter the 15-K grid resistor (of the second tube) for a pattern displaying a *single* peak. Finally, place the vertical probe on point F (the output of the 60-cycle preamplifier). The pattern should now take the form of a smoothly rotating ellipse which slowly changes into a straight line at one extreme and opens into a circle at the other.

All may not go smoothly. When the tube of the 1,200-cycle unit is replaced following the adjustment of the 6,000-cycle unit, for example, the 6,000-cycle unit may tend to lock into a higher or lower multiple of the crystal frequency (because of the shunting effect of the 1,200-cycle tube). A simple adjustment of the 10-K variable resistor may cure the difficulty.

At the other extreme, it may be necessary to repeat the whole procedure and find still another value for the original 4.7-K resistor. If so, your luck will improve on the second try because the 1,200-cycle multivibrator will now tend strongly to lock in at its designed frequency. The desired goal has been brought much closer by virtue of previous adjustments.

A permanent indicator of over-all operation, although a rough one, is provided by a small neon-lamp circuit. Test-point L of the indicator is connected directly to one side of the 110-volt power line [*see point L in Figs. 244 and 248*]. Normally, as the line frequency drifts in and out of synchronization with the 60-cycle frequency derived from the crystal, the lamp pulsates gradually from dark to bright and back again in step with the difference frequency of the two. If the multivibrators are not synchronized, the lamp will pulse rapidly.

A 60-cycle, 100-volt electric clock drawing not more than three watts is now connected to the output of the power amplifier. As the gain control of the power amplifier is advanced to produce an output of 110 volts, the motor should start running.

One final pair of adjustments puts the clock in business. It must be regulated (the crystal frequency adjusted as closely as possible to 120 kilocycles) and the hands set for correct time in the local time zone. The control device to regulate the rate at which the clock runs is based on the fact that a piezoelectric crystal can be forced to vibrate faster or slower than its natural

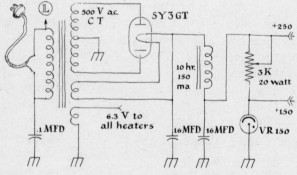

248
Circuit diagram of power supply for quartz-crystal clock

period (within narrow limits) by altering the amount of electrical "push" imparted to the crystal during each vibration by the associated vacuum-tube oscillator — just as the pendulum of a mechanical clock can be made to beat slightly faster or slower than its natural period by altering the amount of energy imparted to or subtracted from the pendulum by the escapement mechanism.

Driving energy for the crystal, in the form of periodic pulses, is taken from the oscillator tube through a variable capacitor which covers a range of 8 to 50 micromicrofarads. This capacitor may be thought of as a rough regulating adjustment. A second variable capacitor (1 to 5 micromicrofarads) is connected between the "hot" side of the crystal and the ground. It shunts a portion of the energy from the tube to the ground, the amount depending upon the setting of the capacitor. This is the "fine" adjustment.

The primary reference frequency in this country is the time signals broadcast by radio station WWV of the National Bureau of Standards. These signals appear on carrier frequencies of 2.5 megacycles, 5 megacycles, 10 megacycles and so on in multiples of 5 megacycles up to 25 megacycles. The signals can be picked up almost anywhere on a short-wave radio. They are accurate to better than one part in 100 million. All WWV carrier frequencies are modulated periodically by time announcements in voice and by a series of pulses or "ticks" which persist for .005 second and commence each second.

Tune in WWV and listen to the seconds tick. Then, by any convenient means, arrange your clock so it will also make audible second ticks. My clock is of the drum-counter type, in which a ratchet coupled to the drum mechanism is moved by a motor-actuated pawl. The movement of the drum begins on the minute and the pawl clicks precisely three seconds later. The clock is set roughly by WWV's voice announcement and regulated by comparing the click of the pawl with the fourth tick (after the minute) of WWV. This is the tick marking the end of the third second. It is possible to judge the interval between the tick of WWV and that of my clock within about a tenth of a second, depending on how far my clock is running ahead of, or behind, WWV.

Note the difference when the new clock is put into operation. At the end of an hour the difference will doubtless have increased or decreased. Rotate the fine adjustment a few degrees and note the setting. Another hour should show the effect of the adjustment. Mark the dial of the regulator control with an arrow to indicate the direction in which the knob must be turned for "fast" and "slow." If the rate requires major adjustment, use the rough control. From this point the task is merely one of narrowing the margin of error. When finally set, the clock should remain with a 10th of a second of WWV for weeks on end.

Some amateurs may live in areas where WWV cannot be heard. It is possible for them to set and regulate the clock with fair accuracy if they can pick up a radio station which broadcasts on a frequency which has a submultiple of 120 kilocycles, such as 600 cycles, 720, 840, 960, 1,080 and so on. The plate circuit of the preamplifier provides access to the crystal frequency through a 10-micromicrofarad capacitor at the point marked "test" [*see circuit diagram, Fig. 244*]. This frequency is compared with that of the broadcasting station by connecting a wire be-

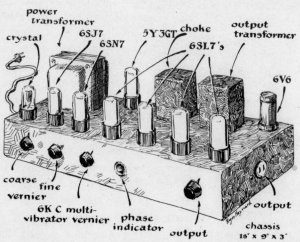

249
Electronic generator of precise frequency to drive electric clock

tween the test point and the external antenna post of the radio receiver, tuning in the station and listening for the beat or difference frequency of the clock and station.

If the receiving set has an internal-loop antenna instead of an external antenna, drape a foot or two of wire (connected to the test point of the clock) over the loop antenna of the set. Adjust the volume of the set so the beat can be heard clearly. The sound will doubtless resemble an undulating or pulsating swish. The rate of the pulsation is equal to the difference frequency between the clock and a submultiple of the carrier frequency. Adjust the regulating controls of the clock for zero beat. The clock will then be as accurate as the frequency of the broadcasting station — which is pretty good.

The adjustment procedures have been outlined in some detail because, as those who undertake the construction of this clock will discover, it is no "cookbook" project. Multivibrators are such fickle critters that each clock must be regarded as an original project in its own right. But the instrument is worth whatever time and patience it costs. Once operating, the 60-cycle output can be further amplified if desired and wired to distant locations for driving all sorts of apparatus, including telescopes, seismograph pens and so on.

7

SOME AFTER-DINNER
EXPERIMENTS

*Many charming experiments can be performed with-
out elaborate apparatus — some require none. How
to investigate the way your eyes present information
to the brain. Directions for building a pseudoscope.
Flea-power engines made with rubber bands or
lighter flints*

IF YOU LIKE TO WHILE AWAY the time performing
experiments that do not require apparatus, you will find much
solace in the mysterious operation of human vision. You already
own a pair of excellent optical instruments for such experimentation: your eyes. With these, plus pencil and paper, you are all
set. If, in addition, you happen to have a pair of pocket mirrors,
a couple of short-focus lenses and a stereoscope, you can really
astonish yourself.

Start by drawing a rectangle about three inches wide and two
inches high and divide it by a horizontal line a quarter of the
way down from the top. Then draw a series of disks diagonally
across the bottom portion which gradually diminish in size, as
shown in Figure 250. Common sense tells you that you have made
a flat drawing. Yet your brain insists that it is a three-dimensional
representation — especially if you judiciously shade the disks.
You get the impression of a series of spheres which run from
the foreground to a "vanishing point" on the horizon. It took
the painters of the Renaissance a century to perfect this trick
of representing three-dimensional reality in two dimensions. The
"projective geometry" on which it is based is today an integral
part of physics.

There is another method of representing three-dimensional

250
Effect of three dimensions achieved
by projective geometry

reality in two dimensions which creates an even more dramatic
visual impression. Make two rectangles, each an inch and a half
wide by an inch and a quarter high. They should be spaced
about two and a half inches apart from center to center. Now
draw a horizontal line through the center of each, dividing the
rectangles into two equal parts from top to bottom.

Next make a shaded, quarter-inch disk precisely in the center
of each horizontal line. Flank the disk in the drawing at left
with an identical pair of disks spaced 3/16 of an inch from it.
Make a similar pair on the horizontal line of the drawing at
right, but space them 5/16 of an inch from the middle disk [see
Fig. 251]. To the casual observer there is certainly nothing in this
pair of drawings to suggest relief in three dimensions. But when
you view the drawing in a stereoscope, which causes the pair of
rectangles to blend into a single image, the disk at left is seen
as a sphere floating in space above the plane of the paper. The
center disk will appear as a sphere in the plane of the paper
while the right one will seem to float in space behind the paper.
With a little practice you can observe this effect without a stereoscope. Locate the drawing about two feet away and place the
index fingers of both hands just outside your eyes. Now, while

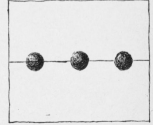

251
Illusion of three dimensions created by stereoscopic drawings

continuing to look at the drawing, move your hands slowly toward the drawing. Your left eye will see the tip of your left index finger and your right eye the tip of your right finger. As your hands advance, you will become conscious of *four* rectangles on the paper. Your brain is accepting the independent images presented by each eye. Now the inner pair of images will gradually overlap. Finally they will blend. When this is accomplished, transfer your full attention to the fused image. It will appear in three dimensions, just as though it were seen through the stereoscope. This is called "wide-eyed" stereoscope seeing.

You can also see the drawings in three dimensions without a stereoscope by the "cross-eyed" method. To achieve this you use only one finger. Place the drawing about two feet away, as before. Now put the tip of one index finger on the bridge of your nose and while looking toward the drawing slowly move your finger toward it, focusing your eyes on the tip. Again you will become conscious of four rectangles on the paper. Gradually, as your finger advances, the innermost pair will fuse as in the wide-eyed method and you will see the center drawing in three dimensions. It will differ from the wide-eyed view, however, in two major respects.

The fused image will be smaller by about a third because, among other things, the optical path between the eyes and paper is now longer. You will also observe that the two outermost spheres will have exchanged position. The sphere at right now floats in front of the plane of the paper and the one at left behind it! The relief has been inverted.

Roger Hayward, who illustrated this volume, has amused himself at odd moments for the past 30 years by learning to make stereoscopic drawings and investigating stereovision. "Three-dimensional drawings are not nearly as hard to do as one would imagine," he writes. "This is due to the tolerance of the eye, provided, of course, you understand what you think you see. If what you appear to see is inconsistent in geometry, that is, in perspective, or inconsistent in the effect of light and shade, the brain is apt to reject the stereoscopic effect. The picture will lack the apparent relief of 3-D and will appear relatively flat.

"This is illustrated by the pairs of drawings in Figure 252. The top pair, which is drawn for cross-eyed viewing, shows a prism lying in front of a screen. Both objects are in the foreground of a long room. The scene is lighted from the upper left; part of a window can be seen in the rear wall. The bottom stereo pair shows the same scene but is drawn to be viewed either by the wide-eyed method or through a conventional stereoscope.

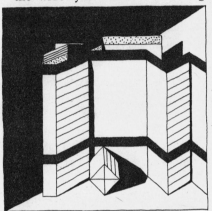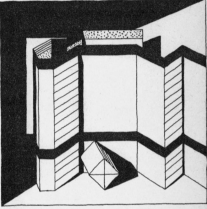

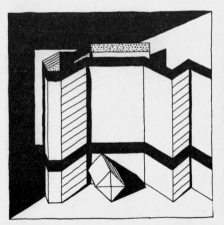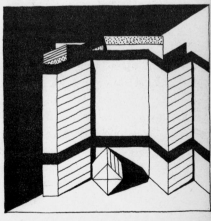

252
Stereoscopic drawings for "cross-eyed" viewing *(top)* and "wide-eyed" viewing *(bottom)*

"Let us assume that you either have access to a stereoscope or have mastered the art of wide-eyed viewing. On examining the drawing you will see the folded screen with a black band along the top and near the bottom. Part of the screen has been folded back and can be seen over the top of its front portion. The prism extends out in front and the screen casts a shadow on the right wall of the room. All this has the effect of a scene viewed in normal perspective with a self-consistent pattern of light and shade, although the pattern is a pretty conventional one.

"Now change to either cross-eyed viewing or substitute the upper drawing for the lower one in the stereoscope. The relief will appear in reverse, near objects seeming smaller than far ones. The folded portion of the screen will seem nearer than the front part, which does not make sense. Other parts of the scene seem to be linked in a fuzzy sort of jumble. From this experiment one can conclude that binocular vision is destroyed when violence is done to the principles of perspective. A far object which partly obscures a near one is nonsense which the mind simply refuses to accept. But if a figure is consistent in perspective and in light and shade, especially if the figure is unfamiliar, the mind will accept it as representing reality, however exotic the forms may appear."

The pseudoscope, described by Roger Hayward

IT IS POSSIBLE TO INVESTIGATE some of the limits within which the mind will accept misinformation from the eyes by means of an instrument called the pseudoscope, a binocular-like device which enjoyed a brief popularity shortly after Sir Charles Wheatstone invented the stereoscope early in the 19th century. Diagrams of four versions of this instrument appear in Figure 253. Pseudoscopes alter the way in which the eyes normally present information to the brain. Some versions interchange the eye positions, in effect causing the left eye to see from the position of the right eye and the right eye from the position of the left. Others combine this interchange with image inversion, exaggregate the spacing between the eyes, and so on.

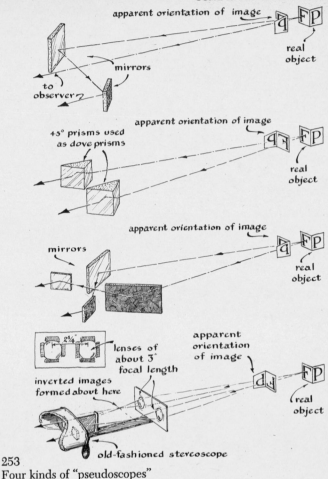

253
Four kinds of "pseudoscopes"

A pseudoscope can easily be made by holding up two hand mirrors, one somewhat to the left of the left eye and the other in front of the right eye. The angles at which the mirrors are held should be such that the image reflected from the mirror at left is directed into the right eye by the mirror at the right. In effect, this causes the right eye to see from a position somewhat to the left of the left eye. The defect of this arrangement is that the optical path for the right eye is longer than that for the left; hence the image presented to the right eye is abnormally small. For objects at a distance of 10 feet or more the difference in image size is of little consequence, however, because of the curious fact that good binocular vision can be had even if one of the images is quite distorted. Accordingly an interesting inversion of relief will appear when the mirrors are adjusted so that the doubly reflected image fuses with the one seen normally by the left eye. The optical arrangement of a pseudoscope of this type is shown at the top of Figure 253.

Other versions of the pseudoscope can be made with prisms, with two sets of mirror pairs, or by mounting a pair of short-focus lenses in the cardholder of a conventional stereoscope. Optical arrangements for these are shown as the second, third and fourth drawings in Figure 253. Holders for the optical parts need not be elaborate. I merely laid the prisms of the second arrangement between two pieces of wood, for example, and held the whole thing together with rubber bands. The mirrors of the third device may be stuck to a small board with sealing wax and adjusted for image fusion while the wax is still soft.

Martin Gardner, who edits the SCIENTIFIC AMERICAN department "Mathematical Games," first called my attention to the stereoscope-pseudoscope represented in the fourth drawing, and suggested an interesting experiment for it — viewing the effect of a small ball rolling inside a round-bottomed bowl. With no shadows to indicate perspective, the mind accepts the inversion perfectly. Released at the edge of the bowl, the ball promptly climbs up one side of what appears to be a mound, rolls down the other side and promptly returns. Finally, after a number of diminishing oscillations, the ball comes to rest on the summit of the mound!

Mackay's miniature heat engines

R. STUART MACKAY of the University of California calls attention to an interesting property of the "flints" used in cigarette lighters. At room temperature they are strongly attracted to a magnet, but when they are heated to 125 degrees centigrade they abruptly become nonmagnetic. In effect, they exhibit the property of bistability with respect to temperature and magnetism. Hence they may be used as the active element in novel heat engines. For example, a quantity of flints (the active material is the metal cerium) could be attached to the bottom of a pendulum and energized by focusing a beam of infrared radiation on them at the point where they pass through the bottom of the swing. A strong magnet would also be located at this point, almost close enough to touch the metal. Once started, the pendulum would continue to swing as long as the infrared was supplied. Because the flints would be heated at the bottom of the swing, they would be strongly attracted to the magnet during the downswing and less strongly attracted to it during the upswing. Accordingly a net transfer of energy from the infrared beam to the pendulum bob would occur.

Mackay suggests that the effect can also be applied to a device for converting heat into rotary motion by fixing a number of flints to the rim of a disk free to turn on an axle. A source of

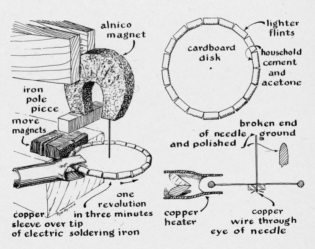

254
A heat engine made out of lighter flints and magnets

heat and a magnet would be located at adjacent points on one side of the disk. A motor of this type has been constructed by Roger Hayward, who reports that it does not run very fast. In fact, he had to fit it with a magnetic bearing to make it run at all. He chanced to have 18 lighter flints at hand and this determined the size of the rotor, which is shown full scale in Figure 254.

The axle was an ordinary sewing machine needle broken near the middle. The sharp end was discarded and the broken end of the remaining part rounded and polished. The eye was then threaded with a quarter-inch of fine copper wire as a stop for a washer made of lucite which supported the disk, as shown in the lower right detail of the drawing. The rounded end of the needle is attracted to one pole of a small alnico magnet clamped in position as shown. The flints are stuck to the edge of the rotor by quick-drying cement which has been thinned with acetone.

Energy to drive the engine is taken from an electric soldering-iron fitted with a short length of copper tubing split at the outer end. The magnet which exerts force on the flints actually consisted of a pair of small alnico bars salvaged from a discarded magnetic ash tray. They were assembled with the north poles and south poles pointing the same way, and were held together with a rubber band. This assembly was placed close enough to the flints to pull the disk about five degrees out of plumb. The split portion of the hot copper tube was placed over the flints at a point as close as possible to the driving magnet. When heat was applied, the rotor turned somewhat unevenly at about a third of a revolution per minute.

Hayward enjoys tinkering with devices for demonstrating basic mechanical principles. Recently he confected two versions of a rubber-band heat engine, with the object of showing how a system becomes increasingly sensitive to external forces as it approaches the condition of instability.

Roger Hayward describes his rubber-band engines

ONE EASY WAY to demonstrate this is to consider the case of two cylinders of unequal diameter standing on end. It takes less force to push over the thinner cylinder. The narrower the cylinder, the closer it comes to the condition of instability.

With a few rubber bands, a needle, some thread and other household objects, you can devise heat engines for demonstrating this principle in more interesting ways.

From a bracket, which can be a laboratory glassware holder, a piece of aluminum foil is suspended on a thread [*see Fig. 255*]. The foil, or bob, can pivot around its midpoint, which is attached to a stretched rubber band. The aluminum foil is curled up at the edge to shade the rubber band from a desk lamp that shines on it.

Turn the bob to the left. The left side of the rubber band is now unshaded. Warmed by the lamp, this part of the rubber shrinks, *i.e.*, contracts. The pivot point accordingly moves slightly to the left. As a result the pendulum now swings to the right.

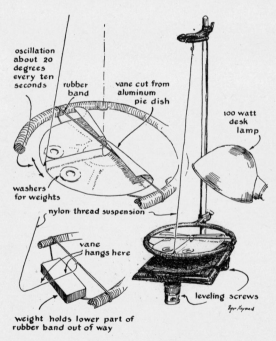

255
An apparatus to demonstrate the effects of near-instability

The curled portion of the bob then shades the warmed portion of the band and exposes the other half to the lamp. The opposite half of the cycle then begins. The apparatus, as here proportioned, will vibrate about 16 cycles per minute over an amplitude of about 10 degrees. I tried observing the shift of the bottom pivot with a small telescope. The motion must be less than a thousandth of an inch, because it was not perceptible.

Save for the leveling screws, which must be capable of exquisite adjustment, the rest of the apparatus is easy to make. Aluminum foil for the bob is easy to cut with ordinary scissors. The 24-gauge weight of foil used for bakery pie-plates is handy. The vane or bob is balanced on the thread by sliding the washers toward or away from the thread. This is quite easy. A wooden structure can be substituted for the lab stand. The thread is N.Y.M.O. sewing thread size A, 300 yards per spool.

Aside from the stability effects, I suppose the two lessons to be learned from this experiment have to do, first, with the phase relationships of the system, and second, with the surprising behavior of rubber when subjected to changes in temperature. The driving force for any oscillator must be out of phase with the displacement, preferably by 90 degrees. In the case of the "figure 4" seismometer suspension, the inertia of the pendulum plus the time lag in warming the rubber combine to approximate 90 degrees.

What about the interesting property of warmed rubber? Unlike most materials, when rubber is stretched the tension increases (up to a point) as it is warmed. I discussed this with Linus Pauling some years ago and he said that you should picture rubber, when under tension, as a bundle of stretched chains, with heat shaking the chains. The harder the chains are shaken (by thermal agitation) the more they pull on the fastenings at their ends. In consequence a stretched rubber band when warmed tends to become shorter and thicker, as a muscle does when exerting a pull, a property which suggests endless experiments.

As far as I know this peculiar form of pendulum, as driven by rubber, is new. It might be used as a thermometer, and measure temperature mixed with earthquakes. Moral: It is easy to

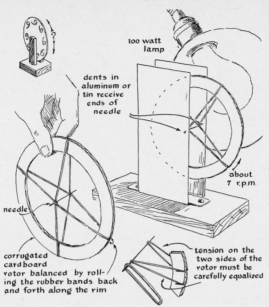

100 watt lamp

dents in
aluminum or
tin receive
ends of
needle

about
7 r.p.m.

needle

corrugated
cardboard
rotor balanced by roll-
ing the rubber bands back
and forth along the rim

tension on the
two sides of the
rotor must be
carefully equalized

256
A heat engine driven by warmed rubber bands

make any device sensitive if you don't care how many things you measure simultaneously. But if the gadget is to unscramble the mixture, measure but one thing, then it is harder to make.

The second system [*see Fig. 256*] shows the same principle applied to a gadget which converts heat into rotary motion. The rim of the wheel is cut from corrugated cardboard with a sharply pointed knife. The rim supports spokes made of rubber bands, and they in turn hold a needle shaft in alignment. You mount this assembly between two plates of thin tin or aluminum. I had the engine running in about an hour, the first 40 minutes being spent in getting the needle to stay in proper alignment. Equalizing the tension on the two sides of the wheel is quite a chore. The needle tends to turn sideways and dump off the bands. Then you start all over. You must next adjust the bands until the wheel balances perfectly when in its bearings. The balancing act, however, is not too difficult. If the wheel persists in coming to rest with an unbalanced section down, you move the outer tips of the bands until it is balanced all around. Now you shine a 50-watt lamp close to one side of the shield. The wheel will start rotating at about seven revolutions per minute.

For the upcoming generation who would like a wheel intended to run forever without an external source of power, we submit the classical perpetual motion machine shown in the upper-left corner of the drawing. The principle: Sixes become nines as the wheel turns. Whether this increase in numerical imbalance can generate counterclockwise rotation I leave to you.

X.

A Closing Challenge

The amateur is invited to design experiments of his own

HAVING INVITED you throughout this volume to repeat some of the classic experiments devised for separating fact from fancy, we close on a more challenging note: Why not design an experiment of your own?

You begin with two requisites — an interesting set of observations and a clearly stated question. From these you construct a theory and then devise an experiment to test the worth of your tentative guess.

As a starter, consider the charming little puzzle that was submitted to the readers of SCIENTIFIC AMERICAN magazine by Ernest Hunter Wright, the retired former head of the Department of English at Columbia University. Many readers theorized about the problem and submitted logical guesses to Dr. Wright. But nobody, to my knowledge, has thus far put the question to nature in the form of a rigorously controlled experiment. So the puzzle must be categorized as "unsolved."

Here, then, in the propounder's own words, is a scientific challenge worthy of your talents.

E. H. Wright presents the puzzle of the skipping stones

WITH THE LUCK OF A LAYMAN, I have had the novel experience of seeing several of the men who plucked the heart out of the atom's mystery scratch their heads in vain for the solution of a problem which I now submit to a wider audience.

We all think we know what happens when we skip a stone across a water surface. We believe that it bounces over the water in a series of successively shorter leaps until it finally stops and sinks. Of course the number and the length of the leaps vary with the smoothness of the water, the size and shape of the stone, the speed and skill of the throw, and other conditions, but by and large the missile seems to act about as I have said.

I am fairly sure it does no such thing. I think a stone does not behave on water in the way described, because I *know* it does not on sand — the hard, wet sand at the water's edge. So first let me tell you what the stone does on the sand, and how I came to know about it.

I found it out in the course of a long walk along the beach. I had been skipping pebbles over the water. (By the way, I wish someone could tell me precisely why beach pebbles are always flattened rather than spherical — no geologist has given me a satisfactory answer.) Because the water rolling into the beach was too rough for good performance, I decided to see how a pebble would behave on the hard, wet sand. On this surface, of course, it would leave little marks recording its travel.

When I saw the marks left in the sand by my first pebble, I think I must have been as astonished as old Crusoe on beholding the first footprint of his man Friday! The first bounce of the pebble was only four inches long; the next was nearly seven feet; then came another short hop of only four inches; then a leap of about five feet; then again the four-inch hop, and so on for seven big hops punctuated by the four-inch ones. Each short skip was unmistakably recorded by two neat little marks in the sand. After the seventh repetition the pebble ceased this strange behavior and merely jumped along with successively shorter strides until it stopped. The total number of hops was about 20 — my average on hard sand.

I kept skipping pebbles all the afternoon, for mile after mile along the beach. I tried them in all shapes and sizes, over every contour of terrain that I could find, at every angle at which it was possible to launch them. I tried all the variations I could think of, and I went back a second day and tried them all again. With never an exception the result was just about the same.

Now I fancy the same thing happens on the water, though in the water there is no imprint left to tell the story. A proper record with a camera would give us the answer. In the sand, at least, the story is quite clear, and a very pretty story it is — as pretty as the tracks of some little animal in the fresh snow.

As yet I have no explanation for these facts. I have put the problem before several physicists of high distinction, but so far have received no answer in return. Somewhere there must be an answer for my little riddle. Who will find it?

I may save some trouble if I say that two or three suggestions have already been tested and found wanting. One was that each of the double marks is the result of the pebble's turning over when it strikes the sand. I can imagine no reason why the pebble should turn over, and at all events I can certify from scrutiny that the stone does not turn over — and so can the companions who have watched it with me.

Another suggestion was that the pebble, striking the sand at a tilt, might hit with its rear end first, do a little flop and strike with its front end before taking off for the long leap. But this supposes a precision of timing and a uniformity of tilt at each landing which are beyond all credence, and besides, why would a big stone make its flop within the same space (four inches) as a tiny one? As a matter of fact the marks in the sand show that the stone usually strikes the sand flat, and all the observers agree with me that there is no flop.

The only other suggestion so far is that the pebble's spin around its vertical axis may account for its strange action. Why such a spin should make it behave the way it does is not clear to me, but we do not need to labor the question, because I have thrown pebbles without any spin (it can be done) and they all left the same mincing steps in the sand.

So what scientist, professional or amateur, wants to go down to the beach with all the needful instruments and find the answer to my riddle? I shall be glad to go along if I am wanted; I can throw pretty well.

REFERENCES
FOR FURTHER READING

ASTRONOMY

AMATEUR TELESCOPE MAKING (4th ed.). A. G. Ingalls, Scientific American, Inc., 1943. This handbook launched the hobby. It is the cornerstone volume in the libraries of most amateur telescope makers.

AMATEUR TELESCOPE MAKING, ADVANCED. A. G. Ingalls. Scientific American, Inc., 1937. A gold mine of information for transforming the simple telescope into a precision instrument for astronomical research.

AMATEUR TELESCOPE MAKING, BOOK III. A. G. Ingalls. Scientific American, Inc., 1953. A compendium of hard-to-find information on optical design, vacuum coating of optical elements, and design of special instruments, including monochromators, spectrographs and Schmidt cameras.

PROCEDURES IN EXPERIMENTAL PHYSICS. John Strong. Prentice-Hall, 1938. Techniques for blowing, grinding and polishing glass; the production of thin reflecting films of metal; the principles of kinematical design.

TELESCOPES AND ACCESSORIES. George Z. Dimitroff and James G. Baker. The Blakiston Co., 1945. A comprehensive description of the instrumentation found in modern astronomical observatories.

HANDBOOK FOR OBSERVING THE SATELLITES. Neale E. Howard. Thomas Y. Crowell Co., 1958. For the beginner. Simple techniques for observing and fixing the orbital position and velocity of man-made satellites.

THE SKY OBSERVER'S GUIDE. Newton Mayall, Margaret Mayall and Jerome Wyckoff. Golden Press, 1957. A clear, delightful introduction to the technique of finding your way around in the sky.

THE OBSERVER'S HANDBOOK. Royal Astronomical Society of Canada, Toronto, Canada. An ephemeris issued annually.

THE AMERICAN EPHEMERIS AND NAUTICAL ALMANAC. United States Naval Observatory. U. S. Government Printing Office. A strictly professional ephemeris listing the position, orbital elements and related information on all major celestial bodies (issued annually).

INTRODUCTION TO ASTRONOMY. Cecelia Payne-Gaposchkin. Prentice-Hall, 1954. A survey text for laymen.

EXPLORING THE DISTANT STARS. Clyde B. Calson. G. P. Putnam's Sons, 1958.

EXPERIMENTAL SPECTROSCOPY. Ralph A. Sawyer. Prentice-Hall, 1944. An ideal reference for the beginner; clear, authoritative and comprehensive.

ARCHAEOLOGY

BEGINNING IN ARCHAEOLOGY. Mary Kenyon. Frederick A. Praeger, 1953. A how-to-get-started guide for the inexperienced amateur.

THE TESTIMONY OF THE SPADE. Geoffrey Bibby. Alfred A. Knopf, 1956. A fascinating review of the prehistory of Europe; how it has been traced from seemingly unrelated scraps of evidence turned up by archaeological techniques.

THE AMERICAN ABORIGINES, THEIR ORIGIN AND ANTIQUITY. D. Jenness. University of Toronto Press, 1933.

EARLY MAN. George Grant MacCurdy. J. B. Lippincott Co., 1937.

ANCIENT MAN IN NORTH AMERICA. W. M. Wormington. Denver Museum of Natural History.

NOTES ON IROQUOIS ARCHAEOLOGY. Alanson Skinner. Museum of the American Indian, Heye Foundation, 1921.

RIVER BASIN PAPERS. Douglas Osborne and others. *Smithsonian Institution Bureau of American Ethnology Bull. 166,* U. S. Government Printing Office.

BIOLOGY

A SOURCEBOOK FOR THE BIOLOGICAL SCIENCES. Evelyn Morholt, Paul F. Brandwein and Alexander Joseph. Harcourt, Brace and Co., 1958. An excellent compendium of techniques, procedures, demonstrations, projects and suggestions for the beginner in biological experimentation.

GENERAL BIOLOGY. Gordon Alexander. Thomas Y. Crowell Co., 1956. A comprehensive general text for students planning to major in biology, with outstanding discussions of morphology, physiology, taxonomy and genetics.

THE MICROTOMIST'S FORMULARY AND GUIDE. Peter Gray. The Blakiston Co., 1954. Perhaps the most comprehensive work ever published on the preparation of specimens for microscopic examination. A *must* for the shelves of every amateur microscopist.

HANDBOOK OF BIOLOGICAL DATA. W. S. Spector. W. B. Saunders Co., 1956. An effectively organized and useful reference.

CELLS AND SOCIETIES. J. T. Bonner. Princeton University Press, 1954.

BIOLOGY OF THE DESERTS. J. L. Clouds-ley-Thompson. Institute of Biology, London, England, 1954.

EXPERIMENTS IN GENERAL BIOLOGY. G. Du Shane and D. Regnery. W. H. Freeman and Co., 1950.

PRINCIPLES OF GENERAL BIOLOGY. M. Gardiner. The Macmillan Co., 1952.

A SOURCEBOOK IN ANIMAL BIOLOGY. T. Hall. McGraw-Hill Book Co., 1951.

THE BIOTIC WORLD AND MAN. L. Milne and M. Milne. Prentice-Hall, 1953.

THE NATURAL SCIENCES

THE AMATEUR NATURALIST'S HANDBOOK. Vinson Brown. Little, Brown and Co., 1948. An invaluable guide for the beginner, yet comprehensive enough to satisfy the needs of advanced amateurs.

EXPLORING THE EARTH AND ITS LIFE IN A NATURAL HISTORY MUSEUM. James L. McCreery. J. B. Lippincott Co., 1952.

THE FASCINATING ANIMAL WORLD. Alan Devoe. McGraw-Hill Book Co., 1951.

ECOLOGY OF ANIMAL PARASITES. Jean G. Baer. University of Illinois Press, 1951.

BIRDS OF AMERICA (3 volumes). T. Gilbert Pearson and others. Garden City Publishing Co., 1944.

A FIELD GUIDE TO AMPHIBIANS AND REPTILES. Roger Conant. Houghton Mifflin Co., 1954.

BEGINNER'S GUIDE TO SEASHORE LIFE. L. A. Hausman. G. P. Putnam's Sons, 1949.

FIELD BOOK OF INSECTS. Frank E. Lutz. G. P. Putnam's Sons, 1950.

INSECT FACT AND FOLKLORE. Lucy W. Clausen. The Macmillan Co., 1954. An amusing and brilliant debunking of popular misconceptions.

SPIDER BOOK. J. H. Comstock. Comstock Publishing Assoc., 1948.

THE BUTTERFLY BOOK. W. J. Holland. Doubleday & Co., 1931.

THE MOTH BOOK. W. J. Holland.

Doubleday-Page, 1908. The all-time classic in its field.

FUN WITH YOUR MICROSCOPE. Raymond F. Yates. D. Appleton-Century Co., 1943.

BIOCHEMISTRY AND PHYSIOLOGY OF PROTOZOA. S. H. Hutner and André Lwoff. Academic Press, 1955.

FIELD MANUAL OF PLANT ECOLOGY. Frank C. Gates. McGraw-Hill Book Co., 1949.

AN INTRODUCTION TO THE PLANT KINGDOM. Norman H. Russell. C. V. Mosby Co., 1958.

THE EARTH SCIENCES

MINERALS AND HOW TO STUDY THEM. Edward Salisbury Dana. John Wiley & Sons, 1949. The number-one book for the serious amateur mineralogist.

A FIELD GUIDE TO ROCKS AND MINERALS. Frederick P. Pough. Houghton Mifflin Co., 1953. An indispensable pocketbook of mineral identification simple enough in concept for the beginner yet adequately meeting the needs of the professional prospector. A *must*.

GEOLOGY. O. D. von Engeln and Kenneth E. Caster. McGraw-Hill Book Co., 1952. A basic text covering the history of igneous rocks, the structure, process and forms of sedimentation phenomena, and a detailed discussion of the four major geologic eras.

PHYSICAL METEOROLOGY. J. C. Johnson. Technology Press of The Massachusetts Institute of Technology, 1954. The reaction of the atmosphere to the forces of its environment, including a review of the earth's heat budget, natural and artificially stimulated precipitation, atmospheric electricity and the physics of the upper atmosphere. (A working knowledge of elementary calculus is assumed.)

ELEMENTARY SEISMOLOGY. Charles F. Richter. W. H. Freeman and Co.,

1958. An excellent introduction to the theory and practice of seismology, including instrumentation and the analysis of seismic waves, with a chronology of the science from 373 B.C. to date.

AN INTRODUCTION TO THE THEORY OF SEISMOLOGY. K. E. Bullen. Cambridge University Press, 1953. A mathematical exposition of seismic wave behavior and the theory of seismographs. (Presumes a working knowledge of advanced mathematics.)

THE EARTH'S CRUST. L. Dudley Stamp. Crown Publishers, 1951. A delightful explanation of the dynamics of the earth's ever-changing crust, with special emphasis on mountain building and the processes responsible for the creation of "scenery." Illustrations in full color.

CLOUD PHYSICS. D. W. Perrie. John Wiley & Sons, 1950. A review of the dynamics of weather with discussions of the formation, forms and classifications of clouds, techniques of cloud observation, the relation of clouds to weather forecasting and the optical and electrical phenomena associated with them.

ATMOSPHERIC ELECTRICITY. J. Alan Chalmers. Pergamon Press, 1957.

THE URANIUM PROSPECTOR'S GUIDE. Thomas J. Ballard and Quentin E. Conklin. Harper & Brothers, 1955.

NUCLEAR PHYSICS

ON AN EXPANSION APPARATUS FOR MAKING VISIBLE THE TRACKS OF IONIZING PARTICLES IN GASES AND SOME RESULTS OBTAINED BY ITS USE. C. T. R. Wilson in *Proceedings of the Royal Society of London*, Series A, Vol. 87, No. 595, pages 277-292; September 19, 1912. A classic of scientific literature and a *must* for your reading list, even if nuclear physics holds only casual interest for you.

THE ELECTRON. Robert Andrews Millikan. University of Chicago Press, 1924. An absorbing account of how the electron's charge was measured by the physicist who made the original experiment. Another scientific classic.

WHAT ARE COSMIC RAYS? P. Auger. University of Chicago Press, 1945.

AN INTRODUCTION TO THE THEORY OF RELATIVITY. P. G. Bergmann. Prentice-Hall, 1942.

ELEMENTARY NUCLEAR THEORY. H. A. Bethe. John Wiley & Sons, 1947.

EXPERIMENTAL NUCLEAR PHYSICS. K. T. Bainbridge. John Wiley & Sons, 1953.

THE SCINTILLATION COUNTER. J. W. Coltman and F. H. Marshall. *Physical Review* (72, 528), 1947.

FIRST DESCRIPTION OF VAN DE GRAAFF GENERATOR. R. J. Van de Graaff, K. T. Compton and L. C. Van Atta. *Physical Review* (43, 149), 1933.

FIRST DESCRIPTION OF THE CYCLOTRON. E. O. Lawrence and M. S. Livingston. *Physical Review* (40, 19), 1932.

A SOURCE BOOK IN PHYSICS. W. F. Magie. McGraw-Hill Book Co., 1935.

IONIZATION CHAMBERS AND COUNTERS. B. B. Rossi and H. H. Staub. McGraw-Hill Book Co., 1949.

INTRODUCTORY NUCLEAR PHYSICS. David Halliday. John Wiley & Sons, 1955.

NUCLEAR MAGNETIC RESONANCE. Edward Raymond Andrew. Cambridge University Press, 1955.

RADIATION COUNTERS AND DETECTORS. C. C. H. Washtell. Philosophical Library, 1958.

MATHEMATICAL MACHINES

DESIGN OF SWITCHING CIRCUITS. W. Keister and others. D. Van Nostrand Co., 1952. An exhaustive treatment of the design of circuits for solving problems in logic by the use of electromechanical relays.

LOGICAL DESIGN OF ELECTRICAL CIRCUITS. Rene A. Higonnet and Rene A. Grea. McGraw-Hill Book Co., 1958. The application of Boolian algebra and other mathematical methods to the design of circuits commonly employed in digital computers.

GIANT BRAINS OR MACHINES THAT THINK. Edmund Callis Berkeley. John Wiley & Sons, 1949. A popular explanation of digital computers and how they work.

THE THEORY OF MATHEMATICAL MACHINES. Francis J. Murray. King's Crown Press, 1947.

MODERN INSTRUMENTS AND METHODS OF CALCULATION. E. H. Horsburgh. G. Bell and Sons, Ltd., 1914.

MATHEMATICS AND THE IMAGINATION. Edward Kasner and James Newman. Simon and Schuster, 1940.

THE NATURE OF NUMBER. Roy Dubisch. The Ronald Press Co., 1952.

AERODYNAMICS

AERODYNAMICS FOR MODEL AIRCRAFT. Avrum Zier. Dodd, Mead and Co., 1942. A simple, well-organized handbook for the designer of model aircraft. It requires no mathematical ability beyond high-school algebra.

EXPERIMENTS WITH AIRPLANE INSTRUMENTS. Nelson F. Beeler and Franklin M. Branley. Thomas Y. Crowell Co., 1953. How to build altimeters, air-speed indicators, gyrostabilizers and related flight instruments from materials commonly found in the home; how to experiment with them.

THE AERODYNAMICS OF POWERED FLIGHT. Robert L. Carroll. John Wiley & Sons, 1960. A professional treatise on the characteristics and design of full-scale aircraft.

AIRPLANE AERODYNAMICS. Daniel O.

Dommash, Sydney S. Sherry and Thomas F. Connolly. Pitman Publishing Co., 1957.

THE ROCKET HANDBOOK FOR AMATEURS. Lt. Charles M. Pankin. John Day Co., 1959. A beginner's manual covering the safe design, construction and launching of small rockets.

THE ROCKET MANUAL FOR AMATEURS. Capt. Bertrand R. Brinely. Ballantine Books, 1960. A comprehensive review of small-rocket design, with special emphasis on safety.

ROCKET PROPELLANTS. Francis A. Warren. Reinhold Publishing Co., 1958. A review of rocket fuels, explaining the techniques of compounding both solid and liquid propellants.

INSTRUMENTAL SATELLITES AND INSTRUMENTAL COMETS. Krafft A. Hericke, Interavia, Vol. II, No. 12, December, 1956.

THE COMPLETE BOOK OF OUTER SPACE. Willy Ley and Wernher von Braun. Gnome Press, 1953.

PRINCIPLES OF GUIDED MISSILE DESIGN. Arthur S. Locke. D. Van Nostrand Co., 1955.

OPTICS, HEAT AND ELECTRONICS

THE WONDER OF LIGHT. Hy Ruchlis. Harper & Brothers, 1960. A delightful picture story about how and why we see. It includes a fascinating series of optical experiments for you to do with simple apparatus at home.

FUNDAMENTALS OF OPTICS. Francis A. Jenkins and Harvey E. White. McGraw-Hill Book Co., 1950. A comprehensive reference for the advanced amateur.

MODERN COLLEGE PHYSICS. Harvey E. White. D. Van Nostrand Co., 1956. An excellent reference.

INTRODUCTION TO MODERN PHYSICS. C. H. Blanchard and others. Prentice-Hall, 1958.

VACUUM TECHNIQUE. Saul Dushman. John Wiley & Sons, 1949. A classic.

THE MICROSCOPE AND ITS USE. J. Munoz and Harry A. Charipper. Chemical Publishing Co., 1943.

PHASE MICROSCOPY. Alva H. Bennett. John Wiley & Sons, 1951.

MECHANISMS AND MOTION. K. H. Hunt. John Wiley & Sons, 1959.

THE DETECTION AND MEASUREMENT OF INFRA-RED RADIATION. R. A. Smith, F. E. Jones and R. P. Chasmar. Clarendon Press, 1957.

THE RADIO AMATEUR'S HANDBOOK. American Radio Relay League, 1960. The number-one reference book for radio hams and amateurs interested in electronics (issued annually).

ELECTRONICS: EXPERIMENTAL TECHNIQUES. William C. Elmore and Matthew Sands. McGraw-Hill Book Co., 1949. A must for experimenters interested in the application of electronics to noncommunications fields such as computers, remote control and telemetry.

ELECTROMAGNETICS. John D. Kraus. McGraw-Hill Book Co., 1953. A comprehensive reference for advanced amateurs concerned with electromagnetic theory and design.

TRANSISTOR CIRCUIT HANDBOOK FOR THE HOBBYIST. Semiconductor Division, Sylvania Electric Products, Inc., 1960. An invaluable aid for the beginner in semiconductor experimentation.

AN INTRODUCTION TO JUNCTION TRANSISTOR THEORY. R. D. Middlebrook. John Wiley & Sons, 1957. For the advanced amateur with a working knowledge of elementary calculus.

TRANSISTOR ENGINEERING REFERENCE HANDBOOK. H. E. Marrows. John F. Rider, Publisher, Inc., 1956. An intensely practical reference outlining circuit design methods and listing the parameters of commercially available devices.

MAGNETIC AMPLIFIER ENGINEERING. George M. Attura. McGraw-Hill Book Co., 1959.

INDEX

Abrasives
  dispenser for, 9
  kits for grinding glass, 10
Accelerator
  particle, 344-60
  tube for atomic particle, 346
  Van de Graaff electrostatic, 487
Acetone, 144
Activated alumina, 144
Adsorbents, chromatographic, 144
Aerodynamics, 413-60
  bathtub, 439-46
  simple experiments in, 414
Aeroelasticity, 438
African agamid, 211
After-dinner experiments, 546-58
Air
  carbon dioxide, content of, 137
  flow at low speed, 418
  foil, B-7, 417
  foil, shape designation of, 420
  formulas for velocity of
    flow, 435, 436
Airplane models, indoor, 415
Albumin, staining of, 161
Algae, how to cultivate, 117-22
Alpha particles, how to determine
  energy of, 332
Alpha ray tracks, 318
Alpha rays, identification of, 329
Aluminizing telescope mirrors, 17
Aluminum, 222
American Bird Banding
  Association, 194
American eagle, 200
American Interplanetary
  Society, 448
American Rocket Society, 448
Amphibians, 202-13

Amplifier
  electromechanical, for
    wind tunnel, 419
  for electronic seismograph, 242
Analemma, 75
Anemometer, 418
Angleworms, as snake food, 212
Animal species, number of, 463
Antheraea mylitta (silkworm), 185
Antibiotics, 111
Apatite, 220
Aperture, advantages of small
  telescopic, 30
Apiezon-W wax, vapor
  pressure of, 349
Aquariums
  gravel for, 208
  for reptiles, 206
Aquatic turtles, 209
Archaeological "digs,"
  prerequisites of, 95
Archaeology, 85-101
Archaic occupation, Indian, 92
Area, methods of determining
  irregular, 399
Argyll, Duke of, 176
Aristotle, 463
Armillary, 74
Arsenic, odor of, 225
Artesian wells, 258
Artificial food for hummingbirds, 169
Artificial-pond culture medium, 120
Assawompsett Pond, 90
Astrolabe, 266
Astronomy, 3-81
Astrospectrograph, 38
Atlas, Attacus (moth), 185
Atmosphere, 281
  detection of stellar, 60